MKSAP®16

Medical Knowledge Self-Assessment Program®

Rheumatology

Welcome to the Rheumatology section of MKSAP 16!

In the pages that follow, we discuss approaches to the patient with rheumatic disease, principles of therapeutics, rheumatoid arthritis, osteoarthritis, fibromyalgia, spondyloarthritis, systemic lupus erythematosus, systemic sclerosis, Sjögren syndrome, mixed connective tissue disease, infectious arthritis, and other clinical challenges. All of these topics are uniquely focused on the needs of generalists and subspecialists *outside* of rheumatology.

The publication of the 16th edition of Medical Knowledge Self-Assessment Program heralds a significant event, culminating 2 years of effort by dozens of leading subspecialists across the United States. Our authoring committees have strived to help internists succeed in Maintenance of Certification, right up to preparing for the MOC examination, and to get residents ready for the certifying examination. MKSAP 16 also helps you update your medical knowledge and elevates standards of self-learning by allowing you to assess your knowledge with 1,200 all-new multiple-choice questions, including 96 in Rheumatology.

MKSAP began more than 40 years ago. The American Board of Internal Medicine's examination blueprint and gaps between actual and preferred practices inform creation of the content. The questions, refined through rigorous face-to-face meetings, are among the best in medicine. A psychometric analysis of the items sharpens our educational focus on weaknesses in practice. To meet diverse learning styles, we offer MKSAP 16 online and in downloadable apps for tablets, laptops, and phones. We are also introducing the following:

High-Value Care Recommendations: The Rheumatology section starts with several recommendations based on the important concept of health care value (balancing clinical benefit with costs and harms) to address the needs of trainees, practicing physicians, and patients. These recommendations are part of a major initiative that has been undertaken by the American College of Physicians, in collaboration with other organizations.

Content for Hospitalists: This material, highlighted in blue and labeled with the familiar hospital icon (◼), directly addresses the learning needs of the increasing number of physicians who work in the hospital setting. MKSAP 16 Digital will allow you to customize quizzes based on hospitalist-only questions to help you prepare for the Hospital Medicine Maintenance of Certification Examination.

We hope you enjoy and benefit from MKSAP 16. Please feel free to send us any comments to mksap_editors@acponline.org or visit us at the MKSAP Resource Site (mksap.acponline.org) to find out how we can help you study, earn CME, accumulate MOC points, and stay up to date. I know I speak on behalf of ACP staff members and our authoring committees when I say we are honored to have attracted your interest and participation.

Sincerely,

Patrick Alguire, MD, FACP
Editor-in-Chief
Senior Vice President
Medical Education Division
American College of Physicians

Rheumatology

Committee

Anne R. Bass, MD, FACP, Editor[1]
Associate Professor of Clinical Medicine
Division of Rheumatology
Weill Cornell Medical College
Rheumatology Fellowship Program Director
Hospital for Special Surgery
New York, New York

Virginia U. Collier, MD, MACP, Associate Editor[2]
Hugh R. Sharp, Jr. Chair of Medicine
Christiana Care Health System
Newark, Delaware
Professor of Medicine
Jefferson Medical College of Thomas Jefferson University
Philadelphia, Pennsylvania

Juliet Aizer, MD, MPH[2]
Professor of Clinical Medicine
Division of Rheumatology
Weill Cornell Medical College
Hospital for Special Surgery
New York, New York

W. Winn Chatham, MD, FACP[2]
Professor of Medicine
University of Alabama at Birmingham
Clinical Immunology and Rheumatology
Birmingham, Alabama

John D. Fitzgerald, MD, PhD[1]
Associate Clinical Professor of Medicine
University of California at Los Angeles
Los Angeles, California

Michael H. Pillinger, MD[2]
Associate Professor of Medicine and Pharmacology
Director of Rheumatology Training
New York University School of Medicine
NYU Hospital for Joint Diseases
New York, New York

Lisa R. Sammaritano, MD, FACP[1]
Associate Professor of Clinical Medicine
Division of Rheumatology
Weill Cornell Medical College
Hospital for Special Surgery
New York, New York

Editor-in-Chief

Patrick C. Alguire, MD, FACP[1]
Senior Vice President, Medical Education
American College of Physicians
Philadelphia, Pennsylvania

Deputy Editor-in-Chief

Philip A. Masters, MD, FACP[1]
Senior Medical Associate for Content Development
American College of Physicians
Philadelphia, Pennsylvania

Senior Medical Associate for Content Development

Cynthia D. Smith, MD, FACP[2]
American College of Physicians
Philadelphia, Pennsylvania

Rheumatology Clinical Editor

Virginia U. Collier, MD, MACP[2]

Rheumatology Reviewers

Lois J. Geist, MD, FACP[1]
John D. Goldman, MD, FACP[1]
Phillip M. Hall, MD, FACP[1]
Carlos J. Lozada, MD, FACP[2]
Asher A. Tulsky, MD, FACP[1]
Robert B. Zurier, MD[1]
John J. Zurlo, MD[2]

Rheumatology Reviewers Representing the American Society for Clinical Pharmacology & Therapeutics

Anne N. Nafziger, MD, FACP[2]
Lisa von Moltke, MD[2]

Rheumatology ACP Editorial Staff

Megan Zborowski[1], Staff Editor
Sean McKinney[1], Director, Self-Assessment Programs
Margaret Wells[1], Managing Editor
John Haefele[1], Assistant Editor

ACP Principal Staff

Patrick C. Alguire, MD, FACP[1]
Senior Vice President, Medical Education

D. Theresa Kanya, MBA[1]
Vice President, Medical Education

Sean McKinney[1]
Director, Self-Assessment Programs

Margaret Wells[1]
Managing Editor

Valerie Dangovetsky[1]
Program Administrator

Becky Krumm[1]
Senior Staff Editor

Ellen McDonald, PhD[1]
Senior Staff Editor

Katie Idell[1]
Senior Staff Editor

Randy Hendrickson[1]
Production Administrator/Editor

Megan Zborowski[1]
Staff Editor

Linnea Donnarumma[1]
Assistant Editor

John Haefele[1]
Assistant Editor

Developed by the American College of Physicians

1. Has no relationships with any entity producing, marketing, re-selling, or distributing health care goods or services consumed by, or used on, patients.

2. Has disclosed relationships with entities producing, marketing, re-selling, or distributing health care goods or services consumed by, or used on, patients. See below.

Conflicts of Interest

The following committee members, reviewers, and ACP staff members have disclosed relationships with commercial companies:

Juliet Aizer, MD, MPH
Honoraria
Biotronik

W. Winn Chatham, MD, FACP
Research Grants/Contracts
Human Genome Sciences, Genentech, Merck Serono, UCB Pharma, Eli Lilly, Anthera
Honoraria
Bristol-Myers Squibb

Virginia U. Collier, MD, MACP
Stock Options/Holdings
Celgene, Pfizer, Merck, Schering-Plough, Abbott, Johnson and Johnson, Medtronic, McKesson, Amgen

Carlos J. Lozada, MD, FACP
Speakers Bureau
Amgen, Pfizer, The Rheumatology Education Group

Anne N. Nafziger, MD, FACP
Consultantship
Adamas Pharmaceuticals, Antisoma (Xanthus), Bristol-Myers Squibb, Canyon Pharmaceuticals, CE3, Cubist, Dominion Diagnostics, InterMune, Inc., Population Council, Sirtris (now GlaxoSmithKline), ViroPharma

Michael H. Pillinger, MD
Research Grants/Contracts
Takeda Inc.

Cynthia D. Smith, MD, FACP
Stock Options/Holdings
Merck and Company

Lisa von Moltke, MD
Employment
Genzyme Corporation

John J. Zurlo, MD
Research Grants/Contracts
Gilead Pharmaceuticals

Acknowledgments

The American College of Physicians (ACP) gratefully acknowledges the special contributions to the development and production of the 16th edition of the Medical Knowledge Self-Assessment Program® (MKSAP® 16) made by the following people:

Graphic Services: Michael Ripca (Technical Administrator/ Graphic Designer) and Willie-Fetchko Graphic Design (Graphic Designer).

Production/Systems: Dan Hoffmann (Director, Web Services & Systems Development), Neil Kohl (Senior Architect), and Scott Hurd (Senior Systems Analyst/Developer).

MKSAP 16 Digital: Under the direction of Steven Spadt, Vice President, ACP Digital Products & Services, the digital version of MKSAP 16 was developed within the ACP's Digital Product Development Department, led by Brian

Sweigard (Director). Other members of the team included Sean O'Donnell (Senior Architect), Dan Barron (Senior Systems Analyst/Developer), Chris Forrest (Senior Software Developer/Design Lead), Jon Laing (Senior Web Application Developer), Brad Lord (Senior Web Developer), John McKnight (Senior Web Developer), and Nate Pershall (Senior Web Developer).

The College also wishes to acknowledge that many other persons, too numerous to mention, have contributed to the production of this program. Without their dedicated efforts, this program would not have been possible.

Introducing the MKSAP Resource Site (mksap.acponline.org)

The MKSAP Resource Site (mksap.acponline.org) is a continually updated site that provides links to MKSAP 16 online answer sheets for print subscribers; access to MKSAP 16 Digital, Board Basics® 3, and MKSAP 16 Updates; the latest details on Continuing Medical Education (CME) and Maintenance of Certification (MOC) in the United States, Canada, and Australia; errata; and other new information.

ABIM Maintenance of Certification

Check the MKSAP Resource Site (mksap.acponline.org) for the latest information on how MKSAP tests can be used to apply to the American Board of Internal Medicine for Maintenance of Certification (MOC) points.

RCPSC Maintenance of Certification

In Canada, MKSAP 16 is an Accredited Self-Assessment Program (Section 3) as defined by the Maintenance of Certification Program of The Royal College of Physicians and Surgeons of Canada (RCPSC) and approved by the Canadian Society of Internal Medicine on December 9, 2011. Approval of this and other Part A sections of MKSAP 16 extends from July 31, 2012, until July 31, 2015. Approval of Part B sections of MKSAP 16 extends from December 31, 2012, to December 31, 2015. Fellows of the Royal College may earn three credits per hour for participating in MKSAP 16 under Section 3. MKSAP 16 will enable Fellows to earn up to 75% of their required 400 credits during the 5-year MOC cycle. A Fellow can achieve this 75% level by earning 100 of the maximum of 174 *AMA PRA Category 1 Credits*™ available in MKSAP 16. MKSAP 16 also meets multiple CanMEDS Roles for RCPSC MOC, including that of Medical Expert, Communicator, Collaborator, Manager, Health Advocate, Scholar, and Professional. For information on how to apply MKSAP 16 CME credits to RCPSC MOC, visit the MKSAP Resource Site at mksap.acponline.org.

The Royal Australasian College of Physicians CPD Program

In Australia, MKSAP 16 is a Category 3 program that may be used by Fellows of The Royal Australasian College of Physicians (RACP) to meet mandatory CPD points. Two CPD credits are awarded for each of the 174 *AMA PRA Category 1 Credits*™ available in MKSAP 16. More information about using MKSAP 16 for this purpose is available at the MKSAP Resource Site at mksap.acponline.org and at www.racp.edu.au. CPD credits earned through MKSAP 16 should be reported at the MyCPD site at www.racp.edu.au/mycpd.

Continuing Medical Education

The American College of Physicians is accredited by the Accreditation Council for Continuing Medical Education (ACCME) to provide continuing medical education for physicians.

The American College of Physicians designates this enduring material, MKSAP 16, for a maximum of 174 *AMA PRA Category 1 Credits*™. Physicians should claim only the credit commensurate with the extent of their participation in the activity.

Up to 14 *AMA PRA Category 1 Credits*™ are available from July 31, 2012, to July 31, 2015, for the MKSAP 16 Rheumatology section.

Learning Objectives

The learning objectives of MKSAP 16 are to:
- Close gaps between actual care in your practice and preferred standards of care, based on best evidence
- Diagnose disease states that are less common and sometimes overlooked and confusing
- Improve management of comorbid conditions that can complicate patient care
- Determine when to refer patients for surgery or care by subspecialists
- Pass the ABIM Certification Examination
- Pass the ABIM Maintenance of Certification Examination

Target Audience

- General internists and primary care physicians
- Subspecialists who need to remain up-to-date in internal medicine
- Residents preparing for the certifying examination in internal medicine
- Physicians preparing for maintenance of certification in internal medicine (recertification)

Earn "Same-Day" CME Credits Online

For the first time, print subscribers can enter their answers online to earn CME credits in 24 hours or less. You can submit your answers using online answer sheets that are provided at mksap.acponline.org, where a record of your MKSAP 16 credits will be available. To earn CME credits, you need to answer all of the questions in a test and earn a score of at least 50% correct (number of correct answers divided by the total number of questions). Take any of the following approaches:

1. Use the printed answer sheet at the back of this book to record your answers. Go to mksap.acponline.org, access the appropriate online answer sheet, transcribe your answers, and submit your test for same-day CME credits. There is no additional fee for this service.

2. Go to mksap.acponline.org, access the appropriate online answer sheet, directly enter your answers, and submit your test for same-day CME credits. There is no additional fee for this service.

3. Pay a $10 processing fee per answer sheet and submit the printed answer sheet at the back of this book by mail or fax, as instructed on the answer sheet. Make sure you calculate your score and fax the answer sheet to 215-351-2799 or mail the answer sheet to Member and Customer Service, American College of Physicians, 190 N. Independence Mall West, Philadelphia, PA 19106-1572, using the courtesy envelope provided in your MKSAP 16 slipcase. You will need your 10-digit order number and 8-digit ACP ID number, which are printed on your packing slip. Please allow 4 to 6 weeks for your score report to be emailed back to you. Be sure to include your email address for a response.

If you do not have a 10-digit order number and 8-digit ACP ID number or if you need help creating a username and password to access the MKSAP 16 online answer sheets, go to mksap.acponline.org or email custserv@acponline.org.

Permission/Consent for Use of Figures Shown in MKSAP 16 Rheumatology Multiple-Choice Questions

The figure shown in Self-Assessment Test Item 62 is reprinted with permission from Physicians' Information and Education Resource (ACP PIER). Philadelphia, PA: American College of Physicians.

Disclosure Policy

It is the policy of the American College of Physicians (ACP) to ensure balance, independence, objectivity, and scientific rigor in all of its educational activities. To this end, and consistent with the policies of the ACP and the Accreditation Council for Continuing Medical Education (ACCME), contributors to all ACP continuing medical education activities are required to disclose all relevant financial relationships with any entity producing, marketing, re-selling, or distributing health care goods or services consumed by, or used on, patients. Contributors are required to use generic names in the discussion of therapeutic options and are required to identify any unapproved, off-label, or investigative use of commercial products or devices. Where a trade name is used, all available trade names for the same product type are also included. If trade-name products manufactured by companies with whom contributors have relationships are discussed, contributors are asked to provide evidence-based citations in support of the discussion. The information is reviewed by the committee responsible for producing this text. If necessary, adjustments to topics or contributors' roles in content development are made to balance the discussion. Further, all readers of this text are asked to evaluate the content for evidence of commercial bias and send any relevant comments to mksap_editors@acponline.org so that future decisions about content and contributors can be made in light of this information.

Resolution of Conflicts

To resolve all conflicts of interest and influences of vested interests, the ACP precluded members of the content-creation committee from deciding on any content issues that involved generic or trade-name products associated with proprietary entities with which these committee members had relationships. In addition, content was based on best evidence and updated clinical care guidelines, when such evidence and guidelines were available. Contributors' disclosure information can be found with the list of contributors' names and those of ACP principal staff listed in the beginning of this book.

Hospital-Based Medicine

For the convenience of subscribers who provide care in hospital settings, content that is specific to the hospital setting has been highlighted in blue. Hospital icons (H) highlight where the hospital-only content begins, continues over more than one page, and ends.

Educational Disclaimer

The editors and publisher of MKSAP 16 recognize that the development of new material offers many opportunities for error. Despite our best efforts, some errors may persist in print. Drug dosage schedules are, we believe, accurate and in accordance with current standards. Readers are advised, however, to ensure that the recommended dosages in

MKSAP 16 concur with the information provided in the product information material. This is especially important in cases of new, infrequently used, or highly toxic drugs. Application of the information in MKSAP 16 remains the professional responsibility of the practitioner.

The primary purpose of MKSAP 16 is educational. Information presented, as well as publications, technologies, products, and/or services discussed, is intended to inform subscribers about the knowledge, techniques, and experiences of the contributors. A diversity of professional opinion exists, and the views of the contributors are their own and not those of the ACP. Inclusion of any material in the program does not constitute endorsement or recommendation by the ACP. The ACP does not warrant the safety, reliability, accuracy, completeness, or usefulness of and disclaims any and all liability for damages and claims that may result from the use of information, publications, technologies, products, and/or services discussed in this program.

Publisher's Information

Unauthorized Use of This Book Is Against the Law

MKSAP 16 ISBN: 978-1-938245-00-8
(Rheumatology) ISBN: 978-1-938245-06-0

Printed in the United States of America.

For order information in the U.S. or Canada call 800-523-1546, extension 2600. All other countries call 215-351-2600. Fax inquiries to 215-351-2799 or email to custserv@acponline.org.

Errata and Norm Tables

Errata for MKSAP 16 will be available through the MKSAP Resource Site at mksap.acponline.org as new information becomes known to the editors.

MKSAP 16 Performance Interpretation Guidelines with Norm Tables, available July 31, 2013, will reflect the knowledge of physicians who have completed the self-assessment tests before the program was published. These physicians took the tests without being able to refer to the syllabus, answers, and critiques. For your convenience, the tables are available in a printable PDF file through the MKSAP Resource Site at mksap.acponline.org.

Table of Contents

Systemic Lupus Erythematosus

Systemic Sclerosis

Sjögren Syndrome

Mixed Connective Tissue Disease

Crystal-Induced Arthropathies

Infectious Arthritis

Idiopathic Inflammatory Myopathies

Rheumatology High-Value Care Recommendations

The American College of Physicians, in collaboration with multiple other organizations, is embarking on a national initiative to promote awareness about the importance of stewardship of health care resources. The goals are to improve health care outcomes by providing care of proven benefit and reducing costs by avoiding unnecessary and even harmful interventions. The initiative comprises several programs that integrate the important concept of health care value (balancing clinical benefit with costs and harms) for a given intervention into various educational materials to address the needs of trainees, practicing physicians, and patients.

To integrate discussion of high-value, cost-conscious care into MKSAP 16, we have created recommendations based on the medical knowledge content that we feel meet the below definition of high-value care and bring us closer to our goal of improving patient outcomes while conserving finite resources.

High-Value Care Recommendation: A recommendation to choose diagnostic and management strategies for patients in specific clinical situations that balance clinical benefit with cost and harms with the goal of improving patient outcomes.

Below are the High-Value Care Recommendations for the Rheumatology section of MKSAP 16.

- Do not obtain an antinuclear antibody test in patients with nonspecific symptoms such as fatigue and myalgia or in patients with fibromyalgia.
- The diagnosis of periarthritis (bursitis, tendinitis) is based upon the history and physical examination; laboratory testing and imaging are unnecessary (see Item 59 and Item 76).
- Do not perform an MRI in patients with suspected carpal tunnel syndrome, because the diagnostic utility of MRI in this setting is unclear (see Item 81).
- Methotrexate may be used as the initial disease-modifying antirheumatic drug (DMARD) for rheumatoid arthritis treatment; this agent is usually better tolerated than other DMARDs and also has good efficacy, long-term compliance rates, and a relatively low cost (see Item 28 and Item 67).
- When sacroiliitis is suspected, begin with plain radiography and only proceed to MRI of the sacroiliac joints in patients with high clinical suspicion and negative plain radiographs (see Item 41).
- Patients with ankylosing spondylitis are monitored clinically; do not use periodic CT or MRI to monitor disease activity and response to treatment.
- Treat patients with podagra (inflammation of the first metatarsophalangeal joint) empirically for gout and do not perform joint aspiration, because gout is common and infection uncommon in this location.
- Do not use uric acid–lowering drugs for gout prophylaxis in patients who have had single or very rare (<2 per year) attacks; these patients can be managed expectantly, because next attacks may be quite delayed.
- Do not treat patients with asymptomatic hyperuricemia (see Item 52).
- A kidney or lung biopsy is unnecessary in patients with a classic presentation of granulomatosis with polyangiitis (also known as Wegener granulomatosis) and positive c-ANCA (antiproteinase-3 antibodies); reserve biopsy for patients with atypical presentations.

Rheumatology

Approach to the Patient with Rheumatic Disease

Inflammatory Versus Noninflammatory Pain

Distinguishing between inflammatory and noninflammatory joint pain is critical in evaluating patients with musculoskeletal conditions (**Table 1**). Inflammation may be the only symptom that distinguishes psoriatic arthritis from osteoarthritis or systemic lupus erythematosus (SLE) from fibromyalgia.

Joint pain is associated with loss of function. Noninflammatory pain arises from sources such as prostaglandins, cathepsin, chemokines, and growth factors. Cytokines (interleukin [IL]-1, IL-6, and tumor necrosis factor [TNF]) are increasingly recognized sources of inflammatory pain.

Inflammatory pain can be distinguished from noninflammatory pain by the presence of redness, heat, and/or swelling. Subjective manifestations of joint inflammation include morning stiffness for more than 60 minutes as well as constitutional symptoms such as fatigue and malaise; objective findings include soft-tissue swelling around the joint, joint effusions, joint erythema, and warmth.

KEY POINTS

- Inflammatory joint pain can be distinguished from noninflammatory pain by the presence of redness, heat, and/or swelling of the joint.

- Patients with joint inflammation typically have morning stiffness, fatigue, and malaise.

The Musculoskeletal Examination

Identifying the source of pain is essential when determining the cause of musculoskeletal symptoms. Patients may frequently refer to their symptoms as "joint pain" (for example, shoulder or hip), although the source may be periarticular (for example, rotator cuff or trochanteric bursa).

Palpation of the joint can determine the presence of tenderness, warmth, or swelling. Pain associated with direct palpation of the joint line suggests arthritis or a joint-associated pathology (for example, meniscal injury). Pain associated with the surrounding soft tissues can suggest other pathology (for example, bursitis, ligamentous strain, or tendinitis). Examination for the presence of swelling can be difficult. The capsule from many joints extends beyond the immediate joint line. The suprapatellar bursa, which is a reflection of the true knee joint capsule along the distal femur, is perhaps the best known example. To examine for a knee effusion, palpate this potential space while compressing the suprapatellar bursa. Similarly with other joints (for example, metacarpophalangeal joints), it is important to envelop the potential joint space (support the palmar aspect of the joint) while compressing the medial and lateral joint lines.

Examination of the joint for passive and active range of motion is also important. Pain with passive range of motion (in which the joint is rotated but the tendons are not actively engaged) suggests an arthritic condition. Pain with active resisted range of motion (in which the joint is immobilized while the patient tries to move the extremity) suggests tendon pathology. Overuse of a tendon or excessive strain across a

TABLE 1. Features of Inflammatory Versus Noninflammatory Pain

Feature	Inflammatory Pain	Noninflammatory Pain
Physical examination findings	Synovitis; erythema; warmth; soft-tissue swelling	No synovitis; bony enlargement may occur in osteoarthritis
Morning stiffness	>60 min	<30 min
Constitutional symptoms	Fever; fatigue	Generally absent
Synovial fluid	Leukocyte count >2000/µL (2.0 × 10⁹/L), predominantly neutrophils	Leukocyte count <2000/µL (2.0 × 10⁹/L), less than 50% neutrophils
Other laboratory findings	Elevated inflammatory markers (ESR, CRP); anemia of chronic disease	Inflammatory markers usually normal or minimally elevated
Arthritis imaging studies	Symmetric joint-space narrowing; periarticular osteopenia; erosions	Asymmetric joint-space narrowing; osteophytes; subchondral sclerosis

CRP = C-reactive protein; ESR = erythrocyte sedimentation rate.

deconditioned muscle may lead to localized pain syndromes (**Table 2**).

Arthritis

Diagnosing arthritis relies on pattern recognition. The type of arthritis can be established by determining the duration of symptoms (acute versus chronic), number of affected joints, whether symptoms and signs point to an inflammatory or noninflammatory condition, and whether joint involvement is symmetric or asymmetric.

Monoarticular Arthritis

Monoarticular arthritis is classified as acute or chronic. Acute monoarticular arthritis can be noninflammatory (traumatic hemarthrosis, internal derangement) or inflammatory (crystalline or septic). In the setting of acute monoarticular arthritis, joint aspiration is needed to evaluate for infectious arthritis (see Joint Aspiration). Suspicion for infectious arthritis should be guided by clinical presentation and examination. Hematogenous sources for infection or local skin breaks should be sought.

Chronic inflammatory monoarticular arthritis (signs of inflammation present ≥6 weeks) should raise concern for mycobacterial, fungal, or *Borrelia burgdorferi* infection. Synovial fluid analysis alone may be inadequate for diagnosis; therefore, systemic evidence of infection (serologies or other laboratory tests) or synovial biopsy may be required to establish the diagnosis. Chronic noninflammatory monoarticular arthritis is usually caused by osteoarthritis.

Oligoarthritis

Acute inflammatory oligoarthritis (involvement of two to four joints) may be caused by gonorrhea or rheumatic fever. Chronic inflammatory oligoarthritis can be caused by spondyloarthritis or a connective tissue disease. Chronic noninflammatory oligoarthritis is usually caused by osteoarthritis.

Polyarthritis

Acute polyarthritis (involvement of more than four joints) can be caused by viral infections (parvovirus B19, HIV, hepatitis B, rubella) or may be an early manifestation of a chronic

---

TABLE 2. Common Overuse Syndromes

Region	Etiology	Symptoms	Examination Findings
Shoulder	Rotator cuff tendinitis	Pain in upper outer arm; pain with overhead activities or reaching behind the back	Pain on abducting arm between 30 and 150 degrees; less pain on passive motion of shoulder
	Biceps tendinitis	Pain in anterior shoulder; pain worsens when lifting heavy objects	Pain on palpation of biceps tendon
Elbow	Lateral epicondylitis	Pain at lateral epicondyle; pain when carrying briefcase/purse or gripping steering wheel	Tender lateral epicondyle
Wrist	de Quervain tenosynovitis	Pain along radial aspect of wrist	Positive Finkelstein test (pain grabbing thumb and stretching abducens tendon) or pain palpating the tendon
	Carpal tunnel syndrome	Pain and paresthesia in palmar aspect of first three digits and radial aspect of the fourth	Positive Tinel sign (symptoms reproduced by tapping palmar aspect of wrist with flat end of reflex hammer)
Hand	Trigger finger	Locking of finger on flexion; pain and crepitus on palpation of tendon sheath	Flexor tendon nodule on palmar aspect of metacarpophalangeal joint
Buttocks	Ischial bursitis (weaver's bottom)	Pain in buttocks, worsens when sitting	Pain on palpation of ischium
	Piriformis syndrome	Pain in buttocks with symptoms of sciatica	Pain on deep palpation of buttocks in region of sciatic notch
Hip	Trochanteric bursitis	Pain in lateral hip, worsens when lying on that side	Pain on palpation over lateral trochanter of the hip
Knee	Pes anserine bursitis	Pain just below knee at anteromedial aspect of the tibia when exercising or climbing stairs	Tenderness at anteromedial aspect of the tibia just below the knee
Foot	Plantar fasciitis	Pain on bottom of the heel when walking	Tenderness along medial aspect of the base of the heel

inflammatory polyarthritis, which is often caused by rheumatoid arthritis, SLE, or spondyloarthritis (such as psoriatic arthritis) (**Table 3**).

Extra-Articular Manifestations of Rheumatic Disease

Dermatologic Manifestations

Skin manifestations are common in patients with rheumatic conditions (**Table 4**) (**Figure 1** and **Figure 2**) and may also reflect consequences of drug therapy.

Fever

With any systemic inflammatory condition, fever may be one of the cardinal findings. Certain arthritic conditions are classically associated with fever, including adult-onset Still disease, familial Mediterranean fever, tumor necrosis factor receptor–associated periodic syndrome, and cryopyrin-associated syndromes (see Other Systemic Inflammatory Diseases, Familial Autoinflammatory Diseases). Fever is also common in SLE but rarely occurs in rheumatoid arthritis.

Inflammatory Eye Disease

Inflammatory arthritis and other autoimmune disorders may involve the eye (**Table 5**). Rheumatic conditions with a higher prevalence of ocular comorbid conditions warrant special attention.

Patients with pauciarticular juvenile inflammatory arthritis have a high incidence of iritis or uveitis (particularly when the patient has positive antinuclear antibody serologies), which can be asymptomatic until damage occurs, warranting regular ophthalmologic evaluation. Uveitis has a broad rheumatic differential. In an otherwise asymptomatic patient with uveitis, a chest radiograph (to rule out sarcoidosis), HLA-B27 (for possible spondyloarthritis), and ANCA (for granulomatosis with polyangiitis [also known as Wegener granulomatosis]) should be obtained.

Up to 25% of patients with rheumatoid arthritis have eye involvement, with almost any structure of the eye affected. Keratoconjunctivitis sicca (dry eyes) is the most common ocular condition in rheumatoid arthritis. The most vision-threatening condition involves scleral melt, in which inflammation can cause a defect in the scleral structure, leading to herniation of the vitreous material through the scleral wall.

A common cause of dry eyes is Sjögren syndrome (inflammation of lacrimal and other exocrine glands), which may occur as its own entity or as a common comorbidity in other autoimmune conditions. In addition to evaluation for ocular disease in patients with rheumatic disease, physicians need to consider systemic autoimmune conditions in patients with eye disease.

TABLE 3. Inflammatory Chronic Polyarthritis

Condition	Pattern of Joint Involvement	Extra-articular Features	Diagnostic Studies
Rheumatoid arthritis	Symmetric; involves small joints (wrist, MCP, PIP, MTP) but also involves hips, knees, elbows, shoulders, and cervical spine	Rheumatoid nodules; dry eyes and mouth; interstitial lung disease; Felty syndrome (splenomegaly, leukopenia, leg ulcers)	Rheumatoid factor; anti-CCP; acute phase reactants; erosive changes on radiograph
Systemic lupus erythematosus	Symmetric polyarthritis with large and small joint involvement	Fever; rash; serositis; kidney disease; neurologic disease	ANA and other serologies; no erosions on radiograph
Spondyloarthritis			
Ankylosing spondylitis	Sacroiliac and spinal involvement; symmetric; large joints (shoulders, hips)	Uveitis	Calcification of anterior longitudinal ligament of spine on radiograph; sacroiliitis; HLA B27 positive
Psoriatic arthritis	Asymmetric oligoarthritis or polyarthritis; DIP joint preference; dactylitis (sausage digits)	Psoriasis	"Pencil-in-cup" deformities; erosions and osteophytes on radiograph
Reactive arthritis (formerly known as Reiter syndrome)	Asymmetric oligoarthritis; knee and ankle involvement; enthesitis; Achilles tendinitis; plantar fasciitis; sacroiliitis	Uveitis; keratoderma blennorrhagicum; *Chlamydia*; enteropathic infection	HLA B27 positive; sacroiliitis
Inflammatory bowel disease–associated arthritis	Asymmetric; sacroiliac joints; knees; feet	Crohn disease; ulcerative colitis	Sacroiliitis; HLA B27 positive in cases of axial involvement

ANA = antinuclear antibodies; CCP = cyclic citrullinated peptide; DIP = distal interphalangeal; MCP = metacarpophalangeal; MTP = metatarsophalangeal; PIP = proximal interphalangeal.

TABLE 4. Dermatologic Manifestations of Rheumatic Disease

Condition	Manifestation
Systemic lupus erythematosus	Butterfly (malar) rash
	Photosensitive rash
	Discoid lupus erythematosus rash
	Subacute cutaneous lupus erythematosus rash
	Oral ulcerations (ulcers on the tongue or hard palate that are usually painless, unlike canker sores)
	Alopecia
	Lupus profundus (painful, indurated subcutaneous swelling with overlying erythema of the skin)
Dermatomyositis	Gottron papules (erythematous plaques on extensor surfaces of MCP and PIP joints)
	Macular erythema (shawl and V sign)
	Heliotrope rash (violaceous rash on the upper eyelid)
	Mechanic's hands (dry, cracked fingers and hands)
	Nailfold capillary abnormalities
Amyopathic dermatomyositis	Above skin findings without myositis findings
Systemic sclerosis	Skin thickening (limited disease involves face and skin distal to elbows/knees; diffuse disease involves skin proximal to distal forearms/knees)
	Nailfold capillary changes
Vasculitis	Purpuric lesions
	Cutaneous nodules
	Ulcers
Behçet disease	Oral and genital ulcers
	Erythema nodosum (painful, erythematous nodules on the pretibial region)
Sarcoidosis	Erythema nodosum
Psoriatic arthritis	Psoriasis typically on extensor surfaces, umbilicus, gluteal fold, scalp, and behind ears (erythematous scaly plaques); pustular psoriasis on palms and soles; arthritis may precede rash by up to 10 years
	Nail pitting
	Onycholysis
Reactive arthritis	Keratoderma blenorrhagicum (psoriasiform rash on soles, toes, palms)
	Circinate balanitis (psoriasiform rash on penis)
Adult-onset Still disease	Evanescent, salmon-colored rash on the trunk and proximal extremities
Rheumatic fever (secondary to streptoccocal infection)	Erythema marginatum
Lyme disease	Erythema chronicum migrans
	Acrodermatitis atrophicans

MCP = metacarpophalangeal; PIP = proximal interphalangeal.

Lung Disease

Rheumatoid arthritis may be associated with pneumonitis (bronchiolitis obliterans with organizing pneumonia or interstitial lung disease), rheumatoid nodules in the lungs, and pleural effusions. Progressive systemic sclerosis can cause interstitial lung disease that usually occurs within the first 2 years of onset. CREST (calcinosis, Raynaud phenomenon, esophageal dysmotility, sclerodactyly, and telangiectasia) syndrome is associated with pulmonary arterial hypertension, often in the absence of pulmonary parenchymal disease. Lupus can manifest with pneumonitis or pleural effusions.

Cavitary nodules, consolidation, or wedge infarcts may be present in the lungs of patients who have granulomatosis with polyangiitis. Patients with microscopic polyangiitis may have hemoptysis and diffuse infiltrates present on chest radiograph. Churg-Strauss syndrome often manifests as an eosinophilic pneumonitis. Polyarteritis nodosa typically spares the lungs.

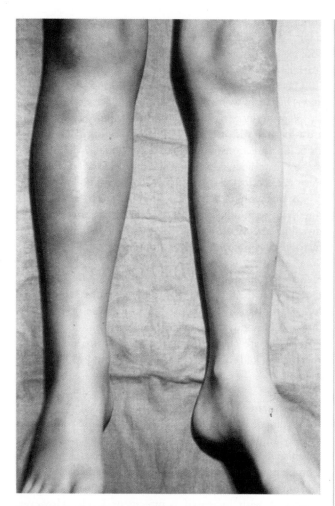

FIGURE 1. The subcutaneous nodules and plaques on this patient's shins are consistent with erythema nodosum.

(c) 2012 American College of Rheumatology. Used with permission.

TABLE 5. Ocular Manifestations of Systemic Inflammatory Conditions

Ocular Presentation	Associated Systemic Rheumatic Disease

Uveitis	Spondyloarthritis
	   Ankylosing spondylitis
	   Reactive arthritis
	   Inflammatory bowel disease
	Sarcoidosis
	Behçet disease
	Juvenile rheumatoid arthritis
	Granulomatosis with polyangiitis
	(also known as Wegener
	granulomatosis)

Episcleritis	Spondyloarthritis Vasculitis Inflammatory bowel disease
Scleritis	Rheumatoid arthritis Relapsing polychondritis Inflammatory bowel disease
Retinal disease	Giant cell arteritis Vasculitis Antiphospholipid syndrome

Diarrhea

Inflammatory bowel disease can be associated with a seronegative chronic inflammatory polyarthritis primarily affecting the larger joints and the sacroiliac joints. Reactive arthritis may occur after enteric infection with *Salmonella*, *Shigella*, *Yersinia*, *Campylobacter*, or *Clostridium*. Other less common conditions in which diarrhea and arthritis are present include Whipple disease and celiac disease.

Musculoskeletal and Rheumatic Manifestations

Systemic conditions have several common rheumatic manifestations. Diabetes mellitus is often associated with Dupuytren contractures or adhesive capsulitis of the shoulder. Carpal tunnel syndrome can be associated with either hypothyroidism or diabetes. See **Table 6** for a list of associations.

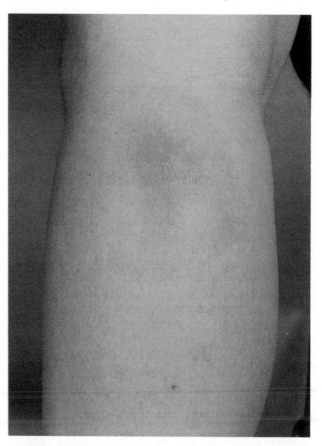

FIGURE 2. Erythema chronicum migrans manifests as large, expanding, erythematous annular lesions. Central clearing may develop as these lesions increase in size.

TABLE 6. Musculoskeletal and Rheumatic Manifestations of Systemic Conditions

Condition	Musculoskeletal/Rheumatic Manifestation
Diabetes mellitus	Dupuytren contracture
	Adhesive capsulitis of the shoulder
	Diabetic amyotrophy (ischemia of large muscle group)
	Carpal tunnel syndrome
	Diffuse idiopathic skeletal hyperostosis
Hypothyroidism	Arthralgia
	Myopathy (with elevated serum creatine kinase)
Hyperthyroidism	Osteoporosis
	Myopathy (serum creatine kinase not elevated)
Hyperparathyroidism	Calcium pyrophosphate deposition disease
	Osteoporosis
Acromegaly	Arthralgia
	Bone pain
	Calcium pyrophosphate deposition disease
Sickle cell disease	Sickle crisis
	Avascular necrosis
Hemophilia	Hemarthroses
Carcinoma	Paraneoplastic syndrome
	Inflammatory polyarthritis
	Dermatomyositis
Myeloma/lymphoma/leukemia	Cryoglobulinemia
	Amyloidosis
	Arthritis (particularly in children)

Laboratory Studies

Laboratory studies are very useful in the diagnosis of rheumatic disease and for monitoring disease activity and medication toxicity. A comprehensive metabolic survey and complete blood count are beneficial to monitor possible effects of rheumatic conditions or their treatments on the liver, kidney, and bone marrow.

Tests That Measure Inflammation

Erythrocyte Sedimentation Rate

Erythrocyte sedimentation rate (ESR) is a common laboratory study used to distinguish inflammatory and noninflammatory conditions and to monitor disease activity. Inflammatory states (rheumatic conditions, infections, and malignancies) are associated with markedly elevated fibrinogen levels and, therefore, elevated ESR. However, other conditions such as pregnancy, diabetes mellitus, and end-stage kidney disease may increase fibrinogen levels in the absence of inflammation, producing a "falsely elevated" ESR. Anemia and macrocytosis are associated with an increased ESR because of rheostatic properties. ESR increases with age and is higher in women.

Low fibrinogen states such as liver failure or heart failure are associated with artificially low ESR. Factors that affect the shape or attraction of erythrocytes, including rouleaux formation (myeloma, polycythemia vera), sickle cell disease, and microcytosis (including spherocytosis), may also lower ESR.

A markedly elevated ESR (>100 mm/h) should alert physicians to conditions such as giant cell arteritis, multiple myeloma, metastatic cancer, or other overwhelming inflammatory states (infection or autoimmune disease).

C-Reactive Protein

C-reactive protein (CRP) is an acute phase reactant; therefore, in contrast to ESR, it is a direct measure of inflammation and responds more quickly to changes in disease state. CRP levels are elevated in giant cell arteritis, polymyalgia rheumatica, and rheumatoid arthritis but tend to be normal in lupus.

Complement

Complement is an integral part of the immune response; it acts to augment inflammation and damage to invading organisms and serves as a chemotactant to leukocytes. Complement production and consumption increase during inflammation; consequently, most inflammatory states are associated with increased complement levels. However, SLE, cryoglobulinemic vasculitis, and urticarial vasculitis are immune complex–mediated diseases that consume complement, resulting in low levels of complement when the disease is active. C3 and C4 are the commonly measured complement components. CH50 assay is useful for detecting complement deficiencies anywhere in the complement pathway but is more expensive and difficult to perform than C3 and C4 measurement.

Antibody Tests

Most persons do not produce levels of antinuclear antibodies (ANA) above the laboratory limits of normal, but low-titer ANA can be detected in some healthy persons, particularly women and the elderly. Of those without rheumatic disease, up to 30% have ANA titers of 1:40, 13% have titers of 1:30, and 3% have titers of 1:320. Therefore, ANA testing is not indicated unless there are symptoms and signs that lead to a clinical suspicion of lupus or another connective tissue disease. More than 95% of patients with SLE have a positive ANA; therefore, a negative ANA argues strongly against the presence of lupus. When clinical suspicion exists, a strong ANA titer (for example, 1:160 or higher) warrants further testing for other manifestations of lupus (complete blood count, serum creatinine level, urinalysis, and other autoantibody testing) or referral to a specialist.

Other autoantibodies have more specificity for autoimmunity and are often associated with specific conditions or disease patterns (**Table 7**).

KEY POINTS

- Inflammatory states are associated with elevated erythrocyte sedimentation rate (ESR); however, conditions such as pregnancy, diabetes mellitus, and end-stage kidney disease may produce a "falsely elevated" ESR.

- C-reactive protein is a direct measure of inflammation that responds more quickly to changes in disease state than erythrocyte sedimentation rate.

- Because low-titer antinuclear antibodies (ANA) can be detected in some healthy persons, ANA testing should be used judiciously in patients with only marginal signs and symptoms supportive of a rheumatic disease.

Imaging Studies

Imaging studies aid in the diagnosis of rheumatic conditions, help to follow the progress of disease, and serve as illustrative teaching aids for the patient.

Radiography

Radiography is essential in the evaluation of patients with established inflammatory arthritis to determine if erosions are

TABLE 7. Autoantibodies in Rheumatic Conditions

Autoantibody	Rheumatic Condition	Sensitivity/Specificity	Comments
ANA	SLE	Lupus: 95% sensitivity; poor specificity	Screening tool for autoimmunity
Anti–double-stranded DNA	SLE	Lupus: 60% sensitivity; Crithidia IFA or Farr assays more specific than ELISA	Correlates with lupus disease activity, especially kidney disease
Anti-Smith	SLE	SLE: 30% sensitivity and 99% specificity	Most specific test for SLE
Anti-U1-RNP	MCTD; SLE	100% sensitivity	High titer seen in MCTD (>1:10,000)
Anti-Ro/SSA; anti-La/SSB	Sjögren syndrome; SLE; RA; PSS	Sjögren syndrome: 70% sensitivity; SLE: 30% sensitivity	Sicca symptoms; in SLE, associated with neonatal lupus (rash and conduction block)
Anti–Scl-70	Diffuse PSS	10%-30% sensitivity	Pulmonary fibrosis
Anticentromere	Limited PSS (CREST)	10%-30% sensitivity	Pulmonary hypertension
c-ANCA (antiproteinase-3)	Granulomatosis with polyangiitis (also known as Wegener granulomatosis)	90% sensitivity when disease is active	N/A
p-ANCA (antimyeloperoxidase)	Microscopic polyangiitis (MPA); Churg-Strauss syndrome (CSS)	MPA: 80% sensitivity; CSS: 60% sensitivity	Atypical p-ANCA (antimyeloperoxidase negative) can be seen in inflammatory bowel disease
Anti-Jo-1	Myositis	20%-30% sensitivity	Interstitial lung disease
Rheumatoid factor	RA; Sjögren syndrome; cryoglobulinemia	RA: 70% sensitivity; not specific for RA	RF is an antibody to Ig and hence many false positives (for example, hepatitis C, SLE); 30% of patients with RA are RF negative
Anti–cyclic citrullinated peptide	RA	RA: 70% sensitivity; more specific for RA than RF	Positive in up to one third of RF-negative RA patients; associated with erosions; predicts disease progression in patients with undifferentiated arthritis
Antihistone	Drug-induced SLE	Drug-induced SLE: 95% sensitivity	Also seen in some patients with native lupus
Cryoglobulins	Vasculitis; hepatitis C; myeloma; SLE; RA	Type II cryoglobulin seen in all patients with cryoglobulinemic vasculitis	Can be an epiphenomenon in connective tissue diseases

ANA = antinuclear antibodies; CREST = calcinosis, Raynaud phenomenon, esophageal dysmotility, sclerodactyly, and telangiectasia; ELISA = enzyme-linked immunosorbent assay; IFA = immunofluorescent assay; MCTD = mixed connective tissue disease; N/A = not applicable; PSS = progressive systemic sclerosis; RA = rheumatoid arthritis; RF = rheumatoid factor; RNP = ribonucleoprotein; SLE = systemic lupus erythematosus.

present (**Table 8**). It may take 12 months of disease activity for erosions to become detectable on plain radiograph. In patients with osteoarthritis, radiography is useful in evaluating the severity of joint-space loss and other bony changes. However, radiographs have significant limitations because they are two-dimensional shadows of three-dimensional structures. For example, the position of the knee during an anterior view may significantly affect the appearance of joint-space findings. (Cartilage loss may be greater or less in the flexed view than in the extended view.) A gouty or rheumatoid erosive lesion imaged *en face* may not be visible or may appear as a simple cyst. At least two views are usually needed to verify findings.

CT and MRI

CT and MRI provide greater detail than plain radiography and may be useful if initial radiographs are negative and clinical suspicion is high. CT is the best modality to image bone, whereas MRI reveals fine detail of soft-tissue structures such as cartilage, synovium, tendons, and ligaments. However, these imaging modalities are expensive and more complicated to read than radiographs; interpretation of CT and MRI findings in the office is often difficult and requires greater reliance on the consulting radiologist's report.

Advanced imaging is often needed to show sacroiliac joint abnormalities. Plain radiographs of sacroiliac joints are difficult to interpret owing to the anatomy of the joint. CT of the joint can provide evidence of erosive changes in the bone, whereas MRI can demonstrate active inflammation and the presence of synovitis or bony edema.

Ultrasonography

The use of ultrasonography to evaluate patients with rheumatic diseases is rapidly increasing. Ultrasonography is relatively inexpensive, can scan across three-dimensional structures, and may be used concurrently with physical examination to evaluate moving structures (for example, tendon evaluations). The addition of a Doppler signal can evaluate blood flow, identify arteries or veins (for example, to be avoided during tendon or joint injections), or evaluate the vascularity of synovial proliferation. The skill of the operator is associated with quality of the evaluation and findings.

Joint Aspiration

Joint aspiration is useful in discriminating between inflammatory and noninflammatory effusions. It is essential when diagnosing infectious arthritis and distinguishing between infectious arthritis and acute crystalline arthropathy. Infectious arthritis may be indistinguishable from an acute gout attack because fever, peripheral leukocytosis, and elevated levels of acute phase reactants can be present in both conditions. When a septic joint is considered in the differential diagnosis, aspiration is needed to confirm or rule out the etiology. Aspirated synovial fluid should be sent for cell count and differential, Gram stain with culture, and crystal analysis. There is no absolute cutoff of synovial fluid leukocyte counts for ruling out septic arthritis; however, patients with counts greater than 50,000/µL (50 × 10⁹/L) with polymorphonuclear cell predominance have a high likelihood of infection. Synovial fluid leukocyte counts less than 2000/µL (2.0 × 10⁹/L) are usually associated with noninflammatory etiologies. The presence of crystals does not rule out infection if suspicion is high.

Under a polarized light, needle-like urate crystals are negatively birefringent (bending light in the sinister or negative direction). The crystals are yellow when parallel to the axis of the polarized field and blue when perpendicular to the axis. Calcium pyrophosphate crystals are rhomboid, blue, and weakly (not as vivid) positively birefringent.

TABLE 8. Radiographic Findings of Common Rheumatic Conditions

Rheumatic Condition	Radiographic Findings
Rheumatoid arthritis	Bony erosions; periarticular osteopenia; subluxations; soft-tissue swelling; MCP and PIP involvement on hand radiograph
Psoriatic arthritis	Destructive arthritis with erosions and osteophytes; DIP involvement; "pencil-in-cup" deformity on hand radiograph; arthritis mutilans
Osteoarthritis	Asymmetric joint-space narrowing; osteophytes; subchondral sclerosis and cystic changes; degenerative disk disease with collapse of disks; degenerative joint disease with facet joint osteophytes; these findings lead to spondylolisthesis (anterior/posterior misalignment of the spine) and kyphosis
Ankylosing spondylitis	Sacroiliitis; squaring of the vertebral bodies; bridging vertical enthesophytes
Diffuse idiopathic skeletal hyperostosis	Calcification of the anterior longitudinal ligament; bridging horizontal syndesmophytes
Calcium pyrophosphate deposition disease	Chondrocalcinosis, most commonly of the knees, shoulders, wrists, pubic symphysis

DIP = distal interphalangeal; MCP = metacarpophalangeal; PIP = proximal interphalangeal.

- Radiography is essential in the evaluation of patients with established inflammatory arthritis to determine if erosions are present.
- In patients with osteoarthritis, radiography is useful in evaluating the severity of joint-space loss and other bony changes.
- Joint aspiration is useful in discriminating between inflammatory and noninflammatory effusions and is essential when diagnosing infectious arthritis and crystalline arthropathy.
- Synovial fluid leukocyte counts less than $2000/\mu L$ $(2.0 \times 10^9/L)$ are usually associated with noninflammatory etiologies and counts above $50,000/\mu L$ $(50 \times 10^9/L)$ are suspicious for infection.

Principles of Therapeutics

Evaluation of Disease Progression

Several formal instruments are available to measure disease activity and progression to assess patient response to pharmacotherapy.

The Disease Activity Score (DAS) is used for patients with rheumatoid arthritis and provides a composite based on objective and subjective indices. Parameters include number of swollen and tender joints, global disease activity on a visual analogue scale, and measurement of erythrocyte sedimentation rate (ESR) or C-reactive protein (CRP) level. The DAS28 is a shorter version of this tool that assesses a smaller number of joints; it is commonly used in clinical trials and clinical practice.

The American College of Rheumatology (ACR) improvement criteria for rheumatoid arthritis (ACR 20, 50, and 70) document the percentage of patients experiencing 20%, 50%, or 70% improvement in tender and swollen joints plus three of five other criteria (ESR or CRP; patient global assessment; physician global assessment; pain; disability/function). ACR responses are commonly used as end points in clinical trials.

For other rheumatic diseases, specific instruments address the unique clinical aspects of a particular condition. The Western Ontario and McMaster Universities Osteoarthritis Index is the standard assessment tool for osteoarthritis of the knee and hip. The Bath Ankylosing Spondylitis Disease Activity Index is recommended for measuring the signs and symptoms of ankylosing spondylitis. Several indices measure lupus disease activity, including the Systemic Lupus Erythematosus Disease Activity Index, the Systemic Lupus Activity Measure, and the British Isles Lupus Assessment Group Index.

The Health Assessment Questionnaire (HAQ) provides a patient-based assessment of function in daily activities such as grooming, feeding, and ambulating; these measures reliably predict disease morbidity and mortality. Briefer versions of the HAQ (for example, the Multidimensional HAQ) and other instruments (for example, the Routine Assessment of Patient Index Data 3 [RAPID3]) are also available. Health assessment instruments such as these can be applied to virtually all forms of rheumatic disease.

- Instruments such as the Disease Activity Score and the Health Assessment Questionnaire are used to measure rheumatic disease activity and progression as well as overall patient function and wellness.

Anti-Inflammatory Agents

Anti-inflammatory agents reduce heat, redness, swelling, and pain as well as improve function. Although these agents generally ameliorate signs and symptoms, they do not alter the course or prognosis of disease.

NSAIDs

NSAIDs are anti-inflammatory, analgesic, and antipyretic agents that inhibit cyclooxygenase (COX) enzymes and thereby block prostaglandin generation. Reduction in prostaglandin E_2 provides most of the anti-inflammatory and analgesic effects of NSAIDs. Because prostaglandin E_2 maintains the gastric lining and kidney blood flow, NSAIDs may promote gastric ulcers, kidney disease, and hypertension. NSAIDs can also occasionally induce pulmonary airway constriction and inflammation (aspirin-sensitive asthma), a result of shunting arachidonic acid (the prostaglandin precursor) into leukotriene synthesis.

The discovery of two cyclooxygenases (COX-1 and COX-2), with COX-1 playing a more homeostatic role and COX-2 playing a more inflammatory role, led to the development of selective COX-2 inhibitors. Selective inhibition of COX-2 enzymes reduces pain and inflammation while causing less gastrointestinal toxicity than nonselective inhibitors and may not promote asthma. Because COX-2–derived prostaglandins participate in maintaining kidney function, selective COX-2 inhibitors are not safer for the kidney than nonselective COX inhibitors and may exacerbate kidney disease and hypertension.

Some selective COX-2 inhibitors, including rofecoxib and valdecoxib, increase cardiovascular risk and have been withdrawn from the market; at present, celecoxib is the only selective COX-2 inhibitor that is clinically available. Data suggest that most NSAIDs—whether COX-selective or not—convey some cardiovascular risk and should be

TABLE 9.	Common Risks for NSAID Adverse Events
Age over 60 years
History of gastritis or ulcers
History of alcohol use
History of kidney disease
History of chronic systemic illness (such as diabetes mellitus or rheumatoid arthritis)
History of cardiovascular disease
History of hypertension
Helicobacter pylori infection
Use of NSAIDs at maximal doses
Use of multiple NSAIDs simultaneously
Coadministration of corticosteroids
Coadministration of anticoagulants

employed with caution in patients with cardiovascular risk. One exception may be naproxen, which appears to reduce cardiovascular risk.

Proton pump inhibitors significantly reduce the gastrointestinal toxicity of NSAIDs. In contrast, H_2 blockers can mask gastrointestinal symptoms without reducing NSAID gastrointestinal toxicity and should be avoided.

NSAIDs should be utilized conservatively at the lowest effective dose and for the shortest period possible. However, many patients require high doses and/or chronic use for symptom relief. NSAIDs should be used carefully in high-risk patients (**Table 9**), and prophylaxis for toxicities (for example, use of a proton pump inhibitor or aspirin for cardiovascular prophylaxis) should be strongly considered.

When NSAIDs are used primarily to treat pain rather than to reduce inflammation (as in osteoarthritis), simple analgesics should be considered as alternatives.

Analgesics

Acetaminophen is generally safe within its therapeutic range, although its potency is limited and liver toxicity may occur at doses only incrementally greater than those required for treatment. Tramadol combines the dual actions of engaging opiate receptors and raising serotonin and nor-epinephrine levels; it is more potent than acetaminophen and has a low potential for abuse. Pure opioids may cause drowsiness and constipation and can be addictive; these agents should be reserved for patients who do not achieve pain relief by other methods.

Colchicine

Colchicine is commonly used to treat gout, pseudogout, and familial Mediterranean fever. The best-established mechanism of action is impairment of microtubule assembly; however, colchicine may have multiple mechanisms of action such as inhibiting the inflammasome (the intracellular complex that activates interleukin [IL]-1). The anti-inflammatory effects of colchicine appear to be directed at myeloid lineage cells, particularly neutrophils and macrophages. Toxicities include gastrointestinal intolerance, bone marrow suppression, and neuromyopathy. Colchicine is renally excreted, and toxicity is increased in patients with kidney disease. Dosing should be adjusted for glomerular filtration rate, and colchicine should be used with caution in patients with significant kidney impairment.

Corticosteroids

Corticosteroids are potent inhibitors of immunity and inflammation. Mechanisms of action are complex, relating mainly to the activities of corticosteroid receptors in altering expression of pro- and anti-inflammatory genes. Corticosteroids treat virtually all inflammatory conditions and may have disease-modifying effects in rheumatoid arthritis. However, corticosteroids have many potential side effects (**Table 10**) and should be prescribed at the lowest effective dose and for the shortest period possible. Strategies to ameliorate risk should always be considered. Calcium and vitamin D supplementation are always indicated. Addition of a bisphosphonate such as alendronate is indicated for most (especially older and/or post-menopausal) patients requiring long-term corticosteroid use (≥7.5 mg/d for more than 3 months) to prevent osteoporosis. In some conditions, a disease-modifying agent such as azathioprine or methotrexate should be considered once initial corticosteroid treatment has stabilized the inflammatory state. In some forms of arthritis, intra-articular injections of a corticosteroid such as triamcinolone or methylprednisolone acetate may maximize local efficacy while minimizing systemic consequences.

TABLE 10.	Potential Toxicities of Corticosteroids
Hypertension
Diabetes mellitus
Fluid retention; edema
Weight gain; obesity
Avascular necrosis
Gastric ulcers
Anxiety; insomnia
Psychosis
Myopathy
Cataracts; glaucoma
Hypercholesterolemia; atherosclerosis
Immune suppression; infection
Seizures

- NSAIDs have beneficial anti-inflammatory, analgesic, and antipyretic effects but can promote gastric ulcers, kidney disease, hypertension, and cardiovascular disease.
- The selective cyclooxygenase-2 inhibitor celecoxib and/or coadministration of a proton pump inhibitor with an NSAID can reduce the risk of NSAID gastropathy.
- Calcium, vitamin D, and (in most cases) a bisphosphonate are indicated to prevent osteoporosis in patients requiring long-term corticosteroid therapy.

Disease-Modifying Antirheumatic Drugs

Disease-modifying antirheumatic drugs (DMARDs) are immunosuppressive agents that can slow or block autoimmune damage to joints and other organs.

Nonbiologic Disease-Modifying Antirheumatic Drugs

Methotrexate

Methotrexate is the gold standard therapy for rheumatoid arthritis and an important treatment for other forms of inflammatory arthritis and autoimmunity such as psoriatic arthritis, systemic vasculitis, and polymyositis. This agent is a folic acid antagonist; however, the mechanism of its benefit in rheumatic diseases may relate not to folic acid antagonism but to its ability to raise extracellular adenosine levels.

Methotrexate toxicities include macrocytic anemia and drug-induced hepatitis. Regular monitoring (every 2 to 3 months) of liver chemistry tests and complete blood counts is mandatory, and this drug should be avoided in patients with liver disease or risk thereof, including regular alcohol consumption. Other methotrexate complications include nodulosis and (rarely) pneumonitis. Coadministration of folic or folinic acid reduces methotrexate toxicity without appreciably reducing its efficacy in rheumatoid arthritis. Methotrexate is highly teratogenic and abortifacient; this agent must be discontinued at least 3 months prior to pregnancy.

Hydroxychloroquine

Hydroxychloroquine is commonly used to treat rheumatoid arthritis and lupus. This agent provides only modest benefit for rheumatoid arthritis but has an excellent side-effect profile. In patients with lupus, hydroxychloroquine can prevent disease flares and may reduce morbidity and mortality. The mechanism of action appears to involve inhibition of antigen processing and costimulatory activation. The most important toxicity is visual loss resulting from retinal pigment deposition.

Although this occurrence is rare at the doses usually employed (200 to 400 mg/d), baseline and subsequent regular retinal examinations permit preclinical detection and drug discontinuation in patients who develop ocular toxicity. Although hydroxychloroquine is a pregnancy risk category C medication, expert consensus states that it is relatively safe in pregnancy and should not be discontinued.

Sulfasalazine

Sulfasalazine is a congener of a salicylate and a sulfapyridine molecule. This agent is used in inflammatory bowel disease to deliver 5-aminosalicylate to the colon; in inflammatory arthritis, it may be the sulfapyridine moiety that has the disease-modifying role. Sulfasalazine is moderately effective in rheumatoid arthritis. Potential toxicities include gastrointestinal symptoms, headache, agranulocytosis, and hepatitis. Sulfasalazine can also cause reversible oligospermia. This agent is considered relatively safe during pregnancy.

Leflunomide

Leflunomide blocks pyrimidine biosynthesis and targets lymphocytes, which lack pyrimidine salvage pathways. Leflunomide is roughly as effective as methotrexate for rheumatoid arthritis; its use in other diseases is less well explored. Toxicities include liver and hematopoietic abnormalities, infection, and interstitial lung disease. Leflunomide is extremely teratogenic and must not be used during or prior to pregnancy.

This agent has an extremely long half-life (months) and undergoes enterohepatic circulation. In the event that the drug must be withdrawn (in advance of pregnancy or owing to serious toxicity), a cholestyramine regimen (three times daily for 8 days) is administered to remove the drug from the body. After cholestyramine treatment, leflunomide levels must be measured twice prior to conception to confirm removal of the drug (reduction of M1 metabolite levels to <0.02 mg/L).

Azathioprine

Azathioprine is typically used as a corticosteroid-sparing or maintenance agent in lupus, vasculitis, and polymyositis. Azathioprine metabolism involves the enzyme thiopurine methyltransferase (TPMT); because patients with TPMT deficiency are more prone to azathioprine toxicity, some rheumatologists advocate checking a TPMT activity level prior to drug initiation. Patients with normal TPMT activity can experience azathioprine toxicity; therefore, laboratory monitoring is still necessary in this setting. Active azathioprine metabolites are also degraded by xanthine oxidase; therefore, the drug should be avoided or used with great caution in patients taking allopurinol or febuxostat. Although azathioprine should not be employed routinely in pregnancy, it may be used in pregnant patients strongly requiring an immunosuppressive agent.

Cyclophosphamide

Cyclophosphamide, a potent alkylating agent, has long been used to treat life-threatening lupus and systemic vasculitis. However, this potent immunosuppressant has numerous potentially severe adverse events, including leukopenia, anemia, increased rate of bacterial and fungal infections, hemorrhagic cystitis and bladder cancer, lymphoma, and other (long-term) malignancies. Because toxicity is common, close monitoring of complete blood counts with differential, liver chemistry tests, and urinalysis at regular intervals is critical. Cyclophosphamide is never used in pregnancy unless the life of the mother is at stake.

Mycophenolate Mofetil

Mycophenolate mofetil was developed to prevent transplant rejection but in recent years has been used as a treatment for lupus, particularly lupus nephritis. This agent's active metabolite is mycophenolic acid, which inhibits inosine monophosphate dehydrogenase (an enzyme in the purine synthetic pathway). Mycophenolic acid preferentially inhibits T and B lymphocytes. Studies suggest that mycophenolate mofetil may be at least as effective as cyclophosphamide for lupus nephritis and lupus maintenance but with fewer, and milder, side effects. This agent is also increasingly used as a corticosteroid-sparing agent in conditions such as systemic vasculitis and polymyositis. Mycophenolate mofetil is teratogenic and should not be used in pregnancy.

Cyclosporine

Cyclosporine is an immunosuppressant agent that preferentially targets T cells and demonstrates efficacy in several rheumatic and autoimmune diseases, including rheumatoid arthritis, lupus, inflammatory myositis, psoriasis, pyoderma gangrenosum, and inflammatory bowel disease. Toxicity is relatively common (hypertension, nephrotoxicity, tremor, hirsutism); therefore, cyclosporine is mainly used as a third-line agent in rheumatic diseases.

KEY POINTS

- Patients taking methotrexate should not consume alcohol and require regular assessment of liver and hematopoietic function.
- Methotrexate is highly teratogenic and abortifacient; this agent must be discontinued at least 3 months prior to pregnancy.
- Patients taking hydroxychloroquine are at risk for retinal toxicity and require baseline and follow-up retinal examinations.
- Patients taking leflunomide who plan to become pregnant or who develop toxicity must discontinue the agent and undergo an 8-day course of cholestyramine elimination therapy.
- Cyclophosphamide toxicities are common; careful monitoring for infection and bone marrow, liver, and bladder toxicity is mandatory.

Biologic Disease-Modifying Antirheumatic Drugs

General Considerations

Biologic agents offer greater specificity for targeted immune suppression with improved efficacy and fewer side effects (**Table 11**). Because of the degree of immune suppression, monitoring for opportunistic infections or infectious complications in patients taking biologic immune modulators is necessary, as is holding doses of biologic therapy during intercurrent infections that require antimicrobial therapy.

Surveillance for latent tuberculosis with tuberculin skin testing or interferon-γ release assay is indicated prior to use of all biologic agents. Additional testing with chest radiography should be considered for patients with risk factors for latent tuberculosis. Subsequent tuberculosis screening is indicated on a periodic basis, as well as for any exposures that might place a patient at risk.

Although many biologic agents have been studied in the context of background therapy with traditional DMARDs, concurrent use of two or more biologic agents is not recommended, because infection rates are significantly increased, with minimal, if any, added efficacy.

Live vaccines should be avoided in patients taking biologic immune modulators. Primary immunization responses to killed vaccines may be suboptimal in the context of treatment with abatacept or rituximab, a consideration that may be relevant for patients due for immunization(s), and vaccination is best undertaken prior to initiation of either agent.

Tumor Necrosis Factor-α Inhibitors

Tumor necrosis factor (TNF)-α inhibitors have been shown to decrease disease activity and inhibit the progression of structural damage in rheumatoid arthritis, with the greatest efficacy observed when used in combination with weekly methotrexate. TNF-α inhibitors are highly effective in suppressing cutaneous and articular disease in psoriatic arthritis. Joint symptoms (axial and peripheral) are improved in patients with ankylosing spondylitis, although treatment has not been shown to delay fusion of axial joints. TNF-α monoclonal antibody inhibitors (but not etanercept) are also beneficial in managing uveitis, oral and genital lesions of Behçet disease, inflammatory bowel disease, and pyoderma syndromes. Clinical responses occur within weeks of initiating treatment.

Although very well tolerated as a class, TNF-α inhibitors may impair innate host defenses, resulting in the delay of resolution of intercurrent infections; treatment should be withheld until the infection has resolved. TNF-α inhibitors are also associated with reactivation of tuberculosis as well as fungal infections, including histoplasmosis and coccidioidomycosis, and viral infections such as hepatitis B. No complications have been reported regarding their use in patients with intercurrent hepatitis C infection or in patients

TABLE 11. Biologic Agents in the Management of Rheumatic Disease

Agent	Target	Indications	Toxicity Monitoring
Etanercept (TNFR:Fc)	TNF-α	Rheumatoid arthritis; psoriatic arthritis; ankylosing spondylitis	Tuberculosis surveillance
Infliximab (anti–TNF-α mAb)	TNF-α	Rheumatoid arthritis; psoriatic arthritis; ankylosing spondylitis; inflammatory bowel disease	Tuberculosis surveillance
Adalimumab (anti–TNF-α mAb)	TNF-α	Rheumatoid arthritis; psoriatic arthritis; ankylosing spondylitis; inflammatory bowel disease	Tuberculosis surveillance
Certolizumab pegol (anti–TNF-α pegol)	TNF-α	Rheumatoid arthritis; psoriatic arthritis; ankylosing spondylitis	Tuberculosis surveillance
Golimumab (anti–TNF-α mAb)	TNF-α	Rheumatoid arthritis; psoriatic arthritis; ankylosing spondylitis	Tuberculosis surveillance
Abatacept (CTLA4:Fc)	T-cell costimulation	Rheumatoid arthritis	Tuberculosis surveillance
Ustekinumab (anti–IL-12/IL-23 mAb)	IL-12/IL-23	Psoriatic arthritis; inflammatory bowel disease	Tuberculosis surveillance
Rituximab (anti-CD20 mAb)	CD20+ B cells	Rheumatoid arthritis; ANCA-associated vasculitis	IgG levels
Belimumab (anti-BLyS mAb)	BLyS/BAFF	SLE	IgG levels
Tocilizumab (anti–IL-6R mAb)	IL-6 receptor	Rheumatoid arthritis	Lipid profile; complete blood count; liver chemistry tests; tuberculosis surveillance
Anakinra (IL-1R antagonist)	IL-1β receptor	Rheumatoid arthritis; adult-onset Still disease	Complete blood count
Rilonacept (IL-1β trap)	IL-1β	Cryopyrin-associated syndromes; refractory gout	Complete blood count
Canakinumab (anti–IL-1β mAb)	IL-1β	Cryopyrin-associated syndromes	Complete blood count

BAFF = B-cell–activating factor; BLyS = B-lymphocyte stimulator; CTLA4 = cytotoxic T-lymphocyte antigen 4; IL = interleukin; mAb = monoclonal antibody; R = receptor; SLE = systemic lupus erythematosus; TNF = tumor necrosis factor.

with HIV infection well controlled with highly active anti-retroviral therapy.

Other less common side effects include psoriasiform skin eruptions, demyelinating syndromes, and drug-induced lupus erythematosus, and discontinuation of TNF-α inhibitors is indicated.

Lymphoma has been reported in patients taking TNF-α inhibitors, although it remains uncertain if the prevalence is greater than would be expected among patients with rheumatoid arthritis. TNF-α inhibitors should be discontinued in this setting. There also is a higher rate of nonmelanoma skin cancer in patients taking TNF-α inhibitors, but overall cancer incidence is not reported to be higher than expected in patients with rheumatoid arthritis.

Abatacept

Abatacept is a fusion protein of CTLA4, a molecule expressed on activated human T cells and the Fc portion of human IgG. This agent binds to antigen-presenting cells and blocks costimulatory signals to T lymphocytes. Abatacept is given as a monthly intravenous infusion. The time to maximum clinical response (6 months) is longer than that observed with TNF-α inhibitors (2 to 3 months).

Abatacept is recommended for patients with moderate or high disease activity and poor prognostic features who have had an inadequate response to sequential nonbiologic DMARDs or methotrexate in combination with other DMARDs. This agent also can be effective in patients who have had an inadequate response to TNF-α inhibition. Abatacept may be associated with an increased risk of lymphoma and lung cancer as well as flares of COPD. Because of its potent immunosuppressive activity, it should not be used concurrently with most other biologic agents (particularly TNF-α inhibitors and anakinra) and with caution with other immunosuppressive medications used to treat rheumatoid arthritis because of an increased risk of infection.

Rituximab

Rituximab is a chimeric monoclonal antibody that depletes CD20+ B-cell lymphocytes. Depletion of CD20+ B cells from the peripheral blood is rapid and persists for 6 to 12 months. In placebo-controlled studies, peripheral B-cell depletion using rituximab is associated with improvement in disease activity measures as well as reduction in joint erosion development in patients with rheumatoid arthritis. This drug is approved for use in combination with methotrexate in patients who have not adequately responded to TNF-α inhibitor therapy.

Rituximab also has been shown to be as effective as cyclophosphamide in inducing remission in patients with ANCA-associated vasculitis. Although uncontrolled studies report improvement in some domains of systemic lupus erythematosus (SLE) disease activity (particularly resolution of immune-mediated cytopenias), placebo-controlled studies of rituximab in SLE have thus far failed to show efficacy.

Treatment with rituximab has not been associated with a significant increase in infections. However, severe infusion reactions can occur, and rare cases of progressive multifocal leukoencephalopathy associated with JC virus reactivation have been reported.

Tocilizumab

Tocilizumab is a chimeric (mouse-human) monoclonal antibody with specificity for the IL-6 receptor and is given as an intravenous infusion. Blocking the biologic effects of IL-6 attenuates B and T lymphocyte activation, leukocyte migration, osteoclast activation, and hepatic synthesis of acute phase reactants. Tocilizumab is FDA approved to treat patients with rheumatoid arthritis who have experienced an inadequate response to TNF-α inhibitors. This agent may be associated with leukopenia, thrombocytopenia, and elevated serum aminotransferase levels. Increases in serum lipid levels occur frequently and should be monitored. Reactivation of tuberculosis and invasive fungal infections can occur, and rare instances of gastric and intestinal rupture have been reported.

Ustekinumab

Ustekinumab is a human genome–derived monoclonal reagent with specificity for the p40 subunit shared by IL-12 and IL-23. Blocking IL-12 attenuates the maturation and activation of the Th1 lineage of T cells responsible for elaboration of inflammatory cytokines, including TNF-α and interferon-γ; blocking IL-23 attenuates the maturation and survival of Th17 cells, a subset of T cells implicated in the pathogenesis of several autoimmune disorders, including Crohn disease, psoriasis/psoriatic arthritis, and rheumatoid arthritis. Higher than expected rates of infection or malignancy have not been observed in controlled studies of ustekinumab, but vigilance for mycobacterial, fungal, and *Salmonella* infections is recommended given the role of IL-12 and IL-23 in host defense against these pathogens.

Belimumab

Belimumab is a monoclonal antibody with specificity for B-cell–activating factor (BAFF), also referred to as B-lymphocyte stimulator (BLyS). BAFF mediates the maturation and survival of immature B cells to antibody-secreting plasmablasts, and its levels are elevated in patients with SLE and Sjögren syndrome. Belimumab, which blocks the biologic activity of soluble BAFF (BLyS), has been FDA approved for treatment of SLE based on demonstrated decreases in autoantibody titers and disease activity measures.

Interleukin-1β Inhibitors

IL-1β inhibitors have proved beneficial in the treatment of adult-onset Still disease (anakinra) and the cryopyrin-associated periodic fever syndromes (rilonacept and canakinumab) but have been disappointing in the treatment of rheumatoid arthritis. IL-1β inhibitors are also occasionally used to manage refractory gout.

KEY POINTS

- Monitoring for opportunistic infections or infectious complications in patients taking biologic immune modulators is necessary, as is holding doses of biologic therapy during intercurrent infections that require antimicrobial therapy.
- Surveillance for latent tuberculosis with tuberculin skin testing or interferon-γ release assay is indicated prior to use of all biologic agents.
- Combination of immunomodulating biologic agents should be avoided; infection rates are significantly increased and there is minimal, if any, added efficacy.
- Tumor necrosis factor α inhibitors in combination with methotrexate provide the most effective means to reduce rheumatoid arthritis symptoms and structural damage.
- Tumor necrosis factor α inhibitors are effective in suppressing cutaneous and articular disease in psoriatic arthritis and in improving joint symptoms (axial and peripheral) in patients with ankylosing spondylitis.

Urate-Lowering Therapy

Urate-lowering therapy is indicated for patients who experience repeated gout attacks (typically two or more per year) or develop tissue deposits of urate (tophi). These agents block the production or promote the excretion or degradation of uric acid. Because urate-lowering therapy may increase the risk of gout attacks for 3 to 6 months or longer after initiation, concurrent prophylaxis with an anti-inflammatory agent, most commonly low-dose colchicine, is required.

Allopurinol

Allopurinol is a purine analog that inhibits xanthine oxidase and thereby blocks urate production. This agent can lower serum urate levels regardless of the cause of hyperuricemia. Allopurinol is approved for use in doses up to 800 mg/d; the dose should be titrated to a target predefined serum urate level (<6.0 mg/dL [0.35 mmol/L]). Typical doses range from 100 to 400 mg/d.

Sensitivity to allopurinol includes rash, bone marrow failure, hepatic failure, and Stevens-Johnson syndrome. Allopurinol should be discontinued immediately in patients who develop rash, although desensitization is possible. Some controversy exists regarding the safety of allopurinol in patients with kidney failure, with past investigators suggesting that such patients may be more susceptible to allopurinol hypersensitivity. A more recent consensus suggests that patients with kidney disease will tolerate allopurinol if it is started at a low dose and titrated, with careful monitoring, until a conservative target urate level is achieved (but not exceeded). Allopurinol should be avoided or used with extreme caution in patients taking another purine analog drug such as azathioprine or 6-mercaptopurine.

Febuxostat

Febuxostat is a newer xanthine oxidase inhibitor used to lower uric acid. This agent is not a purine analog and therefore appears to be safe for patients with allopurinol sensitivity. In contrast to allopurinol, febuxostat is FDA approved for patients with mild to moderate kidney failure. Febuxostat should be titrated to target serum urate levels (<6.0 mg/dL [0.35 mmol/L]); however, the dose range (40 or 80 mg/d) is narrower than that of allopurinol. Possible toxicities include liver function abnormalities, which are often transient. Febuxostat should be avoided in patients taking azathioprine or 6-mercaptopurine.

Probenecid

Probenecid inhibits the renal tubule transporter URAT1 to block retention of urate. This agent is only effective in patients who underexcrete uric acid (documented by a 24-hour urine collection) and is ineffective in patients with kidney disease. Probenecid may increase the risk of kidney stones; therefore, patients taking probenecid must hydrate aggressively, and the drug should be avoided in patients with a high risk for stones (for example, a history of prior stones or tophaceous gout).

Uricase

Pharmacologic restoration of uricase (urate oxidase) represents a theoretically viable urate-lowering approach. Rasburicase, the fungally derived uricase, is used to prevent or treat tumor lysis syndrome. However, rasburicase is highly immunogenic and is not an option for chronic use. Pegloticase is a pegylated recombinant mammalian uricase that has received FDA approval for treatment-failure gout. It is less immunogenic than rasburicase, but allergic and anaphylactic reactions may still occur. Pegloticase rapidly decreases serum uric acid levels and may help resolve tophaceous deposits.

KEY POINT

- Urate-lowering agents are indicated for patients who experience recurrent gout attacks or develop tophi.
- Allopurinol should be discontinued immediately in patients who develop a rash.

Rheumatoid Arthritis

Rheumatoid arthritis is a systemic disorder of unknown cause in which chronic inflammation may lead to joint destruction and disability. Joint damage occurs rapidly early in the disease course and correlates with the cumulative exposure to inflammation. Early recognition and aggressive management are critical to control inflammation, reduce damage, and improve outcomes. Without treatment, most patients develop significant disability and shortened life expectancy.

The annual incidence is approximately 30 per 100,000 persons worldwide, with a prevalence of 1% in white persons and a female predominance. The disease can develop at any age, but peak age of onset is between 30 and 55 years. Patients with rheumatoid arthritis have a greater than average prevalence of coronary artery disease, which may cause reduced life expectancy.

Pathophysiology and Risk Factors

Environmental and genetic factors are important in the pathogenesis of rheumatoid arthritis. In established disease, proinflammatory cytokines such as tumor necrosis factor (TNF) α induce the production of degradative enzymes and promote osteoclast activation, leading to cartilage damage and bone erosion.

Genetic Factors

Heritable factors account for 50% to 65% of the risk for developing rheumatoid arthritis. HLA and non-HLA genes convey susceptibility. The "shared epitope," an amino acid motif shared by several HLA-DRB chains (DR4, DR14, and DR1), is a strong risk factor. More recently, polymorphisms in other genes have been implicated such as the TNF-α promoter PTPN22 (a phosphatase involved in T- and B-cell signaling) and STAT4 (a transcription factor responsive to cytokines). The magnitude of risk with individual polymorphisms appears small.

Hormones

Epidemiologic studies suggest a hormonal influence on the development of rheumatoid arthritis. The risk is reduced in women who have had children and may be further reduced in women who have breast fed for 1 year or more. Disease activity often subsides during pregnancy and flares postpartum. Men with rheumatoid arthritis usually have lower levels of androgenic hormones and higher concentrations of estradiol.

Antibodies

The association of rheumatoid arthritis with rheumatoid factor has long suggested a pathogenic role for antibodies. The more recent association of rheumatoid arthritis with anti-citrullinated protein or peptide antibodies (such as anti–cyclic citrullinated peptide [CCP] antibodies) has supported this concept. The presence of rheumatoid factor or anti-CCP antibodies in the blood is associated with an increased risk of subsequent diagnosis. However, rheumatoid factor and anti-CCP antibodies are neither necessary nor sufficient to cause the disease. Rheumatoid factor is absent in 30% of patients with rheumatoid arthritis, and anti-CCP antibodies are absent in 40% of patients with the disease. Rheumatoid factor is also present in up to 10% of healthy persons.

Environmental Factors

Smoking is a strong risk factor for developing rheumatoid arthritis, particularly with longer duration of cigarette use and in CCP-positive carriers of the shared epitope. Nicotine may not be as important as other elements in cigarettes; smokeless tobacco is not associated with rheumatoid arthritis. The risk of developing the disease decreases after smoking cessation.

There is an increased risk in miners and construction workers, possibly related to inhalation of particular dusts and fibers. Asbestos and silica exposures also have been linked to the disease. Although infections have long been suspected as triggers for rheumatoid arthritis, a definitive association has not yet been confirmed. Finally, there is a higher risk in persons with lower socioeconomic status, suggesting additional unknown environmental risk factors.

KEY POINTS

- Risk factors for rheumatoid arthritis include heritable factors such as the "shared epitope," hormonal influences, and environmental factors.

- Rheumatoid factor and anti–cyclic citrullinated peptide antibodies are associated with an increased risk of rheumatoid arthritis; however, these antibodies are neither necessary nor sufficient to cause the disease.

- Smoking is a strong risk factor for developing rheumatoid arthritis that decreases after cessation.

Diagnosis

Clinical Manifestations

Although rheumatoid arthritis may present as an oligoarthritis with an asymmetric distribution, the disease frequently becomes more symmetric over time. In up to 50% of patients who present with polyarthritis, joint inflammation is self-limited and resolves within 6 months. If the disease remains active after 6 months, it usually persists on a chronic relapsing or progressive course.

Most patients with rheumatoid arthritis have a symmetric polyarthritis involving small, medium, and large joints that is associated with prolonged (>60 minutes) morning stiffness. The metacarpophalangeal and proximal interphalangeal joints of the hands; the wrists; and the metatarsophalangeal joints of the feet are almost always affected (**Table 12**). The shoulders, elbows, hips, knees, ankles, and cervical spine are also commonly involved. The distal interphalangeal joints and lumbar spine are spared.

Examination reveals soft, boggy, or fluctuant swelling and tenderness at involved joints. Warmth and redness are not always present. With active joint inflammation, there is pain on active and passive motion, and range of motion may be limited. With accumulation of joint damage, joint alignment may be altered, resulting in deformity and joint dysfunction (**Figure 3**). Active inflammation or joint deformities may cause entrapment neuropathies, most commonly carpal tunnel syndrome.

Evaluation

Laboratory Studies

Several laboratory abnormalities are useful in demonstrating the presence of an inflammatory process, including an elevated erythrocyte sedimentation rate (ESR), an elevated C-reactive protein (CRP) level, anemia of chronic disease, thrombocytosis, and hypoalbuminemia. Some patients with rheumatoid arthritis do not have any of these findings, and none is specific for rheumatoid arthritis. Synovial fluid analysis demonstrates elevated leukocyte counts with neutrophilic predominance, similar to that seen in other forms of inflammatory arthritis.

Rheumatoid factor, an antibody that recognizes the Fc portion of an IgG molecule, is present in 70% of patients with rheumatoid arthritis but is also prevalent in other autoimmune diseases, including mixed cryoglobulinemia (100%), Sjögren syndrome (70%), and systemic lupus erythematosus (20% to 30%), and is present in up to 10% of the healthy population.

Approximately 60% of patients with rheumatoid arthritis form antibodies to CCP, a particular anti-citrullinated peptide. Anti-CCP antibody assays are commercially available. The specificity of anti-CCP antibodies for rheumatoid arthritis is 95%, far greater than that of rheumatoid factor (approximately 80%). The presence of higher titers of either rheumatoid factor or anti-CCP antibodies or the presence of both antibodies increases the likelihood of a patient being diagnosed with

TABLE 12. Musculoskeletal Manifestations of Rheumatoid Arthritis

Feature	Findings	Comments
Joint inflammation	Morning stiffness Joint tenderness Soft-tissue swelling Palpable joint effusion Local warmth Pain on active and passive range of motion	Assess duration of morning stiffness by asking "How long does it take from when you wake up in the morning until you feel as good as you are going to feel for the rest of the day?"

Distribution of joint involvement	Symmetric
	Initially small joints
	Progresses proximally to larger joints
	Commonly involves the:
	   Metacarpophalangeal joints
	   Proximal interphalangeal joints
	   Wrist joints
	   Metatarsophalangeal joints
		Distal interphalangeal joint involvement is uncommon (seen in psoriatic arthritis, osteoarthritis)

Joint damage	Decreased range of motion Contractures Ulnar deviation Subluxation Cervical instability Basilar invagination	Marginal erosions may be evident earliest at the 5th metatarsophalangeal joint Cartilage degradation causes joint-space narrowing Ankylosis can occur in long-standing disease
Periarticular involvement	Bursitis Tenosynovitis Tendinopathy Swan neck and boutonnière deformities Flexion contractures Popliteal and ganglion cysts	Olecranon bursitis and rotator cuff tendinopathy are common Tenosynovitis can cause trigger finger Tenosynovitis is less prominent than in spondyloarthritis Popliteal (Baker) cysts are contiguous with the knee joint
Muscular weakness	Disuse atrophy Drug-induced myopathy (corticosteroids and other drugs)	Interosseous and quadriceps muscles are common sites of atrophy from disuse
Decreased bone quality	Periarticular osteopenia Generalized loss of bone mineral density Increased risk of fracture	Risk of fracture may be underestimated by bone mineral density alone

the disease. However, the absence of both rheumatoid factor and anti-CCP antibodies does not rule out rheumatoid arthritis. Finally, up to 40% of patients with rheumatoid arthritis have positive antinuclear antibody test results, which is a nonspecific finding.

Imaging Studies

Plain radiographs of affected joints may reveal periarticular osteopenia, erosions, and symmetric joint-space narrowing. Erosive changes first develop at the joint margins where the synovium inserts on bone, and cartilage is absent (**Figure 4**). Although erosive changes may not occur in early disease, baseline radiographs of the hands and feet should be obtained for prognostic purposes and repeated at intervals to assess disease progression over time.

MRI can detect bone erosions earlier in the course of the disease than plain radiographs. Bone marrow edema and synovial proliferation on MRI are predictive of subsequent erosions, but this is not yet an accepted measure of disease activity. Ultrasonography can detect the presence of synovitis, but its role in standard clinical practice has not been established.

KEY POINTS

- Most patients with rheumatoid arthritis have a symmetric polyarthritis involving small and large joints that is associated with prolonged morning stiffness.
- Plain radiographs of affected joints may reveal periarticular osteopenia, erosions, and symmetric joint-space narrowing; MRI may detect bone erosions earlier in the course of rheumatoid arthritis.

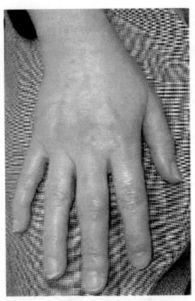
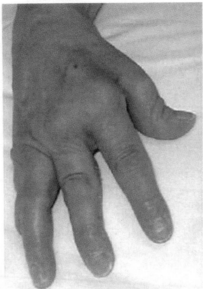
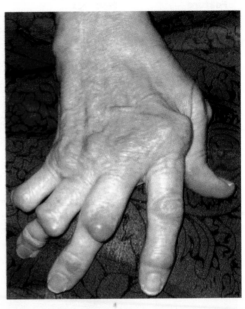

FIGURE 3. Involvement of the hands in rheumatoid arthritis. Early rheumatoid arthritis with mild fusiform soft-tissue swelling of the proximal interphalangeal joints (*left panel*). Moderate to severe rheumatoid arthritis with synovitis of the metacarpophalangeal joints and swan neck deformities of the second and third digits (*center panel*). Severe deforming rheumatoid arthritis with ulnar deviation, multiple rheumatoid nodules, and proximal interphalangeal joint subluxations (*right panel*).

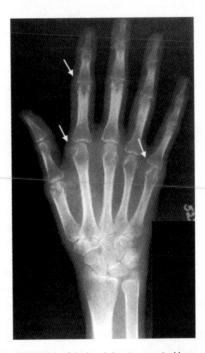

FIGURE 4. Radiograph of the hand showing marginal bone erosions.

Reprinted with permission from Yee AMF and Paget SA, eds. Expert Guide to Rheumatology. Philadelphia: American College of Physicians; 2004.

Complications and Extra-Articular Manifestations

Rheumatoid arthritis causes a spectrum of extra-articular sequelae such as Felty syndrome (characterized by pancytopenia, splenomegaly, and leg ulcers); rheumatoid vasculitis; rheumatoid nodules (**Figure 5**); scleritis with scleral ulceration; and interstitial lung disease (**Table 13**). Long-standing, poorly controlled disease may also result in secondary amyloidosis. Aggressive use of effective therapeutic agents has decreased the prevalence of many of these manifestations.

There is increased recognition of the relationship between chronic inflammation and cardiovascular disease, with rheumatoid arthritis as the prototype. Rheumatoid arthritis is a risk factor for the development of coronary artery disease, independent of traditional cardiovascular risk factors. Use of methotrexate and TNF-α inhibitors can reduce the cardiovascular risk that occurs in these patients.

Patients with rheumatoid arthritis have an increased risk for low bone mass and fracture because of decreased mobility, corticosteroid use, and the inflammatory process. Bone mineral density alone does not fully reflect the increased risk of fracture. The World Health Organization has incorporated rheumatoid arthritis in the Web-based fracture risk calculator FRAX to estimate the risk of fracture.

Evidence of early joint erosions, an increased number of affected joints, elevation in ESR or CRP levels, the presence of rheumatoid nodules, and greater functional impairment later in the disease course are associated with poorer outcome in patients with rheumatoid arthritis.

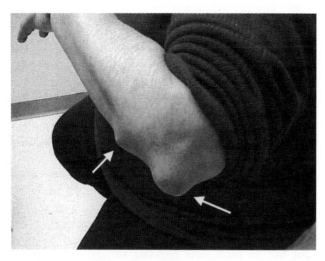

FIGURE 5. Nodules in rheumatoid arthritis.

Reprinted with permission from Yee AMF and Paget SA, eds. Expert Guide to Rheumatology. Philadelphia: American College of Physicians; 2004.

KEY POINTS

- Rheumatoid arthritis may cause Felty syndrome; rheumatoid vasculitis; rheumatoid nodules; scleritis with scleral ulceration; and interstitial lung disease.
- Rheumatoid arthritis is a risk factor for developing coronary artery disease, independent of traditional cardiovascular risk factors.

Management

Management of rheumatoid arthritis is aimed at eliminating inflammation quickly, maintaining remission, avoiding joint injury, and preserving function. Tight, targeted control, with adjustment of treatment regimens as needed to achieve and maintain low disease activity, is associated with improved outcomes. Controversy remains regarding the appropriate treatment regimen after remission has been achieved. After joint damage has occurred, therapy focuses on preventing progressive damage, maximizing function, and relieving pain. Therapy must be individualized and adverse effects minimized. Monitoring intervals vary according to disease severity.

Disease activity and damage must be monitored in patients with rheumatoid arthritis. Fatigue, weight loss, morning stiffness, joint pain, functional limitations, and measurement of acute phase reactants are assessed at each visit.

Composite disease activity measures such as the Disease Activity Score or the Stanford Health Assessment Questionnaire are essential components of the assessment and monitoring of patients with rheumatoid arthritis. These measures facilitate clinical decision making and allow therapy to target optimal outcomes (see Principles of Therapeutics, Evaluation of Disease Progression).

Radiographic monitoring allows assessment for any interval development of joint-space narrowing or erosion. Progressive joint damage on plain radiographs is evidence of an insufficient therapeutic regimen.

KEY POINTS

- Fatigue, weight loss, morning stiffness, joint pain, functional limitations, and measurement of acute phase reactants must be frequently assessed in patients with rheumatoid arthritis.
- Radiographic monitoring of patients with rheumatoid arthritis allows for assessment of joint-space narrowing or erosion; progressive joint damage on plain radiographs is evidence of an insufficient therapeutic regimen.

TABLE 13. Extra-Articular Manifestations of Rheumatoid Arthritis

System	Findings
Constitutional	Fatigue
	Weight loss
Dermatologic	Rheumatoid nodules
	Leg ulcers (Felty syndrome)
	Rheumatoid vasculitis
Ophthalmologic	Episcleritis
	Scleritis
	Keratoconjunctivitis sicca
Hematologic	Anemia of chronic disease
	Thrombocytosis
	Pancytopenia and splenomegaly (Felty syndrome)
	Large granular lymphocyte syndrome
Cardiovascular	Premature coronary artery disease
	Chronic heart failure
	Pericarditis
	Secondary amyloidosis
Pulmonary	Exudative pleural effusions
	Interstitial fibrosis
	Pulmonary nodules
	Bronchiolitis obliterans organizing pneumonia
	Bronchiectasis, bronchiolectasis
	Cricoarytenoid disease producing stridor
Gastrointestinal	Dry mouth
Renal	Secondary amyloidosis
Neurologic	C1-C2 subluxation
	Peripheral neuropathy
	Mononeuritis multiplex (vasculitis)

NSAIDs and Corticosteroids

NSAIDs may provide symptomatic relief but do not alter disease course. Corticosteroids are capable of reducing inflammation rapidly, although adverse effects are common, particularly with greater dose and duration. Intra-articular or oral corticosteroids are often used to reduce inflammation initially while other agents become effective. High-dose corticosteroids are generally only required for extra-articular manifestations (see Principles of Therapeutics, Anti-Inflammatory Agents).

Disease-Modifying Antirheumatic Drugs

Disease-modifying antirheumatic drugs (DMARDs) can reduce or block joint damage (see Principles of Therapeutics, Disease-Modifying Antirheumatic Drugs). The choice for initial DMARD therapy depends on disease duration, disease activity, and prognostic factors. Subsequent therapy should take into consideration the patient's response to prior regimens.

Nonbiologic Disease-Modifying Antirheumatic Drugs

Methotrexate and leflunomide can be effective as initial monotherapy for patients with rheumatoid arthritis of any duration or degree of activity. Methotrexate is the gold standard therapy, because it is usually better tolerated than other DMARDs and has good efficacy, long-term compliance rates, and relatively low cost.

Hydroxychloroquine, sulfasalazine, and minocycline are suggested as initial monotherapy only in patients with relatively short disease duration, low disease activity, and no evidence of erosive disease. Hydroxychloroquine may be effective in combination with methotrexate in a more diverse set of patients, including those with longer disease duration, greater disease activity (moderate or high), and poor prognostic features (such as erosive changes).

Combination therapy with sulfasalazine, methotrexate, and hydroxychloroquine may be used in patients with poor prognostic features and moderate or high levels of disease activity.

Biologic Disease-Modifying Antirheumatic Drugs

If remission of rheumatoid arthritis is not achieved and maintained with nonbiologic DMARDs, biologic DMARDs may be an option. However, the increased cost of these agents is a consideration in their use. Principles associated with the use of biologic DMARDs as well as specific toxicities and recommended monitoring are discussed in the Biologic DMARDs section of the Principles of Therapeutics chapter.

For patients with moderate or high disease activity, TNF-α inhibitors (etanercept, infliximab, adalimumab, golimumab, and certolizumab pegol) may be reasonable alternatives for initial therapy, depending on disease duration and prognostic features. However, there is no clear difference in efficacy of the various TNF-α inhibitors. Choice of a particular medication should take into consideration the differing routes of administration (intravenous infusion versus subcutaneous injection) and dosing intervals.

Use of methotrexate in conjunction with a TNF-α inhibitor is associated with further reductions in disease activity and radiographic progression. In patients unable to take methotrexate, use of an alternative nonbiologic DMARD may also provide benefit. Patients who discontinue a TNF-α inhibitor because of inefficacy may respond well to another agent in this class. Response to a third TNF-α inhibitor after two others have failed is less common.

Abatacept is recommended for patients with moderate or high disease activity and poor prognostic features who have had an inadequate response to sequential nonbiologic DMARDs or methotrexate in combination with other DMARDs. This agent also can be effective in patients who have had an inadequate response to TNF-α inhibition. Abatacept may be associated with an increased risk of lymphoma and lung cancer as well as flares of COPD.

Rituximab, the anti-CD20 B-cell depleting monoclonal antibody, is FDA approved for the treatment of moderately to severely active rheumatoid arthritis in combination with methotrexate in patients who have had an inadequate response to TNF-α inhibitor therapy. Rituximab may also be considered for patients with high disease activity and poor prognostic features despite sequential nonbiologic DMARDs or methotrexate in combination with other DMARDs. Patients who are rheumatoid factor positive may be more likely to respond to rituximab. Infusion reactions are common, particularly with the initial infusion. Corticosteroids just prior to the infusion decrease the frequency and intensity of infusion reactions. Human antichimeric antibodies of unclear significance may develop.

Tocilizumab is an interleukin (IL)-6 receptor antagonist approved by the FDA for the treatment of rheumatoid arthritis in patients with moderate to high disease activity after inadequate response to one or more TNF-α inhibitors.

Although biologic agents are routinely combined with methotrexate, combinations of biologic DMARDs should be avoided, because there is no proven significant additional benefit and an increased risk of serious adverse events such as infection may occur.

KEY POINTS

- Methotrexate or leflunomide may be effective as initial monotherapy for patients with rheumatoid arthritis of any duration or degree of activity.

- In patients with rheumatoid arthritis, tumor necrosis factor α inhibitors can be used as initial therapy for moderate or high disease activity.

- Use of methotrexate in conjunction with a tumor necrosis factor α inhibitor is associated with further reductions in disease activity and radiographic progression in patients with rheumatoid arthritis.

Surgical Therapy

With more effective medical therapy now available, surgical treatment of rheumatoid arthritis is less frequently required. Surgical interventions maintain a role in minimizing pain and maximizing function in select patients. Surgical treatment can complement pharmacologic treatment for active disease; synovectomy may help control stubborn monoarthritis. Surgery may also be required to repair articular and periarticular damage such as tendon repair for tears or impending rupture; osteotomy for realignment; joint fusion for stabilization; and joint arthroplasty. If muscle atrophy is present preoperatively, postoperative rehabilitation can be challenging. For patients in need of multiple procedures, the sequence of the procedures impacts rehabilitation and outcome.

Specific risks encountered in patients with rheumatoid arthritis must be considered in perioperative management. The cervical spine should be evaluated with radiographs in flexion and extension for evidence of atlantoaxial subluxation and dynamic instability that could result in cord compression during intubation. Patients with anemia of chronic disease may require blood transfusions after surgery with significant blood loss. Patients with rheumatoid arthritis are at increased risk for infectious complications associated with prosthetic joints. Perioperative use of rheumatoid arthritis medications must balance the risk of adverse events (such as infection) with the risk of perioperative disease flare, which can impair mobility, delay rehabilitation, and require additional medication. Discontinuation of NSAIDs may be necessary to reduce bleeding risk, and alternative perioperative analgesic regimens may be required. In general, methotrexate may be continued perioperatively because it helps to prevent postoperative arthritis flares and is not associated with a significant increased risk of postoperative infection. TNF-α inhibitors should be held perioperatively.

Nonpharmacologic Management

Educating patients with rheumatoid arthritis about their disease is appropriate. Smoking cessation should be encouraged. Discussion of the benefit of rest for acutely inflamed joints is necessary, along with the importance of physical and occupational therapy to maintain function of articular and periarticular structures. Patient counseling on strategies to modify their risks of fracture and atherosclerosis is beneficial. Nutritional support that targets ideal body weight should be provided. Administration of inactive influenza and pneumococcal vaccines is advised for patients taking immunosuppressive agents. Live vaccines should be avoided in patients on biologic therapies but may be safe with low-dose nonbiologic DMARDs and low-dose prednisone.

KEY POINTS

- Surgical interventions may be required to repair articular and periarticular damage in patients with rheumatoid arthritis.
- Nonpharmacologic management of rheumatoid arthritis includes smoking cessation, rest, physical and occupational therapy, and nutritional support.

Rheumatoid Arthritis and Pregnancy

Although most women with rheumatoid arthritis demonstrate clinical improvement during pregnancy, it may be challenging to reduce therapy in anticipation of conception to minimize fetal toxicity (see Principles of Therapeutics). Medication use in nursing mothers is challenging, as is caring for an infant while struggling with active rheumatoid arthritis. Flares are common during the postpartum period. Potential strategies must be reviewed with each patient in coordination with her obstetrician.

Methotrexate must be discontinued 3 months prior to conception. Leflunomide also must be discontinued, and pregnancy avoided until the drug is no longer detectable in the serum; cholestyramine may be used to hasten the elimination of leflunomide from the body. Sulfasalazine can cause reversible oligospermia; men are advised to discontinue this agent for 3 months prior to conception. NSAIDs and aspirin may interfere with implantation when taken during early pregnancy.

Greater disease activity during pregnancy is associated with small gestational age and preterm delivery. When needed, NSAIDs are often used during the second trimester but should be avoided in the third trimester because of the risk of premature closure of the ductus arteriosus and interference with labor. Low-dose corticosteroids are frequently used but should be avoided if possible before 14 weeks of gestation because of the risk of cleft palate. Corticosteroid use can contribute to gestational diabetes and hypertension. Hydroxychloroquine and sulfasalazine are often used during pregnancy. Although uncertainty remains regarding the safety of TNF-α inhibitors during pregnancy, they are usually held prior to conception. Placental antibody transport can lead to levels of monoclonal antibodies that are higher in cord blood than in the mother.

NSAIDs and low-dose prednisone are considered safe during lactation, but methotrexate should be avoided.

KEY POINT

- Discontinuation of disease-modifying antirheumatic drugs such as methotrexate and leflunomide is indicated prior to conception.

Osteoarthritis

Pathophysiology

Osteoarthritis is the most common musculoskeletal condition, affecting 80% of patients aged 55 years or older and 95% of patients aged 65 years or older.

The development of osteoarthritis is a biomechanical process whereby joints respond pathologically to mechanical stress, resulting in cartilage degradation and changes in subchondral bone. Acute injury (for example, anterior cruciate ligament tear of the knee) or repetitive injury (due to overuse or obesity) can result in cartilage injury, joint laxity, and abnormal joint mechanics that lead secondarily to osteoarthritis.

Risk Factors

The strongest risk factors for osteoarthritis are advancing age, obesity, female gender, joint injury (caused by occupation, repetitive use, or trauma), and genetic factors. Studies involving twins suggest that genetic factors account for 60% to 70% of the risk of osteoarthritis. Risk factors vary somewhat depending on the joint involved. For example, obesity is the most important modifiable risk factor for osteoarthritis of the knee. The incidence of knee osteoarthritis is also increased by injury or occupations with repetitive bending. The prevalence of osteoarthritis of the hip and knee is nearly two times higher in women than in men. Osteoarthritis of the hand has strong female and genetic predilections; it is also associated with obesity, suggesting that the effects of obesity may be metabolic or cytokine-driven as well as mechanical.

KEY POINTS

- Acute or repetitive injury can result in cartilage injury, joint laxity, and abnormal joint mechanics that lead secondarily to osteoarthritis.
- The strongest risk factors for osteoarthritis are advancing age, obesity, female gender, joint injury, and genetic factors.
- Obesity is the most important modifiable risk factor for osteoarthritis of the knee.

Clinical Features and Classification

Pain and loss of function are the hallmark features of osteoarthritis. Although classified as noninflammatory, osteoarthritis can be associated with flares of inflammation, and the presence of inflammation correlates with disease progression. Symptoms usually worsen with activity. Morning stiffness may occur, although it usually lasts less than 30 minutes.

Osteoarthritis of the hand typically leads to bony enlargement of the proximal and distal interphalangeal joints, with bone spurs that result in Bouchard and Heberden nodes

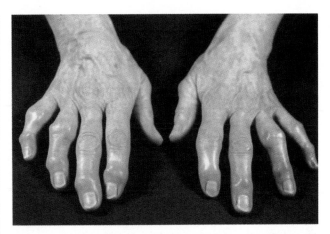

FIGURE 6. Heberden and Bouchard nodes at the distal and proximal interphalangeal joints, respectively.

(c) 2012 American College of Rheumatology. Used with permission.

(**Figure 6**). Involvement of the carpometacarpal joint is also common and leads to "squaring" of the contour of the joint (**Figure 7**).

Asymmetric joint-space narrowing of the knee can result in valgus (lateral joint-space narrowing and knocked knee) or varus (medial joint-space narrowing and bow-legged) deformities (**Figure 8**). During normal gait, the patient's center of gravity focuses over the medial tibiofemoral joint. Therefore, medial joint-space narrowing is the more common osteoarthritis finding in patients with knee osteoarthritis.

Osteoarthritis of the spine may lead to loss of spine mobility. Foraminal or canal stenosis can develop as a result of bone spurs or disk degeneration (resulting in disk bulges or fragmentation), leading to nerve root impingement (cervical radiculopathy, sciatica, pseudoclaudication [from lumbar spinal stenosis], or myelopathy [from cervical spinal stenosis]).

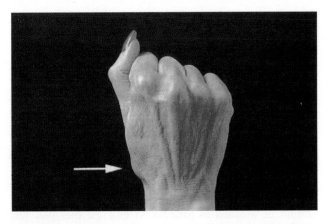

FIGURE 7. "Squaring" of the carpometacarpal joint in a patient with hand osteoarthritis.

(c) 2012 American College of Rheumatology. Used with permission.

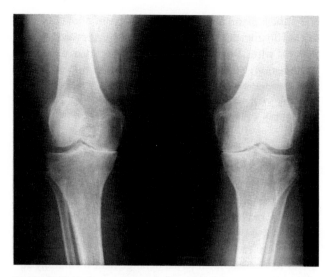

FIGURE 8. Radiograph of the knees showing medial joint-space narrowing (with varus deformities) and subchondral sclerosis.

Primary Osteoarthritis

Primary osteoarthritis generally affects the axial skeleton, weight-bearing joints (hip and knee), and hand (proximal and distal interphalangeal and carpometacarpal joints). The cause of joint damage is unknown. Onset can begin as early as the fourth decade, and prevalence increases steadily with age. Women and black persons have higher prevalence rates.

Secondary Osteoarthritis

Secondary osteoarthritis may result from joint injury or metabolic diseases such as chondrocalcinosis, acromegaly, or hemochromatosis. If osteoarthritis is observed in an atypical joint (such as metacarpophalangeal joints), one of the metabolic diseases such as hemochromatosis should be considered; iron studies and genetic tests should be ordered. Secondary osteoarthritis can also develop in joints previously damaged by inflammatory conditions such as rheumatoid arthritis or infection.

Erosive Osteoarthritis

Erosive osteoarthritis typically involves the hand and occurs predominantly in women. Flares of joint inflammation involve the proximal and distal interphalangeal joints and are associated with erythema, swelling, and severe pain. Radiographs reveal erosions of these joints as well as bone spurs and ankylosis. Between flares, clinical examination of erosive hand osteoarthritis may be indistinguishable from noninflammatory hand osteoarthritis.

Diffuse Idiopathic Skeletal Hyperostosis

Diffuse idiopathic skeletal hyperostosis (DISH) is characterized by calcification of the spinal ligaments, which causes large, flowing osteophytes. Typically there is little disk-space narrowing. Thoracic involvement is common. DISH also causes calcification of the entheses (where tendons or ligaments insert into bone), which may result in Achilles or calcaneal spurs as well as "whiskering" (calcification of the origin of the quadriceps muscles along the iliac crest, for example).

DISH most commonly occurs in obese men older than 40 years of age. Patients may be asymptomatic or may describe stiffness and reduced range of motion, particularly at the thoracic spine. Some studies demonstrate elevated levels of insulin-like growth factor 1 and growth hormone in patients with DISH, suggesting that metabolic factors play a role in pathogenesis.

DISH is diagnosed by the presence of flowing osteophytes across four contiguous vertebrae (**Figure 9**). Because thoracic involvement occurs in DISH, documenting the characteristic radiographic findings in this area may improve the sensitivity of imaging in diagnosing the condition relative to either lumbar or cervical radiography alone. Radiographs of DISH and ankylosing spondylitis have similarities; however, ankylosing spondylitis demonstrates vertical

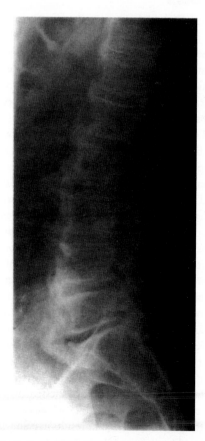

FIGURE 9. Radiograph of the lumbar spine showing diffuse idiopathic skeletal hyperostosis, characterized by flowing ossification along the anterolateral aspects of the vertebral bodies.

bridging syndesmophytes rather than the flowing osteophytes that occur in DISH, and sacroiliitis is not seen in patients with DISH.

KEY POINTS

- Primary osteoarthritis generally affects the axial skeleton, weight-bearing joints (hip and knee), and hand (interphalangeal and carpometacarpal joints).
- Secondary osteoarthritis may result from joint injury or metabolic diseases and can develop in joints previously damaged by inflammatory conditions.
- Erosive osteoarthritis is characterized by flares of joint inflammation involving the proximal and distal interphalangeal joints, which is associated with erythema, swelling, and severe pain.
- Radiographs of diffuse idiopathic skeletal hyperostosis (DISH) and ankylosing spondylitis have similarities; however, ankylosing spondylitis demonstrates vertical bridging syndesmophytes rather than the flowing osteophytes that occur in DISH.

Diagnosis

Osteoarthritis should be suspected in patients 40 years or older who have chronic joint pain without significant morning stiffness in the knee, hip, spine, proximal interphalangeal joints, distal interphalangeal joints, or carpometacarpal joints. Patients have minor or absent joint inflammation on physical examination. Diagnosis can be confirmed on plain radiographs.

Hand osteoarthritis can be distinguished from rheumatoid arthritis by the pattern of joint involvement and associated symptoms. Osteoarthritis typically involves bony enlargement of the proximal interphalangeal and distal interphalangeal joints along with the carpometacarpal joint, whereas rheumatoid arthritis involves synovial swelling of the metacarpophalangeal and proximal interphalangeal joints (and less likely bony enlargement). Rheumatoid arthritis typically is symmetric and associated with signs of inflammation (elevated erythrocyte sedimentation rate or C-reactive protein and morning stiffness).

Hip osteoarthritis is manifested by joint pain often described as groin pain or buttock pain exacerbated by weight bearing. Radiographs reveal joint-space narrowing (most prominent at the superior weight-bearing surface) and femoral or acetabular osteophytes. Knee osteoarthritis that involves the tibiofemoral joint is manifested by pain that is worse when standing or walking, whereas osteoarthritis involving the patellofemoral joint results in pain when climbing or descending stairs or when sitting in a chair for a prolonged period.

Regional soft-tissue pain syndromes, including bursitis, tendinitis, meniscal or labral tears in weight-bearing joints, and muscle spasm in patients with back pain, should be considered in the differential diagnosis (see Approach to the Patient with Rheumatic Disease, The Musculoskeletal Examination). Inflammatory arthritis can develop in patients with previously established osteoarthritis; therefore, radiographic evidence of osteoarthritis should not be used alone to establish a diagnosis.

Imaging Studies

Radiographic findings in osteoarthritis include joint-space narrowing, osteophytes, subchondral sclerosis, bony cyst formation, and eburnation (deformation of joint surface). However, radiographic severity correlates poorly with severity of symptoms.

MRI is rarely indicated for osteoarthritis but may be useful to evaluate for internal derangement if clinically suspected (for example, meniscal, ligamentous, or labral tears). MRI can identify areas of subchondral bone marrow edema that correlate with symptoms of pain. Bone marrow edema has also been associated with radiographic progression of osteoarthritis.

KEY POINTS

- Osteoarthritis should be suspected in patients older than 40 years with chronic joint pain involving the knee, hip, spine, proximal interphalangeal joints, distal interphalangeal joints, or carpometacarpal joints.
- Patients with osteoarthritis do not have significant morning stiffness (<30 minutes) and may have minor or absent joint inflammation on physical examination.
- Radiographic findings in patients with osteoarthritis include joint-space narrowing, osteophytes, subchondral sclerosis, bony cyst formation, and eburnation; however, radiographic severity correlates poorly with severity of symptoms.

Management

Nonpharmacologic Interventions

Numerous evidence-based nonpharmacologic interventions are available for patients with osteoarthritis. The Arthritis, Diet, and Activity Promotion Trial (ADAPT) examined the impact of weight loss, exercise, or combination therapy versus general healthy lifestyle recommendations. The diet and exercise groups showed significant improvement in pain, function, walking distance, and stair climbing at 6 months that persisted after 18 months, with the greatest improvements seen in those using combination therapy with weight loss and exercise. Interventions aimed at improving biomechanics are also helpful for osteoarthritis, particularly of the hip and knee, such as unloading braces.

Patient education programs (such as the Arthritis Foundation Self-Management Program or monthly case worker phone calls) help those with osteoarthritis learn to make adaptations to their limitations. Patients participating in such programs report reduced disabilities.

For patients with knee osteoarthritis with predominantly unilateral involvement (such as medial joint-space loss), unloading the involved side of the knee with an unloading brace can transfer the load to the other side of the knee and reduce pain. However, recent studies of lateral shoe wedges, which work on the same principle, demonstrated that they were not effective in the treatment of medial compartment knee osteoarthritis. Physical therapy can help strengthen muscles and improve alignment, thus reducing stress borne by the arthritic joint.

Use of a cane or other assistive device can significantly unload a knee or hip and improve gait, mobility, and pain level. Instruction on the proper use of a cane is necessary: the cane is placed in the hand contralateral to the symptomatic joint and swings forward as the affected limb swings forward. For osteoarthritis of the hand, adaptive devices such as large grip utensils, writing instruments, and key holders can reduce force across arthritic joints.

Although an initial randomized control trial demonstrated benefit for acupuncture over sham acupuncture and patient education, a recent follow-up study did not support these findings.

Pharmacologic Therapy

Pharmacologic therapy should be considered complementary to nonpharmacologic therapy. Analgesics such as acetaminophen can provide relief similar to NSAIDs; given their safer profile, they should be considered as first-line agents, especially for elderly patients. NSAIDs should be reserved for those who do not respond to acetaminophen.

Cyclooxygenase-2 inhibitors, which have been shown to have decreased frequency of gastrointestinal bleeding, may be an option for patients who are at a low risk for cardiovascular disease and have a significant risk of gastrointestinal toxicity.

There have been mixed results about the effectiveness of glucosamine and chondroitin. Studies supporting their use have demonstrated small beneficial effects; however, larger nonindustry-sponsored trials and meta-analyses have questioned these findings.

Topical creams, including anti-inflammatory agents (methyl salicylate, diclofenac), capsaicin, or other modalities (irritant oils to provide heat and evaporating creams to provide cold), can provide symptomatic relief. Lidocaine patches have been shown to be helpful for knee osteoarthritis.

In patients with refractory osteoarthritis, judicious use of low-dose opioids can maintain function and alleviate pain. Chronic use of opioids carries the risk of dependence, potential for abuse, constipation, urinary retention, cognitive impairment, and falls.

Intra-articular Injection

Corticosteroids

When a single joint or a few joints cause pain that is disproportionate to other joints and limits function, intra-articular corticosteroids may be effective in providing pain relief and improving function. The amount and duration of pain relief vary by patient; furthermore, there is no good method for identifying who might respond well. Successful injections provide pain relief for an average of 3 months.

The dose of corticosteroids depends upon the size of the joint, ranging from 10 mg of methylprednisolone (in the interphalangeal joint) to 80 mg (in the hip). Risks of injection, including pain, bleeding, and infection, should be discussed with the patient before the injection. Potential long-term risks from repeated injection may occur, including atrophy of the cartilage; therefore, the general recommendation calls for no more than three injections per year in a single joint. Rare adverse effects include fat atrophy and depigmentation of the skin.

Hyaluronic Acid

Hyaluronic acid injections provide significant relief for osteoarthritis of the knee. These injections are typically administered in a series of three weekly injections, although single-injection alternatives now exist. Hyaluronic acid injections are expensive but provide similar pain relief to corticosteroid injections; however, pain relief can last longer (3 to 6 months), and there are no limitations on repeat injections. Pain relief typically begins after the series of injections has been completed. Hyaluronic acid injections are most effective when injected into a dry joint after the effusion is drained.

Surgical Intervention

Conservative measures may be less effective when osteoarthritis is advanced, and a well-conducted study has demonstrated that arthroscopy is not effective in treating advanced knee osteoarthritis. When pain or loss of function significantly impacts quality of life, the benefits and risks of joint replacement surgery should be discussed. The decision to undergo joint replacement surgery is based on the patient's symptoms and quality of life, rather than the radiographic severity of the osteoarthritis.

Because joint replacement is elective surgery, the risks of surgery (prosthetic joint infection, deep venous thrombosis/pulmonary embolism, myocardial infarction, prosthesis loosening, or death from anesthesia and/or the procedure) should be discussed with the patient and balanced with the benefits of surgery.

The effectiveness of joint replacement surgery varies by joint. There are excellent data regarding the effectiveness of hip and knee replacement surgery, with 90% of patients reporting satisfaction with surgery. Pain reduction and functional status among postsurgical patients is similar to the status of patients without arthritis.

CONT.

Rehabilitation from knee surgery takes longer than for hip surgery, with patients sometimes requiring 3 months of rehabilitation before experiencing significant relief. Patients typically achieve the full benefits of replacement surgery by 6 months, but improvement may continue through 12 and 24 months after surgery. Physical rehabilitation after surgery is vigorous and is important for optimal outcomes; this should be considered when advising patients about possible joint replacement. A recent study suggests a 25% increase in the risk of fracture 2.5 to 5 years after hip arthroplasty (with protection in bisphosphonate users). This needs to be confirmed in future trials.

Ideally, patients should have realistic expectations for the procedure, be motivated to participate in rehabilitation, and have good social support. Although morbid obesity can shorten the long-term survival of the prosthesis, short-term outcomes are similar in obese and non-obese patients.

KEY POINTS

- Diet, exercise, physical therapy, and assistive devices such as a cane are beneficial for patients with osteoarthritis.
- Analgesics such as acetaminophen are considered first-line agents in those with osteoarthritis, especially elderly patients.
- When a single joint or a few joints cause pain that is disproportionate to other joints and limits function, intra-articular corticosteroids may be effective in providing pain relief and improving function.
- The decision to undergo joint replacement surgery is based on the patient's symptoms and quality of life, rather than the radiographic severity of the osteoarthritis.

Fibromyalgia

Fibromyalgia is a central pain sensitivity syndrome characterized by widespread pain and tenderness in which sensory processing systems are altered, producing allodynia and hyperalgesia. Abnormalities in neuropeptide levels and abnormal functional neuroimaging studies support a neurobiologic mechanism. Psychosocial factors appear to play a complex and important role.

Epidemiology

Fibromyalgia affects approximately 2% of the U.S. population and has a female predominance. Physical and emotional stressors are often temporally associated with the onset and exacerbation of symptoms. Association with other pain syndromes, including irritable bowel syndrome and irritable bladder, pelvic pain, vulvodynia, headache, and temporomandibular

jaw pain, is common. Fibromyalgia also may occur in patients with inflammatory and noninflammatory musculoskeletal conditions. First-degree relatives of patients with fibromyalgia are more likely to have fibromyalgia, mood disorders, and migraines.

Evaluation and Diagnosis

Patients with fibromyalgia have diffuse pain described as myalgia, arthralgia, or paresthesia. Mood disorders and fatigue are common and are often associated with sleep disturbance and cognitive dysfunction. Tenderness is generalized, classically more prominent at defined tender points (**Figure 10**). Fibromyalgia does not cause any other abnormalities on physical examination, routine laboratory testing, or imaging.

The 1990 American College of Rheumatology classification criteria for fibromyalgia focuses on widespread pain and tenderness at specific locations (**Table 14**). The 2010 preliminary diagnostic criteria provide an alternative tool for diagnosis, which emphasizes symptoms over tender points. These criteria can be particularly useful for practitioners with

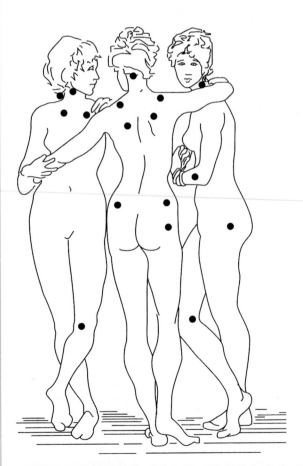

FIGURE 10. Tender point locations for the 1990 criteria for the classification of fibromyalgia (The Three Graces, after Baron Jean-Baptiste Regnault, 1793, Louvre Museum, Paris).

TABLE 14. American College of Rheumatology 1990 Criteria for the Classification of Fibromyalgia[a]

Criterion 1. History of Widespread Pain
Definition: Pain in the right and left side of the body and above and below the waist and axial skeletal pain (cervical spine, anterior chest, thoracic spine, or low back). Shoulder and buttock pain is considered as pain for each involved side. Low back pain is considered lower segment pain.

Criterion 2. Pain in 11 of 18 Tender Point Sites on Digital Palpation
Definition: Pain, on digital palpation, must be present in at least 11 of the following 18 sites:
Occiput: bilateral, at the suboccipital muscle insertions
Low cervical: bilateral, at the anterior aspects of the intertransverse spaces C5–C7
Trapezius: bilateral, at the midpoint of the upper border
Supraspinatus: bilateral, at origins, above the scapula spine near the medial border
Second rib: bilateral, at the second costochondral junctions, just lateral to the junctions of upper surfaces
Lateral epicondyle: bilateral, 2 cm distal to the epicondyles
Gluteal: bilateral, in upper outer quadrants of buttocks in anterior fold of muscle
Greater trochanter: bilateral, posterior to the trochanteric prominence
Knee: bilateral, at the medial fat pad proximal to the joint line
Digital palpation should be performed with an approximate force of 4 kg (8.8 lb). For a tender point to be considered "positive" for pain, the patient must state that the palpation was painful. "Tender" is not to be considered "painful."

[a]Patients are said to have fibromyalgia if both criteria are satisfied. Widespread pain must have been present for at least 3 months. The presence of a second clinical disorder does not exclude the diagnosis of fibromyalgia.

From Wolfe F, Smythe HA, Yunus MB, et al. The American College of Rheumatology 1990 criteria for the classification of fibromyalgia: report of the multicenter criteria committee. Arthritis Rheum. 1990;33:160-172. [PMID: 2306288] Reproduced with permission of John Wiley & Sons, Inc.

less experience performing a formal tender point evaluation. This tool includes a severity scale with potential utility for longitudinal monitoring.

Treatment

Related comorbidities, including sources of pain, sleep disruption, and mood disorders, must be addressed when establishing treatment modalities for patients with fibromyalgia.

Nonpharmacologic Therapy

Educating patients about fibromyalgia can provide reassurance and improve outcomes. Nonpharmacologic therapy is the cornerstone of treatment and should be initiated in all affected patients. Regular aerobic exercise has been shown to be effective in this setting. Exercise regimens should be individualized and titrated up to 30 minutes most days of the week. Physical therapy may also be helpful. Cognitive behavioral therapy has been shown to be beneficial but is not always covered by insurance plans.

Pharmacologic Therapy

The serotonin-norepinephrine reuptake inhibitors (SNRIs) duloxetine and milnacipran are FDA approved for use in fibromyalgia and are effective in patients with or without depression. Data on selective serotonin reuptake inhibitors are equivocal. The antiepileptic medications pregabalin (FDA approved) and gabapentin (off-label) are also used to treat fibromyalgia. Tricyclic antidepressants (such as amitriptyline) and cyclobenzaprine are moderately effective, but side effects are common. Opioid analgesics should be avoided.

KEY POINTS

- Fibromyalgia is characterized by widespread pain and tenderness in which sensory processing systems are altered, producing allodynia and hyperalgesia.

- Related comorbidities, including sources of pain, sleep disruption, and mood disorders, must be addressed when establishing treatment modalities for patients with fibromyalgia.

- Nonpharmacologic therapy such as regular aerobic exercise, physical therapy, and cognitive behavioral therapy is the cornerstone of fibromyalgia treatment and should be initiated in all affected patients.

- Various serotonin-norepinephrine reuptake inhibitors, antiepileptic medications, and tricyclic antidepressants can be beneficial in the treatment of patients with fibromyalgia.

Spondyloarthritis

Spondyloarthritis (formerly known as spondyloarthropathy or the seronegative spondyloarthropathies) refers to a spectrum of inflammatory disorders, including ankylosing spondylitis, psoriatic arthritis, inflammatory bowel disease (IBD)–associated arthritis, and reactive arthritis (formerly known as Reiter syndrome). Manifestations of the various forms of spondyloarthritis overlap; there is a shared tendency to develop inflammation and calcification of entheses and new bone formation.

Pathophysiology

Genetic Predisposition

Spondyloarthritis frequently clusters in families, and HLA-B27 is the strongest genetic risk factor. Approximately 95% of patients with ankylosing spondylitis are HLA-B27 positive, and first-degree relatives of patients with ankylosing spondylitis have an increased risk of developing the disease. Ankylosing spondylitis is rare in populations with a low prevalence of HLA-B27 such as sub-Saharan Africans, and cases that do occur in these populations are usually not associated with HLA-B27.

Other forms of spondyloarthritis share an association with HLA-B27 but to a lesser degree. The association of HLA-B27 with psoriatic arthritis and IBD-associated arthritis is only noted in patients with axial involvement. HLA-B27 is present in a few patients with reactive arthritis, but there are conflicting data on whether HLA-B27 is predictive of a worse outcome in these patients.

Environmental Triggers

Gastrointestinal and genitourinary tract infections are implicated in the development of reactive arthritis. Bacterial fragments have been identified in joints, but cultures are sterile. Bacterial DNA has been detected in the synovium of patients with reactive arthritis and osteoarthritis as well as those without arthritis; the significance of this finding is unclear.

HIV infection is associated with increased severity of psoriatic arthritis and reactive arthritis; testing for HIV is indicated in patients with sudden onset or unexplained worsening of their disease. A temporal relationship exists between psoriatic arthritis and recent trauma in some patients, and repeated microtrauma may explain its predilection for the knees and elbows. Enteric bacteria are suspected to play a role in the intestinal and extraintestinal inflammation that occurs in IBD. No infectious triggers have been identified in association with ankylosing spondylitis.

KEY POINTS

- HLA-B27 is the strongest genetic risk factor for spondyloarthritis; 95% of patients with ankylosing spondylitis are HLA-B27 positive.
- Gastrointestinal and genitourinary tract infections are implicated in the development of reactive arthritis.
- HIV infection is associated with increased severity of psoriatic arthritis and reactive arthritis; testing for HIV is indicated in patients with sudden onset or unexplained worsening of their disease.

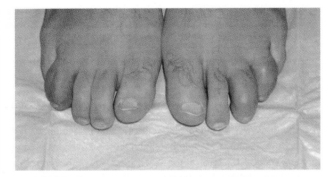

FIGURE 11. "Sausage-shaped" digits caused by dactylitis in a patient with reactive arthritis.

Reprinted with permission from Moore G. Atlas of the Musculoskeletal Examination. Philadelphia: American College of Physicians; 2003.

Classification

Characteristic features of spondyloarthritis include both axial and peripheral arthritis, enthesitis, and dactylitis (**Figure 11**) as well as dermatologic, ophthalmologic, and gastrointestinal inflammation. Despite these commonalities, patterns of articular and extra-articular involvement vary across the spectrum of spondyloarthritis. Certain findings tend to cluster depending on whether there is associated psoriasis, IBD, preceding infection, or none of these features (**Table 15**).

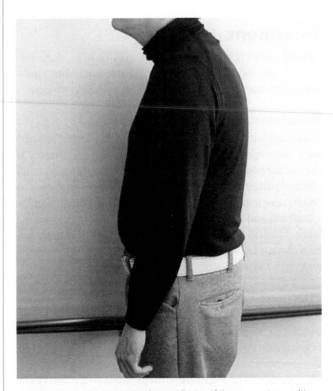

FIGURE 12. This patient has forward flexion of the upper spine resulting in the characteristic stooped posture associated with ankylosing spondylitis.

TABLE 15. Clinical Features of Spondyloarthritis

	Ankylosing Spondylitis	Psoriatic Arthritis	IBD-Associated Arthritis	Reactive Arthritis
Musculoskeletal				
Axial involvement	Axial involvement predominates; initially involves the SI joints and lower spine, progressing cranially	May occur at any level; may start in the cervical spine	May be asymptomatic but can follow a course similar to ankylosing spondylitis	Less common than in other forms of spondyloarthritis
Peripheral manifestations	Enthesitis with or without asymmetric large-joint oligoarthritis; hip involvement can cause significant functional limitation; shoulders can also be involved	Various patterns, most commonly polyarticular; DIP involvement is associated with nail involvement; dactylitis and tenosynovitis; arthritis mutilans	Frequently corresponds with activity of bowel disease; nonerosive; occasionally a more persistent destructive pattern	Enthesitis and asymmetric large-joint oligoarthritis; usually self-limited; nonerosive; some patients experience recurrent or persistent arthritis; may develop features of other forms of spondyloarthritis
Dermatologic		Psoriasis typically precedes joint involvement; nail pitting; onycholysis	Pyoderma gangrenosum; erythema nodosum	Keratoderma blenorrhagicum; circinate balanitis
Ophthalmologic	Uveitis (typically anterior, unilateral, recurrent)	Conjunctivitis is more common than uveitis (anterior, can be bilateral, insidious, or chronic)	Uveitis (anterior, can be bilateral, insidious, or chronic); conjunctivitis, keratitis, and episcleritis are rare	Conjunctivitis is more common than uveitis
Gastrointestinal	Asymptomatic intestinal ulcerations		Crohn disease; ulcerative colitis	Prior GI infection in some patients
Genitourinary	Urethritis (rare)		Nephrolithiasis	Prior GU infection in some patients; noninfectious urethritis, prostatitis, cervicitis, and salpingitis
Cardiovascular	Aortic valve disease; aortitis; conduction abnormalities; CAD	Association with traditional CAD risk factors	Thromboembolism	
Pulmonary	Restrictive lung disease from costovertebral rigidity; apical fibrosis (rare)			
Bone Quality	Falsely elevated bone mineral density from syndesmophytes; increased risk of spine fracture	Increased risk of fracture; multifactorial	High risk for vitamin D deficiency, low bone density, and fracture	Localized osteopenia

CAD = coronary artery disease; DIP = distal interphalangeal; GI = gastrointestinal; GU = genitourinary; IBD = inflammatory bowel disease; SI = sacroiliac.

Ankylosing Spondylitis

Ankylosing spondylitis affects approximately 0.1% of the U.S. population. This disorder has a male predominance, and peak age of onset is between 20 and 30 years. Patients classically present with progressive inflammatory back pain and stiffness. Other organs may also be affected (see Table 15). Initially, pain can be localized to the low back, buttocks, or posterior thighs. With time, inflammation and bony changes usually ascend the spine, producing a stooped posture with limited mobility of the spine and chest (**Figure 12**, previous page). Rigidity increases the risk of fracture, myelopathy, and radiculopathy. Disease activity typically fluctuates, with slow progression of bony changes, including ankylosis. Back pain in patients with advanced disease can be a sign of vertebral fracture; even without a history of trauma, back pain that is new, worsening, or different in character should prompt consideration of spine imaging.

Clinical manifestations associated with worse outcomes include limited lumbar motion; oligoarthritis with hip involvement; dactylitis; greater disease activity; elevated erythrocyte sedimentation rate (ESR); associated psoriasis, IBD, or uveitis; poor response to NSAIDs; radiographic progression; and functional impairment. Sociodemographic factors such as male gender, onset before age 16 years, cigarette smoking, occupations involving spine flexibility or vibration, and lower level of education are also associated with worse outcomes. The modest increase in mortality that occurs in ankylosing spondylitis is attributable to secondary amyloidosis, cardiovascular complications, accidents, and suicide.

Psoriatic Arthritis

Psoriatic arthritis can affect up to 30% of patients with psoriasis. When patients with psoriasis develop arthritis, psoriatic arthritis should be considered, although osteoarthritis is also common. Skin cell turnover in psoriasis may also increase the risk of gout. Characteristic features of psoriatic arthritis include enthesitis, dactylitis, tenosynovitis, arthritis of the distal interphalangeal joints, asymmetric oligoarthritis, and spondylitis (see Table 15).

Approximately 15% of patients who present with psoriatic arthritis are found to have previously undiagnosed psoriasis. Patients who have features consistent with psoriatic arthritis should be examined closely for psoriasiform skin lesions on the umbilicus, gluteal cleft, extensor surfaces, posterior auricular region, and scalp. Nails should be examined for pitting or onycholysis (**Figure 13**). Nail scrapings can be useful to exclude fungus as a cause of nail changes. Another 15% of patients develop skin involvement after the onset of arthritis. Skin and joint symptoms usually do not correlate well, although both may respond to the same therapies.

There are five patterns of joint involvement in psoriatic arthritis: involvement of the distal interphalangeal joints (**Figure 14**); asymmetric oligoarthritis with less than five joints involved; symmetric polyarthritis (similar to that of rheumatoid arthritis); arthritis mutilans (extensive osteolysis of the digits with striking deformity); and spondylitis.

Although spondyloarthritis was initially recognized for the absence of rheumatoid factor and termed "seronegative," rheumatoid factor is present in up to 10% of patients with psoriatic arthritis. Anti–cyclic citrullinated peptide (anti-CCP) antibodies have been detected in a similar percentage (5% to 15%). When present, anti-CCP antibodies correlate with erosive disease in psoriatic arthritis. Titers ≥ 1:40 are seen in nearly 50% of patients, although only 14%

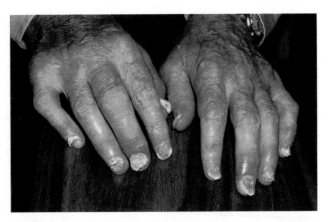

FIGURE 14. This patient with psoriatic arthritis has onycholysis and onychodystrophy.

are ≥ 1:80. Anti–double-stranded DNA antibodies may form after exposure to tumor necrosis factor (TNF)-α inhibitors but have also been reported in 3% of patients prior to any use of such agents.

The coexistence of erosive or lytic changes with new bone formation at the entheses is characteristic of psoriatic arthritis (**Figure 15**).

Inflammatory Bowel Disease–Associated Arthritis

Nearly 50% of patients with IBD develop musculoskeletal symptoms. Although uncommon, arthritis may develop prior to gastrointestinal manifestations. Peripheral arthritis may be acute and remitting with a pauciarticular distribution commonly involving the knee. This usually occurs early in the course of bowel disease, correlates with bowel inflammation, and resolves without specific intervention or destruction to the joints. Peripheral arthritis can also be chronic or relapsing, with prominent involvement of the metacarpophalangeal joints and less correlation with intestinal inflammation.

Axial involvement occurs in up to 20% of patients, particularly in men. Patients may develop radiographic sacroiliitis and spondylitis with or without inflammatory back pain. Axial disease tends not to parallel intestinal disease. Enthesitis develops in 10% of patients.

Patients with IBD are at increased risk of infectious arthritis on the basis of their disease and immunosuppressive treatment; these patients may also develop avascular necrosis related to use of corticosteroids.

Reactive Arthritis

Reactive arthritis is a postinfectious, aseptic arthritis that occurs in both men and women, with an annual incidence estimated at approximately 30 per 100,000 persons. Approximately one third of patients manifest the classic triad of arthritis, urethritis, and conjunctivitis (see Table 15). The classic pathogens (*Chlamydia trachomatis, Yersinia,*

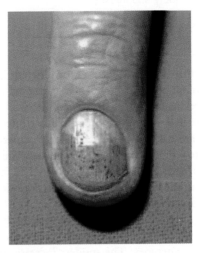

FIGURE 13. Nail pitting in a patient with psoriasis.

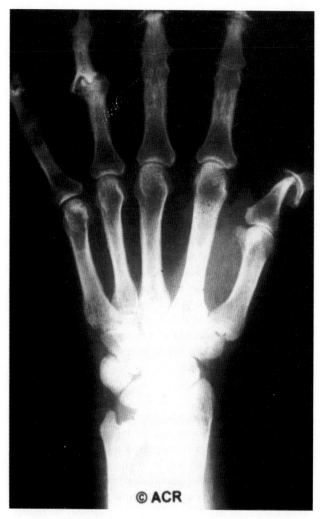

FIGURE 15. Radiograph showing "pencil-in-cup" deformities of the distal interphalangeal joints of the thumb and middle fingers. These deformities are caused by erosive changes associated with psoriatic arthritis.

(c) 2012 American College of Rheumatology. Used with permission.

Salmonella, Shigella, and *Campylobacter*) infect mucous membranes of the gastrointestinal or urogenital tract. *Clostridium difficile* and *Chlamydophila pneumoniae* may also be pathogenic. Infections triggered by these organisms may cause urethritis or diarrhea, although patients may be asymptomatic. Arthritis, usually oligoarticular, develops several days to weeks after the infection.

Urethritis also may develop as a feature of the inflammatory process, without active genitourinary infection and without any history of infection. Oral ulcers, genital lesions such as circinate balanitis, nail changes as seen in psoriasis, and rashes such as keratoderma blenorrhagicum (**Figure 16**) can occur, but none of these findings exclusively occurs in reactive arthritis.

Reactive arthritis is usually self-limited and remits within 6 months without causing erosive damage. About 25% of

patients develop a chronic persistent arthritis and may develop features of psoriatic arthritis, IBD-associated arthritis, or ankylosing spondylitis. Patients may experience recurrent acute arthritis, which may relate to new infections.

KEY POINTS

- Ankylosing spondylitis is characterized by progressive inflammatory back pain and stiffness; onset is between 20 and 30 years of age with a male predominance.
- Pain associated with ankylosing spondylitis may be localized to the low back, buttocks, or posterior thighs; with time, inflammation and bony changes usually ascend the spine, producing a stooped posture with limited mobility of the spine and chest.
- Characteristic features of psoriatic arthritis include enthesitis, dactylitis, tenosynovitis, arthritis of the distal interphalangeal joints, asymmetric oligoarthritis, and spondylitis.
- An inflammatory peripheral arthritis and sacroiliitis may accompany inflammatory bowel disease.
- Detection of pathogens such as *Chlamydia trachomatis* in patients with arthritis, urethritis, conjunctivitis, and/or enthesitis supports a diagnosis of reactive arthritis.

Diagnosis

The 2009 Assessment of SpondyloArthritis International Society (ASAS) criteria allow for early diagnosis of patients across the spectrum of spondyloarthritis, emphasizing the distinction between axial and peripheral involvement (**Table 16**).

Spondyloarthritis should be considered in patients with inflammatory back pain younger than 40 years (**Table 17**). In

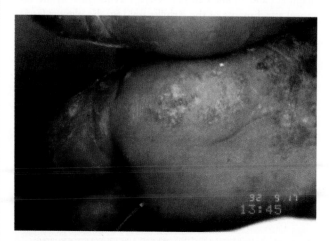

FIGURE 16. Hyperkeratotic skin lesions of keratoderma blenorrhagicum in reactive arthritis.

TABLE 16. Assessment of SpondyloArthritis International Society Classification Criteria for Axial Spondyloarthritis[a]

Sacroiliitis on imaging[b] plus at least one spondyloarthritis feature listed below

    or

HLA-B27 plus at least two other spondyloarthritis features listed below

Spondyloarthritis features:

  Inflammatory back pain

  Arthritis

  Enthesitis

  Dactylitis

  Uveitis

  Psoriasis

  Crohn disease or ulcerative colitis

  Family history for spondyloarthritis

  HLA-B27

  Elevated C-reactive protein level

  Good response to NSAIDs

[a]In patients with back pain for 3 or more months and onset before the age of 45 years; sensitivity is 82.9%, and specificity is 84.4%.

[b]Sacroiliitis on imaging: acute inflammation on MRI or definite radiographic sacroiliitis.

Reproduced from Rudwaleit M, van der Heijde D, Landewé R, et al. The development of Assessment of SpondyloArthritis international Society classification criteria for axial spondyloarthritis (part II): validation and final selection. Ann Rheum Dis. 2009;68:777-783. [PMID: 19297344] With permission from B M J Publishing Group.

the absence of radiographic or MRI evidence of sacroiliitis, the diagnosis of "preradiographic" axial spondyloarthritis can be made if the patient has at least two clinical diagnostic criteria and is positive for HLA-B27.

Patients without back pain, but with peripheral arthritis, enthesitis, or dactylitis in the proper clinical context may fit criteria for peripheral spondyloarthritis. Axial and peripheral manifestations of spondyloarthritis often coexist. Spinal mobility, disease activity, and physical function should be assessed at diagnosis and monitored periodically. Tenderness at the calcaneal attachments of the Achilles tendon, the plantar fascia,

TABLE 17. Assessment of SpondyloArthritis International Society Inflammatory Back Pain Criteria[a]

| Age at onset <40 years |
| Insidious onset |
| Improvement with exercise |
| No improvement with rest |
| Pain at night with improvement upon getting out of bed |

[a]In patients with back pain for 3 or more months. At least four parameters must be present. Sensitivity is 77.0%, and specificity is 91.7%.

Reproduced from Sieper J, van der Heijde D, Landewé R, et al. New criteria for inflammatory back pain in patients with chronic back pain: a real patient exercise by experts from the Assessment of SpondyloArthritis international Society (ASAS). Ann Rheum Dis. 2009;68(6):784-788. [PMID: 19147614] With permission from B M J Publishing Group.

costochondral junctions, and other entheses suggests enthesitis. Improvement with NSAIDs can help distinguish enthesitis from fibromyalgia.

Laboratory Studies

Rheumatoid factor and anti-CCP antibodies are typically negative in patients with spondyloarthritis. C-reactive protein (CRP) levels and ESR correlate with disease activity in some patients, particularly those with peripheral disease. Most patients with ankylosing spondylitis have ESR and CRP levels in the normal range. In patients with IBD, acute phase reactants usually parallel intestinal inflammation.

HIV testing should be considered in patients with reactive or psoriatic arthritis, particularly in those with severe skin manifestations. Stool cultures and urine samples for *C. trachomatis* are suggested in patients with reactive arthritis even in the absence of gastrointestinal or genitourinary symptoms, although the organism may have already been cleared. Significant elevations of IgA or IgM levels above population controls may provide evidence of antecedent infection with certain organisms associated with reactive arthritis, including *Yersinia* and *Salmonella*. Serologic testing for *C. trachomatis* lacks requisite specificity.

Imaging Studies

A single anteroposterior radiograph of the pelvis provides a view of the sacroiliac joints and the hips (**Figure 17**) and is indicated for patients with suspected spondyloarthritis. The earliest changes typically occur at the iliac portion of the sacroiliac joint where the subchondral bone becomes less distinct. Erosive changes can subsequently produce irregularity of the cortex. In late disease, the joint space may be obliterated. Sacroiliitis may be evident on plain radiographs in only 40% of patients with ankylosing spondylitis even after 10 years of disease. If the diagnosis remains in question, MRI of the sacroiliac joints should be considered to evaluate for local

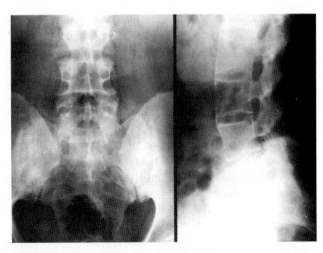

FIGURE 17. Sacroiliitis and sacroiliac joint fusion.

bone marrow edema, which occurs in acute sacroiliitis. CT can detect erosive or sclerotic changes when plain radiographs are insufficient; however, MRI is preferred for the detection of active inflammation and does not expose patients to the radiation of a CT.

Radiographs of the spine may be normal. Early changes of ankylosing spondylitis include squaring of the vertebral bodies. In more advanced disease, calcification of the anterior longitudinal ligament and proliferative changes (such as sclerosis, syndesmophyte formation, and ankylosis) may occur. The "bamboo spine" refers to the appearance of bridging syndesmophytes extending across the entire spine. Atlantoaxial (C1-C2) subluxation can also develop.

Calcification and productive bony changes may also be evident on radiographs of peripheral joints, frequently at sites of chronic or recurrent enthesitis. Erosive changes and osteolysis may be present, particularly in psoriatic arthritis. With hip involvement, joint-space narrowing is typically concentric.

Ultrasonography has greater sensitivity for the detection of enthesitis than the physical examination, although the clinical significance of this is unclear. Ultrasonography can detect synovitis and guide aspirations and injections.

Periodic monitoring of patients with lateral radiographs of the spine (in patients with axial disease) and/or of the hands and feet (in patients with peripheral arthritis) is recommended. Periodic evaluation of other joints, including hips, should be considered based on symptoms and physical examination findings. Although bone marrow edema may resolve with treatment, MRI is not currently recommended for routine monitoring.

KEY POINTS

- Spondyloarthritis should be considered in patients with inflammatory back pain who are younger than 45 years of age.

- Axial and peripheral manifestations of spondyloarthritis often coexist; spinal mobility, disease activity, and physical function should be assessed at diagnosis and monitored periodically.

- Rheumatoid factor and anti–cyclic citrullinated peptide antibodies are typically negative in patients with spondyloarthritis.

- HIV testing should be considered in patients with reactive or psoriatic arthritis, particularly in those with severe skin manifestations.

- A single anteroposterior radiograph of the pelvis is indicated for suspected spondyloarthritis and provides a view of the sacroiliac joints and the hips.

- MRI is the preferred alternative study for detection of inflammation of the sacroiliac joints if spondyloarthritis is highly suspected but plain radiographs are negative.

Treatment

The various forms of spondyloarthritis are treated similarly, but important differences exist in the management of axial and peripheral arthritis. Generally, NSAIDs are first-line therapy. Nonbiologic disease-modifying antirheumatic drugs (DMARDs) are helpful in peripheral arthritis but have no role in the management of axial manifestations. TNF-α inhibition can be helpful in severe or persistent axial, peripheral, and extra-articular manifestations. Treatment of reactive arthritis differs somewhat from the other forms of spondyloarthritis partly because of the relatively favorable prognosis.

Axial Involvement

NSAIDs are first-line therapy for axial arthritis because of their efficacy and relatively low cost. Up to 80% of patients respond to anti-inflammatory doses taken on a regular basis. If one NSAID does not provide relief after 2 weeks, another agent may be tried. Corticosteroid injections into sacroiliac joints can reduce local inflammation. Exercise regimens focus on postural training, maintaining flexibility, and reducing falls and fractures.

TNF-α inhibitors effectively control symptoms of axial inflammation in most patients, although radiographic progression may continue (**Figure 18**). Efficacy is greater in patients with a shorter duration of disease; it remains to be seen whether early initiation of TNF-α inhibitors will prevent radiographic changes. Patients who do not respond to one TNF-α inhibitor may respond to another agent in this class.

Surgical interventions, including cervical fusion and vertebral wedge osteotomy, can be helpful in patients with cervical instability and deformity, respectively. Perioperative

FIGURE 18. MRI of the lumbar spine in a patient with ankylosing spondylitis pre– and post–tumor necrosis factor α inhibitor therapy. The left panel shows edema immediately adjacent to the L4 to L5 endplates (*asterisks*) and immediately subjacent to the superior endplate of L5 (*arrow*). The right panel shows the lumbar spine after tumor necrosis factor α inhibitor therapy was initiated and reveals resolution of active enthesitis by fatty marrow replacement (*arrow*).

management includes attention to possible cervical disease, spinal rigidity, and reduced chest expansion.

Peripheral Involvement

Mild symptoms of peripheral arthritis and enthesitis are often controlled with NSAIDs. NSAIDs may be associated with flares of intestinal inflammation in IBD, although data are conflicting. Corticosteroid injections for arthritis and enthesitis can be beneficial. Care should be taken to avoid injection through psoriatic plaques. Systemic corticosteroids are generally avoided in patients with psoriasis, because they can be associated with a flare of skin manifestations.

Nonbiologic DMARDs, including methotrexate, sulfasalazine, cyclosporine, and leflunomide, should be considered in patients with moderate or severe peripheral inflammation or mild peripheral inflammation that occurs despite the use of NSAIDs or corticosteroids. Sulfasalazine is commonly used for peripheral arthritis and enthesitis, although it has not been found to be effective at treating the dermatologic manifestations of psoriasis. This agent is also effective for both intestinal and extraintestinal manifestations of IBD-associated arthritis. Methotrexate can be effective in the treatment of both peripheral arthritis and skin manifestations associated with psoriatic arthritis. Although these nonbiologic DMARDs have modest efficacy in reducing evidence of inflammation, none has been shown to inhibit radiographic progression.

TNF-α inhibitors have shown greater efficacy at controlling peripheral musculoskeletal inflammation than nonbiologic DMARDs and can inhibit peripheral radiographic progression. These agents improve skin and nail manifestations of psoriasis, intestinal and extraintestinal manifestations of IBD, overall function, and quality of life. TNF-α inhibitors are recommended for patients with evidence of ongoing peripheral inflammation or progressive radiographic changes despite nonbiologic DMARD use and can be considered for initial treatment for patients with poor prognostic features (such as polyarticular inflammation, elevated ESR, evidence of joint damage, impaired function, and decreased quality of life). Although etanercept is effective for peripheral and axial joint inflammation in Crohn disease, it is not effective for intestinal inflammation. Infliximab, adalimumab, and certolizumab pegol are effective for both articular and intestinal manifestations. Paradoxically, some patients treated with TNF-α inhibitors for indications other than psoriasis or psoriatic arthritis develop psoriasis that improves with discontinuation of the drug. Combination of a TNF-α inhibitor with methotrexate is associated with greater benefits in psoriatic arthritis but not in ankylosing spondylitis. Ustekinumab, a monoclonal antibody against IL-12/IL-23, is effective in the treatment of psoriasis, and early studies also suggest efficacy in psoriatic arthritis.

In patients with significant joint damage, surgical options such as total hip arthroplasty may be helpful.

Reactive Arthritis

Active infections should be treated with standard antibiotic regimens in patients with reactive arthritis as in those without reactive arthritis. Enteric infections associated with reactive arthritis may be self-limited and often resolve before the patient is diagnosed with reactive arthritis. Antibiotic treatment for resolved or unproven enteric infection is not recommended and is not indicated for patients with reactive arthritis caused by enteric infection.

When *C. trachomatis* infection is detected, antibiotic treatment is indicated for the patient and his or her sexual partner(s) to avoid reinfection and spread of infection. A recent study reported improved clinical outcomes with prolonged combination antibiotic treatment for patients with reactive arthritis and evidence of persistent chlamydial joint involvement. Further studies are required to evaluate a possible role for prolonged antibiotic treatment.

Although NSAIDs do not alter the course of reactive arthritis, these agents provide symptomatic relief. Corticosteroid injections can reduce local inflammation in affected joints and entheses. If NSAIDs and corticosteroid injections are insufficient, systemic corticosteroids and other immunosuppressive agents may be options. Sulfasalazine has been shown to have some efficacy. If sulfasalazine is contraindicated or if inflammation persists, TNF-α inhibitors can be considered, although data for their use are limited. After articular and extra-articular inflammation resolves, immunosuppression can be discontinued.

KEY POINTS

- When tolerated, NSAIDs are first-line therapy for patients with spondyloarthritis.

- In patients with spondyloarthritis, nonbiologic disease-modifying antirheumatic drugs can be helpful in peripheral arthritis but have no role in the management of axial manifestations.

- Tumor necrosis factor α inhibitors are beneficial for patients with spondyloarthritis who have severe or persistent axial, peripheral, or extra-articular manifestations.

- Antibiotic treatment is not indicated for patients with reactive arthritis caused by enteric infection unless an active infection is present.

Systemic Lupus Erythematosus

Systemic lupus erythematosus (SLE) is characterized by a wide range of organ involvement, multiple autoantibodies, and a broad spectrum of disease severity with intermittent exacerbations and remissions.

Pathophysiology

The cause of SLE is multifactorial, representing a combination of genetic susceptibility and environmental stimuli that leads to autoimmunity with tissue inflammation and damage. Several susceptibility genes have been identified; however, no single genetic polymorphism causes SLE. Triggering of the innate immune system (the nonspecific, or generic, mechanisms of the immune system response to infection) by viruses or endogenous ribonucleoprotein is thought to lead to production of type I interferons important in lupus pathogenesis. Autoantibodies appear early in the course of disease and generally target nucleic acid and/or nucleic acid–binding proteins. Immune complex deposition promotes complement activation, which results in tissue damage.

Proposed environmental factors include ultraviolet light, viral infection, tobacco, and drugs such as hydralazine and procainamide. The significance of the marked female predominance in SLE is unclear; increased levels of estrogen or epigenetic modification of the X chromosome may play a role.

Epidemiology

The incidence of SLE has tripled over the past 40 years, and prevalence in the United States is currently 20 to 122 per 100,000 persons. There is a marked female predominance, especially during reproductive years (in which the female-to-male ratio is 9:1); the ratio is lower in childhood and postmenopause. Symptom onset is most common during childbearing years. Prevalence varies among ethnic groups and is two to three times greater in nonwhite persons. Socioeconomic factors may play a possible role.

KEY POINTS

- Systemic lupus erythematosus is characterized by a wide range of organ involvement, multiple autoantibodies, and a broad spectrum of disease severity with intermittent exacerbations and remissions.

- There is a marked female predominance in systemic lupus erythematosus, especially during reproductive years, and the disorder is two to three times greater in nonwhite persons.

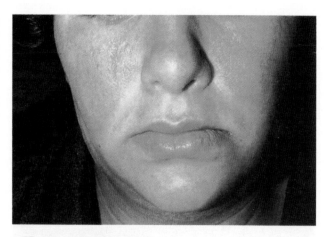

FIGURE 19. Butterfly rash.

Clinical Manifestations

Nonspecific constitutional symptoms in SLE are common and include fever, fatigue, and weight loss.

Mucocutaneous Manifestations

Mucocutaneous manifestations occur in 90% of patients with SLE, with photosensitivity in more than two thirds of patients. Common lupus rashes are summarized in **Table 18**.

Butterfly (malar) rash occurs in 30% of patients (**Figure 19**). Discoid lupus erythematosus rash occurs in 5% to 25% of patients with SLE but more commonly occurs as a distinct cutaneous entity (**Figure 20**).

Alopecia, a common manifestation of active disease, is reversible when not caused by discoid scarring. Mucosal ulcerations occur on the hard palate, tongue, or buccal mucosa and are typically painless; nasal ulcers are usually found on the lower nasal septum. Biopsy specimens of both affected and unaffected skin characteristically show immunofluorescence staining with immunoglobulin and complement deposits at the dermal-epidermal junction, which is termed a positive "lupus band test."

Musculoskeletal Manifestations

Musculoskeletal symptoms affect 90% of patients with SLE. Arthralgia and arthritis predominantly affect the hands,

Rash	Characteristics	Comments
Acute cutaneous lupus erythematosus	Erythematous; flat or raised; affects malar areas, forehead, chin, other sun-exposed areas	Malar rash spares the nasolabial folds; nonscarring
Subacute cutaneous lupus erythematosus	Erythematous annular rings with crusted margins and central hypopigmentation; affects forearms, shoulders, neck, upper torso	Associated with anti-Ro/SSA and anti-La/SSB antibodies; less common papulosquamous form resembles psoriasis; nonscarring
Discoid lupus erythematosus	Discrete erythematous, infiltrated plaques with follicular plugging; affects face, neck, scalp, ear canals, upper torso	Scarring: heals with depressed central scars, atrophy, hypo- and hyperpigmentation, and irreversible alopecia in the scalp
Lupus profundus	Panniculitis (inflammation of the fat layer)	Presents with painful nodules

TABLE 18. Common Rashes in Patients with Systemic Lupus Erythematosus

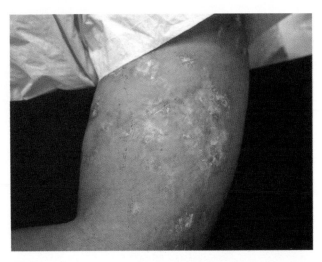

FIGURE 20. Discoid lupus erythematosus, characterized by erythematous and hypopigmented, scarred, atrophic, discoid plaques with raised borders.

wrists, and knees. Arthritis is usually nonerosive and non-deforming. Tendon inflammation may lead to tendon rupture or to Jaccoud arthropathy in 5% to 10% of patients. Jaccoud arthropathy is a chronic nonerosive deformity of the hands that is reducible, because it is due to tendon inflammation rather than joint destruction; it is seen in SLE as well as in rheumatic fever and is similar in appearance to rheumatoid arthritis.

Inflammatory myositis with proximal muscle weakness develops in 4% to 10% of patients; creatine kinase levels are usually elevated, and muscle biopsy is similar to polymyositis. Chronic generalized myalgia in the absence of muscle inflammation may represent fibromyalgia, which occurs in up to 25% of patients. Proximal muscle weakness with normal creatine kinase levels may indicate corticosteroid-induced myopathy.

Other musculoskeletal complications of SLE may be related to disease or therapy. Osteonecrosis affects 5% to 12% of patients, most commonly in the hips and knees. Patients present with weight-bearing pain without obvious signs of inflammation. Corticosteroid use and the presence of antiphospholipid antibodies confer increased risk, and affected joints often require joint replacement.

Osteoporosis occurs in up to 25% patients with SLE and is a common late complication. Increased risk of osteoporosis appears to be related to corticosteroid use, lupus disease activity, decreased physical activity, and avoidance of sun. A high index of suspicion for osteoporotic fracture should be maintained for patients with SLE, especially those treated with long-term corticosteroids. If initial plain radiographs are negative, CT is indicated to rule out osteoporotic fracture. Women with SLE report five times as many fractures as age-matched controls, with half occurring before menopause.

Kidney Manifestations

Kidney disease affects 50% to 75% of patients with SLE. Nonwhite patients are more frequently affected and have a poorer kidney prognosis. Early signs are proteinuria, hematuria, and cellular casts. When uncontrolled, kidney involvement leads to decreased kidney function, hypertension, edema, and, ultimately, kidney failure.

Nephritis frequently occurs in otherwise asymptomatic patients, and routine monitoring of urinalysis, kidney function, and urine protein excretion is indicated. Biopsy is usually necessary for diagnosis and prognostic information, but corticosteroid therapy should be started promptly when nephritis is suspected, even if a biopsy has not yet been obtained. Biopsy findings are not altered by corticosteroid treatment for at least 6 weeks.

Anti–double-stranded DNA antibody titers and complement levels commonly correlate with disease activity in proliferative nephritis. Once the diagnosis is established, proliferative nephritis requires the addition of an immunosuppressive agent (usually cyclophosphamide or mycophenolate mofetil) to corticosteroid therapy to optimize the long-term renal prognosis.

Kidney biopsy results are interpreted according to revised classification criteria from the International Society of Nephrology and Renal Pathology Society (see MKSAP 16 Nephrology). Lupus nephritis class strongly impacts kidney prognosis. In addition to the presence of class IV, biopsy findings indicating a poor prognosis include the presence of cellular crescents and interstitial fibrosis. Clinical factors associated with progressive kidney failure include older age, black ethnicity, low hematocrit (<26%), and elevated serum creatinine (>2.4 mg/dL [212.2 µmol/L]). In patients requiring kidney transplantation, recurrence of lupus nephritis is infrequent.

Neurologic Manifestations

Neurologic manifestations can occur in about 15% to 95% of patients at some point in the disease course (although estimates vary widely) and represent an important cause of morbidity and mortality in SLE. The American College of Rheumatology has established validated case definitions for 19 central and peripheral nervous system manifestations with varying severity (**Table 19**), which are collectively referred to as neuropsychiatric systemic lupus erythematosus (NPSLE). The term lupus cerebritis has been replaced by these more specific case definitions of NPSLE. Neurologic and psychiatric conditions due to lupus must be distinguished from other causes of nervous system abnormalities that occur in SLE, including medication effects, metabolic abnormalities, and infection. Severe NPSLE syndromes, including demyelination and transverse myelitis, are rare. Stroke may be due to active lupus inflammation or antiphospholipid antibodies.

TABLE 19. Neuropsychiatric Manifestations of Systemic Lupus Erythematosus

Central Nervous System
Aseptic meningitis
Cerebrovascular disease
Demyelinating syndrome
Headache
Movement disorder (such as chorea)
Seizure disorder
Myelopathy
Acute confusional state
Anxiety disorder
Cognitive dysfunction
Mood disorder
Psychosis
Peripheral Nervous System
Acute inflammatory demyelinating polyradiculoneuropathy (such as Guillain-Barré syndrome)
Autonomic neuropathy
Mononeuropathy (single or monoplex)
Myasthenia gravis
Cranial neuropathy
Plexopathy
Polyneuropathy

Adapted from the American College of Rheumatology nomenclature and case definitions for neuropsychiatric lupus syndromes. Arthritis Rheum. 1999;42(4):599-608. [PMID: 10211873] Reproduced with permission of John Wiley & Sons, Inc.

Cardiovascular Manifestations

Pericarditis is the most frequent cardiac manifestation of SLE and occurs in 20% of patients, but progression to tamponade is unusual. Myocarditis is reported but is rare (<5%).

Cardiac valve involvement is common and is strongly associated with antiphospholipid antibodies. Up to 60% of patients have evidence of valvular heart disease on screening echocardiograms. Asymptomatic sterile vegetations (Libman-Sacks endocarditis) may lead to embolization or superimposed infective endocarditis.

The prevalence of atherosclerosis is increased in patients with SLE and often occurs early. Women with lupus between the ages of 33 and 44 years have more than a 50-fold increased risk of myocardial infarction compared with age-matched controls. Patients with SLE are at high risk for accelerated atherosclerosis and may have an atypical presentation of cardiac ischemia. Electrocardiography to evaluate for cardiac ischemia is essential for patients with SLE presenting with acute chest discomfort of any type, even for patients who are younger in age or have atypical symptoms, because of the increased risk of atherosclerotic disease in this group. A history of intermittent or progressive chest symptoms merits evaluation with cardiac stress testing. Traditional risk factors are responsible for part, but not all, of the increased risk of atherosclerosis; disease-specific relative risk is 7.5 and is attributed to effects of chronic inflammation leading to vascular damage.

Pulmonary Manifestations

Pleuritis is the most common pulmonary manifestation of SLE, occurring in 30% to 60% of patients. Parenchymal disease is less frequent but more serious, including acute pneumonitis, interstitial lung disease, diffuse alveolar hemorrhage (a severe manifestation with a mortality rate of 50% to 90%), shrinking lung syndrome (secondary to diaphragmatic dysfunction), pulmonary embolism, and pulmonary hypertension.

Hematologic Manifestations

Hematologic manifestations of SLE include anemia, leukopenia, and thrombocytopenia. Anemia may be due to Coombs-positive hemolytic anemia, anemia of chronic disease, or kidney disease. Asymptomatic lymphopenia occurs in conjunction with active disease as a result of antilymphocyte antibodies; neutropenia is rarely due to SLE. Immunosuppressive medications may cause leukopenia that must be differentiated from active SLE. Idiopathic thrombocytopenic purpura is often the first symptom of SLE. Mild thrombocytopenia occurs in up to 50% of patients, but less than 5% of patients develop life-threatening thrombocytopenia with platelet counts less than $20,000/\mu L$ ($20 \times 10^9/L$).

The Antiphospholipid Syndrome

The antiphospholipid syndrome is defined by the presence of antiphospholipid antibodies and typical clinical manifestations. This disorder may occur as an independent syndrome (primary antiphospholipid syndrome) or secondary to underlying SLE. Antiphospholipid antibodies include anticardiolipin antibodies, anti-β2-glycoprotein I antibodies, and the lupus anticoagulant and are found in 30% to 40% of patients with SLE.

Clinical criteria for the diagnosis of the antiphospholipid syndrome are arterial or venous thrombosis and pregnancy loss or complications; other manifestations include livedo reticularis (a lattice-like skin rash), thrombocytopenia, valvular heart disease, and microangiopathic kidney insufficiency. It is important to differentiate the vasculopathy of the antiphospholipid syndrome from SLE-related inflammatory complications such as vasculitis; the antiphospholipid syndrome is treated with anticoagulation, whereas SLE requires immunosuppressive therapy. Catastrophic antiphospholipid syndrome is an uncommon life-threatening manifestation, with acute onset of thrombosis in at least three organ systems; mortality rates approach 50% despite therapy.

Gastrointestinal Manifestations

Gastrointestinal symptoms, including nausea, abdominal pain, and diarrhea, are frequent in SLE and are most often due to medication side effects or superimposed infection. Lupus-related manifestations include dysmotility, mesenteric vasculitis, serositis, and protein-losing enteropathy. Pancreatitis and hepatic involvement are rare.

Malignancy

A slight increase in cancer risk occurs in patients with SLE, although it is unclear whether this is related to disease or therapy. Increased standardized incidence ratios are reported for non-Hodgkin and Hodgkin lymphoma, lung cancer, and hepatobiliary cancer. Although lymphadenopathy is a common finding, localized or unusually large palpable lymph nodes merit evaluation with biopsy to evaluate for lymphoma. Women with SLE have an 11-fold higher prevalence of premalignant cervical dysplasia; prevalence is highest in those taking long-term immunosuppressive medications. H

KEY POINTS

- Nephritis frequently occurs in otherwise asymptomatic patients with systemic lupus erythematosus; routine monitoring of urinalysis, kidney function, and urine protein excretion is indicated.

- Neurologic manifestations of systemic lupus erythematosus include headache, cognitive dysfunction, mononeuropathy, seizure, and stroke.

- Cardiovascular manifestations of systemic lupus erythematosus include pericarditis, myocarditis, valvular disease, atherosclerosis, and myocardial infarction.

- Clinical criteria for diagnosis of the antiphospholipid syndrome are arterial or venous thrombosis and pregnancy loss or complications; other manifestations include livedo reticularis (a lattice-like skin rash), thrombocytopenia, valvular heart disease, and microangiopathic kidney insufficiency.

Diagnosis

The diagnosis of SLE depends on recognition of characteristic multisystem disease and exclusion of infection and malignancy. Autoantibody tests are important, but even those specific for SLE do not make the diagnosis in the absence of typical clinical manifestations.

The American College of Rheumatology criteria for the diagnosis of SLE for use in clinical trials are useful as a guideline in evaluating individual patients (**Table 20**). Clinical diagnosis is based on history, physical examination, routine laboratory tests, and autoimmune serologies.

A detailed history is important in establishing prior symptoms that may not have prompted previous medical evaluation. Physical examination may reveal inflammatory changes in the skin or joints and other signs of systemic disease. Routine laboratory tests, including urinalysis, may indicate internal organ involvement such as cytopenia or kidney

TABLE 20. American College of Rheumatology Criteria for the Diagnosis of Systemic Lupus Erythematosus

Criteria[a]	Definition
Malar rash	Fixed erythema, flat or raised, over the malar eminences
Discoid rash	Erythematous, circular, raised patches with keratotic scaling and follicular plugging; atrophic scarring may occur
Photosensitivity	Rash after exposure to ultraviolet light
Oral ulcers	Oral and nasopharyngeal ulcers (observed by physician)
Arthritis	Nonerosive arthritis of ≥2 peripheral joints, with tenderness, swelling, or effusion
Serositis	Pleuritis or pericarditis (documented by electrocardiogram, rub, or evidence of effusion)
Kidney disorder	Urinalysis: 3+ protein or >0.5 g/d; cellular casts
Neurologic	Seizures or psychosis (without other cause)
Hematologic	Hemolytic anemia or leukopenia (<4000/µL [4.0 × 10⁹/L]) or lymphopenia (<1500/µL [1.5 × 10⁹/L]) or thrombocytopenia (<100,000/µL [100 × 10⁹/L]) in the absence of offending drugs
Immunologic	Anti–double-stranded DNA, anti-Smith, and/or antiphospholipid antibodies
ANA	An abnormal titer of ANA by immunofluorescence or an equivalent assay at any point in the absence of drugs known to induce ANA

ANA = antinuclear antibodies.

[a]Any combination of 4 or more of the 11 criteria, well documented at any time during a patient's history, makes it likely that the patient has systemic lupus erythematosus (specificity and sensitivity are 95% and 75%, respectively).

Reproduced from Hochberg MC. Updating the American College of Rheumatology revised criteria for the classification of systemic lupus erythematosus. Arthritis Rheum. 1997;40(9):1725. [PMID: 9324032] Reproduced with permission of John Wiley & Sons, Inc.

disease. The erythrocyte sedimentation rate is often elevated as a nonspecific indicator of inflammation.

Autoantibodies are the hallmark of diagnosis but must be interpreted with caution and in context. The presence of antinuclear antibodies (ANA) suggests the possibility of SLE, but the ANA test is not specific for lupus. Positive ANA tests may occur in patients with other autoimmune diseases, infection, and malignancy. Asymptomatic low-titer (1:40) ANA has been reported in up to 30% of the general population. A persistent high titer (>1:640) of ANA is more likely to be clinically significant. ANA titer does not fluctuate with the level of disease activity. The ANA immunofluorescence pattern can provide additional information; the rim pattern suggests antibodies to double-stranded DNA.

Suggestive clinical symptoms and a positive ANA should be followed by more specific autoantibody testing.

CONT. Anti–double-stranded DNA and anti-Smith antibodies are specific for SLE (**Table 21**). Several tests for anti–double-stranded DNA antibodies are available, including enzyme-linked immunosorbent assay (most sensitive) and immunofluorescence (Crithidia) and radioimmunoassay (Farr) assays (more specific).

Decreased complement levels (CH50, C3, or C4) are common and reflect immune complex–mediated activation; fluctuation in levels may parallel lupus activity, but decreased levels are not specific for lupus.

Differential Diagnosis

The differential diagnosis of SLE is broad and includes other connective tissue diseases, viral or other infections, and malignancy. Parvovirus B19 virus in particular can cause joint pain with transiently positive autoimmune serologies.

Undifferentiated Connective Tissue Disease

Undifferentiated connective tissue disease (UCTD) refers to mild CTD with a positive ANA and autoimmune symptoms that do not meet criteria for a specific CTD. UCTD may remain stable or may evolve over time to a more well-differentiated disorder. Treatment is dictated by the nature and severity of symptoms.

Drug-Induced Lupus Erythematosus

Diagnosis of drug-induced lupus erythematosus (DILE) is based on clinical presentation, history of medication use, and usual resolution of symptoms within 6 weeks of drug discontinuation. DILE typically causes rash, arthritis, pleuropericarditis, cytopenia, and fever. In classic DILE, autoantibodies typically include ANA, anti–single-stranded DNA, and anti-histone antibodies. Anti–double-stranded DNA and anti-Smith antibodies are uncommon, and complement levels are usually normal. Procainamide, hydralazine, and methyldopa are historically associated with a classic DILE presentation.

Recently implicated drugs include minocycline and tumor necrosis factor (TNF)-α inhibitors. In contrast to the historically associated drugs, TNF-α inhibitors appear to induce lupus-like disease with positive anti–double-stranded DNA antibodies and rare kidney and central nervous system involvement. **H**

KEY POINTS

- Antinuclear antibody assay, complete blood count, metabolic panel, urinalysis, and erythrocyte sedimentation rate are appropriate laboratory studies for patients who have symptoms of systemic lupus erythematosus.

- Patients with symptoms suggestive of systemic lupus erythematosus and the presence of antinuclear antibodies should undergo testing for antibodies to anti–double-stranded DNA, anti-Smith, anti-U1-ribonucleoprotein, anti-Ro/SSA, and anti-La/SSB as well as complement levels.

- Patients with classic drug-induced lupus erythematosus typically have antinuclear, antihistone, and anti–single-stranded DNA antibodies; anti–double-stranded DNA and anti-Smith antibodies are uncommon, and complement levels are usually normal.

- Drug-induced lupus erythematosus caused by tumor necrosis factor α inhibitors may be associated with positive anti–double-stranded DNA antibodies and rare kidney or neurologic involvement.

TABLE 21. Autoantibodies in Systemic Lupus Erythematosus			
Autoantibody	**Antigen**	**Prevalence (%)**	**Comments**
ANA	Multiple nuclear antigens	99	Sensitive, not specific; useful screening test
Anti–double-stranded DNA	Double-stranded DNA	70	Specific for SLE (when high titer); fluctuates with disease activity and with nephritis
Anti–single-stranded DNA	Single-stranded (denatured) DNA	80-90	Not specific for SLE
Anti-Ro/SSA	Specific RNP	40	Associated with Sjögren syndrome, NLE, and SCLE
Anti-La/SSB	Specific RNP	15	Associated with Sjögren syndrome and NLE
Anti-Smith	Specific small nuclear RNP (associated with spliceosome)	30	Specific for SLE; does not fluctuate with disease activity
Anti-U1-RNP	Specific small nuclear RNP (associated with spliceosome)	30-40	Associated with MCTD when sole autoantibody present
Antihistone	Protein component of nucleosomes	70-80	High frequency in drug-induced lupus (95%)
Antiphospholipid[a]	Phospholipid-binding proteins	30-40	Associated with thrombosis and pregnancy loss

ANA = antinuclear antibodies; MCTD = mixed connective tissue disease; NLE = neonatal lupus erythematosus; RNP = ribonucleoprotein; SCLE = subacute cutaneous lupus erythematosus; SLE = systemic lupus erythematosus.

[a]Includes anticardiolipin, anti-β2-glycoprotein I, and lupus anticoagulant antibodies.

Treatment

Treatment of SLE is determined by the location and severity of inflammation; it is not necessarily dictated by diagnosis. Arthralgia is often treated with NSAIDs. Antimalarial drugs, most commonly hydroxychloroquine, have classically been prescribed for rash and arthritis. Hydroxychloroquine can prevent lupus flares and increase long-term survival and may reduce organ damage, thrombosis, and bone loss. Most patients with lupus—even those on immunosuppressive medications—are likely to benefit from long-term antimalarial therapy.

Low-dose corticosteroids are used for mild rash or joint symptoms, with moderate doses for more active disease. Serious manifestations such as kidney or nervous system involvement, vasculitis, and severe hematologic abnormalities require more aggressive immunosuppression. High-dose corticosteroids are the mainstay of therapy, but when sustained high dosage is necessary, addition of steroid-sparing agents may reduce severe complications of long-term corticosteroid use. Immunosuppressive medications include azathioprine, mycophenolate mofetil, methotrexate, and cyclophosphamide. Cyclophosphamide is generally reserved for lupus nephritis or severe resistant disease but is associated with serious toxicity.

Recent studies suggest that mycophenolate mofetil is as effective as intravenous cyclophosphamide for induction therapy in lupus nephritis with a more favorable side-effect profile, although longer term outcome with mycophenolate mofetil is still unknown. Biologic therapies are under active investigation, but more definitive data are needed to support and direct routine clinical use. Belimumab, which blocks the biologic activity of soluble B-cell–activating factor (BAFF), is FDA approved for treatment of SLE based on demonstrated decreases in autoantibody titers and disease activity measures. To date, controlled double-blind studies of the anti-CD20 inhibitor rituximab have not shown benefit in lupus.

KEY POINTS

- Arthralgia associated with systemic lupus erythematosus can be treated with NSAIDs.
- Hydroxychloroquine can prevent lupus flares and increase long-term survival and may reduce organ damage, thrombosis, and bone loss.
- Cyclophosphamide is generally reserved for lupus nephritis or severe resistant disease but is associated with serious toxicity.
- Mycophenolate mofetil may be as effective as intravenous cyclophosphamide for induction therapy in lupus nephritis with a more favorable side-effect profile, although longer term outcome with mycophenolate mofetil is still unknown.

Reproductive Issues

Given the high risk of cervical dysplasia in patients with lupus, the human papillomavirus vaccine is strongly recommended for patients up to the age of 26 years.

Fertility is generally normal in patients with SLE unless reduced by cyclophosphamide treatment. A rheumatologist and an obstetrician with experience in high-risk pregnancy should monitor pregnant patients for risk factors for poor outcome, including active disease within 6 months of conception, kidney disease, and the presence of antiphospholipid antibodies. Many medications used in SLE are contraindicated in pregnancy; permitted medications include prednisone, hydroxychloroquine, and azathioprine. Pregnancy may increase risk for lupus exacerbation, although the rate of flare is controversial; flare is less likely with inactive disease at conception and continuation of hydroxychloroquine. Patients with lupus have higher rates of maternal and fetal complications; preeclampsia in particular is increased and may be difficult to differentiate from lupus nephritis.

Antiphospholipid antibodies increase the risk of fetal loss; antiphospholipid antibody–positive patients with a history of recurrent early pregnancy loss or a single late pregnancy loss are generally treated during pregnancy with low-dose aspirin and heparin.

Maternal anti-Ro/SSA and anti-La/SSB antibodies are associated with risk for neonatal lupus erythematosus (NLE), an inflammatory condition in the fetus caused by transplacental passage of maternal autoantibodies. NLE affects 20% of offspring of seropositive women and is characterized by a reversible inflammatory rash, elevated liver chemistry test results, and thrombocytopenia that resolve in 6 months with clearance of maternal antibodies. Irreversible congenital heart block occurs in 2% of offspring, who usually require a pacemaker. Seropositive women are monitored during pregnancy with fetal echocardiography starting at 16 weeks' gestation; dexamethasone may be prescribed if heart block is detected, although benefit is uncertain.

Combination oral contraceptives had been avoided in women with SLE owing to concern about flare but are now regarded as an effective contraceptive choice. The SELENA trial showed no increased risk of flare in stable antiphospholipid antibody–negative SLE patients taking oral contraceptives. The increased risk of thrombosis with oral contraceptives precludes their use in antiphospholipid antibody–positive patients; barrier or progesterone-only methods are appropriate for these patients. Hormone replacement therapy has been shown to cause a small increase in mild to moderate flares in stable patients with SLE and may be used cautiously in patients with menopause-related severe vasomotor symptoms if patients are antiphospholipid antibody negative.

- A rheumatologist and an obstetrician with experience in high-risk pregnancy should monitor pregnant patients with systemic lupus erythematosus for risk factors for poor outcome, including active disease within 6 months of conception, kidney disease, and the presence of antiphospholipid antibodies.

- Permitted medications in pregnant patients with systemic lupus erythematosus include prednisone, hydroxychloroquine, and azathioprine.

- The risk for preeclampsia is increased in pregnant patients with systemic lupus erythematosus and may be difficult to differentiate from lupus nephritis.

- Patients with antiphospholipid antibodies who have a history of recurrent early pregnancy loss or a single late pregnancy loss are generally treated during pregnancy with low-dose aspirin and heparin.

- Maternal anti-Ro/SSA and anti-La/SSB antibodies are associated with risk for neonatal lupus erythematosus.

Prognosis

The prognosis of SLE has dramatically improved, with the 5-year survival rate rising from 50% to 96% and the current 10-year survival rate over 90%. Recognition of milder disease and improvements in general medical care and immunosuppressive therapies have contributed to improved outcomes. Prognosis is poorer in black patients, in patients with kidney or central nervous system involvement, and in men. Lupus shows a bimodal pattern of mortality, with early deaths (those within the first year of diagnosis) due to active disease or infection; late deaths are caused by accelerated atherosclerosis and infectious complications of immunosuppressive treatment. Appropriate management of SLE includes follow-up and treatment for active autoimmune disease as well as monitoring or preventive therapy for general medical complications, including infection, osteoporosis, neoplasia, and cardiovascular disease.

- Lupus shows a bimodal pattern of mortality, with early deaths (those within the first year of diagnosis) due to active disease or infection; late deaths are caused by accelerated atherosclerosis and infectious complications of immunosuppressive treatment.

- Appropriate management of systemic lupus erythematosus includes follow-up and treatment for active autoimmune disease as well as monitoring or preventive therapy for general medical complications, including infection, osteoporosis, neoplasia, and cardiovascular disease.

Systemic Sclerosis

Pathophysiology and Epidemiology

Systemic sclerosis is a disorder of unknown cause characterized by vasculopathy with intimal proliferation in small arterioles and fibrosis of the dermis and visceral organs. Early findings in affected skin include perivascular infiltrates of lymphocytes and proliferation of fibroblasts with up-regulated synthesis and secretion of collagen and other matrix proteins. The disorder most commonly affects women, and peak incidence occurs in the third and fourth decades. Severity is likely to be greater among black women.

Classification

Limited cutaneous systemic sclerosis (lcSSc) is characterized by skin involvement that is restricted to the face and distal extremities and does not progress proximal to the distal forearms or knees. CREST (calcinosis, Raynaud phenomenon, esophageal dysmotility, sclerodactyly, and telangiectasia) syndrome is a subset of lcSSc. Patients with lcSSc, including those with CREST, are more likely to develop pulmonary arterial hypertension (PAH) in the absence of other pulmonary manifestations.

Diffuse cutaneous systemic sclerosis (dcSSc) is characterized by skin involvement proximal to the distal forearms and knees. Patients with dcSSc are more likely to develop interstitial lung disease (ILD), serositis, and kidney disease (including scleroderma renal crisis). Systemic sclerosis sine scleroderma is characterized by visceral disease in the absence of skin involvement and has internal organ manifestations similar to those observed in dcSSc.

Diagnosis

Diagnosis of systemic sclerosis is based on the presence of tightness, thickening, and swelling/induration of the digits extending proximal to the metacarpophalangeal joints (**Figure 21**). In the absence of skin changes proximal to the metacarpophalangeal joints, diagnosis may also be

FIGURE 21. The hands of this patient with limited cutaneous systemic sclerosis (CREST) syndrome show shiny, taut skin distal to the metacarpophalangeal joints.

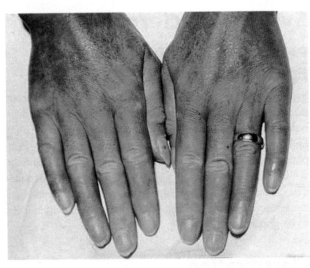

FIGURE 22. Sclerodactyly (skin thickening over the fingers) extending proximal to the metacarpophalangeal joints in a patient with systemic sclerosis.

established in patients manifesting two of the following: sclerodactyly (**Figure 22**), terminal digital pitting (**Figure 23**) or ulceration, or basilar interstitial fibrosis on chest radiograph. Most patients with lcSSc have an antecedent history of Raynaud phenomenon; patients with dcSSc without antecedent Raynaud phenomenon usually develop Raynaud phenomenon when the skin disease becomes apparent or shortly thereafter. Antinuclear antibodies are present in more than 95% of patients with systemic sclerosis, with defined specificities correlating with disease manifestations (Table 22).

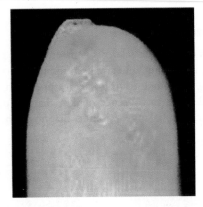

FIGURE 23. Digital pitting (soft-tissue defects and scarring in the pulp space of the distal phalanges) in a patient with systemic sclerosis.

Reprinted with permission from Physician's Information and Education Resource (PIER). Philadelphia: American College of Physicians. Copyright 2012 American College of Physicians.

TABLE 22. Autoantibody Associations in Systemic Sclerosis		
Antibody	**ANA Pattern**	**Clinical Associations**
Anticentromere (kinetochore proteins)	Centromere	lcSSc; PAH
Anti–Scl-70 (DNA topoisomerase-1)	Speckled	dcSSc; ILD
Anti-U3-RNP (fibrillarin)	Speckled	dcSSc; PAH; myositis
Anti-PM-Scl	Nucleolar	Myositis
Anti-Th/To	Nucleolar	lcSSc; PAH

ANA = antinuclear antibodies; dcSSc = diffuse cutaneous systemic sclerosis; ILD = interstitial lung disease; lcSSc = limited cutaneous systemic sclerosis; PAH = pulmonary arterial hypertension; RNP = ribonucleoprotein.

KEY POINTS

- Patients with limited cutaneous systemic sclerosis have skin disease confined to the face and distal extremities and are at risk for pulmonary arterial hypertension.
- Patients with diffuse cutaneous systemic sclerosis are at greater risk for interstitial lung disease, serositis, and scleroderma renal crisis.
- Raynaud phenomenon occurs in most patients with systemic sclerosis.

Clinical Manifestations and Management

There are currently no proven therapies for overall disease modification in systemic sclerosis. However, effective interventions are available for organ-specific manifestations.

Cutaneous Manifestations

Skin disease in lcSSc or dcSSc initially manifests with swelling and puffiness in the digits and hands. Swelling in the dermis usually extends more proximally within 2 years in patients who develop dcSSc. Pruritus may be a presenting manifestation during the early stages of lcSSc and dcSSc. Later in the disease course, the dermis becomes more indurated, initially involving the digits with limitation in interphalangeal joint movement, then extending more proximally in patients with dcSSc. Additional skin manifestations include telangiectasias and dermal calcifications at pressure points, both of which occur more commonly in patients with lcSSc.

Antihistamines and skin emollients are often helpful in managing pruritus. Systemic corticosteroids may decrease digital swelling but should be avoided whenever possible because they are associated with an increased risk of scleroderma renal crisis. The early phases of digital swelling and dermal edema may respond to weekly methotrexate or other immunosuppressive therapies; one open-label trial suggests that the tyrosine kinase inhibitor imatinib may have efficacy in ameliorating skin disease. To date, no therapies have been shown to be consistently effective in treating the indurated phase of skin thickening that occurs in systemic sclerosis. The efficacy of interventions to assess improvement of skin tightening in patients with dcSSc has been complicated by the observation that the skin may soften spontaneously as disease in the dermis evolves into a more atrophic phase.

Musculoskeletal Manifestations

Arthralgia and myalgia are common in patients with systemic sclerosis. An inflammatory nonerosive arthritis may occur that affects large and small peripheral joints. Loss of joint mobility principally involving the interphalangeal joints, wrists, and ankles is attributable to fibrosis of the skin overlying the affected joints. Tendon friction rubs are often palpable over extensor surfaces and are associated with diffuse skin involvement and visceral organ complications. Inflammatory arthritis responds favorably to methotrexate.

A mild noninflammatory myopathy due to increased collagen deposition in skeletal muscle is common in patients with dcSSc; this may be associated with minimal elevation in serum creatine kinase levels but requires no treatment. A few patients may develop an inflammatory myopathy with proximal weakness similar to that seen in patients with idiopathic inflammatory myopathy (polymyositis). These patients may have higher elevations in serum creatine kinase or aldolase levels; corticosteroids can be used with caution (given the association with scleroderma renal crisis), as can weekly methotrexate and other medications (such as azathioprine) used for managing polymyositis.

Vascular Manifestations

In addition to vasospasm giving rise to Raynaud phenomenon, intimal proliferation in terminal arterioles in the microvasculature may cause luminal obliteration, which results in terminal digital pits, ulcers, or gangrene. Abnormal nailfold capillaries (demonstrating dilatation and dropout) are early manifestations, which can be visualized with a handheld ophthalmoscope; their presence is predictive of the development of systemic sclerosis in patients with isolated Raynaud phenomenon. Decreased arteriolar blood flow accounts for many of the visceral manifestations that impact the lungs, myocardium, gastrointestinal tract, and kidneys.

In addition to avoidance of cold exposure, the management of Raynaud phenomenon includes the use of calcium channel blockers, antiplatelet agents, and topical nitrates. The phosphodiesterase-5 inhibitor sildenafil is an effective option for patients who do not respond to or who are intolerant of initial measures. Endothelin receptor antagonists can be effective and are recommended to prevent recurrences of severe digital ulcers. For patients with severe digital ischemia and impending gangrene, aggressive inpatient management with prostacyclin analogues and attention to adequate pain control to minimize sympathetic-mediated vasospasm is employed to avoid loss of a digit. Regional sympathetic blockade is a useful adjunct, and digital sympathectomy is appropriate for patients who do not respond to other interventions and have a digit at risk.

Gastrointestinal Manifestations

Involvement of the alimentary tract occurs in most patients with systemic sclerosis, and gastrointestinal symptoms often antedate the diagnosis of both lcSSc and dcSSc.

Esophageal dysfunction is the most common gastrointestinal manifestation, affecting at least 80% of patients. Decreased lower esophageal sphincter tone results in frequent symptoms of esophageal reflux, and dysmotility affecting smooth muscle in the lower esophagus causes symptoms of dysphagia. Complications of esophageal disease include esophagitis, Barrett esophagus, and aspiration pneumonitis. Management of esophageal disease in systemic sclerosis includes suppression of gastric acid production with a proton pump inhibitor, inclined posture during sleep, and promotility agents such as metoclopramide and octreotide.

Dysmotility involving the stomach, small bowel, and colon may result in a functional ileus and intestinal pseudo-obstruction that is best managed conservatively with bowel rest and proximal decompression as needed. Bacterial overgrowth syndromes, presenting as diarrhea, abdominal bloating, colicky pain, and/or malabsorption with steatorrhea, may also occur in the setting of bowel dysmotility. Diagnosis can be confirmed with glucose hydrogen breath testing. Rotating extended courses of antibiotics targeting bowel flora are helpful in patients with confirmed bacterial overgrowth syndrome.

Gastrointestinal blood loss, occasionally massive, may occur because of bleeding from mucosal telangiectasias. Gastric antral venous ectasia is a common cause of gastrointestinal blood loss and should be considered in patients with systemic sclerosis who present with findings of iron deficiency anemia. Diagnosis is best established with upper endoscopy and can be effectively managed with one or more treatments with laser/photocoagulation.

Primary biliary cirrhosis may occur, most commonly in patients with lcSSc. Wide-mouthed diverticula may be incidentally seen on imaging studies of the colon in patients with systemic sclerosis but are usually not of clinical significance.

Kidney Manifestations

Scleroderma renal crisis (SRC) may occur in patients with systemic sclerosis (particularly dcSSc) as a consequence of intimal proliferation and luminal thrombosis in the afferent renal arterioles, resulting in glomerular ischemia and high levels of renin. SRC is characterized by acute onset of hypertension, azotemia, and microangiopathic hemolytic anemia; however, some patients with evolving SRC may be normotensive.

Corticosteroid therapy is a significant risk factor for SRC and is best avoided whenever possible in patients with dcSSc.

Prompt and aggressive titration of an ACE inhibitor is the cornerstone of SRC treatment. The threshold for starting an ACE inhibitor should be low for patients with dcSSc who develop even mild elevations in blood pressure or otherwise unexplained elevations in serum creatinine levels. Delays in treatment can result in kidney failure. Patients who have experienced SRC should be maintained on an ACE inhibitor even in the setting of kidney failure, because kidney function may improve even months after institution of dialysis. Angiotensin receptor blockers (ARBs) may be an alternative for patients who cannot take an ACE inhibitor, although ARBs are not as effective in managing SRC.

KEY POINTS

- Management of systemic sclerosis targets organ-specific disease manifestations.

- Gastrointestinal symptoms may antedate skin disease in patients with systemic sclerosis, with esophageal dysfunction the most common visceral organ manifestation.

- Enteric telangiectasias and gastric antral venous ectasia may cause gastrointestinal blood loss and iron deficiency in patients with systemic sclerosis.

- ACE inhibitors are effective for managing scleroderma renal crisis and are the treatment of choice for patients with systemic sclerosis who develop hypertension or otherwise unexplained azotemia.

- Patients who experience scleroderma renal crisis should be maintained on an ACE inhibitor even in the setting of kidney failure, because kidney function may improve even months after institution of dialysis.

Pulmonary Manifestations

Lung involvement due to ILD and/or PAH is the primary cause of morbidity and mortality in patients with systemic sclerosis. Other less common pulmonary complications include pleuritis, recurrent aspiration, organizing pneumonia, and hemorrhage from endobronchial telangiectasias. Patients with systemic sclerosis also have a higher than expected risk for developing lung cancer.

Interstitial Lung Disease

ILD most commonly occurs in patients with dcSSc, and patients with elevated antibody titers to anti–Scl-70 have the highest risk for developing ILD. Alveolitis may precede the development of ILD; presenting manifestations include dyspnea, nonproductive cough, and exercise intolerance. Fine bibasilar velcro-like inspiratory crackles are frequently present on physical examination. A restrictive impairment with decreased lung volumes and decreased DLCO are typically present on pulmonary function tests. Chest imaging is best performed with high-resolution noncontrast CT, which is more sensitive than routine radiography in detecting alveolitis and reticular linear opacities present in patients with early stages of lung disease.

Treatment of lung disease with immunosuppressive therapy in patients with systemic sclerosis is generally reserved for those with evidence of alveolitis on high-resolution chest CT scan (ground-glass type appearance) and worsening pulmonary function testing. Cyclophosphamide given orally or intravenously for 1 year with or without low doses of corticosteroids can provide modest benefit to patients with ILD, but the benefits are lost by 24 months of follow-up. Azathioprine may have a role as maintenance therapy following a 6-month course of cyclophosphamide.

Pulmonary Arterial Hypertension

PAH may develop in systemic sclerosis with or without accompanying ILD. Dyspnea and decreased exercise tolerance are the presenting features of PAH. Physical examination findings include an increased pulmonic component of S_2 and persistently split S_2.

In the absence of ILD, a decrease in DLCO corrected for alveolar volume on pulmonary function tests is suggestive of PAH. PAH may be asymptomatic in its early stages; therefore, baseline, then yearly, screening with pulmonary function tests is recommended in all patients with systemic sclerosis without advanced ILD. If right-sided regurgitant valvular lesions are present, echocardiography can provide an estimate of the pulmonary artery systolic pressure; relative dilation of the right ventricle on echocardiography is also suggestive of PAH. Because echocardiographic assessments may overestimate pulmonary artery pressures, direct measurement of the pulmonary artery pressure with right heart catheterization should be undertaken in patients with suspected PAH before proceeding with treatment.

Treatment of PAH in patients with systemic sclerosis includes oxygen supplementation if needed and anticoagulation after the risk of bleeding from telangiectasias has been assessed. Vasodilating agents, including phosphodiesterase-5 inhibitors (such as sildenafil) and prostacyclin analogues (such as iloprost, epoprostenol, and treprostinil), have demonstrated efficacy in relieving symptoms of PAH associated with systemic sclerosis. Nonselective and selective endothelin receptor antagonists (bosentan and ambrisentan, respectively) have also been shown to be effective in improving symptoms and delaying progression of PAH in systemic sclerosis. With appropriate monitoring and assessment of efficacy using 6-minute walk tests and serial right heart catheterization studies, select patients may benefit from a vasodilator in combination with an endothelin receptor antagonist.

Cardiac Manifestations

Primary cardiac involvement in patients with systemic sclerosis is common but often clinically silent. Pericardial effusion

CONT.

is a frequent incidental finding on echocardiogram and in autopsy series but seldom is of a degree to cause tamponade or merit pericardiotomy. Myocardial fibrosis and contraction band necrosis due to coronary vasculopathy may result in cardiomyopathy with systolic or diastolic dysfunction and arrhythmias. Symptomatic cardiomyopathy in patients with systemic sclerosis has a poor prognosis, with 2-year mortality rates exceeding 50%. H

KEY POINTS

- Treatment of pulmonary alveolitis with cyclophosphamide may improve symptoms and delay progression of interstitial lung disease.

  Pulmonary function tests, including assessment of D$_{LCO}$ corrected for alveolar volume, are effective screening measures for detection of pulmonary arterial hypertension in patients with systemic sclerosis without significant interstitial lung disease.

- Right heart catheterization should be performed in patients with systemic sclerosis with suspected pulmonary arterial hypertension.

- Phosphodiesterase-5 inhibitors, prostacyclin analogues, and endothelin receptor antagonists are effective treatments for pulmonary arterial hypertension in patients with systemic sclerosis.

Scleroderma Spectrum Disorders

Morphea is a localized form of scleroderma presenting as one or more indurated plaques confined to the torso and proximal extremities; although histologic findings are identical to those seen in patients with systemic sclerosis, visceral manifestations and a history of Raynaud phenomenon are absent.

Eosinophilic fasciitis presents as woody induration of the extremities sparing the hands and face; peripheral eosinophilia is commonly present. A full-thickness skin biopsy extending down to the fascia overlying muscle demonstrating lymphocytes, plasma cells, and eosinophils infiltrating the deep fascia is highly suggestive in the correct clinical setting.

Scleredema with large, noninflammatory indurated plaques over the shoulder girdle, neck, and upper extremities occurs as a complication of long-standing insulin-dependent diabetes mellitus.

Scleromyxedema is characterized by deposition of mucin with large numbers of stellate fibroblasts in the dermis, presenting as waxy yellow-red papules overlying thickened skin. It affects the face, upper torso, and upper extremities. The condition is frequently associated with paraproteinemia (most commonly IgGλ) and may therefore occur in the setting of multiple myeloma or AL amyloidosis. In a few patients, a mild inflammatory myopathy may accompany the disorder.

Nephrogenic systemic fibrosis presents as brawny, hyperpigmented areas of skin induration that involves the torso and extremities but typically spares the digits. In addition to dermal fibrosis, fibrotic lesions may involve skeletal muscle, resulting in severe contractures; cardiac muscle involvement has also been reported, with attendant high mortality. Most reported cases of nephrogenic systemic fibrosis have occurred in patients with significant impairment of the glomerular filtration rate who have received gadolinium contrast agents for MRI studies.

KEY POINTS

- The absence of Raynaud phenomenon should prompt consideration of causes of skin induration other than systemic sclerosis.

- Morphea is a localized form of scleroderma confined to the torso and proximal extremities that occurs in the absence of visceral disease and Raynaud phenomenon.

- Eosinophilic fasciitis spares the digits and face and may be accompanied by peripheral eosinophilia.

- Nephrogenic systemic fibrosis may involve skeletal and cardiac muscle and most often occurs in patients with impaired kidney function who have received gadolinium contrast agents for MRI studies.

Pregnancy and Systemic Sclerosis

Fertility does not appear to be significantly impacted by systemic sclerosis; however, pregnancy in women with systemic sclerosis is associated with an increased risk of premature birth as well as low-birth–weight full-term infants. Patients with PAH are at risk for decompensation during the later stages of pregnancy and merit close monitoring. The development of SRC during pregnancy is associated with significant mortality and poses the greatest risk to pregnancy. Although ACE inhibitors are otherwise contraindicated in pregnancy because of the risk of fetal malformation, given the high mortality rate associated with SRC, the benefits of ACE inhibitor therapy in this setting are felt to outweigh their risk to the fetus.

KEY POINTS

- Pregnancy in systemic sclerosis is considered high risk and is associated with premature birth and low-birth–weight full-term infants.

- Although ACE inhibitors are otherwise contraindicated in pregnancy because of the risk of fetal malformation, given the high mortality rate associated with scleroderma renal crisis, the benefits of ACE inhibitor therapy in this setting are felt to outweigh their risk to the fetus.

Sjögren Syndrome

Epidemiology and Pathophysiology

Sjögren syndrome is a slowly progressive autoimmune disorder that targets exocrine glands. This condition is characterized by keratoconjunctivitis sicca (dry eyes) and xerostomia (dry mouth) and also causes diverse multisystem manifestations.

Primary Sjögren syndrome affects 0.3% to 0.6% of the U.S. population, with an incidence of 3.9 per 100,000 persons; up to 15% of patients with systemic lupus erythematosus and 25% of patients with rheumatoid arthritis have manifestations of secondary Sjögren syndrome. There is a female predominance (9:1 ratio), and age of onset is most common during the fourth and fifth decades.

Sjögren syndrome is associated with certain HLA-DR and HLA-DQ alleles. Viral agents, including hepatitis C, may serve as triggers of clinical disease. B-cell activation with polyclonal gammopathy is characteristic, and symptoms result from both lymphocytic invasion of epithelial tissues and immune complex–mediated inflammation.

KEY POINTS

- Sjögren syndrome targets the exocrine glands and is characterized by the classic symptoms of dry eyes and dry mouth.
- Sjögren syndrome may present secondary to other connective tissue diseases, most commonly rheumatoid arthritis and systemic lupus erythematosus.

Clinical Manifestations

Although classic symptoms of Sjögren syndrome result from lacrimal and salivary gland involvement, other exocrine glands are also affected. Dry eyes cause gritty sensations or blurriness and may lead to corneal ulcers; dry mouth symptoms include difficulty swallowing, dental caries, and oral candidiasis. Painless parotid gland enlargement occurs in one third of patients. Other symptoms include cough, vaginal dryness, and xerosis (dry skin). Infection is a frequent secondary complication.

Extraglandular involvement occurs in 50% of patients (**Table 23**). Lymphadenopathy is frequent, and 5% of patients ultimately develop B-cell lymphoma. Patients with Sjögren syndrome have up to a 44-fold increased incidence of lymphoma, with extranodal marginal zone B-cell lymphomas of the mucosa-associated lymphoid tissue (MALT) being the most common. Sjögren syndrome usually precedes the diagnosis of lymphoma.

Diagnosis

Diagnosis of Sjögren syndrome is based on the presence of typical symptoms, autoimmune serologies, and exocrine gland dysfunction, but it is often delayed because of the insidious onset of symptoms. Classification criteria have both a sensitivity and specificity of 94% (**Table 24**).

In patients with primary Sjögren syndrome, antinuclear antibodies (speckled pattern) are positive in 80% to 90%; rheumatoid factor in 70% to 90%; anti-Ro/SSA in 60% to 75%; and anti-La/SSB in 40%. Hypergammaglobulinemia is common, with cryoglobulins present in 30% of patients. Abnormal lacrimal and parotid gland function may be documented with the Schirmer test (decreased wetting of tear test strips) and assessment for parotid salivary involvement (see Table 24). Rose Bengal staining may reveal corneal lesions consistent with dryness. Lip biopsy of a minor salivary gland classically demonstrates focal lymphocytic infiltration. Parotid gland biopsy may be indicated to evaluate for lymphoma in the setting of progressive unilateral gland enlargement.

Treatment

Treatment of exocrine manifestations is symptomatic; immunosuppressive regimens generally do not improve gland function. Symptomatic therapy for eyes includes avoidance of medications that reduce tear formation, artificial tears, local immunomodulatory drugs (cyclosporine A), and punctal occlusion (placement of silicone plugs in the tear drainage duct openings of the lower eyelids to increase eye moisture). Sugar-free lozenges, lubricating agents, and muscarinic agonists (pilocarpine and cevimeline) are helpful for oral symptoms.

TABLE 23. Extraglandular Manifestations of Sjögren Syndrome

Organ System	Manifestation
Constitutional	Fatigue; low-grade fever
Skin	Photosensitive rash; palpable purpura
Musculoskeletal	Arthralgia; arthritis; myositis
Gastrointestinal	Hepatomegaly; primary biliary cirrhosis
Pulmonary	Interstitial pneumonitis; chronic bronchitis; bronchiectasis; bronchiolitis obliterans with organizing pneumonia; pseudolymphoma; COPD
Renal	Type I renal tubular acidosis; tubular interstitial nephritis; glomerulonephritis
Hematologic	Anemia; leukopenia; thrombocytopenia
Neurologic	Peripheral neuropathy (motor/sensory); multiple sclerosis–like syndrome; transverse myelitis; transient ischemic attack/cerebrovascular accident; cognitive dysfunction
Vascular	Raynaud phenomenon; small-vessel vasculitis

TABLE 24. American-European Consensus Group Classification Criteria for Sjögren Syndrome

Number	Classification Criteria[a]
1	Dry eye symptoms
2	Dry mouth symptoms
3	Dry eye signs (positive Schirmer test or Rose Bengal test)
4	Characteristic histopathology of lip biopsy
5	Salivary gland involvement documented by decreased unstimulated salivary flow, abnormal parotid sialography, abnormal salivary scintigraphy
6	Anti-Ro/SSA and anti-La/SSB autoantibodies
	Exclusion Criteria
	Previous head and neck radiation; hepatitis C; AIDS; preexisting lymphoma; sarcoidosis; graft-versus-host disease; use of anticholinergic drugs

[a]Primary Sjögren syndrome: any four criteria that includes number 4 or 6 or any three of criteria numbers 3, 4, 5, and 6; secondary Sjögren syndrome: presence of connective tissue disease and criteria number 1 or 2 plus two criteria of numbers 3, 4, and 5.

Reproduced from Classification criteria for Sjögren's syndrome: a revised version of the European criteria proposed by the American-European Consensus Group. Vitali C, Bombardieri S, Jonsson R, et al; European Study Group on Classification Criteria for Sjögren's Syndrome. Ann Rheum Dis. 2002; 61(6):554-558 [PMID: 12006334] with permission from BMJ Publishing Group Ltd.

Mild symptoms such as arthralgia can be treated with NSAIDs, antimalarial agents, or low-dose corticosteroids. Higher doses of corticosteroids and immunosuppressive drugs are used for severe extraglandular manifestations. Treatment with the anti-CD20 agent rituximab has shown promise in a small controlled study.

Prognosis

Most studies describe stable exocrine gland function over time in patients with Sjögren syndrome. The standardized mortality risk is only slightly higher than that of the general population; lymphoma is the primary cause of increased mortality. Clinical and serologic markers associated with lymphoma development occur in 20% of patients and include palpable purpura, low C4 levels, mixed monoclonal cryoglobulinemia, and persistent parotid gland enlargement. MALT lymphoma generally has a good prognosis; however, occasional progression to a poor-prognosis diffuse large B-cell lymphoma may occur.

KEY POINTS

- Extraglandular involvement occurs in 50% of patients with Sjögren syndrome.
- Patients with Sjögren syndrome have a 44-fold increased risk of developing lymphoma.

- The American-European Consensus Group classification criteria for Sjögren syndrome have a sensitivity and specificity of 94%.
- The standardized mortality risk for patients with Sjögren syndrome is only slightly higher than that of the general population; lymphoma is the primary cause of increased mortality.

Mixed Connective Tissue Disease

Mixed connective tissue disease (MCTD) is characterized by overlapping clinical features of systemic lupus erythematosus (SLE), polymyositis, and systemic sclerosis in the presence of high titers of anti-U1-ribonucleoprotein (RNP) antibodies. MCTD has a 10:1 female predominance, and age of onset is generally in the second or third decade.

Clinical Manifestations

Because MCTD is an overlap syndrome, individual clinical features are usually nonspecific (**Table 25**). Typical findings include Raynaud phenomenon, swollen hands, arthritis, and fatigue. Sclerodactyly, esophageal dysmotility, myositis, and pulmonary arterial hypertension (PAH) also may occur. Arthritis is most often nonerosive, but rheumatoid arthritis–like erosions and deformity can occur.

The most frequent cardiac manifestation is pericardial effusion. Exertional dyspnea may develop from interstitial lung disease or PAH. Kidney involvement is uncommon, but membranous glomerulonephritis and renovascular hypertensive

TABLE 25. Clinical Features in Mixed Connective Tissue Disease

Clinical Feature	Prevalence (%)
Arthritis and arthralgia	95
Raynaud phenomenon	85
Gastrointestinal involvement (primarily esophageal dysmotility)	67
Pulmonary involvement (interstitial lung disease and/or pulmonary arterial hypertension)	67
Hand swelling	66
Myositis	63
Sclerodactyly	33
Serositis	27
Kidney disease	10
Nervous system involvement (trigeminal neuropathy is most common)	10

crisis may develop in this setting. Gastrointestinal involvement is similar to that of systemic sclerosis, with esophageal or intestinal dysmotility. Neurologic involvement is rare with the exception of trigeminal neuropathy, which occurs in 25% of patients. Lupus-like inflammatory rash and cytopenia may occur, but hypocomplementemia is uncommon.

Diagnosis

Diagnosis is based on the presence of isolated high titers of anti-U1-RNP antibodies and positive antinuclear antibodies with a high-titer speckled pattern, along with typical symptoms; SLE-specific autoantibodies are absent. Although the presence of anti-U1-RNP antibodies may occur in patients with typical SLE, this does not indicate a diagnosis of MCTD. The differential diagnosis primarily includes other connective tissue diseases and, less commonly, infection or malignancy.

Treatment and Prognosis

Treatment of patients with MCTD is tailored to individual symptoms. NSAIDs, antimalarial agents, corticosteroids, and immunosuppressive medications are used for inflammatory symptoms. Arthritis and fever typically respond to corticosteroids; scleroderma manifestations such as sclerodactyly or vasculopathy do not.

PAH is the main disease-related cause of death and is detected by cardiac catheterization; if detected early, PAH may respond to aggressive cyclophosphamide therapy.

KEY POINTS

- Mixed connective tissue disease is characterized by overlapping clinical features of systemic lupus erythematosus, polymyositis, and systemic sclerosis in the presence of high titers of anti-U1-ribonucleoprotein antibodies.

- Typical findings of mixed connective tissue disease include Raynaud phenomenon, swollen hands, arthritis, and fatigue.

- The most frequent cardiac manifestation of mixed connective tissue disease is pericardial effusion.

- Treatment of patients with mixed connective tissue disease is tailored to individual symptoms.

Crystal-Induced Arthropathies

Gout

Epidemiology

Gout is the most common inflammatory arthritis in the United States (approximately 4%), and its prevalence has increased dramatically in the past several decades. Factors contributing to increased gout prevalence include the aging population, kidney disease, and changes in dietary habits. With rare (usually hereditary) exceptions, gout occurs in adults. Between puberty and middle age, gout occurs almost exclusively in men. Subsequent to menopause, the risk increases in women. Gender differences relate mainly to serum urate levels: men experience serum urate increases around puberty, whereas levels in women rise after menopause. Exceptions to this rule include patients with secondary causes for serum urate elevations (such as kidney failure). Gout is associated with various comorbidities (kidney disease, hypertension, diabetes mellitus, cardiovascular disease, obesity) that complicate disease management.

Pathophysiology

Hyperuricemia

Uric acid is a breakdown product of purines (for example, adenine or guanine), which are consumed through diet or synthesized de novo. High-purine foods include meat (especially organ meats), seafood, and some green vegetables. However, green vegetables may not increase serum urate levels. Obesity contributes to hyperuricemia, although it is difficult to separate obesity from a high-purine diet that causes patients to become overweight. Uric acid synthesis is complex; hereditary abnormalities of the synthetic pathway may occasionally result in hyperuricemia through uric acid overproduction (primary overproduction) (**Figure 24**).

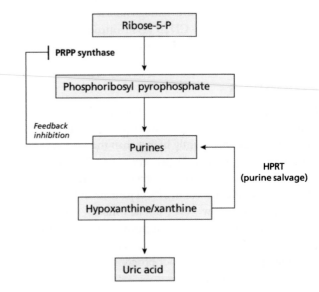

FIGURE 24. Uric acid biosynthesis. The rate-limiting enzyme for purine biosynthesis is phosphoribosyl pyrophosphate (PRPP) synthase; in hereditary cases, PRPP synthase overactivity causes purine and, hence, uric acid overproduction. Purine salvage occurs through the actions of hypoxanthine guanine phosphoribosyl transferase (HPRT); persons with partial HPRT deficiencies generate increased uric acid because of failure to salvage purines, and because purine depletion removes an important feedback inhibition on PRPP synthase.

TABLE 26. Conditions of Increased Cell Turnover Promoting Hyperuricemia

Leukemia and lymphoma, especially acute forms
Hemolytic anemia
Ineffective erythropoiesis
Polycythemia vera
Psoriasis
Tumor lysis due to chemotherapy, especially leukemia and lymphoma
Growth factor treatments (granulocyte-macrophage colony-stimulating factor, granulocyte colony-stimulating factor, erythropoietin)

Additional secondary mechanisms of urate overproduction can promote hyperuricemia in some patients. For example, conditions of increased cell turnover stimulate purine synthesis/breakdown and raise uric acid levels (**Table 26**). Humans and other primates also lack uricase, an enzyme that converts uric acid to the more soluble compound allantoic acid; consequently, all humans have higher serum urate concentrations than those seen in most of the animal kingdom.

Urate Excretion and Underexcretion

Much of the body's urate is eliminated via the kidneys, a regulated process that helps maintain serum urate levels within a limited range (**Figure 25**). Despite apparently normal kidney function, some persons cannot adequately export serum urate and experience hyperuricemia ("primary underexcreters"). Patients with kidney disease (decreased glomerular filtration rate) do not adequately filter urate and also have elevated serum urate levels ("secondary underexcreters"). Weak acids such as lactic acid and keto acids (as in sepsis or diabetes) competitively inhibit renal transporters and block urate excretion. Lead exposure also inhibits renal transporters and raises serum urate levels (lead nephropathy). Dehydration and alkalosis may provoke sodium or proton retention and concomitant urate retention.

Diet has important effects on serum urate. Dietary purine consumption can raise serum urate levels, within a range of about 1 mg/dL (0.06 mmol/L). Diets high in fructose also

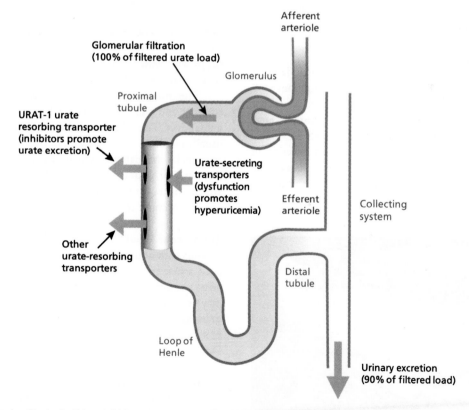

FIGURE 25. Urate handling by the kidney. Soluble serum urate is first filtered by the glomerulus; a decrease in glomerular filtration rate will result in elevated serum urate concentrations ("secondary underexcreters"). In humans, most of the remaining handling of urate in the kidney occurs in the proximal tubule, where multiple organic anion transporters serve to both resorb and secrete urate. Among the urate transporters responsible for urate resorption, URAT-1 appears to play a particularly important role; agents such as probenecid, and to a lesser extent losartan and high-dose salicylates, block URAT-1 to promote urate excretion. Urate transporters that secrete urate into the renal tubule lumen are responsible for keeping serum urate concentrations low; in some persons, one or more of these transporters may be intrinsically inadequate, leading to hyperuricemia despite normal glomerular filtration ("primary underexcreters"). Weak acids, diuretics, and other drugs (ethambutol, pyrazinamide, low-dose aspirin) block secretion at this stage and promote hyperuricemia.

increase serum urate, owing to a unique metabolic pathway. Increases in gout prevalence over the past decades correlate fairly well with expanded use of fructose in commercial foods, including sweetened soft drinks. Alcohol consumption increases the risk of hyperuricemia and gout in a dose-dependent manner. Whereas even moderate consumption of beer (high-purine content) increases serum urate levels, moderate wine consumption (≤1 glass per day) may not raise serum urate levels in most persons. In contrast, some foods can lower serum urate levels. For example, dairy consumption may lower serum urate levels by stimulating uricosuria.

Many drugs alter serum urate levels. Both thiazide and loop diuretics block urate excretion and may be the most clinically relevant. Drugs that are weak acids (such as low-dose salicylates and nicotinic acid) also competitively block urate excretion in the proximal tubule. Isoniazid and pyrazinamide noncompetitively inhibit renal tubular urate excretion; their use in tuberculosis may cause hyperuricemia. On the other hand, some drugs promote urate excretion. High-dose salicylates and the angiotensin receptor blocker losartan inhibit proximal tubule urate resorption (URAT-1 transporter) and have modest urate-lowering effects. In patients with hyperuricemia or gout, consideration should be given to switching from hyperuricemia-promoting agents to equally effective agents without urate-raising potential when such agents are available.

Acute Gouty Inflammation

Formation or release of urate crystals triggers acute inflammation. Crystals may form spontaneously (at concentrations >6.8 mg/dL [0.40 mmol/L]) as a consequence of acute (or chronic) increases in serum urate levels (for example, after dietary indiscretion). In other instances, crystals previously deposited may be liberated by trauma or rapid lowering of serum urate levels (irregular urate dissolution). In all cases, the result is "fresh" crystals that drive inflammatory activation.

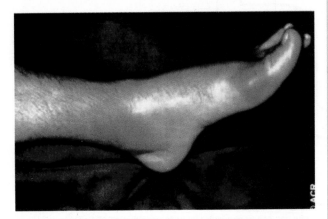

FIGURE 26. This patient has acute gouty arthritis, with intense inflammation around the first metatarsophalangeal joint (podagra) as well as erythema and swelling of the ankle.

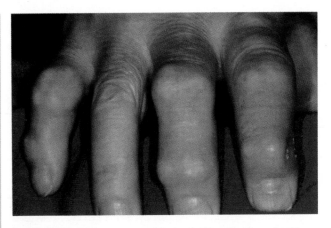

FIGURE 27. Tophaceous gout of the hands. This patient has yellowish, subcutaneous mass-like deposits over the proximal and distal interphalangeal joints of the second, third, and fifth digits. On the distal second digit, one of the tophi has ulcerated.

Clinical Manifestations

Acute and Intercritical Gout

The typical acute gout attack evolves over hours and often starts at night. First attacks most commonly occur at the first metatarsophalangeal joint (podagra) (**Figure 26**), and attacks early in the disease tend to be monoarticular. However, attacks can involve virtually any joint and may be polyarticular; patients with established gout more frequently have polyarticular attacks.

The main symptoms of an acute gout attack are swelling and pain of the affected joint(s), often with low-grade fever. The joint is red, hot, and tender. Gout attacks usually resolve without treatment over days or weeks. After an attack, the patient returns to an asymptomatic state (intercritical gout). However, a history of previous gout attacks makes future attacks more likely and, with time, the attacks are more frequent.

Tophaceous Gout

Patients with gout whose high serum urate levels go unmanaged are at risk for tophi, which are urate crystal deposits often surrounded by local inflammation (**Figure 27**). Tophi may be firm or pasty and usually develop in subcutaneous sites or bursae (such as elbows). Tophi can also develop in cartilage or subchondral bone and cause considerable erosive damage. Occasionally, tophi may become infected.

Chronic Gouty Arthritis

Patients with long-standing gout and established tophaceous disease typically have increased frequency of acute gout attacks and may experience smoldering chronic arthritis.

Diagnosis

Any acute monoarticular or polyarticular inflammatory arthritis in men or postmenopausal women may be indicative of

TABLE 27. Differential Diagnosis of Gout

Condition	Comment
Infected joint	Most important "rule out" in gout; most commonly monoarticular but can be polyarticular; may coexist with acute gout
Pseudogout	Clinically very similar to acute gout; less frequent in the first metatarsophalangeal joint than gout; less commonly polyarticular than gout; may be less inflammatory than gout; may coexist with gout
Basic calcium phosphate deposition	Less common than gout or pseudogout; may mimic gout or pseudogout; crystals not visible on polarizing microscopy
Trauma	May be obvious or occult; rule out fracture; hemarthrosis; trauma may also set off gout or pseudogout attacks
Osteoarthritis	Typically less inflammatory than gout; may occasionally present with "flare"
Reactive arthritis	Often mono- or oligoarticular, lower extremity; onset is typically subacute rather than acute as in gout

acute gout. Differential diagnosis must always include the possibility of a septic joint, because joint infection is a rheumatologic emergency. Pseudogout and other possible diagnoses depend on the pattern of presentation (**Table 27**).

The clinical criteria (**Table 28**) for gout are insufficient to permit a definitive diagnosis of acute gout attack or to rule out infection. (A possible exception is podagra, because gout is common and infection uncommon in the first metatarsophalangeal joint.) Therefore, aspiration of the acutely inflamed joint is indicated in most cases. The presence of needle-shaped, negatively birefringent urate crystals, viewed under polarized microscopy, supports a diagnosis of gout, as does a synovial fluid with a high neutrophil count (>3000/μL [3.0×10^9/L] and often much higher). The acute gout attack is definitively established by identifying neutrophils in synovial fluid that have phagocytosed crystals. The presence of gout does not strictly rule out other conditions; pseudogout and infection may each coexist with acute gout. Gram stain and culture of the synovial fluid, and empiric antibiotic coverage if suspicion of infection is high, are mandatory.

Blood tests and radiographic studies support but cannot establish a diagnosis of acute gout. Appropriate laboratory studies include the following: chemistries to assess kidney function; complete blood count to assess leukocyte count (elevated in infection but also potentially in gout); erythrocyte sedimentation rate and/or C-reactive protein, which are elevated in gout and in other inflammatory conditions; and serum urate concentration. A high serum urate concentration supports but does not establish a diagnosis of gout; a low serum urate concentration argues against but does not rule out gout, because acute gout attacks can be accompanied by transient declines in serum urate. Radiographs in acute gout

typically show nonspecific soft-tissue swelling. Radiographs in patients with a chronic history of gout may show "punched out" lesions in the subchondral bone representing areas of urate deposition, or, in some patients, massive and joint-destroying tophi.

Treatment

NSAIDs, corticosteroids, and colchicine are the appropriate management strategy for acute gout attacks. Choice of treatment is based on relative efficacy and, most importantly, the side-effect profiles of the agents and the risk of toxicity in the individual patient. Because both raising and lowering serum urate levels can precipitate or exacerbate attacks, urate-lowering drugs should be neither initiated nor discontinued during this phase.

Although indomethacin is traditionally used for gout, all NSAIDs can be effective, including selective cyclooxygenase-2 inhibitors. NSAIDs can be started at the maximum approved dose and tapered as the attack responds. Corticosteroids may be administered orally, intravenously, or intra-articularly. Intra-articular corticosteroids decrease local inflammation and minimize systemic exposure, but joint infection must be ruled out prior to injection. Colchicine can be effective early in a gout attack (especially within the first 24 hours, ideally within the first few hours). Treatment of acute attacks with colchicine now consists of a 1.2-mg single dose,

TABLE 28. American College of Rheumatology Criteria for the Classification of Acute Arthritis of Primary Gout

Criteria
The presence of characteristic urate crystals in the joint fluid, OR
A tophus proved to contain urate crystals by chemical means or polarized light microscopy, OR
The presence of six of the following clinical, laboratory, and radiographic findings, even in the absence of crystal identification:
More than one attack of acute arthritis
Maximum inflammation developed within 1 day
Monoarthritis attack
Redness observed over joints
First metatarsophalangeal joint painful or swollen
Unilateral first metatarsophalangeal joint attack
Unilateral tarsal joint attack
Tophus (suspected)
Hyperuricemia
Asymmetric swelling within a joint visible on physical examination or radiography
Subcortical cysts without erosions visible on radiography
Monosodium urate monohydrate microcrystals in joint fluid during attack
Joint fluid culture negative for organisms during attack

Reproduced from Wallace SL, Robinson H, Masi AT, et al. Preliminary criteria for the classification of the acute arthritis of primary gout. Arthritis Rheum. 1977;20(3):895-900. [PMID: 856219] Reproduced with permission of John Wiley & Sons, Inc.

followed 1 hour later by 0.6 mg. This regimen optimizes effectiveness while minimizing toxicity (nausea, vomiting, abdominal pain, and diarrhea; neuromyopathy; bone marrow failure). Occasionally, all of these agents may be contraindicated. In such patients, it may be appropriate to manage pain while allowing the attack to spontaneously subside.

Patients who have had single or very rare attacks do not require prophylaxis and can be managed expectantly, because next attacks in such patients may be quite delayed. In contrast, patients with recurrent episodes (≥2 attacks in 1 year) require urate-lowering therapy to prevent future attacks and occult urate deposition. Xanthine oxidase inhibition by allopurinol or febuxostat blocks urate production and is potentially effective in patients with gout of any cause (see Principles of Therapeutics, Urate-Lowering Therapy). Blockade of the URAT-1 transporter by probenecid increases urate excretion but only in primary underexcreters with normal kidney function; a 24-hour urine uric acid collection is needed to establish that the patient is a primary underexcreter. For convenience, many physicians opt for xanthine oxidase inhibition as an initial strategy. The dose of these agents is not fixed but should be titrated until the patient achieves a target serum urate level of less than 6.0 mg/dL (0.35 mmol/mL). Because urate lowering initially increases the risk for acute attack, patients must be prophylaxed against acute attack (usually with low-dose colchicine) for at least 6 months after starting urate-lowering therapy.

Management of risk factors is part of any urate-lowering strategy. Patients should reduce purine and fructose and increase dairy intake, within the limits of individual tolerance. Weight loss is desirable. Reduction in alcohol consumption is indicated. Medications should be reviewed for any nonessential drugs that contribute to hyperuricemia (for example, diuretics used for hypertension should usually be substituted with other antihypertensives that do not raise serum urate levels). Essential drugs should never be discontinued but may necessitate more aggressive urate-lowering therapy.

Tophaceous deposits can be resolved by reducing serum urate to concentrations that promote solubilization of crystalline urate, which can take years. Tophi are probably best treated with allopurinol or febuxostat because probenecid may promote kidney stones as a consequence of excessive kidney urate delivery. Pegloticase is a recently approved intravenous recombinant uricase that is a potent urate-lowering agent; it may be useful in particularly resistant cases. Many rheumatologists believe that the serum urate target for tophus reduction should be lower than 6.0 mg/dL (0.35 mmol/L), perhaps to the range of ≤5.0 mg/dL (0.29 mmol/L). Tophectomy may occasionally be needed to reduce pain and dysfunction or to debride an infection.

Management of patients with chronic gouty arthritis is based on the individual components of the condition. Short-term anti-inflammatory therapy usually controls acute attacks. In some patients, extended anti-inflammatory use may be needed to bring the arthritis under control. Virtually all patients with chronic gouty arthritis require urate-lowering therapy.

Patients who have moderately elevated serum urate levels but have never had an attack (asymptomatic hyperuricemia) have an increased risk for gout, but a low likelihood of a gout attack in the short term, and therefore do not require prophylaxis. Although studies suggest that hyperuricemia may contribute to several comorbidities (hypertension, kidney disease, cardiovascular disease), there is not yet consensus that these risks are sufficient to warrant chronic urate-lowering therapy, except possibly in patients in whom the serum urate level is exceptionally high. Consideration of lifestyle modifications (such as dietary changes or switching from medications that promote hyperuricemia when alternatives are available) may nonetheless be warranted.

KEY POINTS

- Gout is the most common inflammatory arthritis in the United States (approximately 4%), and its prevalence has increased dramatically in the past several decades.

- Treatment of acute gout attacks should address inflammation only; serum urate levels should be neither raised nor lowered.

- NSAIDs, corticosteroids, and colchicine are effective for treating acute gout, although colchicine is less effective when administered later in the attack.

- Urate-lowering therapy is appropriate for patients who have two or more acute gout attacks in 1 year or have tophi.

- Patients who start urate-lowering therapy should be prophylaxed for at least 6 months to prevent acute gout attacks.

Calcium Pyrophosphate Deposition Disease

Epidemiology and Pathophysiology

Formation of calcium pyrophosphate (CPP) crystals can result in an acute inflammatory state (pseudogout) that resembles gout. Patients with CPP deposition disease are usually older, except (uncommonly) in familial cases. The prevalence is 7% to 10% in patients over the age of 60 years. No gender predilection is recognized. Several endocrinologic and/or metabolic conditions have been associated with CPP deposition, including hyperparathyroidism, hypothyroidism, hemochromatosis, hypophosphatasia, hypomagnesemia, and familial hypocalciuric hypercalcemia.

The mechanisms of CPP crystal formation are incompletely understood but may include abnormal pyrophosphate handling by resident joint cells. Chondrocytes may generate excessive pyrophosphate that combines with extracellular calcium to form crystals. CPP crystals can deposit directly within cartilage (chondrocalcinosis) or may be released into the joint, stimulating joint space inflammation. The mechanisms by which CPP crystals stimulate inflammation appear to be similar to those of urate crystals. Several diseases tend to be associated with CPP deposition disease; the precise relationship between these conditions and CPP deposition remains unclear.

Clinical Manifestations

Patients may experience asymptomatic deposition of CPP within cartilage, detected incidentally on radiographs (chondrocalcinosis). CPP deposits usually are linear below but parallel to the cartilage surface and are commonly located at the cartilaginous structures of the knee (**Figure 28**) and wrist.

CPP crystals within the joint space can precipitate inflammatory reactions. Similar to acute gout, this condition may come on rather suddenly, be precipitated by trauma, and is usually self-limiting. In contrast to gout, pseudogout may be somewhat less inflammatory, less likely to affect the first metatarsophalangeal joint, and less likely to be polyarticular or involve bursae.

Patients with CPP deposition may develop an osteoarthritis-like condition possibly related to CPP effects on cartilage. It can be difficult to distinguish CPP arthropathy from osteoarthritis with accompanying chondrocalcinosis, particularly in joints in which osteoarthritis is common (such as the knee). However, when osteoarthritis and chondrocalcinosis coexist in joints not commonly affected by osteoarthritis (such as the wrist and the second and third metacarpophalangeal joints), a CPP arthropathy is probably present. Similar to osteoarthritis, CPP arthropathy is typically characterized by less than 30 minutes of morning stiffness and joint pain exacerbated by use.

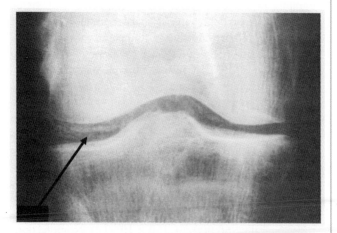

FIGURE 28. Chondrocalcinosis of the knee cartilage. This radiograph shows linearly arranged calcific deposits in the articular cartilage (*arrow*).

Reprinted with permission from Yee AMF and Paget SA, eds. Expert Guide to Rheumatology. Philadelphia: American College of Physicians; 2004.

Diagnosis

A diagnosis of pseudogout should be considered in most patients with acute inflammatory monoarthritis. Increased patient age and a history of pseudogout or CPP-associated conditions can make acute pseudogout more likely. Radiographs of the affected joint reveal soft-tissue swelling. The presence of chondrocalcinosis is consistent with, but not pathognomonic of, pseudogout: chondrocalcinosis can be asymptomatic, and pseudogout can occur without radiographically visible calcium.

Laboratory studies are supportive but not diagnostic. An elevated erythrocyte sedimentation rate and/or C-reactive protein level are typical; hypercalcemia and/or hyperphosphatemia may rarely be present and are presumed in those cases to contribute to crystal deposition. Definitive diagnosis is made by aspirating synovial fluid and examining it under polarizing microscopy for positively birefringent, rhomboid-shaped crystals, neutrophils, and (ideally) crystals within neutrophils. CPP crystals are pale and harder to detect than urate crystals. As in gout, evaluating for joint infection is always the first consideration.

CPP arthropathy is a clinical diagnosis made by observing typical osteoarthritis features, along with chondrocalcinosis, in locations atypical for osteoarthritis. In some instances, a chronic inflammatory condition may result, leading to progressive joint destruction and occasionally a symmetric pattern that can be confused with rheumatoid arthritis.

Treatment

Asymptomatic chondrocalcinosis in the absence of other signs or symptoms needs no treatment. Treatment of acute pseudogout is directed toward suppressing inflammation. NSAIDs, intra-articular or systemic corticosteroids, and colchicine are effective, although colchicine may be less efficacious than in gout. Associated conditions are uncommon but should be identified and treated if possible; however, it is uncertain that such treatment ameliorates the CPP disease. Because CPP deposition cannot be attenuated at the present time, patients requiring prophylaxis for frequent pseudogout attacks should receive standing anti-inflammatory treatment, usually low-dose colchicine or possibly an NSAID. Treatment of chronic CPP arthropathy is directed at relief of symptoms and correction of associated conditions. Total joint replacement may occasionally be warranted.

KEY POINTS

- Calcium pyrophosphate deposition disease is associated with hyperparathyroidism, hypothyroidism, hemochromatosis, hypophosphatasia, hypomagnesemia, and familial hypocalciuric hypercalcemia.
- Calcium pyrophosphate deposition disease may take multiple forms, including asymptomatic chondrocalcinosis; acute inflammatory arthritis (pseudogout); degenerative cartilage disease (osteoarthritis-like); and chronic inflammatory arthritis.

- A diagnosis of pseudogout should be considered in most patients with acute inflammatory monoarthritis, and the diagnosis is made by aspirating synovial fluid and finding birefringent, rhomboid-shaped crystals.

- Treatment of acute pseudogout is directed toward suppressing inflammation with NSAIDs, intra-articular or systemic corticosteroids, or colchicine.

Basic Calcium Phosphate Deposition Disease

Several forms of basic calcium phosphate (BCP), including hydroxyapatite, may deposit as crystals. The biology of these diseases is not well established, although hydroxyapatite may be released from bone. BCP crystal formation is more common in patients ≥50 years of age. BCP crystals may be extremely common (≥50%) in osteoarthritic joints and can cause acute arthritis episodes or a chronic and highly destructive inflammatory arthritis (such as Milwaukee shoulder). BCP crystals may also affect periarticular structures, bursae, or both. In many patients, BCP deposition causes no symptoms. Diagnosis is determined by radiographic appearance and clinical suspicion; the crystals are small and nonbirefringent but can be seen in aggregates after alizarin red or tetracycline staining of synovial fluid or under electron microscopy. Treatment is symptomatic, using NSAIDs, corticosteroids, and colchicine.

KEY POINTS

- Basic calcium phosphate deposition may be asymptomatic, cause severe and destructive large joint arthropathy, or affect periarticular structures.

- Management of basic calcium phosphate deposition disease is symptomatic, using NSAIDs, corticosteroids, and colchicine.

Infectious Arthritis

Bacteria, fungi, and viruses infect joints. Bacterial and fungal infections damage joints, with bacteria often causing damage in days or weeks. Rapid diagnosis and treatment are essential to preserve joint function and to reduce morbidity and mortality.

Diagnosis

Clinical Manifestations and Physical Examination

Infected joints manifest the cardinal signs of inflammation: warmth, redness, swelling, and pain. The degree of inflammation varies with the type and stage of the infection and the response of the host. Vigilance for joint infection in susceptible populations is essential. Joint infections may be monoarticular, polyarticular, or migratory. Most joint infections result from hematogenous spread; therefore, patients should be examined for infectious sources (such as pneumonia, urinary tract infection, endocarditis, or abscess), although often none is identified. Joint infections also result from direct penetration or abrasion of skin; patients should be assessed for a possible point of entry or penetrating object.

Because joint infections can present as part of systemic syndromes, a complete physical examination is mandatory. Specific extra-articular manifestations (rashes, pustules, and other lesions) provide clues to the nature of the infection. When evaluating a patient with an infected joint, the history is often informative. Many patients report preexisting conditions that focus the diagnostic process. The speed of onset (acute, subacute, or chronic) and associated symptoms provide clues to the infection involved. Patients with already damaged joints (such as those with chronic gout or osteoarthritis) are at greater risk for infection in the affected joints; infection should be carefully ruled out in such patients, even in the presence of an apparent alternative explanation (for example, an acute gout attack).

Laboratory and Radiographic Studies

Initial evaluation of a patient with an infected joint includes a complete blood count. An elevated leukocyte count supports a diagnosis of joint infection but is also consistent with other pathologies, including crystal-induced arthritis or nonarticular infection. Erythrocyte sedimentation rate (ESR) and C-reactive protein (CRP) are helpful but nonspecific indicators of inflammation. Blood cultures are essential (even when fever is absent), with most cases of infectious arthritis arising from hematogenous spread, and because even in cases in which the infection arises directly at the joint, the organism may occasionally be identified in the blood cultures. Urinalysis and urine culture may be appropriate. Specific viral titers, along with liver chemistry testing, may be indicated. Early radiographs of infected joints show nonspecific soft-tissue swelling, whereas radiographs taken later can show frank joint destruction and provide clues to the nature of the arthritis. Imaging of other structures (such as chest radiography) to identify primary infectious sources may be warranted.

Joint aspiration is mandatory if infection is suspected and should be performed before initiation of antibiotics to improve the chance of identifying the causative organism whenever possible. Synovial fluid analysis permits assessment of inflammation by measurement of leukocyte counts, as well as Gram stain and culture for bacterial and/or fungal organisms. Inoculation of blood culture bottles may increase the sensitivity of synovial fluid cultures. In bacterial infections, synovial fluid analysis reveals a neutrophilic leukocytosis (typically >50,000/µL [50×10^9/L]). Noninfectious inflammatory arthritis (such as gout or rheumatoid arthritis) can also produce high leukocyte counts, but counts ≥50,000/µL (50×10^9/L) should be presumed infectious

CONT. until proved otherwise. Synovial fluid leukocyte counts ≤50,000/µL (50×10^9/L) do not definitively rule out infection. Although a positive joint fluid culture is the gold standard for diagnosing bacterial infection, cultures from infected joints may be negative, particularly if antibiotics were initiated before synovial fluid aspiration. The physician's judgment, therefore, is paramount. **H**

> **KEY POINTS**
>
> - Rapid diagnosis and treatment of infectious arthritis are essential to preserve joint function and to reduce morbidity and mortality.
>
> - Diagnosis of an infected joint requires a strong index of suspicion, a careful history, a thorough physical examination, and aggressive culturing of joint fluid and other possible infectious sources.
>
> - Joint aspiration is mandatory if infection is suspected and should be performed before the initiation of antibiotics whenever possible.
>
> - A positive joint fluid culture is the gold standard for diagnosing bacterial joint infections, but cultures may be negative even if infection is present, particularly if antibiotics were initiated before synovial fluid aspiration.

Common Causes

Infection with Gram-Positive Organisms

Gram-positive organisms are the most common causes of infectious arthritis, with *Staphylococcus aureus* being the most prevalent. Other gram-positive organisms that infect joints include *Staphylococcus epidermidis* (particularly prosthetic joints) and the *Streptococcus* species (especially in vulnerable individuals such as patients with diabetes mellitus). Most infections with gram-positive organisms are monoarticular and affect large joints (particularly the knee). However, up to 20% of gram-positive infections are polyarticular; these may represent more severe disease, with greater morbidity and mortality. The onset of gram-positive infection is typically rapid (hours to days). Approximately 50% of patients with *S. aureus* infection have positive blood cultures, and Gram stain and synovial fluid culture are high yield.

Infection with Gram-Negative Organisms

Disseminated Gonococcal Infection

Neisseria gonorrhoeae was previously considered the most common joint infection among younger sexually active adults, but its frequency has declined. Contagion is almost exclusively by sexual contact, with women more commonly affected. Two patterns may be encountered. The first involves a single, most often large, joint (such as the knee). Medium-sized monoarticular joint (wrist, ankle) involvement is less common but when present raises the likelihood of gonococcal infection. The second pattern is characterized by fever, chills, tenosynovitis, and a vesiculopustular rash (**Figure 29**). The rash can be subtle with small punctate or pustular lesions occurring at or away from the affected joint. The arthritis appears in an additive or migratory polyarticular pattern (including small joints) that is mild and may present as arthralgia only. Tenosynovitis is common and characteristic, with the dorsa of the hands and feet visibly swollen. The two patterns may overlap in some patients.

Diagnosing gonococcal arthritis requires an appropriate level of suspicion in a susceptible patient. Blood cultures should be taken, and synovial fluid should be aspirated. The clinical microbiology laboratory should be informed if there is a clinical suspicion for gonococcal infection so that samples can be plated directly on Thayer-Martin or other special media. However, the yields of both blood and synovial fluid Gram stain and culture are lower for *N. gonorrhoeae* than that for other bacteria (≤50%). Moreover, synovial fluid cell counts may be only moderately elevated. Therefore, negative joint fluid studies do not rule out gonococcal arthritis when suspicion persists. Systemic gonococcal infection should be confirmed, whenever possible, by direct culture or polymerase chain reaction of specimens from the urethra or urine, cervix, throat, and rectum. Although gonococcal arthritis is typically less destructive than other forms of bacterial arthritis, immediate management is nonetheless required.

Nongonococcal Gram-Negative Organisms

Nongonococcal gram-negative organisms typically produce a rapid onset, monoarticular or occasionally polyarticular arthritis. Gram-negative infections are more common in patients with impaired immunity such as those with diabetes or those over the age of 65 years.

Patients with sickle cell anemia are prone to *Salmonella* infection both systemically and in the joint. Injection drug users are susceptible to gram-negative joint infections owing to contaminated needles; *Pseudomonas* species are classically reported. Based on the route of introduction in these

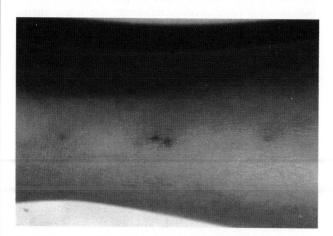

FIGURE 29. Cutaneous lesions associated with disseminated gonococcal infection.

patients, infections may occur in multiple or atypical joints (for example, sternoclavicular and acromioclavicular). Overall, the most common gram-negative joint infections are *Escherichia coli* and *Pseudomonas aeruginosa*. Fever is frequently present, and sepsis can occur. The yield of synovial fluid Gram stain and culture is intermediate between gram-positive and gonococcal infections.

Lyme Arthritis

Joint involvement in Lyme disease (*Borrelia burgdorferi* infection) manifests in two forms. During the early initial infection, patients may develop polyarthralgia. In the mid to late phase of Lyme disease (months to years after infection), a chronic arthritis may occur. Chronic Lyme arthritis manifests gradually and is typically monoarticular, involving a large joint (often the knee, hip, or ankle). Chronic Lyme arthritis is usually less inflammatory than bacterial arthritis, but effusions can be large. Fever is uncommon. The synovial fluid leukocyte count is moderately elevated (10,000 to 20,000/µL [10×10^9/L to 20×10^9/L], predominantly neutrophils). Cultures are negative, although polymerase chain reaction and/or direct microscopic examination of synovial biopsy may confirm the presence of *B. burgdorferi*. Lyme arthritis is usually diagnosed by recognizing a subacute or chronic inflammatory arthritis in the setting of clinical and serologic documentation of Lyme disease (see MKSAP 16 Infectious Disease).

Mycobacterial Infections

Mycobacterium tuberculosis

Mycobacterium tuberculosis is the most common cause of mycobacterial arthritis. Vigilance should be exercised in patients from endemic areas and in those who are immunocompromised.

A minority (1% to 2%) of *M. tuberculosis* infections affect articular structures. Most cases are monoarticular, and arthritis may occur with or without pulmonary infection. Inflammation often develops indolently and is less intense than that seen with gram-positive or gram-negative organisms. Infection may affect an intervertebral disk, accompanied by destructive osteomyelitis involving the adjacent vertebrae (Pott disease); in such cases, a vertebral biopsy is often necessary to definitively establish the diagnosis.

Patients may or may not demonstrate fever and night sweats. The ESR and CRP levels can be markedly elevated. Radiographs of affected joints can show soft-tissue swelling or reveal signs of erosion consistent with prolonged infection. CT and MRI are more sensitive and can be useful when plain radiography is inadequate. A tuberculin skin test is warranted (but can be negative), as is a search for pulmonary or other extra-articular infection. Synovial fluid aspiration or synovial biopsy with culture and staining for acid-fast bacilli can be diagnostic.

Mycobacterium marinum

Mycobacterium marinum is a marine organism present in freshwater and saltwater. *M. marinum* infection typically results from skin puncture with contaminated objects (such as fish hooks) or through contact between fish or water and breaks in the skin (for example, when handling aquarium fish). *M. marinum* infection is usually localized to the area of the puncture, mainly in the skin, tendons, and adjacent joint (such as in a small joint of the hands). Nodular papules may form and then ulcerate. A high index of suspicion is necessary in patients with antibiotic-unresponsive cellulitis-like syndromes, particularly of the hands, and in patients with occupational or lifestyle risk of marine exposure. Diagnosis is based on clinical circumstances and culture of joint fluid or synovial biopsy.

Fungal Infections

Fungi that infect joints include *Candida, Aspergillus, Cryptococcus, Coccidioides, Blastomyces, Sporothrix,* and *Histoplasma* species. Fungal arthritis is rare but is more common in patients who are immunocompromised and in geographically endemic areas. Initial infection is typically through the organism's usual port(s) of entry, with subsequent spread to the joint. Fungal arthritis is usually monoarticular in a large or medium-sized joint; it progresses indolently and is less inflammatory than other bacterial infections. Diagnosis is made by examination and culture of fluid from the affected joint or upon histologic examination of a synovial biopsy.

Viral Infections

Viruses affect joints via direct infection, immune complex–mediated arthritis, or both.

Parvovirus B19

Parvovirus B19 is a DNA virus that replicates in erythroid precursors. Parvovirus outbreaks usually occur in the late winter and spring. Infection is most common in children and manifests as erythema infectiosum (fifth disease), consisting of polyarthralgia, flu-like symptoms, and a characteristic facial rash ("slapped cheek" appearance). Adults usually contract the virus from children; persons at risk include school workers and parents. Because the slapped cheek appearance is atypical in adults, the diagnosis should be suspected in the setting of flu-like illness (fever, polyarthritis in a rheumatoid-like distribution), particularly after exposure to a sick child. Diagnosis is confirmed by documenting IgM anti-parvovirus antibodies. Parvovirus B19 infection is usually self-limited and resolves after several weeks. Occasionally adults may experience waxing and waning arthralgias and myalgias that persist for months to years.

Other Forms of Viral Arthritis

Rubella is a single-strand RNA virus that produces a characteristic syndrome in children and young adults (fever, cough, lymphadenopathy, and a morbilliform rash). Rubella infection and (less frequently) rubella vaccination may affect joint tissues to produce symmetric or migratory polyarthralgia.

Hepatitis B and hepatitis C viruses can cause articular symptoms. Hepatitis B virus causes an acute, symmetric, polyarticular, sometimes severe, immune complex–mediated arthritis and occurs before the appearance of icterus. Patients with chronic hepatitis B infection may manifest polyarthralgia. Patients with hepatitis C infection may also develop polyarthralgia and/or essential mixed cryoglobulinemia with accompanying polyarthritis.

Prosthetic Joint Infections

Prosthetic joint infections are uncommon (1% to 3%) but pose unique challenges. Bacterial organisms propagate as biofilms on the inorganic surfaces of prostheses and can be practically impossible to eradicate while the artificial joint is in place. Prosthetic joints may become infected during implantation; such infections are initially asymptomatic but become apparent ≤3 months after surgery. Alternatively, prosthetic joints may become infected after implantation (>3 months to years) via hematogenous spread. In either case, the joint may be swollen and inflamed or only painful. Leukocyte counts, ESR, and CRP levels are usually elevated. Radiographs may reveal erosion or loosening around the implantation site. Diagnosis requires synovial fluid aspiration or open debridement, along with Gram stain and culture. Orthopedic consultation is mandatory.

Infections in Previously Damaged Joints

Preexisting damage renders joints vulnerable, and patients with arthritis of almost any form (such as osteoarthritis, rheumatoid arthritis, and psoriatic arthritis) are at increased risk for joint infections. In inflammatory forms of arthritis (such as rheumatoid arthritis), immune dysfunction and immunosuppressant treatments may compound the risk of joint infection. Previously damaged joints are more susceptible to both common and uncommon infectious agents. Crystal arthropathies also increase the risk of joint infection, and acute bacterial infections may coexist with acute gout or pseudogout.

KEY POINTS

- Gram-positive organisms are the most common causes of infectious arthritis, with *Staphylococcus aureus* being the most common infecting agent.
- Gonococcal joint infections are more common in young, sexually active adults, and tenosynovitis is common and characteristic.
- Gram-negative nongonococcal joint infections are more common in patients who are immunocompromised.
- Lyme arthritis is usually diagnosed by recognizing a chronic inflammatory arthritis in the setting of clinical and serologic documentation of Lyme disease.
- Diagnosis of a prosthetic joint infection requires synovial fluid aspiration or open debridement, along with Gram stain and culture.

Management

Pharmacologic Therapy

Bacterial infections require rapid initiation of appropriate (often empiric) antibiotic treatment (**Table 29**). However, antibiotic initiation should be deferred long enough for cultures to be obtained. When Gram stain is informative, antibiotic therapy should address the presumed organism, but broader coverage may be warranted pending final identification. The duration needed to treat bacterially infected joints

---

TABLE 29. Empiric and Definitive Antibiotic Treatment for Septic Native Joint Arthritis

Gram Stain Results	Likely or Identified Pathogen	First-Line Therapy	Second-Line Therapy
Gram-positive cocci	*Staphylococcus aureus*, other staphylococcal species	Oxacillin/nafcillin or cefazolin	Cefazolin or nafcillin
	If MRSA is a concern (risk factors or known MRSA carrier)	Vancomycin or linezolid	Teicoplanin
Gram-negative cocci	*Neisseria gonorrhoeae*	Ceftriaxone	Fluoroquinolones
Gram-negative bacilli	Enteric gram-negative bacilli	Ceftriaxone or cefotaxime	Fluoroquinolones
	Pseudomonas aeruginosa	Ceftazidime (plus gentamicin if proven)	Carbapenems, cefepime, piperacillin-tazobactam, fluoroquinolones
Gram stain unavailable	At risk for *N. gonorrhoeae* infection	Ceftriaxone or cefotaxime	
	No risk for *N. gonorrhoeae*; *S. aureus* or gram-negative bacilli are likely	Nafcillin plus ceftazidime	Nafcillin plus a fluoroquinolone

MRSA = methicillin-resistant *Staphylococcus aureus*.

Modified with permission from Physician's Information and Education Resource (PIER). Philadelphia: American College of Physicians. Copyright 2012 American College of Physicians.

CONT.

is not well established but is generally 2 to 4 weeks, with the initial phase of treatment administered intravenously.

Patients with proven or suspected gonococcal arthritis should be treated for disseminated infection with intravenous ceftriaxone or an equivalent. Those with arthralgia or tenosynovitis rather than a frank septic arthritis can be transitioned to oral therapy with ciprofloxacin after symptoms subside. Treatment is usually continued for 7 to 14 days depending on the severity of illness. Empiric doxycycline or azithromycin for chlamydial coinfection should be instituted.

Patients with strongly suspected or proven articular tuberculosis require extended multidrug therapy (three to four drugs, for ≥6 months, with some combination of isoniazid, pyrazinamide, rifampin, ethambutol, and streptomycin) to fully eradicate the organism. *M. marinum* infection is treated with minocycline, clarithromycin, or trimethoprim-sulfamethoxazole but is resistant to isoniazid.

Fungal joint infections require long durations of treatment. Although all known antifungal medications can be effective, specific agents may be most effective, or at least best-studied, for specific fungi.

In most cases, viral arthritis is self-limited, and therapy is directed toward relief of symptoms (for example, NSAIDs). Exceptions may include chronic viruses such as hepatitis B and hepatitis C; infection caused by these agents may require antiviral therapy.

Surgical Management

Thorough drainage of infected joints is essential for successful resolution and for preventing joint damage. Joints that are readily accessible (such as knees) can be managed with either needle aspiration or arthroscopic drainage. Needle aspiration should be performed repeatedly, usually daily, with complete removal of synovial fluid until the fluid ceases reaccumulating. Arthroscopic drainage or open surgical debridement is mandatory when the joint space is irregular, the fluid is loculated, or it is otherwise difficult or impractical to thoroughly and regularly evacuate the joint space using needle drainage. Early orthopedic consultation is strongly recommended.

Tuberculous and fungal infections may also benefit from drainage if fluid accumulation is apparent. Surgical debridement may be required in refractory cases.

Prosthetic joint infection virtually always requires removal of the infected hardware. An antibiotic spacer is usually inserted, and long-term (weeks to months) antibiotic therapy is initiated. Only after complete resolution of the infection can reimplantation be considered. With this approach, the new joint remains uninfected approximately 90% of the time. If the patient is not a candidate for this protocol, surgical debridement and chronic antibiotic suppression may minimize morbidity and mortality.

Patients in the recovery phase of a bacterially or fungally infected joint commonly experience stiffness. Physical or occupational therapy is critical for maintaining and restoring motion. **H**

- Antibiotic therapy should be initiated rapidly and empirically for patients with suspected bacterial infections after collecting fluid from the joint, blood, and other appropriate sites for Gram stain and culture.
- Patients with proven or suspected gonococcal arthritis should be treated for disseminated infection using intravenous ceftriaxone or an equivalent.
- Acute viral arthritis is usually self-limiting and can be managed symptomatically.
- Bacterially infected joints require aggressive drainage by daily needle aspiration, arthroscopy, or (rarely) open debridement; early orthopedic consultation is strongly recommended.
- Eradication of prosthetic joint infection usually requires removal of the infected hardware.

Idiopathic Inflammatory Myopathies

The hallmark of the idiopathic inflammatory myopathies is muscle weakness caused by inflammation, although other organ systems may be involved, especially the skin and lungs. This group of disorders is relatively rare and includes polymyositis, dermatomyositis, and inclusion body myositis (IBM), all of which differ in clinical presentation, histopathologic findings, and associated autoantibody specificities.

Pathophysiology

Genetic and environmental factors are likely to cause the idiopathic inflammatory myopathies. Both HLA and non-HLA genes confer risk. Potential environmental triggers include infectious agents (particularly viruses and parasites), drugs, toxins, ultraviolet radiation, and malignancy. Seasonal variation in incidence supports an environmental effect. Humoral and cellular immune systems are involved, and lymphocytic muscle infiltrates are characteristic. Dermatomyositis results from dysregulation of the humoral system, whereas polymyositis and IBM are caused by T-cell–mediated cytotoxicity.

Epidemiology

Inflammatory myopathies may occur as a manifestation of other connective tissue diseases, particularly systemic lupus erythematosus, systemic sclerosis, and mixed connective tissue disease. Patients with myopathy associated with other connective tissue diseases are usually younger (20 to 40 years of age) and have milder involvement. Myositis also presents as a paraneoplastic autoimmune syndrome in conjunction with malignancy, generally in older patients (>50 years of age).

The combined incidence of polymyositis and dermatomyositis is 5 to 10 per million persons, and prevalence is 50 to 110 per million persons in the United States. Onset may occur at any age, but peak age is between 40 and 60 years. Dermatomyositis has a bimodal distribution with peak of onset in childhood (<18 years) and again in midlife. Women are affected more often than men (ratio of 3:1). Black and Hispanic persons may have more severe disease.

The prevalence of IBM is about 5 to 10 per million persons, and onset is almost exclusively after age 50 years. Men are more commonly affected than women (ratio of 3:1).

Clinical Manifestations

Muscular Manifestations

The classic symptom of dermatomyositis and polymyositis is symmetric proximal muscle weakness with little or no pain; onset is usually acute or subacute with episodic or persistent disease progression. Neck flexor muscles may be involved; in late disease, respiratory muscle weakness may lead to respiratory failure.

In contrast, IBM presentation is insidious and slowly progressive, with weakness in both proximal and distal muscle groups. The quadriceps, wrists, finger flexors, and swallowing muscles are typically involved. Although muscle involvement in IBM is typically symmetric, it may be asymmetric in up to 15% of cases.

Cutaneous Manifestations

Cutaneous findings are characteristic of dermatomyositis and may precede the onset of myositis. Photosensitive rashes occur over the face, chest, and hands. Characteristic rashes include heliotrope rash (**Figure 30**), the V sign, and the shawl sign. Gottron papules are erythematous, violaceous, clumped papules over the extensor surfaces of the metacarpophalangeal

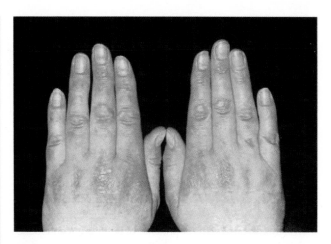

FIGURE 31. Gottron papules affecting the hand joints in a patient with dermatomyositis.

joints, proximal interphalangeal joints, elbows, and knees and are pathognomonic for dermatomyositis (**Figure 31**). Nailfold capillary abnormalities and cuticular hypertrophy also occur. Mechanic's hands may occur in polymyositis and dermatomyositis and are characterized by roughened erythematous hyperkeratotic fissuring of the palmar and lateral aspects of fingers.

Amyopathic dermatomyositis is a rare subset of dermatomyositis that presents as a typical rash in the absence of muscle symptoms. Muscle symptoms may be subclinical in some patients, with myositis seen only on imaging studies or biopsy; however, other patients with amyopathic dermatomyositis show no evidence of muscle inflammation, even on biopsy. Calcinosis over extensor surfaces is usually seen in juvenile dermatomyositis or, less commonly, in patients with a polymyositis-scleroderma overlap syndrome.

> **KEY POINTS**
> - Dermatomyositis and polymyositis manifest as symmetric proximal muscle weakness with little or no pain; onset is usually acute or subacute with episodic or persistent disease progression.
> - Inclusion body myositis manifests as weakness in both proximal and distal muscle groups; presentation of this disorder is insidious and slowly progressive.
> - Gottron papules are pathognomonic for dermatomyositis, and characteristic rashes of this disorder include heliotrope rash, the V sign, and the shawl sign.

Extramuscular Manifestations

Extramuscular manifestations in polymyositis and dermatomyositis include systemic symptoms such as fever, fatigue, and weight loss; Raynaud phenomenon; arthralgia or arthritis; and pulmonary, cardiac, and gastrointestinal symptoms. Extramuscular manifestations are rare in patients with IBM.

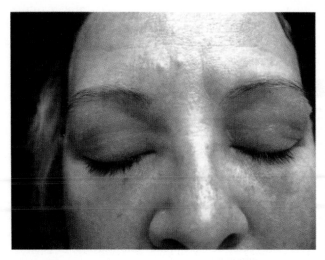

FIGURE 30. Heliotrope rash in a patient with dermatomyositis.

Cardiopulmonary Manifestations

Pulmonary manifestations in polymyositis and dermatomyositis are common and result from interstitial lung disease (ILD), hypoventilation (weakness of respiratory muscles), aspiration pneumonia, and, rarely, pulmonary arterial hypertension. The presence of ILD imparts a poorer prognosis in patients with polymyositis or dermatomyositis. ILD is seen in 65% of patients with polymyositis and dermatomyositis screened with high-resolution CT, not all of whom are symptomatic; in clinical practice, both high-resolution CT and pulmonary function testing are used to evaluate for the presence of this manifestation. ILD may precede onset of muscle symptoms. Clinical manifestations range from asymptomatic to severe progressive cough and dyspnea. ILD is strongly associated with the presence of positive autoantibodies to transfer RNA synthetases, including anti–Jo-1 antibodies (see Diagnosis, Autoantibodies). Various patterns of ILD occur, ranging from nonspecific interstitial pneumonitis (most common) to usual interstitial pneumonia or bronchiolitis obliterans with organizing pneumonia. The pattern of involvement determines corticosteroid responsiveness and, ultimately, prognosis.

Significant cardiac manifestations are uncommon. Subclinical electrocardiogram changes and arrhythmias are frequent, but cardiomyopathy due to myocarditis is rare.

Gastrointestinal Manifestations

Dysphagia caused by weakness of swallowing muscles is common, especially in the setting of IBM, in which it may be an early symptom of disease and may lead to aspiration pneumonia. More generalized bowel hypomotility, similar to that seen in systemic sclerosis, may develop. Bowel vasculitis primarily occurs in juvenile dermatomyositis.

KEY POINTS

- Extramuscular manifestations are rare in patients with inclusion body myositis.
- Interstitial lung disease occurs in 65% of patients with polymyositis and dermatomyositis screened with high-resolution CT, not all of whom are symptomatic.
- Anti–Jo-1 antibodies are associated with interstitial lung disease in patients with inflammatory myopathies.

Diagnosis

Diagnosis is based on the presence of progressive proximal muscle weakness, elevation in muscle-associated enzymes, characteristic electromyographic findings, and chronic inflammation on muscle biopsy. Dermatomyositis is further diagnosed by the characteristic rash found in patients.

Muscle-Related Enzymes

In more than 95% of patients with inflammatory myopathies, muscle-related enzymes, including serum creatine kinase, aldolase, aspartate aminotransferase, and alanine aminotransferase, are elevated and fluctuate with disease activity. The CK-MB isoform of creatine kinase, generally associated with cardiac muscle, may be elevated because of its expression in regenerating muscle. Rarely, patients can have normal muscle enzymes despite muscle inflammation, especially in the presence of significant muscle atrophy and fibrosis or indolent course.

Autoantibodies

Autoantibodies are found in 90% of patients with polymyositis and dermatomyositis (**Table 30**) but are rarely found in IBM. Antinuclear antibodies are found in 80% of patients but are nonspecific. Myositis-specific antibodies are diagnostic for polymyositis and dermatomyositis in the setting of typical symptoms.

Antisynthetase autoantibodies are directed against aminoacyl-transfer RNA synthetase enzymes; the most common (and clinically available) is anti–Jo-1. Autoantibodies to seven other transfer RNA synthetase enzymes have been identified but are less frequent. Antisynthetase autoantibodies are associated with a distinct clinical syndrome (see Table 30).

Antibodies to the signal recognition particle define another serologic and clinical subset; these autoantibodies are found in 5% of patients. Affected patients present with acute onset of severe myositis, cardiac involvement, and dysphagia and have a poor prognosis.

Anti–Mi-2 autoantibodies are detected in 20% of patients with juvenile and adult dermatomyositis and are associated with classic rash, cuticular overgrowth, milder muscle involvement,

TABLE 30. Myositis-Specific Antibodies			
Autoantibody	**Antigen**	**Frequency**	**Clinical Presentation**
Antisynthetase	Aminoacyl-transfer RNA synthetase	30% to 40%	Acute or subacute onset; antisynthetase syndrome, including interstitial lung disease, arthritis, fever, Raynaud phenomenon, mechanic's hands; fair prognosis
Anti–Jo-1 (most common antisynthetase antibody)	Histidyl-transfer RNA	20%	Same as above; interstitial lung disease
Antisignal recognition particle	Signal recognition particle	5%	Acute onset of severe myositis; cardiac involvement; dysphagia; no rash; poor prognosis
Anti–Mi-2	Nuclear helicase protein Mi-2	<10%	Classic dermatomyositis rash; mild myositis; good prognosis

and lower risk of ILD; prognosis is better than that associated with other myositis-specific antibodies.

Myositis-associated antibodies include anti-U1-ribonucleo-protein, anti-PM-Scl, and anti-Ku; these antibodies are nonspecific and are predominantly found in overlap forms of myositis.

Imaging Studies

Muscle imaging with ultrasonography or MRI can identify promising sites for biopsy, and the pattern of muscle involvement can aid in clinical diagnosis. Imaging studies cannot differentiate among inflammatory, metabolic, traumatic, and other myopathies. The sensitivity of ultrasonography in detecting myositis is 83%, and contrast-enhanced ultrasonography can differentiate between edema and increased muscle perfusion associated with myositis.

MRI with fat-suppressed T2-weighted images or short tau inversion recovery sequences also visualizes inflammatory edema suggestive of myositis, fat infiltration, and alterations in muscle size. Given the frequently focal muscle involvement in the idiopathic inflammatory myopathies, use of noninvasive imaging allows identification of high-yield biopsy sites.

Electromyography

Electromyography (EMG) with nerve conduction study can demonstrate the presence of inflammatory myositis and can exclude neuropathic disease. The characteristic triad includes short-duration, small, low-amplitude polyphasic potentials; fibrillation potentials at rest; and bizarre, high-frequency, repetitive discharges. EMG studies themselves disrupt muscle structure and cause local inflammation; as a result, biopsy is indicated for the muscle contralateral to the side of EMG testing.

Muscle Biopsy

Muscle biopsy is the gold standard for diagnosing the idiopathic inflammatory myopathies; it shows a predominantly lymphocytic muscle infiltration with evidence of necrosis and regeneration. Characterization of the infiltration pattern and cell markers allows for the diagnosis of polymyositis, dermatomyositis, or IBM. In dermatomyositis, B cells and CD4-positive T cells are present in perivascular areas and surrounding the muscle fascicles; vascular endothelium appears to be the target tissue. In polymyositis and IBM, cytotoxic CD8-positive T lymphocytes invade the endomysium (within the muscle fascicles), and the primary target is the myofibril itself. The biopsy in IBM can show endomysial inflammation similar to that seen in polymyositis, although the degree of inflammation is generally less than that in polymyositis. Other pathologic findings seen in IBM include rimmed vacuoles and inclusion bodies seen on light microscopy. Filamentous tubules seen on electron microscopy are highly specific for the disease.

Differential Diagnosis

The differential diagnosis for myopathy is broad. Asymptomatic elevation in serum creatine kinase levels and frank muscle weakness can be caused by many other disorders (**Table 31**). Careful history; physical examination; laboratory tests, including autoantibody studies; EMG; ultrasonography or MRI; and biopsy generally lead to the correct diagnosis. Surgical biopsy is preferable to needle biopsy, because it yields adequate tissue to perform pathology and enzyme testing to rule out noninflammatory myopathic disorders. In the case of dermatomyositis, skin biopsy showing an interface dermatitis in the appropriate clinical setting can be enough to establish a diagnosis without muscle biopsy.

KEY POINTS

- In more than 95% of patients with inflammatory myopathies, muscle-related enzymes, including creatine kinase, aldolase, aspartate aminotransferase, and alanine aminotransferase, are elevated and fluctuate with disease activity.

TABLE 31. Differential Diagnosis of Myopathy	
Myopathy	**Common Examples**
Idiopathic inflammatory myopathies	Polymyositis; dermatomyositis; inclusion body myositis
Connective tissue disease–associated	Systemic lupus erythematosus; mixed connective tissue disease; systemic sclerosis
Endocrine disease	Hypothyroidism
Infection-induced myopathies	Bacterial: Lyme disease; pyomyositis
	Viral: influenza; HIV; hepatitis B; hepatitis C
	Parasitic: toxoplasmosis; trichinosis
Drug- or toxin-induced myopathies	Corticosteroids; ethanol; statins; colchicine
Metabolic myopathies	Acid maltase deficiency; McArdle disease
Mitochondrial myopathies	Kearns-Sayre syndrome; Leigh syndrome
Muscular dystrophies	Duchenne dystrophy; Becker dystrophy
Neuromuscular disorders	Amyotrophic lateral sclerosis; myasthenia gravis; Guillain-Barré syndrome

- Muscle imaging with ultrasonography or MRI can identify promising sites for biopsy, and the pattern of muscle involvement can aid in the diagnosis of patients with inflammatory myopathies.
- Electromyography with nerve conduction study can demonstrate the presence of inflammatory myositis and can exclude neuropathic disease.
- Muscle biopsy is the gold standard for diagnosing the idiopathic inflammatory myopathies; results show a predominantly lymphocytic muscle infiltration with evidence of necrosis and regeneration.

Treatment

Initial therapy for polymyositis and dermatomyositis is high-dose corticosteroids, usually at a dose of 1 mg/kg. Therapy is generally continued until serum creatine kinase levels normalize with a slow taper thereafter; clinical symptoms are slower to improve. Proximal weakness that develops after prolonged corticosteroid therapy with normal muscle enzymes suggests corticosteroid-induced myopathy. Immunosuppressive therapy, primarily with methotrexate and azathioprine, is used for corticosteroid-resistant disease and for corticosteroid-sparing; it is also used in poor prognosis groups or in patients with severe extramuscular disease such as ILD. Intravenous immune globulin may also induce and maintain remission for resistant disease or for patients with frequent infectious complications. Physical therapy is important to maintain muscle strength. Dermatomyositis rash may respond to hydroxychloroquine and topical corticosteroids or tacrolimus; sunscreen is an important adjunct therapy. IBM is generally resistant to treatment, although the rate of deterioration may be slowed in some patients with corticosteroids or intravenous immune globulin.

Association with Malignancy

Malignancy is strongly associated with the idiopathic inflammatory myopathies, particularly dermatomyositis; screening for occult malignancy is mandatory in adults with these diseases. Cancer has been identified in 30% of patients with dermatomyositis and 15% of patients with polymyositis, with 60% of malignancies presenting after diagnosis of myositis. The standardized incidence ratios of malignancy in dermatomyositis are 3.0 to 6.2, and in polymyositis, 1.4 to 2.0. The risk of cancer in IBM appears similar to that in polymyositis. Most cancers are detected within 1 year of inflammatory myopathy diagnosis. The most common types of malignancy are adenocarcinomas, with ovarian cancer especially common. Factors associated with underlying malignancy include older age, rapid onset, skin necrosis, periungual erythema, low C4 levels, and low lymphocyte counts. Assessment for cancer should be age- and sex-appropriate, including urinalysis, chest radiography, colonoscopy, prostate-specific antigen in men, and gynecologic

examination with Pap testing and CA-125 in women. Additional testing usually includes pelvic ultrasonography or CT to exclude ovarian cancer. CT of the chest, abdomen, and pelvis is often performed in patients at high risk for cancer. Whole body PET/CT has compared favorably with conventional cancer screening in a recent study.

Prognosis

Survival rates for patients with dermatomyositis and polymyositis have improved over the past 40 years, from a 5-year survival rate of 65% to 75%, to 95% in recent studies; the standard mortality ratio for polymyositis and dermatomyositis is 3.0. Prognosis varies depending on the clinical subset of the myopathy and the presence of underlying malignancy. Survival in patients with IBM appears to be longer than for polymyositis and dermatomyositis. The most common causes of death in patients with idiopathic inflammatory myopathies are malignancies, infections (particularly aspiration pneumonia), profound muscle weakness, cardiovascular disease, and respiratory failure. Overall, the most important predictor of mortality is age, with worsening prognosis with older age at onset. Men as well as black and Hispanic persons also have a poorer prognosis.

KEY POINTS

- Initial treatment for dermatomyositis and polymyositis is high-dose corticosteroids, and physical therapy is important to maintain muscle strength.
- Inclusion body myositis is generally resistant to treatment, although the rate of deterioration may be slowed in some patients with corticosteroids or intravenous immune globulin.
- Screening for occult malignancy is mandatory in adults who are diagnosed with inflammatory myopathies.
- The most important predictor of mortality in inflammatory myopathy is age, with worsening prognosis with older age at onset.

Systemic Vasculitis

Vasculitis is an inflammation of blood vessel walls that causes vessel narrowing, occlusion, aneurysm, or rupture. Several disorders may impact the vasculature in a similar fashion and are important to consider in the differential diagnosis (**Table 32**). Patients with vasculitis frequently have constitutional symptoms and manifestations reflecting inflammation and ischemia in the affected organ(s). The approach to and categorization of vasculitis are based on the caliber of vessels predominantly involved in the primary forms of vasculitis (**Table 33**) as well as the presence of potential infectious triggers, inciting medications, or other underlying autoimmune disorders (**Table 34**).

TABLE 32. Differential Diagnosis of Vasculitis

Disease	Characteristics
Infection (sepsis, endocarditis, hepatitis)	Heart murmur, rash, and/or musculoskeletal symptoms can occur in bacterial endocarditis or viral hepatitis. Obtain blood cultures, hepatitis B and C serologic studies, and an echocardiogram.
Drug toxicity/poisoning	Cocaine, amphetamines, ephedra alkaloids, and phenylpropanolamine may produce vasospasm, resulting in symptoms of ischemia. Perform toxicology screen.
Coagulopathy	Occlusive diseases (disseminated intravascular coagulation, antiphospholipid syndrome, thrombotic thrombocytopenic purpura) can produce ischemic symptoms. Perform coagulation panel and test for hypercoagulability.
Malignancy	Paraneoplastic vasculitis is rare. Any organ system may be affected, but the skin and nervous system are the most common. Vasculitic symptoms may precede, occur simultaneously with, or follow diagnosis of cancer. Lymphoma occasionally may involve the blood vessels and mimic vasculitis. Consider malignancy in patients with incomplete or no response to therapy for idiopathic vasculitis.
Atrial myxoma	Classic triad of symptoms: embolism, intracardiac obstruction leading to pulmonary congestion or congestive heart failure, and constitutional symptoms (fatigue, weight loss, fever). Skin lesions can be identical to those seen in leukocytoclastic vasculitis. Atrial myxomas are rare, but they are the most common primary intracardiac tumor. Myxomas also can occur in other cardiac chambers.
Multiple cholesterol emboli	Typically seen in patients with severe atherosclerosis. Embolization may occur after abdominal trauma, aortic surgery, or angiography. May also occur after heparin, warfarin, or thrombolytic therapy. Patients may have livedo reticularis, petechiae and purpuric lesions, and localized skin necrosis.

TABLE 33. Primary Vasculitic Diseases

Condition	Characteristics
Large-Vessel Vasculitis	
Giant cell arteritis	Headache, visual abnormalities, jaw claudication, constitutional symptoms, polymyalgia rheumatica
Polymyalgia rheumatica	Aching in the shoulders, neck, and hip girdle region; fatigue, malaise
Takayasu arteritis	An inflammatory phase characterized by fever, arthralgias, myalgias, malaise, weight loss; a pulseless phase characterized by arm or leg claudication, hypertension, headache
Medium-Sized Vessel Vasculitis	
Polyarteritis nodosa	Mononeuritis multiplex, hypertension, testicular pain, abdominal pain, arthralgias, fever, weight loss; cutaneous, renal, mesenteric, or nerve involvement
Kawasaki disease	Fever, conjunctivitis, erythema of the oral mucous membranes, erythema or edema of the extremities, cervical lymphadenopathy, coronary aneurysms; occurs in children
Small-Vessel Vasculitis	
Granulomatosis with polyangiitis (also known as Wegener granulomatosis)	Upper-airway disease (sinusitis, epistaxis), mononeuritis multiplex, c-ANCA positivity; pulmonary, ocular, or renal disease
Microscopic polyangiitis	Renal or pulmonary involvement, fever, arthralgias, purpura, mononeuritis multiplex, p-ANCA positivity
Churg-Strauss syndrome	Asthma, rhinitis, sinusitis, migratory pulmonary infiltrates, mononeuritis multiplex, purpura, fever, arthralgias, myalgias; cardiac, renal, or gastrointestinal involvement; 50% of affected patients have positive titers of p-ANCA
Henoch-Schönlein purpura	Purpura, abdominal pain, kidney disease, arthritis; occurs more frequently in children
Essential cryoglobulinemic vasculitis	Purpura, arthralgias, lymphadenopathy, hepatosplenomegaly, kidney disease, mononeuritis multiplex, hypocomplementemia; associated with hepatitis C virus infection
Cutaneous leukocytoclastic vasculitis	Palpable purpura; occurs in patients with connective tissue diseases and as a reaction to drugs or viruses

TABLE 34. Causes of Secondary Vasculitis
Medications
Antimicrobial agents
Vaccines
Antithyroid agents
Anticonvulsant agents
Antiarrhythmic agents
Diuretics
Other cardiovascular drugs
Anticoagulants
Antineoplastic agents
Hematopoietic growth factors
NSAIDs
Leukotriene inhibitors
Psychotropic drugs
Sympathomimetic agents
Allopurinol
Tumor necrosis factor modulatory agents
Interferon alfa
Infections
Hepatitis A, B, and C virus
HIV
Bacterial endocarditis
Parvovirus B19
Neoplasms
Hairy cell leukemia (associated with polyarteritis nodosa)
Other hematologic and solid malignancies
Autoimmune Diseases
Systemic lupus erythematosus
Rheumatoid arthritis
Sjögren syndrome
Inflammatory myopathies
Systemic sclerosis
Relapsing polychondritis
Inflammatory bowel disease
Primary biliary cirrhosis

Large-Vessel Vasculitis

Giant Cell Arteritis

Pathophysiology and Epidemiology

Giant cell arteritis (GCA), also known as temporal arteritis, affects large-caliber vessels that contain internal elastic membranes. In addition to affecting the extracranial arteries of the head and neck, GCA can also involve the thoracic aorta and its major branch vessels; intracranial vessels are rarely affected. Arterial lesions of GCA are characterized by a transmural lymphocytic infiltrate in the vessel wall with disruption of the internal elastic lamina. Although not uniformly present on a given tissue section, multinucleated giant cells within the vessel wall or adventitia are characteristic features. GCA occurs in patients older than 50 years and most commonly affects women (2:1 ratio).

Clinical Manifestations and Diagnosis

Patients with GCA usually have constitutional features, including fever and fatigue; therefore, GCA should be considered in the differential diagnosis of fever of unknown origin or new-onset headache in patients over the age of 50 years. Symptoms of polymyalgia rheumatica with stiffness and pain referable to the hip and shoulder girdle may be the predominant presenting clinical feature. Cranial vessel involvement includes jaw claudication (due to ischemia of the masseter or temporalis muscles), scalp tenderness, and temporal or occipital headache. Inflammation of the ophthalmic artery may cause ischemia of the optic nerve, resulting in visual loss. Involvement of the subclavian vessels may result in upper extremity limb claudication or subclavian steal syndrome. Aortic valve regurgitation may occur with GCA involvement of the proximal ascending aorta.

Physical findings include tenderness and thickening over involved temporal arteries. Involvement of the carotid or subclavian vessels may manifest as audible bruits in the neck or supraclavicular fossa, respectively. Subclavian artery lesions may be associated with attenuation of the ipsilateral radial pulse and a differential systolic blood pressure measured in the ipsilateral/contralateral arms. Typical laboratory findings include a markedly elevated erythrocyte sedimentation rate (ESR) and C-reactive protein (CRP) level. Anemia and thrombocytosis are often present.

Diagnosis of GCA is best established by demonstration of the characteristic histologic lesions within sections of biopsied temporal arteries. Skip lesions are common, and multiple sections of the artery should be analyzed to increase the diagnostic yield of a given temporal artery biopsy. Occasionally, it is necessary to undertake a second contralateral biopsy to establish the presence of suspected GCA. Diagnosis is sometimes made clinically in patients with a highly characteristic presentation, elevated acute phase reactants, and prompt response to treatment.

Imaging of the aortic arch and major branch vessels with CT angiography or MR angiography is indicated when symptoms referable to the cranial arteries are absent, the temporal artery biopsy is negative, or physical findings implicate involvement of the carotid or subclavian vessels. Fusiform luminal narrowing of the carotid, innominate, or subclavian arteries characteristic of GCA may be sufficient to establish the diagnosis.

Management

GCA symptoms respond rapidly to corticosteroids (1 mg/kg/d of prednisone); this rapid response to treatment can be helpful diagnostically. Treatment is indicated immediately in patients clinically suspected of having GCA and should not await results of a temporal artery biopsy. Biopsy findings do not change significantly for at least 4 weeks after corticosteroids are instituted, and prompt treatment is necessary to avoid the development of visual loss.

In most patients, tapering of prednisone is initiated after 4 to 6 weeks, typically performed in 10% decrements every 2 weeks and guided by patient symptoms, ESR, and CRP. Flares commonly occur during tapering and are best managed by increasing the dose of prednisone by 10 mg over the dose that previously controlled the disease. For patients who repeatedly experience flares during prednisone tapering, corticosteroid-sparing immunosuppressive agents, including methotrexate, azathioprine, and mycophenolate mofetil, can be used but are not of proven efficacy.

Low-dose aspirin therapy can minimize the risk of cerebral ischemic events. Patients should be followed expectantly for aortic complications such as aneurysm.

Polymyalgia Rheumatica

Polymyalgia rheumatica is characterized by pain and stiffness in the proximal limbs associated with elevated levels of acute phase reactants. This disorder is associated with GCA and is considered to be in the same spectrum of diseases. Some patients who have polymyalgia rheumatica symptoms ultimately prove to have elderly-onset rheumatoid arthritis.

Clinical Manifestations and Diagnosis

Polymyalgia rheumatica symptoms include pain, stiffness, and limitation in the range of motion of the shoulder and hip girdle muscles. Onset may be insidious or abrupt and accompanied by constitutional symptoms such as fatigue or fever. Physical findings include tenderness over the shoulder girdle musculature and limitation in passive movement of the shoulder or hip joints. Peripheral joint swelling is not observed at onset; this type of swelling should prompt consideration of rheumatoid arthritis as an alternative diagnosis. Laboratory studies reflecting the presence of an acute phase response include elevation in ESR or CRP levels. A mild normochromic normocytic anemia may occur depending on syndrome duration.

Management

Relatively low doses of corticosteroids (primarily prednisone) are used to treat polymyalgia rheumatica symptoms. Corticosteroids can be tapered over a 6-month period in some patients, but others experience flares with tapering and require more prolonged therapy. Methotrexate can be used as a corticosteroid-sparing agent.

Takayasu Arteritis

Pathophysiology and Epidemiology

Takayasu arteritis affects the aorta and its major branches as well as the pulmonary arteries. Histologically, the lesions are similar to those that occur in GCA, with a lymphoplasmacytic and granulomatous infiltrate extending through the vessel wall. There is a female predominance (8:1 ratio), and onset typically occurs between the second and fourth decades.

Clinical Manifestations and Diagnosis

The initial inflammatory phase of Takayasu arteritis is characterized by low-grade fever, fatigue, and malaise with varying degrees of myalgia and arthralgia that may persist for months. The ESR and CRP levels are significantly elevated, and affected patients may experience weight loss. During the early phase, physical findings may include bruits audible over involved carotid, subclavian, renal, or iliac vessels. With more prolonged disease duration, the pulseless phase of the disease evolves, and symptoms of vascular insufficiency such as upper or lower extremity claudication appear. Hypertension may develop as a consequence of renal artery stenosis. Differential systolic blood pressures and pulse deficits in the extremities are apparent on physical examination. In the pulseless, noninflammatory phase, acute phase reactants may be normal.

Diagnosis is established by the demonstration of characteristic narrowing of the aorta or its major branch vessels. Imaging of the entire aorta and major branch vessels using angiography, CT angiography, or MR angiography is indicated in suspected cases (**Figure 32**). The entire aorta may be

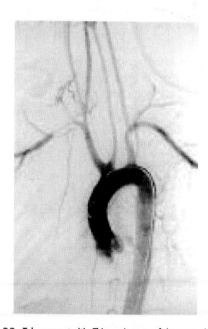

FIGURE 32. Takayasu arteritis. This angiogram of the aorta demonstrates high-grade stenosis of the proximal right subclavian artery as well as the left subclavian artery just below the origin of the left vertebral artery. Incidentally noted is anatomic variation with a common origin of the right brachiocephalic artery and the left common carotid artery.

CONT.

narrowed; branch vessel stenoses typically occur at points adjacent to their origin.

Management

During the inflammatory phase of Takayasu arteritis, high-dose corticosteroids are effective in suppressing vessel inflammation and in resolving accompanying constitutional symptoms. Case series support a role for weekly methotrexate or tumor necrosis factor (TNF)-α inhibitors as corticosteroid-sparing agents; daily oral cyclophosphamide is used for patients with severe or refractory disease. Difficulties in management may arise when the diagnosis is first established in the advanced pulseless stage, because active vessel inflammation may be absent. In such patients, gadolinium-contrast MRI studies and PET scans have been used to determine if inflammation is present in areas of demonstrated stenosis.

Management of vascular insufficiency due to fixed arterial narrowing may require operative revascularization, best undertaken after inflammation in the involved vessels has been controlled. Low-dose aspirin and treatment of any noted elevation in lipid levels are important to minimize complications of premature atherosclerosis that may evolve in affected vessels. **H**

KEY POINTS

- Treatment is indicated immediately in patients clinically suspected of having giant cell arteritis rather than awaiting results of a temporal artery biopsy because of the risk of visual loss.
- Relatively low doses of corticosteroids (primarily prednisone) are used to treat polymyalgia rheumatica symptoms.
- Takayasu arteritis affects the aorta and its major branches as well as pulmonary arteries and typically affects younger women.
- Imaging of the entire aorta and its major branch vessels using angiography, CT angiography, or MR angiography is indicated in patients with suspected Takayasu arteritis.

Medium-Sized Vessel Vasculitis
Polyarteritis Nodosa

Pathophysiology and Epidemiology

Polyarteritis nodosa is characterized by inflammation and necrosis of medium-sized and small muscular artery walls. The inflammatory infiltrates consist of neutrophils and mononuclear cells that invade the vessel wall. Peak age of onset is between 40 and 60 years. Up to 50% of cases occur in the setting of recently acquired hepatitis B virus infection, a more prevalent association in younger patients presenting with polyarteritis nodosa.

Clinical Manifestations and Diagnosis

Patients with polyarteritis nodosa typically present with fever, arthralgia, myalgia, abdominal pain, and weight loss. Most patients have peripheral nerve manifestations, most commonly mononeuropathy or mononeuritis multiplex. Up to one third of patients have renal arteriolar involvement, which presents as renovascular hypertension; glomerulonephritis is not seen. Other presenting features include testicular pain, painful cutaneous nodules, skin ulcers, palpable purpura, and livedo reticularis. There is occasional involvement of the coronary arteries. Polyarteritis nodosa rarely involves the central nervous system or pulmonary vessels. Anemia, leukocytosis, thrombocytosis, and elevation in ESR are typically present.

Diagnosis is best established by the demonstration of necrotizing arteritis in biopsy specimens or characteristic medium-sized artery aneurysms and stenoses on imaging studies of mesenteric or renal arteries using either angiography or CT angiography. Highest yield biopsies are obtained from involved skin, symptomatic muscles, or the sural nerve (when potential involvement is confirmed by abnormal nerve conduction studies). The kidneys should not be biopsied, because the procedure can result in hemorrhage from renal arteriolar aneurysms.

Management

Most patients respond to treatment with high-dose corticosteroids (the equivalent of 1 mg/kg/d of prednisone). Following several weeks of treatment, the dose can be slowly tapered if clinical and laboratory signs of inflammation have abated. Cyclophosphamide is indicated for patients who do not respond to corticosteroids or have significant kidney, gastrointestinal, cardiac, or neurologic involvement. In patients with hepatitis B–associated polyarteritis nodosa, a short course (1 to 2 weeks) of corticosteroids should be given concomitantly with antiviral therapy (such as entecavir). Using this approach, more than 50% of patients with hepatitis B e antigen–positive polyarteritis nodosa respond with resolution of the arteritis as well as seroconversion to anti–hepatitis B e antibody positivity.

Kawasaki Disease

Kawasaki disease is a systemic vasculitis involving medium-sized to small arteries that occurs in children, although there are case reports of the disease occurring in adults with HIV infection.

Clinical Manifestations and Diagnosis

Typical initial presenting features are fever with nonexudative conjunctivitis, pleomorphic erythematous rash, and oral mucositis. Other clinical features include cervical lymphadenopathy and an oligoarticular or polyarticular inflammatory arthritis. Laboratory abnormalities include anemia, leukocytosis, thrombocytosis, and sterile pyuria.

CONT.

As the syndrome evolves, the rash desquamates, initially in the periungual areas and then proximally over the hands and feet. Acute coronary syndrome or peripheral vascular occlusion events may also occur as a consequence of medium-sized artery inflammation. Coronary artery aneurysms occur less commonly in adults than in children with Kawasaki disease.

Management

High-dose salicylates and early administration of intravenous immune globulin are the recommended treatment; corticosteroids are used for those who do not respond to this regimen. Evaluation with echocardiography following resolution is indicated to ascertain whether coronary artery aneurysms have developed. **H**

KEY POINTS

- Up to 50% of cases of polyarteritis nodosa occur in the setting of recently acquired hepatitis B virus infection.

- Patients with polyarteritis nodosa typically present with fever, arthralgia, myalgia, abdominal pain, weight loss, and peripheral neuropathy.

- Diagnosis of polyarteritis nodosa can be established by biopsy of the skin, muscle, or sural nerve that demonstrates neutrophils and monocytes invading the vessel walls.

- Most patients with polyarteritis nodosa respond to treatment with high-dose corticosteroids (the equivalent of 1 mg/kg/d of prednisone); cyclophosphamide is indicated for patients who do not respond to corticosteroids or have significant kidney, gastrointestinal, cardiac, or neurologic involvement.

- Kawasaki disease is a systemic vasculitis involving medium-sized to small arteries that occurs in children and some adults with HIV infection and responds to high-dose salicylates and early administration of intravenous immune globulin.

H Small-Vessel Vasculitis

Antineutrophil Cytoplasmic Antibodies and Associated Vasculitis

The ANCA-associated vasculitides include granulomatosis with polyangiitis (also known as Wegener granulomatosis), microscopic polyangiitis, and Churg-Strauss syndrome. These disorders involve small to medium-sized arteries and may be associated with a "pauci-immune" (lacking immune complexes) glomerulonephritis.

ANCA are present in most patients with these disorders and may be pathogenic. A cytoplasmic immunofluorescence pattern of c-ANCA generally reflects antibodies to serine proteinase-3 and is highly sensitive and specific for granulomatosis with polyangiitis. p-ANCA can be seen in the presence of antibodies to myeloperoxidase or to other antigens. Anti-myeloperoxidase antibodies are associated with microscopic polyangiitis and Churg-Strauss syndrome. p-ANCA antibodies are also present in other conditions such as inflammatory bowel disease.

Granulomatosis with Polyangiitis

Clinical Manifestations and Diagnosis

Granulomatosis with polyangiitis is a systemic necrotizing vasculitis that predominantly affects the upper and lower respiratory tract and kidneys. More than 70% of patients have upper airway manifestations such as sinusitis or nasal, inner ear, or laryngotracheal inflammation. The disease is highly destructive if untreated, potentially resulting in cartilage erosion with nasal septal perforation and saddle nose deformity.

Ocular involvement includes scleritis, uveitis, keratitis, and inflammatory retro-orbital pseudotumor with extraocular muscle dysfunction and proptosis. Purpura and ulcers are common skin manifestations. Mononeuritis multiplex may also occur.

Pulmonary manifestations can present as cough, hemoptysis, and pleurisy. Characteristic radiographic findings include multifocal infiltrates or nodules, some of which may cavitate; diffuse opacities are seen in patients with pulmonary hemorrhage (**Figure 33**).

Pauci-immune glomerulonephritis occurs in up to 80% of patients. Although glomerulonephritis may be the presenting

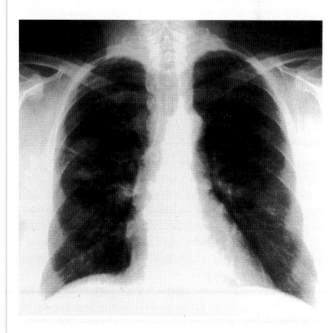

FIGURE 33. Radiograph showing pulmonary nodules in a patient with granulomatosis with polyangiitis (also known as Wegener granulomatosis).

Reprinted with permission from Yee AMF and Paget SA, eds. Expert Guide to Rheumatology. Philadelphia: American College of Physicians; 2004.

CONT.

manifestation, it is most often preceded by respiratory tract manifestations.

Diagnosis is best established by lung or kidney biopsy. Diagnostic lung tissue findings include the presence of vasculitis, acute and chronic inflammation, and sometimes the presence of granulomas. Although biopsy of sinus or tracheal tissue may reveal evidence of inflammation, the diagnostic yield of these procedures is very low. The characteristic kidney lesion is a necrotizing focal segmental or diffuse glomerulonephritis without significant immune deposits. The presence of antiproteinase-3 antibodies is sufficient to establish a diagnosis in patients with classic upper airway manifestations, pulmonary infiltrates/nodules, and urinary abnormalities consistent with glomerulonephritis. Biopsy is often required in patients with less classic presentations.

Management

Initial treatment consists of high-dose corticosteroids accompanied by a 3- to 6-month course of oral cyclophosphamide. Biweekly intravenous cyclophosphamide can be used as an alternative to daily oral dosing, although the relapse rate may be higher. B-cell depletion therapy with rituximab has been shown in a randomized trial to be equally as efficacious as cyclophosphamide in treating initial disease manifestations or disease relapses.

Following remission using any of these approaches, corticosteroid therapy is tapered off, cyclophosphamide is stopped, and treatment is continued an additional 18 months with azathioprine or weekly methotrexate. Up to 90% of patients achieve remission, but relapses are frequent. Relapse rates are higher when methotrexate is used to induce remission, and this use is usually reserved for patients with disease confined to the upper airways. Trimethoprim-sulfamethoxazole given every other day can minimize the occurrence of opportunistic *Pneumocystis* infection and may prevent disease relapse by inhibiting potential flares triggered by bacterial infection.

Microscopic Polyangiitis

Clinical Manifestations and Diagnosis

Microscopic polyangiitis is a necrotizing vasculitis that predominantly affects the lungs and kidneys. Patients of any age may be affected, but peak incidence occurs between 30 and 50 years. Patients frequently present with rapidly progressive glomerulonephritis or pulmonary hemorrhage. Other manifestations include fever, arthralgia, purpuric skin rash, and mononeuritis multiplex.

Antimyeloperoxidase antibodies are present in 60% to 85% of patients. Given the lack of sensitivity and specificity of p-ANCA and antimyeloperoxidase antibody tests, diagnosis is best confirmed with biopsy of the affected skin, lung, or kidney. Lung biopsy reveals a necrotizing small-vessel vasculitis or pulmonary capillaritis. Kidney biopsy reveals pauci-immune focal or diffuse necrotizing glomerulonephritis

indistinguishable from that seen in granulomatosis with polyangiitis. The skin biopsy may reveal necrotizing arteritis of small arterioles in the dermis.

Management

Treatment is the same as for granulomatosis with polyangiitis. High-dose corticosteroids plus either cyclophosphamide or rituximab should be given to induce remission. After the disease is suppressed, patients treated with cyclophosphamide should be transitioned to azathioprine or weekly methotrexate. However, vigilance for disease reactivation is important given the high frequency of relapse.

Churg-Strauss Syndrome

Clinical Manifestations and Diagnosis

Churg-Strauss syndrome is a systemic vasculitis in the spectrum of hypereosinophilic disorders that most often occurs in the setting of antecedent asthma, allergic rhinitis, or sinusitis. Patients typically present with significant eosinophilia (>10%), migratory pulmonary infiltrates, purpuric skin rash, and mononeuritis multiplex; fever, arthralgia, and myalgia are also common presenting features. Cardiac involvement with eosinophilic cardiomyopathy, gastrointestinal lesions, and glomerulonephritis is less common, although cardiac disease accounts for more than 50% of reported mortality. The kidney lesion in Churg-Strauss syndrome is a necrotizing pauci-immune glomerulopathy.

Diagnosis is usually established by biopsy-confirmed eosinophilic tissue infiltration or necrotizing small-vessel vasculitis involving small arteries or veins. Only 40% of patients are positive for p-ANCA at the time of diagnosis, usually with specificity for myeloperoxidase. Patients who are positive for p-ANCA usually have manifestations of vasculitis such as glomerulonephritis and mononeuritis multiplex, whereas those who are negative for p-ANCA experience more eosinophilic infiltrative disease such as pneumonitis and cardiomyopathy.

Management

Most patients respond quickly to high-dose corticosteroids, and 80% to 90% of patients achieve full remission. Oral or intravenous cyclophosphamide is also recommended for patients with neurologic, gastrointestinal, kidney, or cardiac involvement. Relapses are frequent, and maintenance therapy with azathioprine or methotrexate is recommended for an additional 12 to 18 months following remission. **H**

KEY POINTS

- Granulomatosis with polyangiitis (also known as Wegener granulomatosis) predominantly affects the upper and lower respiratory tract and kidneys and is associated with antiproteinase-3 antibodies (c-ANCA).

- The presence of antiproteinase-3 antibodies (c-ANCA) is sufficient to establish a diagnosis of granulomatosis with polyangiitis in patients with classic presentations; however, biopsy of the lung or kidney may be required in patients with atypical presentations.
- Microscopic polyangiitis predominantly affects the lungs and kidneys and is associated with antibodies to myeloperoxidase (p-ANCA).
- High-dose corticosteroid therapy accompanied by a 3- to 6-month course of cyclophosphamide or corticosteroids plus rituximab is used to induce remission of granulomatosis with polyangiitis and microscopic polyangiitis.
- Churg-Strauss syndrome is associated with eosinophilia and typically occurs in the setting of antecedent rhinitis, sinusitis, or asthma.

Cryoglobulinemic Vasculitis

Pathophysiology

Cryoglobulins are immunoglobulins that precipitate from serum in the cold. Type I cryoglobulins are monoclonal immunoglobulins that self-aggregate and are associated with Waldenstrom macroglobulinemia and multiple myeloma; they may also be seen in patients with Sjögren syndrome or B-cell lymphoma who develop monoclonal paraproteins. Type I cryoglobulins may be associated with vasculitis and nephritis but are more commonly associated with hyperviscosity syndromes.

Type II cryoglobulins are rheumatoid factors that are monoclonal IgM or IgA immunoglobulins with specificity for the Fc portion of IgG; this subtype is most often associated with vasculitis and most commonly occurs in the setting of viral infections with hepatitis C or HIV. Type III cryoglobulins are polyclonal rheumatoid factors; vasculitis associated with type III cryoglobulins is most often seen in the setting of autoimmune disorders such as systemic lupus erythematosus, Sjögren syndrome (in the absence of associated monoclonal paraprotein), or rheumatoid arthritis.

Attention to appropriate specimen handling is critical to detecting the presence of circulating cryoglobulins, including collecting the blood in prewarmed tubes without anticoagulant and allowing blood to clot at 37.0 °C (98.6 °F) before and during centrifugation.

Clinical Manifestations and Diagnosis

Cutaneous purpura, mononeuritis multiplex, and an immune complex glomerulonephritis are the primary presenting features of cryoglobulinemic vasculitis. Serum levels of C3 and C4 are usually low. Although only 5% of patients with hepatitis C infection develop a cryoglobulin-associated syndrome, more than 80% of patients with type II cryoglobulin syndromes have active infection with hepatitis C.

Management

Most patients with hepatitis C–associated cryoglobulinemia respond to antiviral therapy with interferon alfa and ribavirin. A short course of corticosteroids may be required to suppress the acute phase of inflammation and vasculitis. For patients with severe manifestations, including kidney failure, digital gangrene, and severe neurologic disease, a 2- to 3-week course of plasma exchange is employed. In patients with refractory disease or in whom antiviral therapy is not feasible or tolerated, a course of B-cell depletion treatment with rituximab may be of benefit. A similar treatment strategy is undertaken in patients with cryoglobulinemic vasculitis not associated with hepatitis C or hepatitis B infection, employing cyclophosphamide in lieu of antiviral therapy.

Henoch-Schönlein Purpura

Clinical Manifestations and Diagnosis

Although Henoch-Schönlein purpura most commonly occurs in children, the syndrome may affect adults with greater severity. Presenting features include a purpuric rash predominantly affecting the distal lower extremities, arthritis, abdominal pain, and hematuria. Attacks are usually self-limited and resolve in several weeks, although a subset of patients experience persistent progressive kidney disease. Onset in men over the age of 50 years is commonly associated with solid tumors or myelodysplastic syndrome.

Skin biopsy specimens reveal the presence of leukocytoclastic vasculitis with deposits of IgA demonstrated on immunofluorescent studies. Kidney biopsies obtained in patients with persistent hematuria and proteinuria or kidney disease following attacks of Henoch-Schönlein purpura reveal a glomerulonephritis with IgA deposition consistent with lesions seen in patients with IgA nephropathy. The kidney disease may be aggressive in some patients with transition to diffuse proliferative glomerulonephritis.

Management

A short course of moderate-dose corticosteroids (20- to 40-mg/d prednisone) may decrease the duration and severity of skin and joint symptoms associated with attacks of Henoch-Schönlein purpura. Although corticosteroids have little impact on the development and progression of associated IgA nephropathy, patients with proliferative glomerulonephritis may respond to high-dose corticosteroids and monthly cyclophosphamide. Evaluation for underlying malignancy is indicated for patients who are over the age of 50 years, particularly men.

Cutaneous Leukocytoclastic Vasculitis

Clinical Manifestations and Diagnosis

Leukocytoclastic vasculitis involving the skin presents as palpable purpura, tender nodules, persistent urticaria, or shallow ulcers (**Figure 34**). Lesions most commonly manifest on the distal lower extremities. Biopsy specimens reveal neutrophils

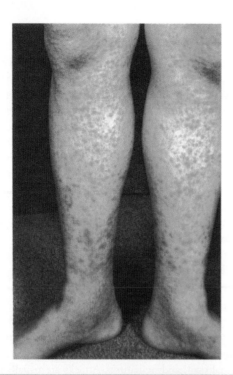

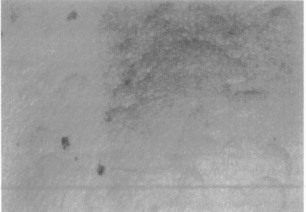

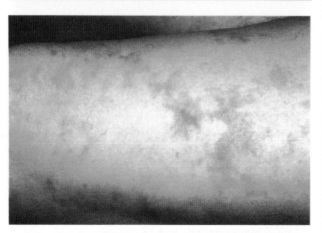

FIGURE 34. Dermatologic manifestations of cutaneous leukocytoclastic vasculitis. The top panel shows palpable purpura, the center panel shows urticaria, and the bottom panel shows livedo reticularis.

Reprinted with permission from Alguire PA. Internal Medicine Essentials for Clerkship Students 2. Philadelphia: American College of Physicians; 2009.

and mononuclear cells invading the walls of dermal capillaries, arterioles, and venules with characteristic nuclear fragments (dust). The differential diagnosis for leukocytoclastic vasculitis is broad, with approximately 40% of cases rendered idiopathic but the remaining 60% of cases associated with an identifiable autoimmune disease (most often systemic lupus erythematosus), offending drugs, antecedent/intercurrent infection, hematologic malignancy, or systemic vasculitis (see Table 34).

Management

Removal of offending drugs or treatment of the triggering infectious cause may be sufficient treatment. Symptomatic and persistent leukocytoclastic vasculitis from any cause may respond favorably to NSAIDs, colchicine, or dapsone. Urticarial lesions are best managed with antihistamines combining H1 and H2 blocking agents. Urticarial vasculitis is a frequent cutaneous complication of lupus, and patients with persistent urticarial vasculitis who have high titers of antinuclear antibodies and/or other clinical features of lupus respond favorably to treatment with hydroxychloroquine. Low to moderate doses of corticosteroids can be used when these agents prove ineffective, with use of corticosteroid-sparing agents such as weekly methotrexate or azathioprine for patients with corticosteroid-dependent lesions. **H**

KEY POINTS

- Vasculitis due to cryoglobulins is most often associated with type II cryoglobulins in the setting of viral infection with hepatitis C or HIV.

- Although only 5% of patients with hepatitis C infection develop a cryoglobulin-associated syndrome, more than 80% of patients with type II cryoglobulin syndromes have active infection with hepatitis C.

- Henoch-Schönlein purpura is characterized by purpuric rash, arthritis, abdominal pain, and hematuria and may be associated with malignancy in patients over the age of 50 years.

- Approximately 60% of cases of leukocytoclastic vasculitis are associated with an identifiable autoimmune disease (most often systemic lupus erythematosus), offending drugs, antecedent/intercurrent infection, hematologic malignancy, or systemic vasculitis; the remaining 40% are idiopathic.

Other Systemic Inflammatory Diseases

Behçet Disease

Behçet disease is characterized by oral and genital ulcerations; uveitis; skin lesions; articular, gastrointestinal, and nervous system involvement; and vasculitis. Biopsy specimens reveal neutrophil and mononuclear cell infiltration of involved tissues, small-vessel vasculitis, venulitis, and thrombosis. This disease is associated with HLA-B51, which imparts a five-fold increased risk. There is an increased prevalence of Behçet disease in persons living along the Silk Road (from Asia to the Mediterranean Sea), most likely related to a high background prevalence of HLA-B51 among these populations. There are 80 to 370 cases per 100,000 persons in Turkey but only 0.12 to 0.33 cases per 100,000 persons in the United States. Peak age of onset is between 20 and 40 years. Mortality is associated with male gender, early age of onset, frequent disease flares, and arterial involvement.

Clinical Manifestations and Diagnosis

Nonscarring oral ulcers on the mucous membranes or tongue are often the presenting symptom of Behçet disease (**Figure 35**). Genital ulcers are deep, painful, and scarring (**Figure 36**). Ocular disease can manifest as posterior or anterior uveitis and can result in blindness. Skin manifestations include erythema nodosum, pseudofolliculitis, acneiform nodules, superficial migratory thrombophlebitis, and pathergy, in which a pustule-like lesion or papule appears 48 hours after skin prick by a 20- to 21-gauge needle. Oligoarthritis occurs in 50% of patients. Intestinal lesions can be indistinguishable from those of ulcerative colitis.

Behçet disease of the central nervous system involves the brainstem, basal ganglia, or cerebral white matter. Involvement of the vasa vasorum may result in large-vessel aneurysms that can thrombose or rupture. Pulmonary artery aneurysms can manifest as hemoptysis.

Criteria for diagnosis are the presence of recurrent oral ulcerations plus at least two of the following: recurrent genital ulcers, eye lesions, skin lesions, or pathergy without an alternative explanation.

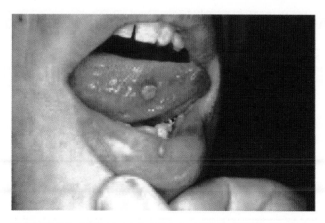

FIGURE 35. Aphthous oral ulcerations in a patient with Behçet disease.

Reprinted with permission from Physician's Information and Education Resource (PIER). Philadelphia: American College of Physicians. Copyright 2012 American College of Physicians.

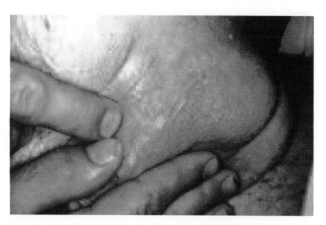

FIGURE 36. Genital ulcerations in a patient with Behçet disease.

Reprinted with permission from Physician's Information and Education Resource (PIER). Philadelphia: American College of Physicians. Copyright 2012 American College of Physicians.

Treatment

Topical corticosteroids, colchicine, or thalidomide can be used to treat mucosal lesions in Behçet disease. Ocular disease is managed with topical, intraocular, or systemic corticosteroids; however, corticosteroids alone do not prevent blindness in patients with retinal vasculitis. Azathioprine, cyclosporine, and cyclophosphamide are used along with corticosteroids for serious ocular or visceral disease. Case series suggest that tumor necrosis factor (TNF)-α inhibitors such as infliximab are effective and are recommended for patients with serious refractory disease.

KEY POINT

- Criteria for the diagnosis of Behçet disease are the presence of recurrent oral ulcerations plus at least two of the following: recurrent genital ulcers, eye lesions, skin lesions, or pathergy without an alternative explanation.

Relapsing Polychondritis

Clinical Manifestations

Relapsing polychondritis is a rare relapsing-remitting inflammatory disorder characterized by chondritis of the ears, nose, and respiratory tract; ocular inflammation; and nonerosive seronegative inflammatory polyarthritis. One third of patients have an associated connective tissue disease, vasculitis, myelodysplastic condition, or malignancy. This disease has an equal male-to-female ratio, and onset is most likely between the ages of 40 and 60 years.

Painful, erythematous swelling of the auricular cartilage occurs in most patients (**Figure 37**). Inflammation of the nasal cartilage occurs in up to 50% of patients. Over time, inflammation may destroy cartilage with loss of structure to the affected organ, leading to cauliflower ear or saddle nose

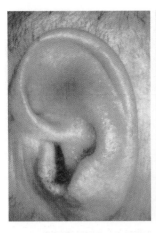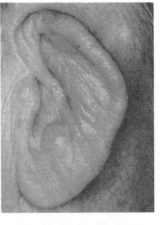

FIGURE 37. Early relapsing polychondritis showing redness and swelling of the auricle (*left panel*). Late relapsing polychondritis showing loss of structural integrity of cartilage, resulting in a floppy ear appearance (*right panel*).

(c) 2012 American College of Rheumatology. Used with permission.

deformity. Ocular involvement is common and can manifest as conjunctivitis, episcleritis, scleritis, uveitis, retinal vasculitis, or proptosis (due to swelling of periorbital structures).

Relapsing polychondritis can also cause laryngotracheal disease, leading to hoarseness or stridor. Musculoskeletal manifestations include inflammation of the parasternal joints or a nonerosive arthritis of peripheral joints. Vasculitis may occur, affecting vessels of any size. Patients may also have aortic and mitral valve insufficiency.

Diagnosis

Diagnosis of relapsing polychondritis can be made by biopsy of the affected cartilage but is not necessary if sufficient clinical criteria are present (**Table 35**). Because respiratory tract involvement is prevalent, pulmonary function testing with flow volume loops is indicated for patients diagnosed with or suspected of having relapsing polychondritis.

Treatment

Mild disease can be managed with NSAIDS, corticosteroids, or dapsone. For organ-threatening involvement or refractory disease, methotrexate, azathioprine, cyclosporine, or cyclophosphamide can be used. Recent case reports suggest a possible role for TNF-α inhibitors.

KEY POINT

- Relapsing polychondritis is characterized by chondritis of the ears, nose, and respiratory tract; ocular inflammation; and nonerosive seronegative inflammatory polyarthritis and is primarily a clinical diagnosis.

Adult-Onset Still Disease

Adult-onset Still disease (AOSD) is characterized by daily spiking fever, evanescent rash, and arthritis. Elevated levels of interleukin (IL)-1, IL-6, IL-18, and TNF-α have been noted in this condition, which shares characteristics with the so-called autoinflammatory diseases (see Familial Autoinflammatory Diseases).

The incidence rate is 0.16 per 100,000 persons in the United States, with a female predominance. AOSD may occur at any age, but peak age of onset is between 16 and 35 years.

Clinical Manifestations

AOSD typically occurs abruptly with high fever, rash, and joint pain (**Table 36**). Fever is quotidian, usually reaching 39.0 °C (102.2 °F), lasting less than 4 hours, and peaking in early evening. An evanescent, salmon-colored rash appears on the trunk and proximal extremities. Arthralgia and arthritis occur in most patients, most commonly in the wrists, knees,

TABLE 35. Diagnostic Criteria for Relapsing Polychondritis		
	Prevalence	
Criteria[a]	**Presentation (%)**	**Total (%)**
Bilateral auricular chondritis	40	85
Nasal chondritis	20	50
Nonerosive seronegative inflammatory polyarthritis	35	50
Ocular inflammation	20	50
Respiratory tract involvement		
Laryngotracheal involvement	26	48
Laryngobronchial involvement	15	23
Hearing loss, tinnitus, or vertigo	9	30

[a]Diagnosis can be made in the presence of three of the above criteria; chondritis at two sites plus a response to corticosteroids or dapsone; or one criteria plus histological confirmation.

With permission from Springer Science+Business Media: Primer on the Rheumatic Diseases, Relapsing Polychondritis, 13 Edition, 2008, page 452, Stone, JH, Crofford LeJ, White PH, table 22-1, Adapted from Isaak BL, Liesegang TJ, Michet CJ Jr. Opthalmology 1986; 93:681-689, by permission of Opthalmology.

TABLE 36. Clinical Manifestations of Adult-Onset Still Disease

Clinical Manifestation	Patients Affected (%)
Fever	82-100
Rash	51-94
Arthralgia	11-100
Arthritis	68-100
Sore throat	35-92
Myalgia	56-84
Lymphadenopathy	32-74
Liver chemistry test abnormalities	50-75
Splenomegaly	14-65
Pleuritis or pericarditis	10-53

CONT.

and ankles, although any joint may be involved. Radiographic changes in the wrist are common, with joint-space narrowing that may progress to ankylosis.

Diagnosis

Diagnosis of AOSD is based on typical clinical presentation with exclusion of infection and malignancy, particularly leukemia and lymphoma. Laboratory abnormalities include leukocytosis, anemia, thrombocytosis, elevated erythrocyte sedimentation rate, and abnormal liver chemistry tests. Serum ferritin levels are particularly elevated (≥1000 ng/mL [1000 µg/L]) and fluctuate with disease activity.

Hemophagocytic syndrome, a potentially deadly complication, may be associated with AOSD and should be suspected in the presence of pancytopenia. Vasculitis and autoinflammatory syndromes may be confused with AOSD. Although some patients may have low-titer antinuclear antibodies, the presence of leukocytosis and the absence of other autoantibodies or hypocomplementemia help to distinguish AOSD from lupus.

Treatment

Treatment is empiric and generally includes corticosteroid therapy. If corticosteroid therapy fails or prolonged corticosteroids are required, immunosuppressive agents (most commonly methotrexate) are introduced. Reports suggest efficacy of IL-1 and IL-6 inhibitors as well as TNF-α inhibitors in refractory cases. Only 15% of patients respond to NSAIDs.

KEY POINTS

- Adult-onset Still disease is characterized by daily spiking fever, rash, arthritis, and elevated serum ferritin levels.

- The clinical diagnosis of Adult-onset Still disease can be made after infection, lymphoma, and leukemia have been ruled out.

Familial Autoinflammatory Diseases

Familial autoinflammatory diseases are inherited systemic disorders characterized by intermittent episodes of fever and other systemic manifestations such as joint pain, abdominal pain, and rash (**Table 37**). These disorders are caused by inherited defects in the innate immune system (the arm of the immune system that provides immediate, but nonspecific, responses to infection). Familial Mediterranean fever is the most common of these diseases, with a prevalence of 1 in 250 to 1 in 1000 among persons of Turkish, Armenian, and Sephardic Jewish descent.

KEY POINTS

- Familial autoinflammatory diseases are inherited systemic disorders characterized by intermittent episodes of fever and other systemic manifestations such as joint pain, abdominal pain, and rash.

- Familial Mediterranean fever is the most common of the familial autoinflammatory diseases, with a prevalence of 1 in 250 to 1 in 1000 among persons of Turkish, Armenian, and Sephardic Jewish descent.

Diseases of Collagen

Osteogenesis Imperfecta

Osteogenesis imperfecta (OI) occurs in 1 per 10,000 births and is most commonly caused by mutations in the gene for type I collagen. The disorder is manifested by brittle bones, blue sclerae, and dentinogenesis imperfecta.

Type I OI is the most common and mildest form, characterized by fractures starting in childhood that decrease in frequency after puberty. Types II and III are severe and result in perinatal death or severe skeletal abnormalities in infancy.

Diagnosis is made by evaluating production of type I collagen by fibroblasts obtained from skin biopsy. Although studies have demonstrated efficacy of cyclical intravenous pamidronate in reducing bone pain and increasing bone mineral mass in children with severe variants of OI, bisphosphonates are not generally used in mildly affected patients.

Ehlers-Danlos Syndrome

Ehlers-Danlos syndrome (EDS) occurs in 1 per 5000 births and is characterized by mutations in the structure, expression, or processing of types I, III, and V collagen. Classic EDS is associated with mutations in the gene for type V collagen and is manifested by smooth, velvety, hyperextensible skin; joint hypermobility; delayed wound healing with atrophic scarring; and easy bruising. Vascular EDS is associated with mutations in the gene for type III collagen and is manifested by arterial fragility and thin, translucent skin. Aneurysms, arteriovenous

TABLE 37.	Familial Autoinflammatory Diseases					
	FMF	**TRAPS**	**HIDS**	**FCAS**	**MWS**	**NOMID**
Inheritance	Autosomal recessive	Autosomal dominant	Autosomal recessive	Autosomal dominant	Autosomal dominant	Autosomal dominant
Age at onset	65% <10 years of age; 90% <20 years of age	50% <10 years of age; up to 5th decade	Usually <5 years of age	<1 year of age	Childhood	Neonatal period
Ethnicity	Mediterranean	All	Northern European	European	European	All
Clinical Manifestations						
Attack (time)	12-72 h	Days to weeks	3-7 days	12-24 h	1-2 days	Progressive
Abdominal	Pain; serositis	Pain; serositis	Pain; vomiting	Nausea	Pain	—
Pleuritis	Common	Common	Rare	—	Rare	Rare
Arthritis	Monoarthritis of lower extremities	Large joints	Symmetric polyarthritis of large joints	Arthralgia	Arthralgia; oligoarthritis	Epiphyseal overgrowth; contractures
Rash	Erysipeloid on lower legs	Migratory with underlying myalgia	Diffuse maculopapular	Cold-induced; urticaria-like	Urticaria-like	Urticaria-like
Other Manifestations	High risk for amyloidosis	Conjunctivitis; periorbital edema	Cutaneous vasculitis; lymphadenopathy; elevated IgD	Conjunctivitis; headache; amyloidosis	Sensorineural deafness; conjunctivitis; amyloidosis	Sensorineural deafness; aseptic meningitis; mental retardation
Treatment	Colchicine	Corticosteroids; TNF-α inhibitors	NSAIDs; corticosteroids	IL-1 receptor antagonist	IL-1 receptor antagonist	IL-1 receptor antagonist

FCAS = familial cold autoinflammatory syndrome; FMF = familial Mediterranean fever; HIDS = hyperimmunoglobulinemia D with periodic fever syndrome; IL = interleukin; MWS = Muckle-Wells syndrome; NOMID = neonatal-onset multisystem inflammatory disease; TNF = tumor necrosis factor; TRAPS = tumor necrosis factor receptor–associated periodic syndrome.

fistulas, arterial dissections, and vessel rupture can occur, as well as bowel and uterine rupture (particularly during pregnancy). Patients with vascular EDS should avoid contact sports, anticoagulants, and unnecessary surgery. Treatment of EDS is supportive.

Marfan Syndrome

Marfan syndrome (MFS) occurs in 1 per 4000 births and is associated with overgrowth of long bones as well as ocular and cardiovascular abnormalities. The skin and aorta contain abnormally low levels of elastin, which has been linked to mutations in the gene for fibrillin, an extracellular matrix protein important in the regulation of sequestered transforming growth factor β. Skeletal findings in patients with MFS include arm span greater than height, pectus excavatum, arachnodactyly (long digits), dural ectasia, a high arched palate, and micrognathia. Ectopia lentis (lens dislocation) occurs in 60% of patients. Mitral valve involvement, ranging from mild valve thickening to prolapse or regurgitation, occurs in 50% of patients. Aortic root aneurysms, which can develop in patients at a young age, represent the leading cause of MFS-associated mortality.

KEY POINTS

- Osteogenesis imperfecta is characterized by brittle bones, blue sclerae, and dentinogenesis imperfecta.

- Classic Ehlers-Danlos syndrome is manifested by smooth, velvety, hyperextensible skin; joint hypermobility; delayed wound healing with atrophic scarring; and easy bruising.

- Vascular Ehlers-Danlos syndrome is characterized by arterial fragility and thin, translucent skin; in addition, aneurysms, arteriovenous fistulas, arterial dissections, and vessel rupture can occur, as well as bowel and uterine rupture (particularly during pregnancy).

- Marfan syndrome is associated with overgrowth of long bones as well as ocular and cardiovascular abnormalities, and the skin and aorta contain abnormally low levels of elastin.

Sarcoidosis

Sarcoidosis is a multisystem disorder characterized by well-formed noncaseating granulomas that infiltrate tissues (see MKSAP 16 Pulmonary and Critical Care Medicine). Although the cause is unknown, reports of seasonal and familial clustering suggest environmental and genetic factors in disease pathogenesis. Sarcoidosis occurs in about 1 per 20,000 persons in the United States. Black persons are more often affected than white persons. The disease can occur at any age, but peak age of onset is between 20 and 40 years.

Clinical Manifestations

CONT.

Sarcoidosis can manifest as a chronic condition or as Löfgren syndrome, an acute, self-limited form of the disease characterized by hilar lymphadenopathy, erythema nodosum, and acute arthritis or tenosynovitis, usually of the ankles. Fever and anterior uveitis may also occur.

Chronic sarcoidosis can involve virtually any organ (**Table 38**). Musculoskeletal involvement occurs in 4% to 38% of patients in whom it is usually the presenting symptom.

TABLE 38.	Organ Involvement in Sarcoidosis
Organ	**Manifestation**
Lung	Pulmonary nodules
	Pulmonary infiltrates
	Pulmonary fibrosis
Skin	Erythema nodosum
	Lupus pernio (indurated, violaceous plaques on the face and ears)
	Plaques
	Papules
Bones	Lytic lesions in long bones of hands and feet
Joints	Arthralgia
	Oligoarthritis
	Polyarthritis
	Tenosynovitis
	Dactylitis
Eyes	Uveitis
	Lacrimal gland inflammation
Salivary glands	Parotitis
Lymph nodes	Hilar and mediastinal lymphadenopathy
	Generalized lymphadenopathy
Nervous system	Brain lesions
	Leptomeningeal involvement
	Myelopathy
	Cranial nerve palsy (especially facial nerve)
	Hypothalamic and pituitary involvement
	Peripheral neuropathy
Liver/Spleen	Asymptomatic involvement
	Elevated liver enzymes
Heart	Conduction disease (heart block, sudden death)
	Myocarditis
Endocrine	Hypercalcemia
	Hypervitaminosis D
Muscle	Asymptomatic involvement common
	Myositis is rare

Symmetric oligoarthritis affecting the large joints of the lower extremities occurs most commonly (60% of patients with Löfgren syndrome and 30% with chronic sarcoidosis). There is a strong predilection for ankle involvement, but the knees, wrists, and metacarpophalangeal and proximal interphalangeal joints also can be affected. Asymptomatic lytic bone lesions involving the hands, feet, and long bones occur in nearly 10% of patients.

Diagnosis

In patients with acute lower extremity arthritis and erythema nodosum, Löfgren syndrome can be diagnosed without tissue biopsy if symmetric bilateral hilar lymphadenopathy is demonstrated on chest radiography. In all other cases, tissue biopsy should be performed to confirm the diagnosis of sarcoidosis. Biopsy of erythema nodosum skin lesions is not helpful, because it will reveal nonspecific septal panniculitis even when sarcoidosis is present. Although serum angiotensin-converting enzyme levels are elevated in 75% of patients with chronic sarcoidosis, the test lacks specificity and is therefore of limited use diagnostically.

Treatment

NSAIDs or corticosteroids can be used to treat Löfgren syndrome, which generally resolves within several months. Patients with musculoskeletal involvement may respond to NSAIDs, but one third of patients require corticosteroids for relief of joint pain. Hydroxychloroquine, colchicine, and methotrexate are also sometimes used. H

KEY POINTS

- Sarcoidosis is characterized by well-formed noncaseating granulomas that infiltrate tissues of almost any organ.
- Sarcoidosis can manifest as Löfgren syndrome, an acute, self-limited form of the disease characterized by hilar lymphadenopathy, erythema nodosum, and acute arthritis or periarthritis, usually of the ankles.
- Tissue biopsy is needed to diagnose sarcoidosis except in cases of classic Löfgren syndrome with symmetric hilar lymphadenopathy.

Bibliography

Approach to the Patient with Rheumatic Disease

Abbadie C, Bhangoo S, De Koninck Y, Malcangio M, Melik-Parsadaniantz S, White FA. Chemokines and pain mechanisms. Brain Res Rev. 2009;60(1):125-134. [PMID: 19146875]

Duffy RL. Low back pain: an approach to diagnosis and management. Prim Care. 2010;37(4):729-741. [PMID: 21050954]

Finzel S, Ohrndorf S, Englbrecht M, et al. A detailed comparative study of high-resolution ultrasound and micro-computed tomography for detection of arthritic bone erosions. Arthritis Rheum. 2011;63(5):1231-1236. [PMID: 21538312]

Grönhagen CM, Gunnarsson I, Svenungsson E, Nyberg F. Cutaneous manifestations and serological findings in 260 patients with systemic lupus erythematosus. Lupus. 2010;19(10):1187-1194. [PMID: 20501526]

Leung L, Cahill CM. TNF-alpha and neuropathic pain–a review. J Neuroinflammation. 2010;7:27. [PMID: 20398373]

RDL Reference Laboratory. ANA profiles in ANA-positive rheumatic disease. www.rdlinc.com/pdf/ANA%20profiles%20&%20guide%20to%20interpretation.pdf. Accessed on November 5, 2010.

Schaible HG, von Banchet GS, Boettger MK, et al. The role of proinflammatory cytokines in the generation and maintenance of joint pain. Ann N Y Acad Sci. 2010;1193(1):60-69. [PMID: 20398009]

Waits JB. Rational use of laboratory testing in the initial evaluation of soft tissue and joint complaints. Prim Care. 2010;37(4):673-689. [PMID: 21050950]

Principles of Therapeutics

Askling J, van Vollenhoven RF, Granath F, et al. Cancer risk in patients with rheumatoid arthritis treated with anti-tumor necrosis factor alpha therapies: does the risk change with the time since start of treatment? Arthritis Rheum. 2009;60(11):3180-3189. [PMID: 19877027]

Barnes PJ. Mechanisms and resistance in glucocorticoid control of inflammation. J Steroid Biochem Mol Biol. 2010;120(2-3):76-85. [PMID: 20188830]

Bingham CO 3rd, Looney RJ, Deodhar A, et al. Immunization responses in rheumatoid arthritis patients treated with rituximab: results from a controlled clinical trial. Arthritis Rheum. 2010;62(1):64-74. [PMID: 20039397]

Chan ES, Cronstein BN. Methotrexate–how does it really work? Nat Rev Rheumatol. 2010;6(3):175-178. [PMID: 20197777]

Donohue KE, Gartlehner G, Jonas DE, et al. Systematic review: comparative effectiveness and harms of disease-modifying medications for rheumatoid arthritis. Ann Intern Med. 2008;148(2):124-134. [PMID: 18025440]

Hyrich KL, Deighton C, Watson KD, BSRBR Control Centre Consortium, Symmons DP, Lunt M; British Society for Rheumatology Biologics Register. Benefit of anti-TNF therapy in rheumatoid arthritis patients with moderate disease activity. Rheumatology (Oxford). 2009;48(10):1323-1327. [PMID: 19706737]

Farkouh ME, Greenberg BP. An evidence-based review of the cardiovascular risks of non-steroidal anti-inflammatory drugs. Am J Cardiol. 2009;103(9):1227-1237. [PMID: 19406264]

Jones G, Sebba A, Gu J, et al. Comparison of tocilizumab monotherapy versus methotrexate monotherapy in patients with moderate to severe rheumatoid arthritis: the AMBITION study. Ann Rheum Dis. 2010;69(1):88-96. [PMID: 19297346]

Kamanamool N, McEvoy M, Attia J, Ingsathit A, Ngamjanyaport P, Thakkinstian A. Efficacy and adverse events of mycophenolate mofetil versus cyclophosphamide for induction therapy of lupus nephritis: systemic review and meta-analysis. Medicine. 2010;89(4):227-235. [PMID: 20616662]

Listing J, Strangfeld A, Kekow J, et al. Does tumor necrosis factor alpha inhibition promote or prevent heart failure in patients with rheumatoid arthritis? Arthritis Rheum. 2008;58(3):667-677. [PMID: 18311816]

Ponce de Leon D, Acevedo-Vasquez E, Alvizuri S, et al. Comparison of an interferon-gamma assay with tuberculin skin testing for detection of tuberculosis (TB) infection in patients with rheumatoid arthritis in a TB-endemic population. J Rheumatol. 2008;35(5):776-781. [PMID: 18398944]

Rheumatoid Arthritis

Aletaha D, Neogi T, Silman AJ, et al; American College of Rheumatology; European League Against Rheumatism. Rheumatoid arthritis classification criteria: an American College of Rheumatology/European League Against Rheumatism collaborative initiative. Arthritis Rheumatol. 2010;62(9):2569-2581. [PMID: 20872595]

Cooper GS. Occupational exposures and risk of rheumatoid arthritis: continued advances and opportunities for research. J Rheumatol. 2008;35(6):950-952. [PMID: 18528947]

Finckh A, Bansback N, Marra CA, et al. Treatment of very early rheumatoid arthritis with symptomatic therapy, disease-modifying antirheumatic drugs, or biologic agents: a cost-effectiveness analysis. Ann Intern Med. 2009;151(9):612-621. [PMID: 19884622]

Gaujoux-Viala C, Smolen JS, Landewé R, et al. Current evidence for the management of rheumatoid arthritis with synthetic disease-modifying antirheumatic drugs: a systematic literature review informing the EULAR recommendations for the management of rheumatoid arthritis. Ann Rheum Dis. 2010;69(6):1004-1009. [PMID: 20447954]

Hetland ML, Chistensen IJ, Tarp U, et al; All Departments of Rheumatology in Denmark. Direct comparison of treatment responses, remission rates, and drug adherence in patients with rheumatoid arthritis treated with adalimumab, etanercept, or infliximab. Arthritis Rheum. 2010;62(1):22-32. [PMID: 20039405]

Klareskog L, Catrina AI, Paget S. Rheumatoid arthritis. Lancet. 2009;373(9664):659-672. [PMID: 19157532]

Markatseli TE, Papagoras C, Drosos AA. Prognostic factors for erosive rheumatoid arthritis. Clin Exp Rheumatol. 2010;28(1):114-123. [PMID: 20346251]

Saag KG, Teng GG, Patkar NM, et al; American College of Rheumatology. American College of Rheumatology 2008 recommendations for the use of nonbiologic and biologic disease-modifying antirheumatic drugs in rheumatoid arthritis. Arthritis Rheum. 2008;59(6):762-784. [PMID: 18512708]

Singh JA, Beg S, Lopez-Olivo MA. Tocilizumab for rheumatoid arthritis. Cochrane Database Syst Rev. 2010;(7):CD008331. [PMID: 20614469]

Singh JA, Noorbaloochi S, Singh G. Golimumab for rheumatoid arthritis: a systematic review. J Rheumatol. 2010;37(6):1096-1104. [PMID: 20436075]

Osteoarthritis

Atchia I, Kane D, Reed MR, et al. Efficacy of a single ultrasound-guided injection for the treatment of hip osteoarthritis. Ann Rheum Dis. 2011;70(1):110-116. [PMID: 21068096]

Bennell KL, Bowles KA, Payne C, et al. Lateral wedge insoles for medial knee osteoarthritis: 12 month randomised controlled trial. BMJ. 2011;342:d2912. doi: 10.1136/bmj.d2912. [PMID: 21593096]

Berry PA, Jones SW, Cicuttini FM, Wluka AE, Maciewicz RA. Temporal relationship between serum adipokines, biomarkers of bone and cartilage turnover, and cartilage volume loss in a population with clinical knee osteoarthritis. Arthritis Rheum. 2011;63(3):700-707. [PMID: 21305502]

McAlindon T, Formica M, Schmid CH, Fletcher J. Changes in barometric pressure and ambient temperature influence osteoarthritis pain. Am J Med. 2007;120(5):429-434. [PMID: 17466654]

Moskowitz RW, Williams HJ, Clegg DO. Clinical efficacy and safety of glucosamine, chondroitin sulphate, their combination, celecoxib or placebo taken to treat osteoarthritis of the knee: 2-year results from GAIT. Ann Rheum Dis. 2010;69(8):1459. [PMID: 20525840]

Prieto-Alhambra D, Javaid MK, Judge A, et al. Fracture risk before and after total hip replacement in patients with osteoarthritis: potential benefits of bisphosphonate use. Arthritis Rheum. 2011;63(4):992-1001. [PMID: 21452321]

Sawitzke AD, Shi H, Finco MF, et al. Clinical efficacy and safety of glucosamine, chondroitin sulphate, their combination, celecoxib or placebo taken to treat osteoarthritis of the knee: 2-year results from GAIT. Ann Rheum Dis. 2010;69(8):1459-1464. [PMID: 20525840]

Suarez-Almazor ME, Looney C, Liu Y, et al. A randomized controlled trial of acupuncture for osteoarthritis of the knee: effects of patient-provider communication. Arthritis Care Res (Hoboken). 2010;62(9):1229-1236. [PMID: 20506122]

Wandel S, Jüni P, Tendal B, et al. Effects of glucosamine, chondroitin, or placebo in patients with osteoarthritis of hip or knee: network meta-analysis. BMJ. 2010;341:c4675. [PMID: 20847017]

Fibromyalgia

Arnold LM. Advances in the management of fibromyalgia. CNS Spectr. 2009;14(10 Suppl 8):12-16. [PMID: 20128144]

Buskila D. Developments in the scientific and clinical understanding of fibromyalgia. Arthritis Res Ther. 2009;11(5):242-249. [PMID: 19835639]

Williams DA. The role of non-pharmacologic approaches in the management of fibromyalgia. CNS Spectr. 2009;14(12 Suppl 16):10-12; discussion, 12-14. [PMID: 20568689]

Wolfe F. Fibromyalgia wars. J Rheumatol. 2009;36(4):671-678. [PMID: 19342721]

Wolfe F, Clauw DJ, Fitzcharles MA, et al. The American College of Rheumatology preliminary diagnostic criteria for fibromyalgia and measurement of symptom severity. Arthritis Care Res (Hoboken). 2010;62(5):600-610. [PMID: 20461783]

Spondyloarthritis

De Vos M. Joint involvement in inflammatory bowel disease; managing inflammation outside the digestive system. Expert Rev Gastroenterol Hepatol. 2010;4(1):81-89. [PMID: 20136591]

Maksymowych WP. Spondyloarthritis: lessons from imaging. Arthritis Res Ther. 2009;11(3):222. [PMID: 19519927]

Ritchlin CT, Kavanaugh A, Gladman DD, et al; Group for Research and Assessment of Psoriasis and Psoriatic Arthritis (GRAPPA). Treatment recommendations for psoriatic arthritis. Ann Rheum Dis. 2009;68(9):1387-1394. [PMID: 18952643]

Rudwaleit M, van der Heijde D, Landewe R, et al. The development of Assessment of SpondyloArthritis international Society classification criteria for axial spondyloarthritis (part II): validation and final selection. Ann Rheum Dis. 2009;68(6):777-783. [PMID: 19297344]

Sieper J. Developments in the scientific and clinical understanding of the spondyloarthritides. Arthritis Res Ther. 2009;11(1):208. [PMID: 19232062]

Sieper J, van der Heijde, Landewe R, et al. New criteria for inflammatory back pain in patients with chronic back pain: real patient exercise by experts from the Assessment of SpondyloArthritis International Society (ASAS). Ann Rheum Dis. 2009;68(6):784-788. [PMID: 19147614]

Townes JM. Reactive arthritis after enteric infections in the United States: the problem of definition. Clin Infect Dis. 2010;50(2):247-254. [PMID: 20025528]

van Tubergen AM, Landewé RB. Tools for monitoring spondyloarthritis in clinical practice. Nat Rev Rheumatol. 2009;5(11):608-615. [PMID: 19806152]

Systemic Lupus Erythematosus

Bertsias GK, Boumpas DT. Pathogenesis, diagnosis and management of neuropsychiatric SLE manifestations. Nat Rev Rheumatol. 2010;6(6):358-367. [PMID: 20458332]

Clowse ME, Jamison M, Myers E, James AH. A national study of the complications of lupus in pregnancy. Am J Obstet Gynecol. 2008;199(2):127.e1-e6. [PMID: 18456233]

Helmick CG, Felson DT, Lawrence RC, et al; National Arthritis Data Workgroup. Estimates of the prevalence of arthritis and other rheumatic conditions in the United States. Part I. Arthritis Rheum. 2008;58(1):15-25. [PMID: 18163481]

Hom G, Graham RR, Modrek B, et al. Association of systemic lupus erythematosus with C8orf13-BLK and ITHAM-ITGAX. N Engl J Med. 2008;358(9):900-909. [PMID: 18204098]

Ippolito A, Petri M. An update on mortality in systemic lupus erythematosus. Clin Exp Rheumatol. 2008;26(5 supp 51):S72-S79. [PMID: 19026147]

Klumb EM, Araujo ML, Jesus GR, et al. Is higher prevalence of cervical intraepithelial neoplasia in women with lupus due to immunosuppression? J Clin Rheumatol. 2010;16(4):153-157. [PMID: 20407390]

Pons-Estel GJ, González LA, Zhang J, et al. Predictors of cardiovascular damage in patients with systemic lupus erythematosus: data from LUMINA (LXVIII), a multiethnic US cohort. Rheumatology (Oxford). 2009;48(7): 817-822. [PMID: 19454606]

Pons-Estel G, Alarcón GS, Scofield L, Reinlib L, Cooper GS. Understanding the epidemiology and progression of systemic lupus erythematosus. Semin Arthritis Rheum. 2008;39(4):257-268. [PMID: 19136143]

Ruiz-Irastorza G, Ramos-Casals M, Brito-Zeron P, Khamashta MA. Clinical efficacy and side effects of antimalarials in systemic lupus erythematosus: a systematic review. Ann Rheum Dis. 2010;69(1):20-28. [PMID: 19103632]

Shinjo SK, Bonfá E, Wojdyla D, et al; Grupo Latino Americano de Estudio del Lupus Eritematoso (Gladel). Antimalarial treatment may have a time-dependent effect on lupus survival: data from a multinational Latin American inception cohort. Arthritis Rheum. 2010;62(3):855-862. [PMID: 20131238]

Systemic Sclerosis

Bérezné A, Ranque B, Valeyre D, et al. Therapeutic strategy combining intravenous cyclophosphamide followed by oral azathioprine to treat worsening interstitial lung disease associated with systemic sclerosis: a retrospective multicenter open-label study. J Rheumatol. 2008;35(6):1064-1072. [PMID: 18464307]

Henness S, Wigley FM. Current drug therapy for scleroderma and secondary Raynaud phenomenon: evidence-based review. Curr Opin Rheumatol. 2007;19(6):611-618. [PMID: 17917543]

Ingraham KM, O'Brien MS, Shenin M, Derk CT, Steen VD. Gastric antral vascular ectasia in systemic sclerosis: demographics and disease predictors. J Rheumatol. 2010;37(3):603-607. [PMID: 20080908]

Johnson SR, Feldman BM, Pope JE, Tomlinson GA. Shifting our thinking about uncommon disease trials: the case of methotrexate in scleroderma. J Rheumatol. 2009;36(2):323-329. [PMID: 19040308]

Korn JH, Mayes M, Matucci Cerinic M, et al. Digital ulcers in systemic sclerosis: prevention by treatment with bosentan, an oral endothelin receptor antagonist. Arthritis Rheum. 2004;50(12):3985-3993. [PMID: 15593188]

Steen VD. Pregnancy in scleroderma. Rheum Dis Clin North Am. 2007;33(2):345-358. [PMID: 17499711]

Sjögren Syndrome

Ramos-Casals M, Tzioufas AG, Stone JH, Siso A, Bosch X. Treatment of primary Sjögren syndrome: a systematic review. JAMA. 2010;304(4):452-460. [PMID: 20664046]

Thanou-Stavraki A, James J. Primary Sjögren's syndrome: current and prospective therapies. Semin Arthritis Rheum. 2008;37(5):273-292. [PMID: 17714766]

Voulgarelis M, Moutsopoulos HM. Mucosa-associated lymphoid tissue lymphoma in Sjögren syndrome: risks, management and prognosis. Rheum Dis Clin N Am. 2008;34(4):921-933. [PMID: 18984412]

Mixed Connective Tissue Disease

Jais X, Launay D, Yaici A, et al. Immunosuppressive therapy in lupus- and mixed connective tissue disease-associated pulmonary arterial hypertension: a retrospective analysis of twenty-three cases. Arthritis Rheum. 2008;58(2):521-531. [PMID: 18240255]

Tsai YY, Yang YH, Yu HH, Wang LC, Lee JH, Chiang BL. Fifteen-year experience of pediatric-onset mixed connective tissue disease. Clin Rheumatol. 2010;29(1):53-58. [PMID: 19756834]

Crystal-Induced Arthropathies

Choi HK. A prescription for lifestyle change in patients with hyperuricemia and gout. Curr Opin Rheumatol. 2010;22(2):165-172. [PMID: 20035225]

Lawrence RC, Felson DT, Helmick CG, et al; National Arthritis Data Workgroup. Estimates of the prevalence of arthritis and other rheumatic conditions in the United States. Part II. Arthritis Rheum. 2008;58(1):26-35. [PMID: 18163497]

Pillinger MH, Keenan RT. Update on the management of hyperuricemia and gout. Bull NYU Hosp Jt Dis. 2008;66(3):231-239. [PMID: 18937638]

Richette P, Bardin T, Doherty M. An update on the epidemiology of calcium pyrophosphate dihydrate crystal deposition disease. Rheumatol. 2009;48(7):711-715. [PMID: 19398486]

Infectious Arthritis

Franco-Paredes C, Diaz-Borjon A, Senger MA, Barragan L, Leonard M. The ever-expanding association between rheumatologic diseases and tuberculosis. Am J Med. 2006;119(6):470-477. [PMID: 16750957]

Mathews CJ, Weston VC, Jones A, Field M, Coakley G. Bacterial septic arthritis in adults. Lancet. 2010;375(9717):846-855. [PMID: 20206778]

Ross JJ, Shamsuddin H. Sternoclavicular septic arthritis: review of 180 cases. Medicine. 2004;83(3):139-148. [PMID: 15118542]

Young NS, Brown KE. Parvovirus B19. N Engl J Med. 2004;350:586-597. [PMID: 14762186]

Idiopathic Inflammatory Myopathies

Callen JP. Cutaneous manifestations of dermatomyositis and their management. Curr Rheumatol Rep. 2010;12(3):192-197. [PMID: 20425525]

Fardet L, Dupuy A, Gain M, et al. Factors associated with underlying malignancy in a retrospective cohort of 121 patients with dermatomyositis. Medicine. 2009;88(2):91-97. [PMID: 19282699]

Fathi M, Vikgren J, Boijsen M, et al. Interstitial lung disease in polymyositis and dermatomyositis: longitudinal evaluation by pulmonary function and radiology. Arthritis Rheum. 2008;59(5):677-685. [PMID: 18438901]

Gunawardena H, Betteridge ZE, McHugh NJ. Myositis-specific antibodies: their clinical and pathogenic significance in disease expression. Rheumatology (Oxford). 2009;48(6):607-612. [PMID: 19439503]

Lundberg IE, Forbess CJ. Mortality in idiopathic inflammatory myopathies. Clin Exp Rheumatol. 2008;26(supp 51):S109-S114. [PMID: 19026152]

Selva-O'Callaghan A, Grau JM, Gomez-Cenzano C, et al. Conventional cancer screening versus PET/CT in dermatomyositis/polymyositis. Am J Med. 2010;123(6):558-562. [PMID: 20569766]

Walker UA. Imaging tools for the clinical assessment of idiopathic inflammatory myositis. Curr Opin Rheumatol. 2008;20(6):656-661. [PMID: 18946324]

Systemic Vasculitis

Gaffo AL. Diagnostic approach to ANCA-associated vasculitides. Rheum Dis Clin North Am. 2010;36(3):491-506. [PMID: 20688246]

Gomard-Mennesson E, Landron C, Dauphin C, et al. Kawasaki disease in adults: report of 10 cases. Medicine (Baltimore). 2010;89(3):149-158. [PMID: 20453601]

Iannuzzella F, Vaglio A, Garini G. Management of hepatitis C virus-related mixed cryoglobulinemia. Am J Med. 2010;123(5):400-408. [PMID: 20399313]

Maksimowicz-McKinnon K, Clark TM, Hoffman GS. Limitations of therapy and a guarded prognosis in an American cohort of Takayasu arteritis patients. Arthritis Rheum. 2007;56(3):1000-1009. [PMID: 17328078]

Marie I, Proux A, Duhaut P, et al. Long-term follow-up of aortic involvement in giant cell arteritis: a series of 48 patients. Medicine (Baltimore). 2009;88(3):182-192. [PMID: 19440121]

Pagnoux C, Seror R, Henegar C, et al; French Vasculitis Study Group. Clinical features and outcomes in 348 patients with polyarteritis nodosa: a systematic retrospective study of patients diagnosed between 1963 and 2005 and entered into the French Vasculitis Study Group Database. Arthritis Rheum. 2010;62(2):616-626. [PMID: 20112401]

Ribi C, Cohen P, Pagnoux C, et al; French Vasculitis Study Group. Treatment of Churg-Strauss syndrome without poor-prognosis factors: a multicenter, prospective, randomized, open-label study of seventy-two patients. Arthritis Rheum. 2008;58(2):586-594. [PMID: 18240234]

Stone JH, Merkel PA, Spiera R, et al; RAVE-ITN Research Group. Rituximab versus cyclophosphamide for ANCA-associated vasculitis. N Engl J Med. 2010;363(3):221-232. [PMID: 20647199]

Other Systemic Inflammatory Diseases

Ben-Chetrit E, Touitou I. Familial Mediterranean fever in the world. Arthritis Rheum. 2009;61(10):1447-1453. [PMID: 19790133]

Callewaert B, Malfait F, Loeys B, De Paepe A. Ehlers-Danlos syndromes and Marfan syndrome. Best Pract Res Clin Rheumatol. 2008;22(1):165-189. [PMID: 18328988]

Chatham W. Rheumatic manifestations of systemic disease: sarcoidosis. Curr Opin Rheumatol. 2010;22(1):85-90. [PMID: 19851109]

De Menthon M, Lavalley MP, Maldini C, Guillevin L, Mahr A. HLA-B51/B5 and the risk of Behçet's disease: a systematic review and meta-analysis of case-control genetic association studies. Arthritis Rheum. 2009;61(10):1287-1296. [PMID: 19790126]

Franchini S, Dagna L, Salvo F, Aiello P, Baldissera E, Sabbadine MG. Efficacy of traditional and biologic agents in different clinical phenotypes of adult onset Still's disease. Arthritis Rheum. 2010;62(8):2530-2535. [PMID: 20506370]

Glorieux FH. Osteogenesis imperfecta. Best Pract Res Clin Rheumatol. 2008;22(1):85-100. [PMID: 18328983]

Kent PD, Michet CJ Jr, Luthra HS. Relapsing polychondritis. Curr Opin Rheumatol. 2004;16(1):56-61. [PMID: 14673390]

Kontzias A, Efthimiou P. Adult-onset Still's disease: pathogenesis, clinical manifestations, and therapeutic advances. Drugs. 2008;68(3):319-337. [PMID: 18257609]

Saadoun D, Wechsler B, Desseaux K, et al. Mortality in Behçet's disease. Arthritis Rheum. 2010;62(9):2806-2812. [PMID: 20496419]

Thelier N, Assous N, Job-Deslandre C, et al. Osteoarticular involvement in a series of 100 patients with sarcoidosis referred to rheumatology departments. J Rheumatol. 2008;35(8):1622-1628. [PMID: 18634144]

Yao Q, Furst DE. Autoinflammatory disease: an update of clinical and genetic aspects. Rheumatology. 2008;47(7):946-951. [PMID: 18388145]

Rheumatology
Self-Assessment Test

This self-assessment test contains one-best-answer multiple-choice questions. Please read these directions carefully before answering the questions. Answers, critiques, and bibliographies immediately follow these multiple-choice questions. The American College of Physicians is accredited by the Accreditation Council for Continuing Medical Education (ACCME) to provide continuing medical education for physicians.

The American College of Physicians designates MKSAP 16 Rheumatology for a maximum of 14 *AMA PRA Category 1 Credits*™. Physicians should claim only the credit commensurate with the extent of their participation in the activity.

Earn "Same-Day" CME Credits Online

For the first time, print subscribers can enter their answers online to earn CME credits in 24 hours or less. You can submit your answers using online answer sheets that are provided at mksap.acponline.org, where a record of your MKSAP 16 credits will be available. To earn CME credits, you need to answer all of the questions in a test and earn a score of at least 50% correct (number of correct answers divided by the total number of questions). Take any of the following approaches:

➢ Use the printed answer sheet at the back of this book to record your answers. Go to mksap.acponline.org, access the appropriate online answer sheet, transcribe your answers, and submit your test for same-day CME credits. There is no additional fee for this service.

➢ Go to mksap.acponline.org, access the appropriate online answer sheet, directly enter your answers, and submit your test for same-day CME credits. There is no additional fee for this service.

➢ Pay a $10 processing fee per answer sheet and submit the printed answer sheet at the back of this book by mail or fax, as instructed on the answer sheet. Make sure you calculate your score and fax the answer sheet to 215-351-2799 or mail the answer sheet to Member and Customer Service, American College of Physicians, 190 N. Independence Mall West, Philadelphia, PA 19106-1572, using the courtesy envelope provided in your MKSAP 16 slipcase. You will need your 10-digit order number and 8-digit ACP ID number, which are printed on your packing slip. Please allow 4 to 6 weeks for your score report to be emailed back to you. Be sure to include your email address for a response.

If you do not have a 10-digit order number and 8-digit ACP ID number or if you need help creating a username and password to access the MKSAP 16 online answer sheets, go to mksap.acponline.org or email custserv@acponline.org.

CME credit is available from the publication date of July 31, 2012, until July 31, 2015. You may submit your answer sheets at any time during this period.

Directions

*Each of the numbered items is followed by lettered answers. Select the **ONE** lettered answer that is **BEST** in each case.*

Self-Assessment Test

Item 1

A 52-year-old man is evaluated in the emergency department for a 2-week history of progressive fever and malaise with gradual onset of shortness of breath, pleuritic chest pain, myalgia, arthralgia, and rash. He reports no cough. He has a 15-year history of rheumatoid arthritis, which is well controlled with methotrexate and etanercept; his last flare was 1 year ago. Other medications are naproxen and folic acid.

On physical examination, temperature is 39.0 °C (102.2 °F), blood pressure is 148/94 mm Hg, pulse rate is 90/min, and respiration rate is 22/min. Cardiac examination is normal. Pulmonary examination reveals a left pleural friction rub. There is synovial thickening of the wrists and metacarpophalangeal and proximal interphalangeal joints bilaterally as well as small bilateral knee effusions. A non-blanching purpuric rash is noted over the distal lower extremities.

Laboratory studies:

Hemoglobin	9.8 g/dL (98 g/L)
Leukocyte count	2600/µL (2.6 × 10^9/L)
Platelet count	128,000/µL (128 × 10^9/L)
Erythrocyte sedimentation rate	86 mm/h
Urinalysis	1+ protein; 2-5 erythrocytes/hpf; 5-10 leukocytes/hpf

Chest radiograph reveals blunted costophrenic angles bilaterally without infiltrate.

Blood and urine culture results are pending.

Which of the following is the most appropriate diagnostic test to perform next?

(A) Antinuclear antibody and anti–double-stranded DNA antibody assay
(B) Bone marrow aspiration and biopsy
(C) CT of the chest, abdomen, and pelvis
(D) Rheumatoid factor and anti–cyclic citrullinated peptide antibody assay

Item 2

A 42-year-old woman is evaluated for recurring pain and swelling of the left knee and right ankle that began 5 months ago. At that time, she also had an episode of conjunctivitis as well as dysuria, both of which resolved spontaneously. The joint pain and swelling persisted, and aspiration of the left knee was performed, which revealed leukocytosis without evidence of crystals or bacteria. She started naproxen, which provided some relief; 1 month later, she switched to indomethacin, but there was no improvement. She then began corticosteroid joint injections, which initially provided relief, but now the pain and swelling have recurred. Six months ago she also had an episode of nonbloody diarrhea of 5 days' duration that resolved spontaneously.

On physical examination, vital signs are normal. Cutaneous examination is normal. There is no evidence of conjunctivitis or iritis. Musculoskeletal examination reveals swelling, tenderness, and warmth of the left knee and right ankle.

Rheumatoid factor, antinuclear antibody, and anti–cyclic citrullinated peptide antibody testing is negative. Lyme disease serology results are negative. *Chlamydia trachomatis* and *Neisseria gonorrhoeae* test results are negative.

Radiographs of the left knee and right ankle are normal.

Which of the following is the most appropriate treatment for this patient?

(A) Colchicine
(B) Glucosamine
(C) Nitrofurantoin
(D) Sulfasalazine

Item 3

A 52-year-old man is evaluated for a 5-year history of gradually progressive left knee pain. He has 20 minutes of morning stiffness, which returns after prolonged inactivity. He has minimal to no pain at rest. He reports no clicking or locking of the knee. Over the past several months, the pain has limited his ambulation to no more than a few blocks.

On physical examination, vital signs are normal. BMI is 25. The left knee has a small effusion and some fullness at the back of the knee; the knee is not erythematous or warm. Range of motion of the knee elicits crepitus. There is medial joint line tenderness to palpation, bony hypertrophy, and a moderate varus deformity. There is no evidence of joint instability on stress testing.

Radiographs of the knee reveal bone-on-bone joint-space loss and numerous osteophytes.

Which of the following is the most appropriate next diagnostic step for this patient?

(A) CT of the knee
(B) Joint aspiration
(C) MRI of the knee
(D) No diagnostic testing

Item 4

A 72-year-old woman is evaluated in the emergency department for severe right shoulder pain and swelling. Three weeks ago, she injured her shoulder when falling from a stepladder and went to the emergency department; radiographs of the shoulder revealed soft-tissue swelling. She partially improved, but the pain and swelling recurred after several days and gradually worsened. She has been taking acetaminophen for the pain, with no relief.

On physical examination, temperature is 37.1 °C (98.8 °F), blood pressure is 116/76 mm Hg, pulse rate is 78/min, and respiration rate is 14/min. BMI is 23. The right shoulder is swollen, erythematous, warm, and tender, particularly over the anterior surface. Range of motion of the shoulder elicits pain and is limited.

Radiographs of the right shoulder reveal significant soft-tissue swelling and possible large fluid collection. There is a hazy overlay of calcification around the entire joint, and the joint itself is eroded.

Aspiration of the right shoulder is performed; the fluid is blood tinged. Synovial fluid leukocyte count is 32,000/μL ([32×10^9/L], 82% polymorphonuclear cells). Polarized light microscopy reveals no needle- or rhomboid-shaped crystals. Gram stain and cultures are negative.

Which of the following is the most likely diagnosis?

(A) Basic calcium phosphate deposition disease
(B) Calciphylaxis
(C) Calcium pyrophosphate deposition disease
(D) Osteoarthritis

 Item 5

A 35-year-old woman is evaluated in the emergency department for diffuse dull chest and midepigastric discomfort, weakness, and vomiting that began in the early morning and has progressively worsened throughout the day. At age 14 years, she was diagnosed with lupus nephritis and was treated with high-dose corticosteroids for several years. Since then, she has had intermittent flares of arthritis, rash, alopecia, and pleuropericarditis. She also has hypertension. Medications are hydroxychloroquine, azathioprine, prednisone, and enalapril.

On physical examination, temperature is 37.0 °C (98.6 °F), blood pressure is 146/94 mm Hg, pulse rate is 104/min, and respiration rate is 20/min. Cardiac examination reveals tachycardia and an S_4. The lungs are clear to auscultation. The abdomen is nontender.

Laboratory test results are pending.

Which of the following is the most appropriate initial diagnostic test?

(A) CT angiography of the abdomen
(B) CT pulmonary angiography
(C) Electrocardiography
(D) Right upper quadrant ultrasonography

Item 6

A 32-year-old man is evaluated in the emergency department for a 2-week history of progressive pain and swelling of both ankles. He also has low-grade fever and a painful red left eye with photophobia of 2 days' duration. The patient has no other pertinent personal or family medical history. He takes no medications.

On physical examination, temperature is 38.2 °C (100.7 °F), blood pressure is 128/26 mm Hg, pulse rate is 96/min, and respiration rate is 14/min. BMI is 26. There is ocular injection around the left iris. Slit lamp examination reveals anterior uveitis. The abdomen is nontender. Genital examination is normal. A few tender, erythematous nodules measuring 1 to 3 cm are found on the anterior legs. Swelling of the right knee is present. There is swelling, tenderness, and warmth of the ankles and feet involving the joints and periarticular tissues.

Which of the following is the most appropriate diagnostic test to perform next?

(A) ANCA assay
(B) Chest radiography
(C) Colonoscopy
(D) Urine polymerase chain reaction for *Neisseria gonorrhoeae*

Item 7

A 34-year-old woman is evaluated for a 2-month history of stiffness and swelling of the fingers and wrists as well as myalgia and stiffness in the shoulder girdle and thighs. She also has a 1-year history of chronic diffuse pruritus in the absence of skin rash. She has a 5-year history of Raynaud phenomenon and gastroesophageal reflux symptoms. Medications are ibuprofen and famotidine.

On physical examination, temperature is 36.8 °C (98.2 °F), blood pressure is 130/90 mm Hg, pulse rate is 80/min, and respiration rate is 14/min. The lungs are clear. There is diffuse swelling of the digits of both hands with loss of skin folds. Dilated nailfold capillaries are present. The wrists are tender and swollen, and there is a palpable extensor tendon rub proximal to the left wrist. The patient has difficulty rising from a deep squat without assistance.

Laboratory studies:

Complete blood count	Normal
Creatine kinase	850 units/mL
Serum creatinine	Normal
Thyroid-stimulating hormone	Normal
Antinuclear antibodies	Titer of 1:320
Anti–double-stranded DNA antibodies	Negative
Anti-topoisomerase I (anti–Scl-70) antibodies	Positive
Urinalysis	Normal

Pulmonary function studies:

FVC	90% of predicted
DLCO	90% of predicted

Chest radiograph and echocardiogram are normal.

Which of the following is the most appropriate treatment?

(A) Add cyclophosphamide
(B) Add hydroxychloroquine
(C) Add methotrexate
(D) Add naproxen

Item 8

A 76-year-old woman is evaluated for a 3-month history of left knee pain of moderate intensity that worsens with ambulation. She reports minimal pain at rest and no nocturnal pain. There are no clicking or locking symptoms. She has tried naproxen and ibuprofen but developed dyspepsia; acetaminophen provides mild to moderate relief. The patient has hypertension, hypercholesterolemia, and chronic stable angina. Medications are lisinopril, metoprolol, simvastatin, low-dose aspirin, and nitroglycerin as needed.

On physical examination, vital signs are normal. BMI is 32. Range of motion of the left knee elicits crepitus. There is a small effusion without redness or warmth and tenderness to palpation along the medial joint line. Testing for meniscal or ligamentous injury is negative.

Laboratory studies, including complete blood count and erythrocyte sedimentation rate, are normal.

Radiographs of the knee reveal medial tibiofemoral compartment joint-space narrowing and sclerosis; small medial osteophytes are present.

Which of the following is the next best step in management?

(A) Add celecoxib

(B) Add glucosamine sulfate

(C) MRI of the knee

(D) Weight loss and exercise

Item 9

A 42-year-old woman is evaluated for a 2-month history of fatigue, tingling in the fingers of both hands, and pain radiating into the hands and forearms. She also has difficulty opening bottles. The tingling symptoms occasionally are alleviated when she shakes her hands in the morning, but she typically has 2 to 3 hours of morning stiffness in her wrists and fingers. She takes no medications.

On physical examination, vital signs are normal. BMI is 21. Soft-tissue swelling and tenderness is palpable at the wrists and metacarpophalangeal joints bilaterally. She has sensory loss over the palmar surface of the first three digits and weakness of abduction and opposition of the thumbs bilaterally. The Phalen maneuver produces pain at the wrists and tingling in the hands.

Results from electrodiagnostic studies are consistent with bilateral median neuropathies of the wrist.

Which of the following is the most likely cause of this patient's neuropathy?

(A) Osteoarthritis

(B) Overuse injury

(C) Polymyalgia rheumatica

(D) Rheumatoid arthritis

Item 10

A 23-year-old man is evaluated during a follow-up visit. One month ago, he was diagnosed with systemic lupus erythematosus; treatment with prednisone, 20 mg/d, was initiated, which partially improved his joint pain and swelling. He now reports oral ulcers, ankle swelling, fatigue, nausea, and low-grade fever.

On physical examination, temperature is 38.1 °C (100.6 °F), blood pressure is 146/92 mm Hg, pulse rate is 102/min, and respiration rate is 18/min. Raised malar erythema is present. There is an erythematous ulceration 1 cm in diameter on the hard palate. Musculoskeletal examination reveals tenderness of the metacarpophalangeal joints, proximal interphalangeal joints, and knees with mild synovitis; bilateral pitting ankle edema is present.

Laboratory studies:

Hemoglobin	9.1 g/dL (91 g/L)
Leukocyte count	3900/µL (3.9 × 10⁹/L)
Erythrocyte sedimentation rate	102 mm/h
C3	Decreased
C4	Decreased
Serum creatinine	1.1 mg/dL (97.2 µmol/L)
Antinuclear antibodies	Titer of 1:640 (homogeneous pattern)
Anti–double-stranded DNA antibodies	Positive
Urinalysis	3+ protein; 4-6 erythrocytes/hpf; 4-6 leukocytes/hpf; no erythrocyte casts
24-Hour urine collection for protein	1120 mg/24 h

At this time, prednisone is increased to 60 mg/d.

Which of the following is the most appropriate next step in management?

(A) Intravenous cyclophosphamide

(B) Kidney biopsy

(C) MR angiography of the renal arteries

(D) Mycophenolate mofetil

Item 11

A 27-year-old woman is evaluated during a routine follow-up visit for a 9-year history of systemic lupus erythematosus. She has ongoing symptoms of malar rash and joint pain. She reports no weight loss, sweats, pleuritic chest pain, or alopecia. Eight years ago, she was diagnosed with lupus nephritis (class IV) and treated with intravenous cyclophosphamide; she has not had any recurrence. Current medications are mycophenolate mofetil, prednisone, and hydroxychloroquine.

On physical examination, temperature is 37.4 °C (99.3 °F), blood pressure is 128/84 mm Hg, pulse rate is 78/min, and respiration rate is 18/min. There is a malar erythematous rash and a maculopapular rash over the anterior chest wall. There is new left supraclavicular lymphadenopathy with two 2-cm lymph nodes, and cervical lymphadenopathy is present. The metacarpophalangeal and proximal interphalangeal joints are tender; there is no swelling.

Laboratory studies:

Hemoglobin	11.2 g/dL (112 g/L)
Leukocyte count	4600/µL (4.6 × 10⁹/L)
Platelet count	156,000/µL (156 × 10⁹/L)
Erythrocyte sedimentation rate	38 mm/h
C3	Normal
C4	Normal
Serum creatinine	0.9 mg/dL (79.6 µmol/L)
Anti–double-stranded DNA antibodies	Positive (1+)
Urinalysis	1+ protein; 0-2 erythrocytes/hpf; 0-2 leukocytes/hpf; no erythrocyte casts

Which of the following is the most appropriate management?

(A) Increase mycophenolate mofetil
(B) Increase prednisone
(C) Perform lymph node biopsy
(D) Perform tuberculin skin test

Item 12

A 24-year-old woman is evaluated for a 3-week history of pain and swelling of the right knee and left ankle. She also has urinary frequency and urgency. The patient has no history of tick exposure, skin rash, diarrhea, or abdominal pain. She has not been sexually active in the past month. She takes no medications.

On physical examination, vital signs are normal. Musculoskeletal examination reveals swelling, tenderness, warmth, pain on active and passive range of motion, and a palpable effusion of the right knee; the left ankle is swollen and tender, with pain at the extremes of active range of motion and no significant pain with passive range of motion.

Serologic test results for *Borrelia burgdorferi* are negative. Urinalysis reveals 2+ leukocyte esterase, 18 leukocytes/hpf, and no protein, bacteria, squamous epithelial cells, or erythrocytes.

Aspiration of the right knee is performed; synovial fluid analysis reveals an erythrocyte count of 150/μL and a leukocyte count of 7500/μL (7.5×10^9/L). Gram stain is negative. Synovial fluid culture results are pending.

Which of the following is the most appropriate next step in management?

(A) Antinuclear antibody testing
(B) Rheumatoid factor testing
(C) Synovial fluid polymerase chain reaction testing for *Borrelia burgdorferi*
(D) Urine nucleic acid amplification testing for *Chlamydia trachomatis* and *Neisseria gonorrhoeae*

Item 13

A 68-year-old man is evaluated for a 10-year history of left knee pain associated with osteoarthritis. He is limited in ambulation to two blocks and now has pain at rest, which also disturbs his sleep. He reports only partial relief with NSAIDs and now takes hydrocodone on a regular basis. He has had little benefit from physical therapy and intra-articular corticosteroid injections. He has no other pertinent personal medical history.

On physical examination, temperature is 37.2 °C (99.0 °F), blood pressure is 142/72 mm Hg, pulse rate is 88/min, and respiration rate is 18/min. BMI is 28. The left knee is enlarged. Range of motion of the knee elicits significant crepitus with medial joint line pain. There is no varus or valgus laxity or anterior or posterior laxity.

Radiographs of the knee reveal severe joint-space narrowing of the medial compartment of the joint and mild to moderate narrowing of the patellofemoral joint. There is a tibial osteophyte and subchondral sclerosis.

Which of the following is the most appropriate treatment for this patient?

(A) Arthroscopic lavage
(B) High tibial osteotomy
(C) Hyaluronate injection
(D) Total knee replacement surgery

Item 14

A 74-year-old woman is evaluated for a 2-year history of progressive pain of the fingers and knees, along with morning stiffness lasting 20 minutes. She has no other pertinent personal or family medical history. Her only medication is acetaminophen as needed for pain.

On physical examination, temperature is 37.0 °C (98.6 °F), blood pressure is 118/70 mm Hg, pulse rate is 66/min, and respiration rate is 12/min. BMI is 19. Musculoskeletal examination reveals tenderness, erythema, some soft-tissue swelling, and bony hypertrophy of the second and third metacarpophalangeal joints bilaterally. Bony hypertrophy and fluctuance of the knees is noted bilaterally.

Laboratory studies, including erythrocyte sedimentation rate and serum ferritin, iron, and total iron-binding capacity levels, are normal; transferrin saturation is not elevated. Rheumatoid factor and anti–cyclic citrullinated peptide antibodies are negative.

Radiographs of the hands reveal joint-space narrowing, particularly of the second and third metacarpophalangeal joints; osteophytes, subchondral sclerosis, and linear calcification of the cartilage are noted. The triangular fibrocartilage of the wrists also demonstrates calcification. Radiographs of the knees show diffuse joint-space narrowing with osteophytes and cartilaginous calcification. There are no marginal erosions or periarticular osteopenia.

Which of the following is the most likely diagnosis?

(A) Calcium pyrophosphate arthropathy
(B) Hemochromatosis
(C) Osteoarthritis
(D) Pseudogout
(E) Rheumatoid arthritis

Item 15

A 32-year-old woman seeks preconception counseling. She was diagnosed with rheumatoid arthritis 1 year ago. She has no other pertinent personal or family medical history. Disease activity is controlled with methotrexate. She also takes folic acid.

On physical examination, vital signs are normal. On musculoskeletal examination, there is no synovitis or bony abnormalities. The remainder of the examination is normal.

Laboratory studies, including erythrocyte sedimentation rate and C-reactive protein level, are normal; rheumatoid factor and anti–cyclic citrullinated peptide antibodies are positive. Urine pregnancy test results are negative.

Radiographs of the hands, feet, and cervical spine are normal.

Which of the following is the most appropriate management?

(A) Discontinue methotrexate before conception

(B) Discontinue methotrexate when conception is confirmed

(C) Maintain methotrexate through pregnancy at current dose

(D) Maintain methotrexate through pregnancy with dose adjustment

Item 16

A 58-year-old woman is evaluated for a 3-month history of fatigue and a nonpruritic rash on the chest and arms. The rash worsens with sun exposure. The patient reports no pleurisy, dryness of the eyes or mouth, arthritis, or Raynaud phenomenon.

On physical examination, vital signs are normal. On cutaneous examination, there are no other rashes, alopecia, or oral ulcers. There is no evidence of synovitis. The appearance of the rash is shown.

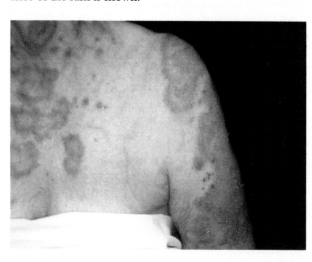

Laboratory studies, including metabolic panel, complete blood count, and urinalysis, are normal. Antinuclear antibody test results are negative, and anti-Ro/SSA antibody test results are positive.

Which of the following is the most likely diagnosis?

(A) Livedo reticularis

(B) Lyme disease

(C) Subacute cutaneous lupus erythematosus

(D) Systemic lupus erythematosus

Item 17

A 47-year-old man is evaluated in the emergency department for a 5-day history of acute swelling and pain of the right knee. He has a 15-year history of gout, with multiple attacks annually; he also has diabetes mellitus and chronic kidney disease. Medications are enalapril, glipizide, and allopurinol.

On physical examination, temperature is 38.2 °C (100.8 °F), blood pressure is 146/88 mm Hg, pulse rate is 96/min, and respiration rate is 15/min. BMI is 27. Several nodules are noted on the metacarpophalangeal and proximal interphalangeal joints and within the olecranon bursa. The right knee is swollen, erythematous, warm, tender, and fluctuant.

Laboratory studies:

Hemoglobin	10.1 g/dL (101 g/L)
Leukocyte count	13,000/µL ([13 × 10⁹/L], 85% neutrophils)
Serum creatinine	2.8 mg/dL (247.5 µmol/L)
Serum uric acid	9.2 mg/dL (0.54 mmol/L)

Radiographs of the knee reveal soft-tissue swelling.

Aspiration drainage of the right knee is performed. Synovial fluid leukocyte count is 110,000/µL ([110 × 10⁹/L], 88% neutrophils). Polarized light microscopy of the fluid demonstrates extracellular and intracellular negatively birefringent crystals. Gram stain is negative for bacteria. Culture results are pending.

Which of the following is the most appropriate initial treatment?

(A) Intra-articular methylprednisolone

(B) Prednisone

(C) Surgical debridement and drainage

(D) Vancomycin plus piperacillin-tazobactam

Item 18

A 42-year-old man is evaluated for a 2-year history of recurrent pain and swelling of the wrists and knees, which limits his ability to walk and cook. He also has a 3-year history of psoriasis affecting the scalp. Scaling recurs periodically, which was initially responsive to topical medications but now is more resistant to treatment. He has no other pertinent personal or family medical history. His only medication is topical clobetasol propionate.

On physical examination, vital signs are normal. Cutaneous examination reveals erythematous plaques in the scalp with thick silver scaling. Nail pitting is present. On musculoskeletal examination, the wrists and knees are swollen and tender, and there is pain on active and passive range of motion.

Rheumatoid factor and anti–cyclic citrullinated peptide antibody test results are negative.

Synovial fluid analysis is compatible with an inflammatory arthritis. There are no crystals. Gram stain and culture results are negative.

Which of the following is the most appropriate treatment for this patient?

(A) Ibuprofen

(B) Methotrexate

(C) Prednisone

(D) Rituximab

Item 19

A 58-year-old man is evaluated for a 6-year history of hand pain accompanied by morning stiffness lasting 30 minutes and a 2-year history of bilateral hip pain. He takes naproxen, which moderately relieves the pain.

On physical examination, vital signs are normal. There is tenderness of both wrists and the metacarpophalangeal joints and pain on flexion and internal rotation of the hips. The wrists and hips have limited range of motion.

Radiographs reveal joint-space narrowing at the hips, metacarpophalangeal joints, and proximal interphalangeal joints; osteophytes are seen at the metacarpophalangeal and hip joints.

Which of the following tests is likely to confirm diagnosis?

(A) Antinuclear antibody assay
(B) Rheumatoid factor
(C) Serum transferrin saturation
(D) Serum uric acid level

Item 20

A 52-year-old man is evaluated for an 8-week history of pain and 2 hours of morning stiffness of the hands that improves with activity. The patient has no pertinent personal or family medical history. He takes no medications.

On physical examination, vital signs are normal. Synovitis is noted at the metacarpophalangeal joints of the second through fifth digits bilaterally with swelling, tenderness, and pain on range of motion. The remainder of the examination is normal.

Laboratory studies, including complete blood count, chemistries, liver chemistry tests, thyroid-stimulating hormone, C-reactive protein, and urinalysis, are normal; erythrocyte sedimentation rate is 13 mm/h, and rheumatoid factor is negative. Parvovirus serology results are negative.

Radiographs of the hands are normal.

Which of the following antibody assays is most helpful in establishing this patient's diagnosis?

(A) Anti–cyclic citrullinated peptide antibodies
(B) Antimitochondrial antibodies
(C) Antineutrophil cytoplasmic antibodies
(D) Antinuclear antibodies

Item 21

A 38-year-old man is evaluated for a 3-year history of pain and stiffness involving the low back. These symptoms are worse in the morning and usually improve with activity. He has no other pertinent personal or family medical history. His only medication is occasional use of acetaminophen, which provides minimal relief.

On physical examination, vital signs are normal. Musculoskeletal examination reveals decreased lumbar spinal mobility.

Laboratory studies are normal except for an elevated erythrocyte sedimentation rate and C-reactive protein level.

An anteroposterior radiograph of the pelvis reveals fusion of the sacroiliac joints bilaterally.

Which of the following is the most appropriate treatment?

(A) Diclofenac
(B) Etanercept
(C) Methotrexate
(D) Sulfasalazine

Item 22

A 24-year-old man is evaluated in the emergency department for a 6-week history of myalgia, abdominal pain, and a 4.1-kg (9-lb) weight loss. The patient has a previous history of injection drug use. He takes no medications.

On physical examination, temperature is 37.5 °C (99.5 °F), blood pressure is 180/110 mm Hg, pulse rate is 90/min, and respiration rate is 18/min. Cardiopulmonary examination is normal. On abdominal examination, there is diffuse tenderness without guarding and no evidence of hepatosplenomegaly. The testes are tender. Livedo reticularis is noted on the lower extremities. There is weakness of left foot eversion; no other focal weakness is noted.

Laboratory studies:

Hematocrit	31%
Leukocyte count	13,000/µL (13 × 10⁹/L)
Erythrocyte sedimentation rate	70 mm/h
Serum creatinine	1.6 mg/dL (141.4 µmol/L)
Hepatitis B surface antigen	Positive
Hepatitis B e antigen	Positive

Mesenteric angiogram reveals aneurysms of mesenteric and renal arteries.

In addition to prednisone, which of the following is the most appropriate treatment?

(A) Entecavir
(B) Infliximab
(C) Mycophenolate mofetil
(D) Rituximab

Item 23

A 64-year-old man is evaluated for a 2-year history of knee osteoarthritis. He has bilateral knee pain that worsens with walking. He has tried topical therapies, physical therapy, and acetaminophen, none of which has provided relief. The patient also has peripheral vascular disease, hyperlipidemia, and hypertension. Medications are hydrochlorothiazide, pravastatin, and a daily aspirin.

On physical examination, temperature is 37.0 °C (98.6 °F), blood pressure is 116/76 mm Hg, pulse rate is 60/min, and respiration rate is 12/min. BMI is 26. Musculoskeletal examination reveals small knee effusions bilaterally, with crepitus and tenderness along the medial joint line.

Laboratory studies, including complete blood count, erythrocyte sedimentation rate, plasma glucose, and serum creatinine, are normal.

Radiographs of the knees, including weight-bearing studies, reveal bilateral medial joint-space narrowing, subchondral sclerosis, and small osteophytes.

Which of the following is the most appropriate treatment for this patient?

(A) Celecoxib
(B) Colchicine
(C) Indomethacin
(D) Prednisone
(E) Tramadol

Item 24

A 67-year-old woman returns to the office 1 week following her initial visit for suspected giant cell arteritis. At that time, prednisone, 60 mg/d, was initiated and a left temporal artery biopsy was performed; the biopsy results were negative for arteritis. She also has hypertension, diabetes mellitus, and chronic kidney disease. Additional medications are atenolol, hydrochlorothiazide, and metformin.

On physical examination, temperature is 38.1 °C (100.5 °F), blood pressure is 130/90 mm Hg, pulse rate is 90/min, and respiration rate is 14/min. Pulses are present in both temporal arteries. Diffuse scalp tenderness is noted. There are no audible bruits over the carotid or subclavian vessels.

Laboratory studies:

Hematocrit	34%
Erythrocyte sedimentation rate	105 mm/h
Serum creatinine	2.1 mg/dL (185.6 μmol/L)
Estimated glomerular filtration rate	38 mL/min/1.73 m²
Urinalysis	Normal

Which of the following is the most appropriate management?

(A) CT angiography of the aortic arch, carotid, and subclavian vessels
(B) Decrease prednisone to 10 mg/d
(C) MR angiography of the aortic arch, carotid, and subclavian vessels
(D) Ultrasound-guided biopsy of the right temporal artery

Item 25

A 42-year-old man is evaluated for swelling, pain, and morning stiffness of the wrists and hands. Six months ago, he was diagnosed with rheumatoid arthritis. The patient drinks two to three alcoholic beverages daily and has a 20-pack-year history of smoking. Medications are hydroxychloroquine, prednisone, naproxen, and folic acid.

On physical examination, temperature is 37.0 °C (98.6 °F), blood pressure is 118/76 mm Hg, pulse rate is

72/min, and respiration rate is 14/min. BMI is 26. Musculoskeletal examination reveals swelling, erythema, and tenderness of the wrists and multiple metacarpophalangeal and proximal interphalangeal joints bilaterally, with decreased range of motion. The knees are swollen with slightly decreased flexion bilaterally.

The comprehensive metabolic profile, including aminotransferase levels, is normal.

Radiographs of the hands reveal periarticular soft-tissue swelling as well as joint-space narrowing of several metacarpophalangeal and proximal interphalangeal joints with periarticular osteopenia.

Prior to initiating methotrexate therapy, which of the following must be discontinued?

(A) Alcohol
(B) Folic acid
(C) Hydroxychloroquine
(D) Prednisone
(E) Smoking

Item 26

A 38-year-old woman is evaluated for a 6-month history of progressive fatigue and dyspnea on exertion. Over the past 2 years she has noted episodes of hand swelling, joint pain, blue color change of her fingers with cold exposure, and difficulty swallowing. She takes no medications.

On physical examination, temperature is 36.9 °C (98.4 °F), blood pressure is 126/84 mm Hg, pulse rate is 88/min, and respiration rate is 18/min. Cardiac examination reveals an accentuated pulmonic component of S_2 and a grade 2/6 holosystolic murmur. Muscle strength is normal.

Laboratory studies reveal a serum creatine kinase level of 312 units/L, an antinuclear antibody titer of 1:1280 (speckled pattern), and high positive anti-U1-ribonucleoprotein antibodies.

Pulmonary function tests show a D_{LCO} of 55% of predicted with normal FEV_1 and lung volumes. Chest radiograph is normal. Electrocardiogram reveals right axis deviation. Echocardiogram shows 2+ tricuspid regurgitation, an enlarged right atrium, normal left and right ventricular function, and an estimated systolic pulmonary artery pressure of 40 mm Hg. High-resolution CT of the chest is normal. Ventilation/perfusion scan results are normal.

Which of the following is the most appropriate next step in management?

(A) Muscle biopsy
(B) Radionuclide stress test
(C) Repeat echocardiography and pulmonary function tests in 1 year
(D) Right heart catheterization

Item 27

A 30-year-old woman is evaluated in the emergency department for a 2-day history of fever, malaise, and progressive swelling and pain of the right knee. Two weeks

CONT.

ago, she played volleyball and fell, abrading both knees. She resumed playing but later developed cellulitis over the left knee; a first-generation cephalosporin was initiated for 7 days. She was subsequently well until the current symptoms developed 2 days ago. She reports no upper respiratory or urinary symptoms and is otherwise healthy. She takes no medications.

On physical examination, temperature is 38.1 °C (100.5 °F), blood pressure is 117/78 mm Hg, pulse rate is 72/min, and respiration rate is 12/min. BMI is 19. Healing abrasions are noted on the anterior surfaces of both knees; there are no rashes or other skin lesions. The right knee is swollen, erythematous, warm, and exquisitely tender, with markedly diminished range of motion and no instability.

Radiographs of the right knee reveal soft-tissue swelling and a large effusion; there are no erosions, punched-out lesions, or other bony changes.

Which of the following is the most likely diagnosis?

(A) Acute gouty arthritis
(B) Anterior cruciate ligament tear
(C) Lyme arthritis
(D) *Staphylococcus aureus* infection

Item 28

A 36-year-old woman is evaluated for a 5-week history of pain and swelling of the fingers accompanied by morning stiffness lasting more than 1 hour. Her only medication is ibuprofen, which provides minimal relief.

On physical examination, vital signs are normal. Musculoskeletal examination reveals tenderness and swelling of the right second, third, and fourth metacarpophalangeal joints and the left third, fourth, and fifth metacarpophalangeal joints. There is no bony enlargement, ulnar deviation, or other abnormalities.

Laboratory studies:

Erythrocyte sedimentation rate	40 mm/h
Rheumatoid factor	43 units/mL (43 kU/L)
Antinuclear antibodies	Negative
Anti–cyclic citrullinated peptide antibodies	Positive
IgM antibodies against parvovirus B19	Negative
Hepatitis B surface antigen	Negative
Hepatitis B surface antibodies	Positive
Hepatitis C virus antibodies	Negative

Radiographs of the hands and wrists are normal.

Which of the following is the most appropriate next step in management?

(A) Etanercept
(B) Hydroxychloroquine
(C) Methotrexate
(D) Reevaluate in 6 weeks

Item 29

A 52-year-old woman is evaluated for a 3-month history of fatigue, a photosensitive malar rash, and hand pain accompanied by morning stiffness. She has no other pertinent personal or family medical history. She takes no medications.

On physical examination, vital signs are normal. There is a 5-mm ulcer on the hard palate. A livedo rash is present on the knees. Tenderness of the metacarpophalangeal and proximal interphalangeal joints is noted; there is no swelling. The remainder of the physical examination is normal.

Initial laboratory studies, including complete blood count, erythrocyte sedimentation rate, and urinalysis, are normal. Antinuclear antibody test results are positive with a titer of 1:160.

Which of the following tests is most specific in confirming this patient's diagnosis?

(A) Anti–double-stranded DNA antibodies
(B) Anti-Ro/SSA and anti-La/SSB antibodies
(C) Anti-U1-ribonucleoprotein antibodies
(D) Antiproteinase-3 antibodies

Item 30

A 26-year-old woman is evaluated in the emergency department. She has a 3-month history of intermittent bloody diarrhea and tenesmus. She was diagnosed with ulcerative colitis 2 months ago and was started on 5-aminosalicylate enemas. The patient also has a 3-week history of left knee and bilateral ankle pain; she tried over-the-counter ibuprofen, but this caused worsening of her bloody diarrhea.

On physical examination, vital signs are normal. The abdomen is diffusely tender without rebound or guarding; hyperactive bowel sounds are noted. Musculoskeletal examination reveals swelling, tenderness, warmth, and pain on active and passive range of motion of the left knee and swelling, tenderness, and pain at the extremes of active range of motion of the ankles.

Synovial fluid analysis is consistent with an inflammatory arthritis. Synovial fluid Gram stain, microscopy for crystals, and culture results are negative.

Plain radiographs of the left knee and ankles are normal.

Which of the following is the most appropriate long-term treatment for this patient?

(A) Etanercept
(B) Methotrexate
(C) Prednisone
(D) Sulfasalazine

Item 31

A 23-year-old woman is evaluated for a 4-month history of a painless indurated plaque on the abdomen that is mildly pruritic. She reports no history of Raynaud phenomenon. She is otherwise healthy and takes no medications.

On physical examination, temperature is 36.9 °C (98.4 °F), blood pressure is 110/60 mm Hg, pulse rate is 70/min, and respiration rate is 12/min. There is a 5 × 10-cm well-demarcated nontender area of induration on the anterior abdomen; the overlying skin texture is smooth with mild blanching erythema. No other skin lesions are present. The remainder of the examination is unremarkable.

Laboratory studies, including complete blood count and urinalysis, are normal. Antinuclear antibody test results are negative.

Results from a skin biopsy reveal perivascular accumulations of lymphocytes in the dermis consistent with scleroderma skin; no pannicular inflammation is present.

Which of the following is the most likely diagnosis?

(A) Diffuse cutaneous systemic sclerosis
(B) Limited cutaneous systemic sclerosis
(C) Linear scleroderma
(D) Morphea

Item 32

A 44-year-old woman is evaluated during a follow-up visit for an 8-month history of rheumatoid arthritis. She is feeling well, with no current joint pain or swelling and less than 10 minutes of morning stiffness. She does not drink alcohol or smoke cigarettes. She has no other pertinent personal medical history. Medications are methotrexate, hydroxychloroquine, and folic acid, all of which were initiated 4 months ago.

On physical examination, temperature is 37.0 °C (98.6 °F), blood pressure is 115/72 mm Hg, pulse rate is 66/min, and respiration rate is 13/min. BMI is 22. Musculoskeletal examination reveals minimal tenderness and no swelling of the right third and left fourth metacarpophalangeal joints. The remainder of the examination is normal.

Laboratory studies reveal normal complete blood count and liver chemistry tests; erythrocyte sedimentation rate is 22 mm/h.

Radiographs of the hands, knees, and feet are normal.

Which of the following is the most appropriate next step in management?

(A) Add etanercept
(B) Discontinue methotrexate
(C) Liver biopsy
(D) Retinal examination

Item 33

A 66-year-old man comes for a preoperative evaluation before total joint arthroplasty of the left knee. He has a 25-year history of rheumatoid arthritis. He has had progressive pain in his left knee with activity, which limits his ability to hike. The patient has similar pain in the right knee, but it is less severe. He reports no recent morning stiffness. He is able to climb two or three flights of stairs without chest pain or shortness of breath. He has no other medical problems and reports no additional symptoms. Medications are methotrexate and folic acid.

On physical examination, temperature is 37.0 °C (98.6 °F), blood pressure is 120/70 mm Hg, pulse rate is 80/min, and respiration rate is 16/min. BMI is 19. Examination of the hands reveals ulnar deviation and swan neck deformities involving the third digit of the right hand and the fourth digit of the left hand. Range of motion of the

knees elicits crepitus and pain, which are worse in the left knee. There is no warmth, redness, swelling, or tenderness. Neurologic examination is unremarkable.

Recent evaluation of liver chemistry tests revealed no abnormalities.

Electrocardiogram and chest radiograph are normal.

Which of the following is the next best step in management?

(A) Cervical spine radiography
(B) Exercise cardiac stress testing
(C) Preoperative spirometry
(D) Screening coagulation studies

Item 34

A 64-year-old man is evaluated during a routine follow-up visit for a 5-year history of rheumatoid arthritis. Four months ago, he began intravenous infusions of tocilizumab to manage synovitis that was not responding to treatment with etanercept; his last infusion was administered 2 weeks ago. The patient also has hypertension. Family history is notable for his father, brother, and uncle with coronary artery disease. Other medications are enalapril, hydrochlorothiazide, methotrexate, prednisone, and naproxen as needed.

On physical examination, temperature is 37.0 °C (98.6 °F), blood pressure is 130/84 mm Hg, pulse rate is 80/min and regular, and respiration rate is 16/min. Auscultation of the heart and lungs is normal, and no edema is present. No synovitis is present on musculoskeletal examination. The remainder of the examination is unremarkable.

Laboratory studies performed before each infusion reveal normal complete blood counts, liver chemistry tests, and serum creatinine levels. A lipid profile obtained 6 months ago revealed a total cholesterol level of 180 mg/dL (4.7 mmol/L) and a LDL cholesterol level of 98 mg/dL (2.5 mmol/L).

Results from a tuberculin skin test obtained before starting tocilizumab treatment were negative.

Which of the following is the most appropriate test to perform next?

(A) Echocardiography
(B) Electrocardiography
(C) Lipid profile
(D) Serum aminotransferase levels
(E) Serum immunoglobulin levels

Item 35

A 42-year-old woman is evaluated for a 3-week history of malaise, rash, chest pain, and increasing pain and swelling of the hands. She was diagnosed with seropositive rheumatoid arthritis 4 years ago, and methotrexate was initiated. The patient started infliximab 9 months ago and did not have recent flares of synovitis.

On physical examination, temperature is 38.1 °C (100.5 °F), blood pressure is 130/80 mm Hg, pulse rate is 88/min, and respiration rate is 18/min. An erythematous macular rash is noted on the sun-exposed areas of the forearms and the face. On cardiopulmonary examination, a pleural friction rub is audible over the left lateral chest wall. The proximal interphalangeal joints of both hands have soft-tissue swelling and are tender to palpation.

Laboratory studies, including complete blood count, complete metabolic profile, and C-reactive protein level, are normal; rheumatoid factor, anti–cyclic citrullinated peptide antibody, and antinuclear antibody test results are positive. Results from a tuberculin skin test taken 6 months ago were negative.

Chest radiograph reveals a small left-sided pleural effusion.

Which of the following is the most appropriate next step in management?

(A) Add hydroxychloroquine
(B) Add rituximab
(C) Discontinue infliximab
(D) Increase methotrexate

Item 36

A 38-year-old man is evaluated in the emergency department for fever and night sweats, as well as severe mid back pain, which has gradually increased over 6 months. The pain is now constant, independent of motion, and not relieved at night. The patient emigrated from Ghana 1 month ago. He has a 3-year history of HIV infection and takes no medications.

On physical examination, the patient appears cachectic and uncomfortable. Temperature is 38.2 °C (100.8 °F), blood pressure is 112/74 mm Hg, pulse rate is 78/min, and respiration rate is 14/min. BMI is 19. Limitation of flexion, extension, and rotation of the spine is noted. The mid thoracic back is tender. Neurologic examination is normal. The remainder of the examination is normal.

Radiographs of the spine reveal disk-space narrowing at the T12-L1 disk with destruction of the inferior surface of the T12 and the superior surface of the L1 vertebrae. MRI of the spine reveals a large irregular intervertebral and paraspinal mass. Chest radiograph is normal.

Which of the following is most likely to provide a diagnosis?

(A) CT myelography
(B) Technetium-99m bone scan
(C) Tuberculin skin test
(D) Vertebral biopsy

Item 37

A 45-year-old man is evaluated for a 10-year history of progressive bilateral knee pain with activity; the pain is worse when standing or walking. The pain is chronic, without acute exacerbations, and he has no other musculoskeletal symptoms. He takes ibuprofen as needed for the pain, with some relief.

On physical examination, vital signs are normal. There is no effusion, erythema, or warmth to palpation. Bony

enlargement is present. There is crepitus with passive range of motion, which is painful and limited.

A radiograph of the knee is shown.

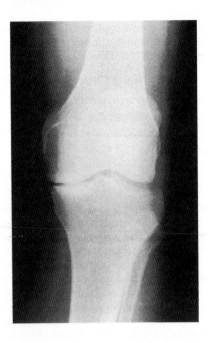

Which of the following is the most likely diagnosis?

(A) Calcium pyrophosphate deposition disease
(B) Gout
(C) Osteoarthritis
(D) Rheumatoid arthritis

Item 38

A 24-year-old woman is evaluated in the emergency department for a 5-day history of fever and right knee pain, which over the past 2 days has progressed to include pain and swelling of the left ankle and right wrist. She has pain on moving the hand and wrist joints and on flexing and extending the fingers and toes. She had been previously well and has no history of trauma. Her only medication is an oral contraceptive.

On physical examination, temperature is 38.4 °C (101.2 °F), blood pressure is 118/76 mm Hg, pulse rate is 86/min, and respiration rate is 13/min. BMI is 21. The oropharynx is unremarkable. The right wrist is swollen, erythematous, warm, and painful, with limited active and passive range of motion. The dorsum of the right hand is swollen, red, and warm; there is tenderness with direct palpation of the extensor tendons, with minimal ability to move the fingers. The right knee is tender to palpation, and there is pain on motion. The left ankle is tender, and the dorsum of the foot is swollen and tender. Findings on cutaneous examination are shown (see next page).

Arthrocentesis is performed. The synovial fluid leukocyte count is 14,400/µL ([14.4 × 10⁹/L], 85% neutrophils). Polarized light microscopy of the fluid is negative for crystals, and Gram stain and cultures are negative.

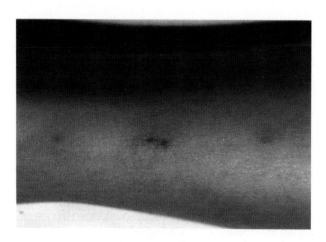

Which of the following is the most likely diagnosis?

(A) Disseminated gonococcal infection
(B) Gout
(C) Rheumatoid arthritis
(D) Staphylococcal arthritis

Item 39

A 23-year-old woman is evaluated for a 3-week history of cough and purulent nasal secretions. She also has hypothyroidism. Family history is negative for autoimmune disorders. Her only medication is levothyroxine.

On physical examination, temperature is 37.9 °C (100.2 °F), blood pressure is 140/86 mm Hg, pulse rate is 90/min, and respiration rate is 18/min. Nasal turbinates are boggy with purulent, blood-streaked secretions. There are scattered expiratory rhonchi on auscultation. There is no skin rash, alopecia, or joint swelling. Neurologic examination is normal.

Laboratory studies:

Hematocrit	32%
Leukocyte count	12,000/µL (12 × 10⁹/L)
Platelet count	440,000/µL (440 × 10⁹/L)
Serum creatinine	Normal
Antinuclear antibodies	Positive
p-ANCA	Positive
Antimyeloperoxidase antibodies	Positive
Urinalysis	Normal

Sputum culture and tuberculin skin testing results are negative. Gram stain is negative.

Chest radiograph shows nodular infiltrates. CT scan of paranasal sinuses reveals opacification of maxillary and ethmoid sinuses as well as normal orbits.

Which of the following is most likely to establish the diagnosis?

(A) Kidney biopsy
(B) Nasal and sinus mucosa biopsy
(C) Open lung biopsy
(D) Pulmonary angiography
(E) Transbronchial lung biopsy

Item 40

A 23-year-old woman is evaluated for a 1-year history of morning stiffness and achiness of the hands as well as Raynaud phenomenon. Two months ago, she experienced a sun-induced rash on the chest and back and patches of discoloration on the hands.

On physical examination, temperature is 36.4 °C (97.5 °F), blood pressure is 106/66 mm Hg, pulse rate is 60/min, and respiration rate is 16/min. The lungs are clear. Erythematous, violaceous, clumped papules over the extensor surfaces of the elbows, metacarpophalangeal joints, and proximal interphalangeal joints are present; there are nailfold capillary abnormalities with cuticular hypertrophy. Bilateral proximal upper and lower extremity weakness is noted; there is tenderness of the metacarpophalangeal and proximal interphalangeal joints bilaterally without synovitis.

Laboratory studies reveal an erythrocyte sedimentation rate of 82 mm/h, a serum creatine kinase level of 650 units/L, and an antinuclear antibody titer of 1:160 (speckled pattern).

Chest radiograph is normal. Electromyography shows muscle irritability without evidence of neuropathy.

Which of the following is the most appropriate initial treatment?

(A) Intravenous immune globulin
(B) Prednisone
(C) Prednisone and azathioprine
(D) Prednisone and methotrexate

Item 41

A 20-year-old man is evaluated for a 6-month history of low back pain accompanied by prolonged morning stiffness. His symptoms improve over the course of the day, but he is now unable to play recreational soccer. Rest, physical therapy, and acupuncture have not improved his symptoms. Use of ibuprofen or diclofenac provides only partial relief. He has no other pertinent medical history and takes no additional medications.

On physical examination, vital signs are normal. There is loss of normal lumbar lordosis, and flexion of the lumbar spine is decreased. The low back and pelvis are tender to palpation. Pain increases when the patient crosses his legs. Reflexes and muscle strength are intact.

Radiographs of the lumbar spine and sacroiliac joints are normal.

Which of the following studies is most likely to establish the diagnosis in this patient?

(A) Bone scan
(B) CT of the sacroiliac joints
(C) MRI of the lumbar spine
(D) MRI of the sacroiliac joints

Item 42

A 36-year-old man is hospitalized for acute kidney injury and hypertension. He was given an intravenous dose of labetalol, and hemodialysis was initiated acutely to facilitate fluid and potassium management. He has a 5-year history of diffuse cutaneous systemic sclerosis. His only medication before hospitalization was omeprazole.

On physical examination following dialysis, temperature is 36.6 °C (97.8 °F), blood pressure is 140/70 mm Hg, pulse rate is 70/min, and respiration rate is 18/min. Cardiac examination reveals regular rhythm without murmurs or extra sounds. Pulmonary auscultation reveals bibasilar crackles. Cutaneous examination reveals sclerodactyly of both hands as well as skin induration of the forearms and anterior chest; there are no digital ulcers or acrocyanosis.

Laboratory studies:

Hematocrit	28%
Leukocyte count	4900/µL (4.9×10^9/L)
Platelet count	90,000/µL (90×10^9/L)
Blood urea nitrogen	40 mg/dL (14.3 mmol/L)
Serum creatinine	5.2 mg/dL (459.7 µmol/L)
Lactate dehydrogenase	480 units/L

Peripheral blood smear reveals several schistocytes. Kidney ultrasound reveals normal-sized kidneys and no hydronephrosis.

Which of the following is the most appropriate treatment?

(A) Bosentan
(B) Lisinopril
(C) Plasma exchange
(D) Sildenafil

Item 43

A 42-year-old man is evaluated during a routine follow-up visit. He was diagnosed with rheumatoid arthritis 1 year ago. At that time, the patient had evidence of early erosions of the metacarpophalangeal joints and positive anti–cyclic citrullinated peptide antibodies. Disease activity persisted on methotrexate but resolved approximately 6 months ago after the addition of adalimumab. The patient now reports no morning stiffness, pain, swelling, or fatigue. He has not had any illnesses or been in contact with sick persons.

On physical examination today, vital signs are normal. Musculoskeletal examination reveals no deformities and no joint swelling or tenderness. Erythrocyte sedimentation rate and C-reactive protein level are normal.

Laboratory studies (9 months ago):

Hepatitis B surface antibody	Positive
Hepatitis B surface antigen	Negative
Hepatitis C virus antibody	Nonreactive
Tuberculin skin testing	Negative

Which of the following is the most appropriate diagnostic test to perform next?

(A) Anti–cyclic citrullinated peptide antibody assay
(B) Bilateral radiographs of the hands and wrists
(C) Repeat hepatitis C virus antibody assay
(D) Repeat tuberculin skin testing
(E) Varicella virus antibody assay

Item 44

A 52-year-old woman is evaluated for a 3-month history of progressive submandibular swelling and tenderness as well as a 3-week history of nonproductive cough and a hoarse voice. She is otherwise healthy and takes no medications.

On physical examination, temperature is 37.7 °C (99.8 °F), blood pressure is 160/105 mm Hg, pulse rate is 100/min, and respiration rate is 18/min. Oral mucous membranes are normal. The right submandibular gland is tender and indurated.

Laboratory studies:

Hematocrit	32%
Leukocyte count	8800/µL (8.8×10^9/L)
Platelet count	483,000/µL (483×10^9/L)
Serum creatinine	1.6 mg/dL (141.4 µmol/L)
Urinalysis	2+ protein; 10-15 erythrocytes/hpf; 0-5 leukocytes/hpf; erythrocyte casts present

Chest radiograph reveals right upper lobe and right lower lobe infiltrates with several cavitary lesions. CT scan of the neck and chest reveals an enlarged right submandibular gland, an inflammatory luminal mass in the trachea subjacent to the larynx, and right upper lobe and right lower lobe patchy infiltrates adjacent to several 1- to 2-cm cavitary lesions; no hilar or paratracheal lymphadenopathy is present. Tuberculin skin test results are negative.

Which of the following is the most likely diagnosis?

(A) Granulomatosis with polyangiitis
(B) Sarcoidosis
(C) Sjögren syndrome
(D) Tuberculosis

Item 45

A 46-year-old woman is evaluated for a 3-month history of pain and swelling of the hands, dyspnea, and wheezing. She has no other pertinent personal or family medical history. She takes naproxen as needed for pain relief.

On physical examination, vital signs are normal. The ears are thickened bilaterally; the right ear has moderate warmth, erythema, and tenderness to palpation. Saddle nose deformity is noted; examination of the nares shows intact mucosa. Tenderness of the metacarpophalangeal and proximal interphalangeal joints is noted; the second and third metacarpophalangeal joints are swollen bilaterally. Pulmonary examination reveals expiratory wheezing in the upper lung fields. The appearance of the ears is shown (see next page).

Laboratory studies reveal a hemoglobin level of 11 g/dL (110 g/L) and an erythrocyte sedimentation rate of 56 mm/h. Antinuclear antibody and ANCA assay results are negative.

Chest radiograph is normal.

Which of the following is the most appropriate diagnostic test to perform next in this patient?

(A) CT of the sinuses
(B) Pulmonary function testing with flow volume loops

(C) Rheumatoid factor

(D) Urine toxicology screen

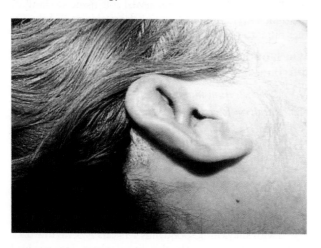

Item 46

A 22-year-old woman is evaluated for a 3-month history of malaise, myalgia, and a 2.2-kg (5-lb) weight loss. She is otherwise healthy. Her only medication is an oral contraceptive.

On physical examination, temperature is 37.8 °C (100.0 °F), blood pressure is 110/70 mm Hg, pulse rate is 80/min, and respiration rate is 14/min. Cutaneous examination reveals no oral ulcers, rash, or alopecia. Cardiac examination is normal without audible murmurs, but a bruit is audible in the left supraclavicular fossa. Radial and dorsalis pedis pulses are symmetrically normal. There is no joint swelling, and muscle strength is normal.

Laboratory studies:

Hematocrit	28%
Leukocyte count	7600/µL (7.6 × 10⁹/L)
Platelet count	480,000/µL (480 × 10⁹/L)
Erythrocyte sedimentation rate	80 mm/h
C-reactive protein	4.5 mg/dL (45 mg/L)
Creatine kinase	Normal
Serum creatinine	Normal
Rheumatoid factor	Negative
ANCA	Negative
Antinuclear antibodies	Negative

Which of the following is the most likely diagnosis?

(A) Adult-onset Still disease

(B) Microscopic polyangiitis

(C) Polyarteritis nodosa

(D) Polymyositis

(E) Takayasu arteritis

Item 47

A 72-year-old woman is evaluated for a 6-month history of increasing pain and swelling of the hands and fingers associated with a 20-year history of osteoarthritis. The pain is worse with activity, and she now has difficulty opening jars and buttoning her shirt. She states that diclofenac no longer provides relief. She takes no other medications.

On physical examination, temperature is 37.0 °C (98.6 °F), blood pressure is 148/78 mm Hg, pulse rate is 88/min, and respiration rate is 18/min. Musculoskeletal examination reveals bilateral firm swelling and tenderness of the second and third proximal interphalangeal joints. The left third distal interphalangeal joint is swollen and red. The remainder of the examination is unremarkable.

Laboratory studies reveal an erythrocyte sedimentation rate of 36 mm/h.

Radiographs of the hands reveal joint-space narrowing of the proximal and distal interphalangeal joints with multiple osteophytes; erosive changes of the distal interphalangeal joints are noted.

Which of the following is the most likely diagnosis?

(A) Erosive hand osteoarthritis

(B) Psoriatic arthritis

(C) Rheumatoid arthritis

(D) Tophaceous gout

Item 48

A 49-year-old woman is evaluated for a 4-week history of purpuric rash, arthralgia, and lower limb paresthesia. She also has a 10-year history of Sjögren syndrome. She has no other pertinent personal or family medical history and takes no medications.

On physical examination, temperature is 36.9 °C (98.4 °F), blood pressure is 140/76 mm Hg, pulse rate is 80/min, and respiration rate is 14/min. Ocular and oral mucous membranes are dry. There is no synovitis. There are nonblanching purpuric papular lesions on the dorsa of the feet and anterior tibial regions.

Laboratory studies:

Complete blood count	Normal
Serum creatinine	1.6 mg/dL (141.4 µmol/L)
C3	46 mg/dL (460 mg/L)
C4	8.6 mg/dL (860 mg/L) (normal range, 13-38 mg/dL [130-380 mg/L])
Rheumatoid factor	186 units/mL (186 kU/L)
Antinuclear antibodies	Titer of 1:160 (speckled pattern)
c-ANCA	Negative
p-ANCA	Positive
Hepatitis B surface antigen	Negative
Hepatitis C virus antibodies	Positive
Hepatitis C virus RNA	Negative
Serum cryoglobulin	Positive
Serum immunoelectrophoresis	IgMK paraprotein present
Urinalysis	2+ protein; 15-20 erythrocytes/hpf; 0-5 leukocytes/hpf; erythrocyte casts present

Skin biopsy results reveal leukocytoclastic vasculitis. Kidney biopsy results reveal early membranoproliferative glomerular lesions with subepithelial and subendothelial immune deposits and glomerular thrombi.

Which of the following is the most likely diagnosis?

(A) Microscopic polyangiitis
(B) Systemic lupus erythematosus
(C) Type I cryoglobulinemic vasculitis
(D) Type II cryoglobulinemic vasculitis

Item 49

A 42-year-old woman is evaluated during a routine follow-up visit. Six months ago, she was diagnosed with polymyositis; at that time, her serum creatine kinase level was 9866 units/L, and antinuclear antibody and anti–Jo-1 antibody test results were positive. Prednisone and azathioprine were initiated with good response. Today, she reports muscle weakness, hand stiffness and achiness, sporadic nonproductive cough, and dyspnea. In addition to azathioprine and low-dose prednisone, she currently takes alendronate.

On physical examination, temperature is 36.6 °C (97.9 °F), blood pressure is 132/68 mm Hg, pulse rate is 86/min, and respiration rate is 20/min. Cardiac examination is normal. Pulmonary examination reveals bibasilar crackles. Hyperkeratotic fissuring of the palms and lateral aspects of the fingers as well as mild cyanosis of the left second and third fingers are noted. There is bilateral quadriceps and deltoid muscle weakness. The metacarpophalangeal and proximal interphalangeal joints are mildly tender without synovitis.

Laboratory studies reveal a normal complete blood count, an erythrocyte sedimentation rate of 45 mm/h, and a serum creatine kinase level of 342 units/L.

Chest radiograph is normal.

Which of the following is the most appropriate next step in management?

(A) Echocardiography
(B) High-resolution CT of the chest and pulmonary function tests
(C) Increase prednisone and azathioprine
(D) Right heart catheterization

Item 50

A 27-year-old woman is evaluated for a 3-week history of progressive swelling and pain of the right second digit. Two months ago, she cut her digit while cleaning an aquarium tank. Over the next several days, a nodular erythematous lesion appeared, and the skin above the lesion gradually became more red and puckered. Treatment with cephalexin failed to resolve the skin infection, which gradually spread proximally. She is now unable to move the joint.

On physical examination, temperature is 37.2 °C (99.0 °F), blood pressure is 118/76 mm Hg, pulse rate is 72/min, and respiration rate is 14/min. BMI is 21. The right second proximal interphalangeal joint is swollen, erythematous, and tender, with minimal range of motion. A nodular erythematous lesion is noted on the palmar surface of the right second digit, proximal to

the distal interphalangeal joint; it has surface ulceration and is surrounded by diffuse swelling and erythema.

Radiographs of the hand reveal soft-tissue swelling of the right second proximal interphalangeal joint and the tissues distal to it.

Which of the following is the most likely cause of the infection?

(A) *Mycobacterium marinum*
(B) *Naegleria fowleri*
(C) *Neisseria gonorrhoeae*
(D) *Sporothrix schenckii*

Item 51

A 62-year-old man is evaluated for a 3-day history of mid back pain, which started after he lifted boxes. He was diagnosed with ankylosing spondylitis 18 years ago; his low back pain and stiffness caused by this disorder have since resolved after starting etanercept 6 years ago.

On physical examination, vital signs are normal. Musculoskeletal examination reveals lower thoracic and upper lumbar spine tenderness; limited thoracic and lumbar motion without pain; and no buttock tenderness.

Radiographs of the spine taken 1 year ago revealed bridging syndesmophytes.

Which of the following is the most appropriate next step in management?

(A) Add prednisone
(B) Discontinue etanercept; begin adalimumab
(C) Epidural corticosteroid injection
(D) Repeat radiographs of the spine

Item 52

A 38-year-old man is evaluated for an abnormal serum urate level of 7.9 mg/dL (0.47 mmol/L) that was obtained at a health screening performed at his place of employment. All other measures from the comprehensive metabolic profile were normal. He drinks two alcoholic beverages each week (usually on the weekend) and eats meat several times weekly. He has no other pertinent medical history; family history is notable for his father who has gout. The patient takes no medications.

On physical examination, temperature is 37.0 °C (98.6 °F), blood pressure is 120/80 mm Hg, pulse rate is 66/min, and respiration rate is 12/min. BMI is 24. The remainder of the examination is unremarkable.

Which of the following is the most appropriate treatment for this patient?

(A) Allopurinol
(B) Colchicine
(C) Hydrochlorothiazide
(D) Probenecid
(E) No treatment

Item 53

A 60-year-old man is evaluated for an 8-month history of progressive, generalized weakness and significant difficulty rising from a chair. He reports occasional fever, muscle aches, and hand pain without swelling. He was diagnosed with Hashimoto disease 15 years ago. His only medication is levothyroxine.

On physical examination, temperature is 37.4 °C (99.3 °F), blood pressure is 128/76 mm Hg, pulse rate is 72/min, and respiration rate is 18/min. No rash is present. Bilateral proximal upper and lower extremity weakness is noted. Distal muscle strength is normal.

There is tenderness of the proximal interphalangeal joints bilaterally without synovitis.

Laboratory studies reveal an erythrocyte sedimentation rate of 56 mm/h, a serum creatine kinase level of 1149 units/L, and a thyroid-stimulating hormone level of 2.0 microunits/mL (2.0 milliunits/L).

Electromyogram shows muscle irritability without evidence of neuropathy. Results from a biopsy of the proximal thigh muscle reveal pronounced lymphocytic infiltration of the endomysium with invasion of intact myofibers; there is no evidence of significant perivascular infiltration, inclusions, or rimmed vacuoles.

Which of the following is the most likely diagnosis?

(A) Dermatomyositis
(B) Hypothyroid myopathy
(C) Inclusion body myositis
(D) Polymyositis

Item 54

A 29-year-old woman is evaluated for a 4-day history of pain and swelling involving the wrists, knees, elbows, and multiple joints of the fingers and hands. She is an elementary school teacher, and several children in her class recently had an illness that included a rash on the cheeks. The patient is otherwise healthy and takes no medications.

On physical examination, temperature is 38.1 °C (100.6 °F), blood pressure is 112/76 mm Hg, pulse rate is 86/min, and respiration rate is 15/min. BMI is 23. A faint morbilliform rash is noted on the arms and trunk. There is swelling and tenderness with erythema of the wrists, knees, and several metacarpophalangeal and interphalangeal joints bilaterally.

Laboratory studies:

Complete blood count	Normal
Erythrocyte sedimentation rate	34 mm/h
Rheumatoid factor	Negative
Antinuclear antibodies	Weakly positive
Anti–streptolysin O antibodies	Negative
IgM antibodies against parvovirus B19	Positive

Which of the following is the most appropriate treatment?

(A) Azithromycin
(B) Hydroxychloroquine
(C) Ibuprofen
(D) Penicillin

Item 55

A 58-year-old man is evaluated for a 6-week history of pain and stiffness of the shoulders and hips accompanied by persistent fever and a 2.2-kg (5-lb) weight loss. He reports no jaw claudication, headache, respiratory symptoms, abdominal pain, or swelling of the peripheral joints. The patient is otherwise healthy and takes no medications.

On physical examination, temperature is 38.6 °C (101.5 °F), blood pressure is 140/70 mm Hg, pulse rate is 100/min and regular, and respiration rate is 16/min. Cardiopulmonary examination is normal. Cutaneous examination reveals no skin rash or temporal or scalp tenderness. There is no lymphadenopathy. Musculoskeletal examination reveals mild pain and limitation at the extremes of shoulder and hip rotation bilaterally. Neurologic examination is unremarkable.

Laboratory studies:

Hematocrit	32%
Leukocyte count	12,000/µL (12 × 10⁹/L)
Platelet count	420,000/µL (420 × 10⁹/L)
Erythrocyte sedimentation rate	103 mm/h
C-reactive protein	6.4 mg/dL (64 mg/L)
Serum creatinine	Normal
Rheumatoid factor	Negative
Antinuclear antibodies	Negative
ANCA	Negative
Urinalysis	Normal

Peripheral blood smear and blood cultures are negative.

Chest radiograph and echocardiogram are normal. Results of bilateral temporal artery biopsies are negative.

Which of the following is the most appropriate diagnostic test to perform next?

(A) Bone marrow biopsy
(B) CT angiography of the neck and chest
(C) Kidney and mesenteric angiography
(D) MRI of the shoulder and hip joints

Item 56

A 74-year-old woman is evaluated during a follow-up visit. One month ago, she was diagnosed with giant cell arteritis and began treatment with prednisone, 60 mg/d. She also takes calcium and vitamin D (25-hydroxy vitamin D) supplementation.

On physical examination, temperature is 37.0 °C (98.6 °F), blood pressure is 122/79 mm Hg, pulse rate is 66/min, and respiration rate is 12/min. BMI is 22. The remainder of the examination is unremarkable.

Bone mineral density test results reveal a T score of -1.5 at the spine.

In addition to tapering the prednisone dose, which of the following is the most appropriate treatment for this patient?

(A) Alendronate
(B) Calcitonin

(C) Estrogen hormone replacement therapy

(D) Hydrochlorothiazide and sodium restriction

(E) Substitute calcitriol (1,25-dihydroxy vitamin D) for vitamin D (25-hydroxy vitamin D)

Item 57

A 67-year-old man is evaluated for a 3-year history of low back pain, which is of moderate intensity and worsens during activities, and a 1-year history of neck pain accompanied by 20 minutes of morning stiffness. He reports no radiating symptoms. He has tried ibuprofen, naproxen, and acetaminophen, with only partial relief. He also has type 2 diabetes mellitus that is treated with glyburide and metformin.

On physical examination, vital signs are normal. BMI is 34. There is decreased range of motion of the cervical, thoracic, and lumbar spine. The patient is unable to touch his toes. Straight-leg-raising test results are normal. There is no tenderness over the sacroiliac joints. Neurologic examination is normal.

A radiograph of the spine is shown.

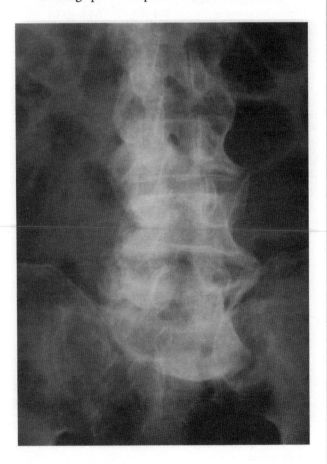

Which of the following is the most likely diagnosis?

(A) Ankylosing spondylitis

(B) Diffuse idiopathic skeletal hyperostosis

(C) Lumbar spinal stenosis

(D) Spondylolisthesis

Item 58

A 48-year-old woman is evaluated in November before the initiation of rituximab for rheumatoid arthritis. Seven years ago, she was diagnosed with rheumatoid arthritis, which has been inadequately controlled with methotrexate and etanercept. She is also due to receive the influenza vaccination. She has no other personal pertinent medical history.

Physical examination findings are unremarkable, and vital signs are normal. Musculoskeletal examination reveals swelling in multiple joints.

Which of the following is the most appropriate next step in management?

(A) Administer intramuscular influenza vaccine

(B) Administer intranasal influenza vaccine

(C) Begin zanamivir

(D) Do not administer any influenza vaccine

Item 59

A 45-year-old man is evaluated for a 3-week history of gradually increasing right elbow pain, which radiates down the dorsal aspect of the right forearm. The patient reports gardening for many hours over the past several weeks, and the pain worsens when gripping a shovel. He reports no neck pain or paresthesia. He takes ibuprofen as needed for the pain, with minimal relief.

On physical examination, vital signs are normal. The neck, shoulders, elbows, and wrists have full passive range of motion without pain. Tenderness of the outer aspect of the right elbow is noted. Extension of the right wrist against resistance elicits pain of the elbow and forearm. Muscle strength and reflexes are normal. The remainder of the examination is unremarkable.

Which of the following is the most likely diagnosis?

(A) Cervical radiculopathy

(B) Lateral epicondylitis

(C) Olecranon bursitis

(D) Osteoarthritis of the elbow

Item 60

A 45-year-old man is evaluated during a routine physical examination. He has a history of ectopia lentis (lens dislocation) since childhood. He has no other pertinent personal history. Family history includes his father who died of a ruptured aortic aneurysm. He takes no medications.

On physical examination, temperature is 36.4 °C (97.6 °F), blood pressure is 140/80 mm Hg, pulse rate is 82/min, and respiration rate is 12/min. BMI is 24. He is 190.5 cm (75 in) tall with an arm span of 195.6 cm (77 in) and has arachnodactyly (long digits). Other skeletal findings noted are a high arched palate, micrognathia, pectus excavatum, and scoliosis. Mild ligamentous laxity is also present. Cardiac examination reveals a grade 2/6 holosystolic murmur at the apex. The remainder of the examination is normal.

Echocardiogram reveals moderate mitral regurgitation and a dilated aortic root.

Which of the following is the most likely diagnosis?

(A) Classic Ehlers-Danlos syndrome

(B) Marfan syndrome

(C) Osteogenesis imperfecta

(D) Vascular Ehlers-Danlos syndrome

Item 61

A 28-year-old woman is evaluated for a 3-week history of increasing frequency and severity of Raynaud phenomenon episodes despite appropriate lifestyle modifications. She also has a 2-day history of persistent severe pain and cyanosis of the right second finger. Four years ago, she was diagnosed with limited cutaneous systemic sclerosis with Raynaud phenomenon, sclerodactyly, and gastroesophageal reflux with dysphagia. Medications are nifedipine and omeprazole.

On physical examination, temperature is 37.1 °C (98.8 °F), blood pressure is 160/90 mm Hg, pulse rate is 105/min, and respiration rate is 16/min. There is sclerodactyly of the digits of both hands. The right second digit is swollen with marked cyanosis and exquisite tenderness of the terminal phalange. No digital ulcerations are present. Radial pulses over both wrists are normal.

Laboratory studies, including complete blood count, serum creatinine, urinalysis, and peripheral blood smear, are normal.

In addition to opioids for pain control, which of the following is the most appropriate next step in management?

(A) Add bosentan

(B) Add enalapril

(C) Arteriography of the right upper extremity

(D) Digital sympathectomy

(E) Intravenous epoprostenol

Item 62

A 42-year-old man is evaluated for a 1-month history of a painful, swollen right finger and a swollen left toe.

On physical examination, vital signs are normal. The right third distal interphalangeal joint is swollen, with localized tenderness to palpation and pain with active and passive range of motion. The appearance of the nails is shown.

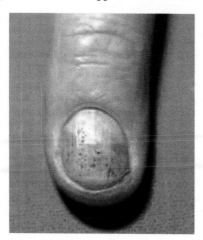

The left second toe is remarkable for fusiform swelling and mild diffuse tenderness, with decreased active and passive range of motion. There is onycholysis of several toenails, including the left second toenail. The remainder of the physical examination is normal.

Which of the following is the most likely diagnosis?

(A) Lyme arthritis

(B) Osteoarthritis

(C) Psoriatic arthritis

(D) Rheumatoid arthritis

Item 63

A 49-year-old man is evaluated for a 10-year history of gout. He is currently asymptomatic but is interested in reducing the frequency of attacks. Previous attacks were rare, but for the past 3 years he has had four to five attacks per year. His father has a history of chronic tophaceous gout. The patient's only medication is ibuprofen as needed for gout attacks.

On physical examination, temperature is 37.0 °C (98.6 °F), blood pressure is 118/80 mm Hg, pulse rate is 72/min, and respiration rate is 13/min. BMI is 29. The general physical examination is normal. There is no evidence of tophi, and the joint examination is unremarkable.

Laboratory studies, including complete blood count, serum chemistries, and liver chemistry tests, are normal; erythrocyte sedimentation rate is 16 mm/h, and serum uric acid level is 9.2 mg/dL (0.54 mmol/L).

Radiographs of the hands and feet are normal.

Which of the following is the most appropriate initial treatment?

(A) Allopurinol

(B) Colchicine

(C) Colchicine and allopurinol

(D) Febuxostat

Item 64

A 28-year-old woman is evaluated for a 4-month history of recurring pruritic and burning red papules on the torso and proximal extremities, with individual lesions lasting up to 24 hours and then resolving. She takes loratadine for the itching.

On physical examination, temperature is 36.9 °C (98.4 °F), blood pressure is 110/70 mm Hg, pulse rate is 70/min, and respiration rate is 14/min. Several 1-cm erythematous papules without scales are present on the torso. There is no scarring or pigment changes on the skin, oral lesions, or joint swelling.

Laboratory studies:

Complete blood count	Normal
Erythrocyte sedimentation rate	18 mm/h
C3	56 mg/dL (560 mg/L)
C4	11 mg/dL (110 mg/L) (normal range, 13-38 mg/dL [130-380 mg/L])
Serum creatinine	Normal

Antinuclear antibodies	Titer of 1:320 (speckled pattern)
Urinalysis	Normal

Results of a skin biopsy of one of the lesions reveal transmural and perivascular infiltration of dermal vessels with lymphocytes.

Which of the following is the most appropriate additional treatment for this patient?

(A) Cyclophosphamide
(B) Hydroxychloroquine
(C) Methotrexate
(D) Mycophenolate mofetil

Item 65

A 52-year-old woman is evaluated for a 3-month history of fatigue as well as pain of the hands and knees that has progressively worsened and is accompanied by 1 hour of morning stiffness. She also has a 15-year history of intermittent low back pain that worsens with activity and is relieved by rest. She takes ibuprofen as needed for the pain, which provides minimal relief.

On physical examination, vital signs are normal. Synovitis of the proximal interphalangeal joints, elbows, left knee, and ankles is noted.

Radiographs of the hands and knees are normal. Aspiration of the left knee reveals a synovial fluid leukocyte count of 12,000/µL (12 × 10^9/L).

Which of the following is the most likely diagnosis?

(A) Fibromyalgia
(B) Osteoarthritis
(C) Polymyalgia rheumatica
(D) Rheumatoid arthritis

Item 66

A 22-year-old woman seeks preconception counseling and treatment of recently diagnosed systemic lupus erythematosus. She reports fatigue and hand pain accompanied by morning stiffness lasting 15 minutes.

On physical examination, vital signs are normal. Malar erythema is noted. There is tenderness of the proximal interphalangeal joints bilaterally; no other synovitis is present. Recent ophthalmologic examination findings, including visual fields, are normal.

Laboratory studies:

Leukocyte count	3300/µL (3.3 × 10^9/L), with an absolute lymphocyte count of 1200/µL (1.2 × 10^9/L)
C3	Normal
C4	Decreased
Serum creatinine	Normal
Antinuclear antibodies	Titer of 1:160 (homogeneous pattern)
Anti–double-stranded DNA antibodies	Positive

IgG-specific anticardiolipin antibodies	Positive
Urinalysis	Normal

Which of the following is the most appropriate treatment?

(A) Azathioprine
(B) Hydroxychloroquine
(C) Mycophenolate mofetil
(D) Prednisone
(E) No treatment at this time

Item 67

A 58-year-old woman is evaluated for a 2-month history of foot pain and stiffness. The pain is localized to the balls of her feet and is associated with 90 minutes of morning stiffness. The patient has tried acetaminophen and applied ice without relief. She otherwise takes no medications.

On physical examination, vital signs are normal. Examination of the feet reveals tenderness and mild swelling across the metatarsal heads of both feet. The remainder of the examination is normal.

Laboratory studies:

Complete blood count	Normal
Complete metabolic panel	Normal
C-reactive protein	1.7 mg/dL (17 mg/L)
Rheumatoid factor	48 units/mL (48 kU/L)
Anti–cyclic citrullinated peptide antibodies	Positive
Antinuclear antibodies	Negative
IgG antibodies against parvovirus B19	Negative
IgM antibodies against parvovirus B19	Negative

Radiographs of the feet are normal.

Which of the following is the most important next step in management?

(A) Colchicine
(B) Methotrexate
(C) NSAIDs
(D) Shoe inserts

Item 68

A 62-year-old man is evaluated for a 5-year history of gout. He currently experiences approximately four attacks per year. His most recent attack was 3 weeks ago; at that time, he was started on daily colchicine. Six months ago, the patient was diagnosed with granulomatosis with polyangiitis (also known as Wegener granulomatosis); he was initially treated with prednisone and cyclophosphamide and was subsequently switched to azathioprine as a maintenance therapy. He has no other pertinent personal medical history.

On physical examination, temperature is 36.9 °C (98.5 °F), blood pressure is 117/72 mm Hg, pulse rate is 72/min, and respiration rate is 15/min. BMI is 27. The remainder of the examination is normal.

Laboratory studies reveal normal complete blood count and serum electrolyte levels; erythrocyte sedimentation rate is 23 mm/h, and serum uric acid level is 8.7 mg/dL (0.51 mmol/L). Estimated glomerular filtration rate is within normal range. 24-Hour urine collection findings are consistent with uric acid underexcretion.

Which of the following is the most appropriate treatment?

(A) Allopurinol
(B) Febuxostat
(C) Pegloticase
(D) Probenecid

Item 69

A 32-year-old man is evaluated for an insidious onset of low back pain of 4 months' duration. The pain occurs in the morning and evening, is mild in intensity, and does not radiate to the legs or buttocks. He has pain at night, and rest does not alleviate the pain. He has tried acetaminophen and naproxen without relief. Family history is significant for an uncle who has spondyloarthritis.

On physical examination, vital signs are normal. Musculoskeletal examination reveals pain and restricted movement on lumbar motion. There is no pain to palpation over the sacroiliac joints.

Laboratory studies reveal a C-reactive protein level of 1.6 mg/dL (16 mg/L).

An anteroposterior radiograph of the pelvis is normal. Radiographs of the lumbar spine are normal. MRI of the lumbosacral spine is normal.

Which of the following is the most appropriate diagnostic test to perform next in this patient?

(A) HLA-B27 testing
(B) Human antichimeric antibody assay
(C) Radiographs of the cervical spine
(D) Rheumatoid factor

Item 70

A 47-year-old man is evaluated for a 3-week history of paresthesia of the left leg and decreased grip strength in the right hand as well as a 6-month history of nonproductive cough. He also has allergic rhinitis with a history of asthma. Medications are fluticasone and inhaled albuterol as needed.

On physical examination, temperature is 37.1 °C (98.8 °F), blood pressure is 150/100 mm Hg, pulse rate is 100/min, and respiration rate is 18/min. There is no rash, and ocular, nasal, and oral mucous membranes are normal. Pulmonary examination reveals scattered expiratory rhonchi. Weak opposition function is noted in the right hand. There is weakness of eversion of the left foot.

Laboratory studies:

Hematocrit	34%
Leukocyte count	12,500/μL (12.5 × 10⁹/L) (44% neutrophils, 32% eosinophils, 15% lymphocytes, 9% monocytes)

Platelet count	410,000/μL (410 × 10⁹/L)
Serum creatinine	1.8 mg/dL (159.1 μmol/L)
Creatine kinase	Normal
c-ANCA	Negative
p-ANCA	Positive
Antimyeloperoxidase antibodies	Positive
Antiproteinase-3 antibodies	Negative
Urinalysis	1+ protein; 5-10 erythrocytes/hpf; 0-5 leukocytes/hpf

Chest radiograph reveals scattered bilateral nodular infiltrates.

Which of the following is the most likely diagnosis?

(A) Churg-Strauss syndrome
(B) Granulomatosis with polyangiitis
(C) Microscopic polyangiitis
(D) Polyarteritis nodosa

Item 71

A 68-year-old man is evaluated for a 1-year history of progressive fatigue, mild dyspnea on exertion, difficulty ambulating, and generalized weakness. He now has difficulty getting out of a chair. He reports no joint or muscle pain. He also has a 15-year history of hypercholesterolemia previously treated with lovastatin, which was discontinued 4 months ago because of his muscle weakness.

On physical examination, temperature is 36.8 °C (98.2 °F), blood pressure is 142/84 mm Hg, pulse rate is 82/min, and respiration rate is 18/min. There is no rash or lymphadenopathy. Cardiac examination is normal. The lungs are clear. Sensation and reflexes are normal. Muscle strength in the quadriceps and wrists is decreased. Hand grip strength is decreased, most notably in the right hand.

Laboratory studies:

Erythrocyte sedimentation rate	32 mm/h
Creatine kinase	430 units/L
Serum creatinine	Normal
Antinuclear antibodies	Negative

Which of the following is the most likely diagnosis?

(A) Dermatomyositis
(B) Inclusion body myositis
(C) Polymyositis
(D) Statin-induced myopathy

Item 72

A 28-year-old woman is evaluated during a follow-up visit for a 1-year history of Raynaud phenomenon. She also has a 3-year history of gastroesophageal reflux symptoms without dysphagia. Her only medication is omeprazole.

On physical examination, temperature is 36.9 °C (98.4 °F), blood pressure is 110/70 mm Hg, pulse rate is 80/min, and respiration rate is 16/min. Cardiopulmonary examination is normal. There is soft-tissue swelling of the digits of both hands. Several telangiectasias are present over the palms and volar aspects of the digits of both hands. There is no proximal skin edema or tightening.

Laboratory studies, including complete blood count, serum creatinine, and urinalysis, are normal. Antinuclear antibody test results reveal a titer of 1:640 (nucleolar pattern).

Which of the following is the most appropriate test to perform next?

(A) Barium esophagography
(B) High-resolution CT of the chest
(C) Pulmonary function tests and echocardiography
(D) Right heart catheterization

Item 73

A 36-year-old woman is evaluated for a 6-month history of fatigue and pain and stiffness of the fingers and knees. She reports weakness and heaviness in her arms and legs. She has a rash on her face, elbows, and hands. Family history is significant for a maternal aunt who has systemic lupus erythematosus. The patient takes no medications.

On physical examination, temperature is 37.6 °C (99.7 °F), blood pressure is 102/60 mm Hg, pulse rate is 76/min, and respiration rate is 18/min. Cutaneous examination reveals mild alopecia; clumped, mildly erythematous papules over the olecranon, metacarpophalangeal joints, and proximal interphalangeal joints bilaterally; and cuticular overgrowth with periungual erythema of all digits. The appearance of the face is shown.

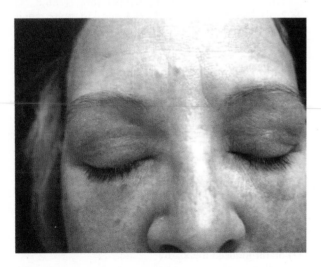

Musculoskeletal examination reveals bilateral quadriceps and deltoid muscle weakness; synovitis of the proximal interphalangeal joints bilaterally; and small bilateral knee effusions. Distal muscle strength is normal.

Laboratory studies:

Complete blood count	Normal
Erythrocyte sedimentation rate	65 mm/h
Blood urea nitrogen	Normal
Creatine kinase	642 units/L
Antinuclear antibodies	Titer of 1:160 (speckled pattern)

Radiographs of the hands, wrists, and knees are normal.

Which of the following is the most likely diagnosis?

(A) Dermatomyositis
(B) Inclusion body myositis
(C) Mixed connective tissue disease
(D) Polymyositis
(E) Systemic lupus erythematosus

Item 74

A 56-year-old woman is evaluated during a follow-up visit for a 6-year history of Sjögren syndrome treated with low-dose hydroxychloroquine and cyclosporine eyedrops. She has had two episodes of cutaneous vasculitis, which resolved with corticosteroids.

On physical examination, temperature is 36.4 °C (97.6 °F), blood pressure is 116/64 mm Hg, pulse rate is 72/min, and respiration rate is 18/min. Oral mucous membranes are dry. There is a new firm, left parotid gland enlargement without tenderness or warmth, reported by the patient to be progressive over several months, with asymmetry of the parotid glands.

Laboratory studies at the time of diagnosis revealed elevated serum immunoglobulin levels; positive mixed monoclonal cryoglobulin levels; and positive rheumatoid factor, antinuclear antibodies, and anti-Ro/SSA antibodies.

Current laboratory studies:

Complete blood count	Normal
Alkaline phosphatase	Normal
Calcium	Normal
Rheumatoid factor	Negative
C3	Normal
C4	Decreased
Antinuclear antibodies	Positive
Anti-Ro/SSA antibodies	Positive

Which of the following is the most appropriate management?

(A) Add pilocarpine
(B) Add prednisone
(C) Bone marrow biopsy
(D) Increase hydroxychloroquine
(E) Parotid gland biopsy

Item 75

A 42-year-old man is evaluated for morning stiffness of the wrists lasting up to 1 hour. He was diagnosed with rheumatoid arthritis 4 months ago and was started on methotrexate and titrated to maximum dose 3 months ago with partial response. He also takes prednisone as needed for joint pain and folic acid daily.

On physical examination, vital signs are normal. Musculoskeletal examination reveals swelling, tenderness, and pain on range of motion of the wrists. No rash or joint deformities are noted. The remainder of the examination is normal.

Laboratory studies reveal a C-reactive protein level of 3.1 mg/dL (31 mg/L); anti–cyclic citrullinated peptide antibodies are positive.

Which of the following is the most appropriate treatment?

(A) Add adalimumab
(B) Discontinue folic acid
(C) Discontinue methotrexate; begin infliximab
(D) Discontinue methotrexate; begin sulfasalazine
(E) Maintain current regimen

Item 76

A 65-year-old woman is evaluated for a 3-week history of nonradiating left hip pain that worsens with walking or lying on her left side. She reports no locking symptoms or paresthesia. Her only medication is ibuprofen as needed, which provides partial relief.

On physical examination, vital signs are normal. BMI is 28. Full range of motion of the hip is present. There is tenderness on the lateral aspect of the hip with direct palpation. Results from a straight-leg-raising test are normal, and reflexes are normal.

Which of the following is the most likely diagnosis?

(A) Iliotibial band syndrome
(B) Lumbar radiculopathy
(C) Osteoarthritis of the hip
(D) Trochanteric bursitis

Item 77

A 62-year-old man is evaluated for a 2-month history of stiffness and swelling of the forearms, thighs, and calves. Four months ago, he experienced severe left shoulder girdle pain; at that time, a noncontrast MRI was performed, demonstrating a partial thickness rotator cuff tear. The patient reports no history of Raynaud phenomenon. He has type 2 diabetes mellitus that is managed with diet. He takes no medications.

On physical examination, temperature is 37.1 °C (98.8 °F), blood pressure is 130/76 mm Hg, pulse rate is 76/min, and respiration rate is 14/min. Symmetric induration without dermal papules is present in the forearms, thighs, and calves. There is no swelling or induration of the upper or lower extremity digits, and the skin over the face and torso has a normal texture.

Laboratory studies:

Hematocrit	36%
Leukocyte count	6700/µL (6.7×10^9/L) (70% neutrophils, 16% lymphocytes, 12% monocytes, 2% eosinophils)
Platelet count	370,000/µL (370×10^9/L)
Erythrocyte sedimentation rate	68 mm/h
Creatine kinase	56 units/mL
Serum creatinine	0.9 mg/dL (79.6 µmol/L)

Which of the following is the most likely diagnosis?

(A) Diabetic scleredema
(B) Diffuse cutaneous systemic sclerosis
(C) Eosinophilic fasciitis
(D) Nephrogenic systemic fibrosis

Item 78

A 16-year-old male adolescent is evaluated in the emergency department for a 2-day history of persistent fever, abdominal pain, and right knee pain. During the past year, he has had three similar episodes, each lasting 2 to 3 days. He feels well between episodes. He takes no medications.

On physical examination, temperature is 38.3 °C (101.0 °F), blood pressure is 142/86 mm Hg, pulse rate is 96/min, and respiration rate is 18/min. There is diffuse abdominal tenderness without rebound and no evidence of hepatosplenomegaly or lymphadenopathy. The right knee has an effusion; flexion of the knee is limited to 100 degrees. A well-demarcated, raised, erythematous, warm, and painful rash is noted on the right lower extremity overlying the shin.

Laboratory studies reveal an erythrocyte sedimentation rate of 42 mm/h and a normal serum ferritin level; antinuclear antibody test results are negative. Urinalysis reveals 1+ protein with no cells or casts.

Which of the following is the most likely diagnosis?

(A) Adult-onset Still disease
(B) Crohn disease
(C) Familial Mediterranean fever
(D) Reactive arthritis

Item 79

A 32-year-old man is evaluated for gout. In the past 2 years, he has had three gout attacks, two of which involved the first metatarsophalangeal joint. The third attack occurred 1 month ago and involved his right knee; the joint was aspirated, and urate crystals were confirmed on polarized light microscopy. He wants to reduce his risk of future attacks; however, he does not want to take medications. The patient eats a low-fat diet high in leafy green vegetables and dairy products and consumes a small amount of fruit weekly. He drinks one glass of wine two or three times a week. He has no history of kidney stones or tophi. Family history is notable for his father and grandfather who have tophaceous gout. His only medication is hydrochlorothiazide for hypertension.

On physical examination, temperature is 37.0 °C (98.6 °F), blood pressure is 116/76 mm Hg, pulse rate is 60/min, and respiration rate is 12/min. BMI is 27. There are no tophi. Musculoskeletal examination is normal.

Laboratory studies, including complete blood count, serum chemistries, and liver chemistry tests, are normal; erythrocyte sedimentation rate is 16 mm/h, and serum uric acid level is 8.6 mg/dL (0.51 mmol/L).

Which of the following is the most appropriate next step in management?

(A) Decrease dairy consumption
(B) Decrease leafy green vegetable consumption
(C) Decrease wine consumption
(D) Increase fruit consumption
(E) Substitute lisinopril for hydrochlorothiazide

Item 80

A 62-year-old man is evaluated for a 2-week history of purpuric lesions on the lower extremities. He is otherwise healthy and takes no medications.

On physical examination, temperature is 37.2 °C (99.0 °F), blood pressure is 160/100 mm Hg, pulse rate is 88/min, and respiration rate is 12/min. The mucous membranes are normal. Tender, nonblanching purpuric papules are present on the feet and distal lower extremities. There is 1+ tibial and pedal edema. No joint swelling is noted.

Laboratory studies:

Hematocrit	28%
Leukocyte count	9500/µL (9.5 × 10⁹/L), with normal differential
Mean corpuscular volume	76 fL
Platelet count	490,000/µL (490 × 10⁹/L)
Reticulocyte count	0.4%
Serum creatinine	1.9 mg/dL (168 µmol/L)
Rheumatoid factor	Negative
Antinuclear antibodies	Negative
c-ANCA	Negative
p-ANCA	Negative
Serum cryoglobulin	Negative
Urinalysis	2+ protein; 15-20 erythrocytes/hpf; 0-5 leukocytes/hpf

Serum immunofixation electrophoresis reveals no paraproteins.

Skin biopsy results confirm leukocytoclastic vasculitis with deposits of IgA.

Which of the following is the most likely diagnosis?

(A) Churg-Strauss syndrome
(B) Henoch-Schönlein purpura
(C) Microscopic polyangiitis
(D) Polyarteritis nodosa
(E) Subacute cutaneous lupus erythematosus

Item 81

A 45-year-old woman is evaluated for a 3-month history of worsening discomfort in the right forearm, right wrist, and right hand accompanied by numbness and tingling in the hand that she can "shake away." The pain is worse at night, at times disrupting her sleep.

On physical examination, vital signs are normal. Neurologic examination shows weakness in her pinch grip and subtle numbness in the second, third, and fourth distal fingers.

Which of the following is the most appropriate next step in management?

(A) Electromyography and nerve conduction study
(B) MRI of the wrist
(C) NSAIDs
(D) Surgical release of the median nerve

Item 82

A 38-year-old woman is evaluated during a routine follow-up visit for a 20-year history of systemic lupus erythematosus. In recent years, disease activity has been quiescent. She currently reports fatigue, alopecia, and occasional hand arthralgia. She seeks advice regarding contraception options other than barrier methods.

The patient was also recently diagnosed with osteoporosis. She had a 22-week fetal loss during her first pregnancy, followed by three successful pregnancies while taking aspirin and enoxaparin. Current medications are hydroxychloroquine, low-dose prednisone, alendronate, calcium, and vitamin D.

On physical examination, temperature is 36.9 °C (98.4 °F), blood pressure is 126/78 mm Hg, pulse rate is 72/min, and respiration rate is 16/min. There is tenderness of the metacarpophalangeal and proximal interphalangeal joints bilaterally.

Laboratory studies:

Complete blood count	Normal
Complement (C3 and C4)	Normal
Serum creatinine	Normal
Antinuclear antibodies	Titer of 1:320 (homogeneous pattern)
Anti–double-stranded DNA antibodies	Positive
IgG-specific anticardiolipin antibodies	Positive
Lupus anticoagulant	Positive
Urinalysis	Normal

Which of the following is the most appropriate contraceptive method for this patient?

(A) Combination estrogen-progesterone oral contraceptive
(B) Etonogestrel/ethinyl estradiol vaginal ring
(C) Intramuscular medroxyprogesterone acetate
(D) Progesterone-containing intrauterine device

Item 83

A 24-year-old man is evaluated in the emergency department for a 3-day history of right eye redness and pain, photophobia, and decreased visual acuity. He has a 2-year history of recurrent, painful oral ulcerations and tender nodules on his shins as well as occasional knee and ankle pain for the past 3 months. His only medication is occasional ibuprofen for joint pain.

On physical examination, temperature is 37.3 °C (99.2 °F), blood pressure is 124/78 mm Hg, pulse rate is 105/min, and respiration rate is 18/min. BMI is 26. On ophthalmologic examination, there is a ciliary flush around the right limbus and a constricted pupil. A slit lamp examination reveals findings consistent with anterior and posterior uveitis; retinal vasculitis is also present. Oral ulcerations varying in size from 3 mm to 1 cm are noted on the inner cheek, palate, and tongue. The lungs are clear. The abdomen is nontender. No bruits are noted. The left knee and right ankle are swollen. Peripheral pulses are normal.

Laboratory test results are pending.

Chest radiograph reveals a prominent right pulmonary artery. CT of the chest demonstrates an aneurysm of the right pulmonary artery.

Which of the following is the most likely diagnosis?

(A) Behçet disease
(B) Granulomatosis with polyangiitis
(C) Polyarteritis nodosa
(D) Sarcoidosis

Item 84

A 36-year-old man is evaluated for a 5-month history of left knee pain and swelling. He is a gardener and frequently scrapes his knees while working in the soil. He has mild but chronic discomfort when walking and at rest. The patient reports no diarrhea or urethral discharge and has been sexually inactive for 2 years. He has a 10-year history of type 2 diabetes mellitus that is managed with insulin.

On physical examination, temperature is 38.0 °C (100.4 °F), blood pressure is 135/77 mm Hg, pulse rate is 78/min, and respiration rate is 12/min. BMI is 20. The left knee is warm and swollen with a palpable effusion. The knee has decreased flexion, and increasing discomfort is noted at the limits of range of motion.

Laboratory studies reveal a leukocyte count of 11,000/µL ([11 × 10⁹/L], 35% lymphocytes) and an erythrocyte sedimentation rate of 48 mm/h.

Radiographs of the left knee reveal soft-tissue swelling and diffuse joint-space narrowing, with periarticular osteopenia. Aspiration of the knee is performed. Synovial fluid leukocyte count is 6500/µL ([6.5 × 10⁹/L], 65% lymphocytes). Polarized light microscopy reveals no crystals. Gram stain is negative.

Subsequent bacterial cultures, Lyme disease titers, rheumatoid factor, and anti–cyclic citrullinated peptide antibody titers are negative. Tuberculin skin test results are negative.

Which of the following is the most appropriate diagnostic test to perform next?

(A) Alizarin red staining of synovial fluid
(B) Anti–streptolysin O antibody titers
(C) MRI of the knee
(D) Synovial biopsy

Item 85

A 34-year-old woman is evaluated during a follow-up visit. She was diagnosed with fibromyalgia 1 year ago. At that time, she received intensive education about her condition,

and an aerobic exercise program was prescribed. Pregabalin was also initiated but was discontinued when she developed hives. She continues to have fatigue, widespread pain, and difficulty sleeping. She currently takes no medications.

On physical examination, vital signs are normal. Musculoskeletal examination reveals multiple tender points but no synovitis or muscle weakness. Screening for mood disorders is negative. The remainder of the examination is normal.

Laboratory studies, including erythrocyte sedimentation rate, C-reactive protein level, and thyroid-stimulating hormone level, are normal.

Which of the following is the most appropriate class of pharmacologic treatment for this patient?

(A) Corticosteroids
(B) NSAIDs
(C) Selective serotonin reuptake inhibitors
(D) Serotonin and norepinephrine reuptake inhibitors

Item 86

A 77-year-old woman is evaluated in the emergency department for a 4-month history of persistent right knee pain and low-grade fever. Three years ago, she underwent right total knee replacement to treat osteoarthritis. Three months ago, a synovial fluid aspirate was positive for methicillin-sensitive *Staphylococcus aureus*, with 2500 leukocytes/µL (2.5 × 10⁹/L). She was treated with intravenous, then oral, nafcillin without improvement.

On physical examination today, temperature is 38.0 °C (100.4 °F), blood pressure is 133/77 mm Hg, pulse rate is 84/min, and respiration rate is 12/min. BMI is 19. There is a vertical well-healed surgical scar across the anterior surface of the right knee. The knee is slightly warm, with pain on passive range of motion.

Current laboratory studies:

Hemoglobin	11.3 g/dL (113 g/L)
Leukocyte count	13,000/µL ([13 × 10⁹/L], 88% neutrophils)
Erythrocyte sedimentation rate	88 mm/h
C-reactive protein	17 mg/dL (170 mg/L)

Radiographs of the right knee reveal prosthetic loosening and periprosthetic lucency of the femur. A repeat synovial fluid aspiration confirms the presence of methicillin-sensitive *Staphylococcus aureus*.

Which of the following is the most appropriate next step in management?

(A) Add diclofenac
(B) Add rifampin
(C) Intravenous vancomycin
(D) Surgical removal of the prosthetic joint

Item 87

A 26-year-old woman is hospitalized for a 3-month history of daily spiking fever, diffuse joint pain, myalgia, intermittent rash, and a 9-kg (20-lb) weight loss.

On physical examination, temperature is 38.4 °C (101.2 °F), blood pressure is 126/68 mm Hg, pulse rate is 92/min, and respiration rate is 16/min. There are enlarged cervical lymph nodes. A salmon-colored rash is noted on the trunk and proximal extremities. Musculoskeletal examination reveals tenderness of the wrists, knees, and ankles without swelling; there is decreased range of motion of the wrists. Hepatomegaly is noted.

Laboratory studies:

Hemoglobin	9.8 g/dL (98 g/L)
Leukocyte count	21,000/µL (21 × 10⁹/L)
Platelet count	560,000/µL (560 × 10⁹/L)
Erythrocyte sedimentation rate	102 mm/h
Ferritin	5250 ng/mL (5250 µg/L)

CT scan of the chest, abdomen, and pelvis reveals diffuse lymphadenopathy. Bone marrow biopsy results are normal. Blood cultures are negative.

Which of the following is the most likely diagnosis?

(A) Adult-onset Still disease
(B) Lymphoma
(C) Parvovirus B19 infection
(D) Systemic lupus erythematosus

Item 88

A 32-year-old woman is evaluated for a 3-year history of progressive tightening of the skin involving the face, upper extremities, torso, and proximal lower extremities as well as a 2-month history of increasing fatigue and exertional dyspnea. She also has Raynaud phenomenon complicated by recurring, painful, terminal digital ulcers; gastroesophageal reflux disease; and hypertension. Medications are enalapril, omeprazole, and nifedipine.

On physical examination, temperature is 36.9 °C (98.4 °F), blood pressure is 130/80 mm Hg, pulse rate is 110/min, and respiration rate is 16/min. Conjunctival pallor is noted. Cutaneous examination reveals sclerodactyly of the fingers with scars on the tips and induration of the skin on the face, forearms, and anterior torso. The remainder of the physical examination is normal.

Laboratory studies:

Hematocrit	24%
Leukocyte count	6400/µL (6.4 × 10⁹/L)
Platelet count	490,000/µL (490 × 10⁹/L)
Mean corpuscular volume	77 fL
Blood urea nitrogen	24 mg/dL (8.6 mmol/L)
Serum creatinine	1.0 mg/dL (88.4 µmol/L)
Ferritin	10 ng/mL (10 µg/L)

In addition to iron replacement therapy, which of the following is the most appropriate management?

(A) Begin erythropoietin
(B) Bone marrow biopsy
(C) Colonoscopy
(D) Hydrogen breath test
(E) Upper endoscopy

Item 89

A 74-year-old man is evaluated during a follow-up visit for a knee injury. One month ago, he was evaluated in the emergency department for a knee sprain that occurred during a tennis game. A radiograph of the knee taken at that time is shown. He was treated with ice, bandaging, and naproxen. The symptoms completely resolved after 5 days, and the patient resumed his normal activities. He has no other pertinent personal or family history.

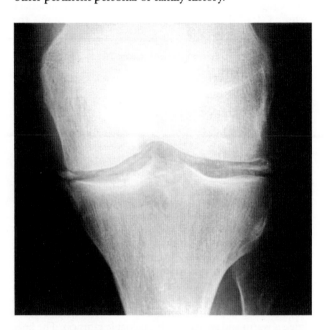

On physical examination today, temperature is 37.0 °C (98.6 °F), blood pressure is 117/74 mm Hg, pulse rate is 63/min, and respiration rate is 12/min. BMI is 21. Examination of the knees reveals no swelling, erythema, or tenderness; there is full range of motion without crepitus. Stability tests reveal no abnormalities. The remainder of the examination is normal.

Laboratory studies, including serum electrolytes, calcium, phosphorus, magnesium, alkaline phosphatase, ferritin, iron, transferrin, and thyroid-stimulating hormone levels, are normal.

Which of the following is the most appropriate treatment?

(A) Colchicine
(B) Intra-articular corticosteroid injection
(C) Intra-articular hyaluronan injection
(D) Naproxen
(E) No treatment

Item 90

A 48-year-old woman is evaluated for thrombocytopenia, which was diagnosed during an evaluation for menorrhagia. She notes easy bruising and a general decrease in energy level. She has had faint cutaneous mottling over the lower extremities for years; cold-induced color changes of the fingers associated with numbness and pain; and migraines several times per month. She also reports three first-trimester miscarriages and two successful pregnancies. Her only medication is ibuprofen for her migraines.

On physical examination, temperature is 36.8 °C (98.2 °F), blood pressure is 126/74 mm Hg, pulse rate is 84/min, and respiration rate is 18/min. The joints are nontender. A grade 2/6 holosystolic murmur at the cardiac apex is noted. The skin findings are shown.

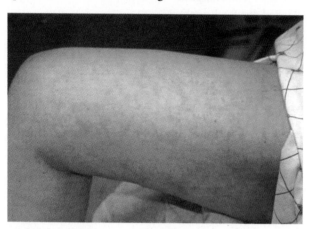

Laboratory studies:

Hemoglobin	11.0 g/dL (110 g/L)
Leukocyte count	6800/μL (6.8 × 10⁹/L)
Platelet count	88,000/μL (88 × 10⁹/L)
Serum creatinine	1.4 mg/dL (123.8 μmol/L)
Prothrombin time	11 s
Activated partial thromboplastin time	41 s
INR	1.0
Urinalysis	2+ protein; no erythrocytes or leukocytes

Which of the following is the most likely diagnosis?

(A) The antiphospholipid syndrome
(B) Immune thrombocytopenic purpura
(C) Myelodysplastic syndrome
(D) Systemic lupus erythematosus

Item 91

A 32-year-old woman is evaluated for possible systemic disease associated with right eye pain and redness. She was recently diagnosed with anterior uveitis by her ophthalmologist. She is otherwise healthy. Her only medication is a topical corticosteroid prescribed by the ophthalmologist.

On physical examination, vital signs are normal. The right eye is red, and there is ocular injection concentrated around the iris. The remainder of the examination is normal.

Which of the following is an appropriate initial test for this patient?

(A) Anti–double-stranded DNA antibody assay
(B) Anti-Ro/SSA antibody assay
(C) Chest radiograph
(D) Rheumatoid factor

Item 92

A 68-year-old woman is evaluated in the emergency department for a 2-day history of swelling of the right knee. She has an 8-year history of right knee osteoarthritis. She also has chronic kidney disease, hypertension, type 2 diabetes mellitus, and a history of peptic ulcer disease. Medications are metformin, omeprazole, enalapril, and aspirin.

On physical examination, temperature is 37.0 °C (98.6 °F), blood pressure is 132/84 mm Hg, pulse rate is 78/min, and respiration rate is 14/min. BMI is 22. On musculoskeletal examination, the right knee is swollen, warm, tender, and erythematous, with limited range of motion. There are no tophi.

Laboratory studies reveal an erythrocyte sedimentation rate of 49 mm/h, a serum creatinine level of 2.1 mg/dL (185.6 μmol/L), and a serum uric acid level of 4.5 mg/dL (0.27 mmol/L).

Aspiration of the right knee is performed. Synovial fluid leukocyte count is 25,000/μL (25 × 10⁹/L), with 85% neutrophils. Polarized light microscopy of the fluid demonstrates numerous rhomboid-shaped positively birefringent crystals seen both extracellularly and within the neutrophils.

Radiographs of the right knee reveal soft-tissue swelling and bilateral medial joint-space narrowing, with linear calcific densities within the plane of the cartilage. Synovial fluid Gram stain is negative for bacteria.

Which of the following is the most appropriate treatment?

(A) Allopurinol
(B) Ibuprofen
(C) Intra-articular triamcinolone
(D) Intravenous vancomycin
(E) Prednisone

Item 93

A 46-year-old man is evaluated for a 2-month history of increasing exertional dyspnea. He also has a 3-year history of diffuse cutaneous systemic sclerosis. He reports no cough, chest pain, or orthopnea. He takes no medications.

On physical examination, temperature is 36.9 °C (98.4 °F), blood pressure is 120/70 mm Hg, pulse rate is 90/min, and respiration rate is 16/min at rest. Cardiac examination reveals normal heart sounds and no gallops or rubs. Chest is clear to auscultation. Cutaneous examination reveals sclerodactyly of the digits of both hands as well as skin edema and induration over the forearms, anterior torso, and anterior thighs.

Laboratory studies:

Complete blood count	Normal
Anti-topoisomerase I (anti–Scl-70) antibodies	Positive

Pulmonary function studies:

FVC	60% of predicted
FEV₁	70% of predicted
Dʟᴄᴏ	32% of predicted

Chest radiograph and echocardiogram are normal.

Which of the following is the most appropriate diagnostic test to perform next?

(A) CT angiography of the chest
(B) High-resolution CT of the chest
(C) Radionuclide exercise stress test
(D) Right heart catheterization

Item 94

A 29-year-old woman is evaluated during a routine examination. She seeks advice in reducing her personal risk of developing rheumatoid arthritis, because her mother was recently diagnosed with the disorder. The patient is asymptomatic. She has a 10-pack-year history of smoking and consumes six alcoholic beverages per week, usually on weekends. She is sedentary and overweight. She takes oral contraceptives.

On physical examination, vital signs are normal. BMI is 29. There is no synovitis or bony abnormalities. The remainder of the examination is normal.

Which of the following lifestyle modifications is most likely to reduce the patient's risk of developing rheumatoid arthritis?

(A) Alcohol cessation
(B) Discontinuation of oral contraceptives
(C) Increased physical activity
(D) Smoking cessation
(E) Weight loss

Item 95

A 36-year-old woman is evaluated for a 2-week history of moderately severe back pain unrelated to trauma. The pain is constant, localized to the center of the mid back without radiation, and worse with walking or lifting. She was diagnosed with systemic lupus erythematosus 17 years ago and was diagnosed with nephritis 15 years ago; she was treated with cyclophosphamide and high-dose prednisone, which was tapered but has been continued at a low dose because of symptoms of arthritis and rash. Other medications are hydroxychloroquine, calcium, and vitamin D.

On physical examination, temperature is 36.8 °C (98.2 °F), blood pressure is 116/72 mm Hg, pulse rate is 82/min, and respiration rate is 18/min. Sensory examination and muscle strength are normal. There is tenderness of the mid thoracic vertebral spine and paraspinal muscles and pain with forward flexion or twisting of the back. The neurologic examination is normal.

A radiograph of the thoracic spine is negative for fracture.

Which of the following is the most appropriate management?

(A) Add cyclobenzaprine
(B) Bed rest for 1 week
(C) CT of the thoracic spine
(D) Physical therapy

Item 96

A 32-year-old man is evaluated in the emergency department for a 1-week history of arthralgia, rash over the hands, burning sensation in the eyes, sore lips and tongue, and fever. Three months ago, he was diagnosed with HIV infection. Medications are efavirenz, emtricitabine, and tenofovir.

On physical examination, temperature is 38.1 °C (100.5 °F), blood pressure is 140/80 mm Hg, pulse rate is 100/min and regular, and respiration rate is 16/min. Bilateral conjunctival hyperemia is present; there is no change in visual acuity. Cracked, red lips and a strawberry tongue are present. The radial and dorsalis pedis pulses are normal, and there are no pleural or pericardial rubs. An erythematous rash is noted on the palms and digits of both hands with signs of desquamation around the nailfolds. There is tenderness to palpation of the wrists, knees, and ankles.

Laboratory studies:

Hematocrit	28%
Leukocyte count	18,000/µL (18×10^9/L)
Platelet count	540,000/µL (540×10^9/L)
Erythrocyte sedimentation rate	76 mm/h
C-reactive protein	1.6 mg/dL (16 mg/L)
Rheumatoid factor	Negative
Antinuclear antibodies	Negative
Urinalysis	Trace protein; 0-4 erythrocytes/hpf; 15-20 leukocytes/hpf; no bacteria

Which of the following is the most likely diagnosis?

(A) Disseminated gonococcal infection
(B) Kawasaki disease
(C) Psoriatic arthritis
(D) Toxic shock syndrome

Answers and Critiques

Item 1   Answer: A

Educational Objective: Diagnose drug-induced lupus erythematosus.

Testing for antinuclear antibodies (ANA), as well as anti–double-stranded DNA antibodies and complement levels, is indicated for this patient with suspected drug-induced lupus erythematosus (DILE) caused by the tumor necrosis factor (TNF)-α inhibitor etanercept. He has new-onset fever, arthralgia, myalgia, nonblanching purpuric rash, pleuritis, pancytopenia, and proteinuria with active urine sediment, all of which are suggestive of a clinical diagnosis of systemic lupus erythematosus (SLE). Although these findings might also be compatible with an infection, he has no focal symptoms or findings to suggest sepsis and has been appropriately tested with blood and urine cultures.

Most patients with DILE caused by TNF-α inhibitors have fever, rash, arthritis, and hematologic abnormalities in the presence of positive ANA as well as anti–double-stranded DNA antibodies. This clinical and serologic profile is in contrast to DILE induced by other medications, which is characterized by positive ANA, antihistone antibodies, and anti–single-stranded DNA antibodies. Nephritis is not common but has been reported in patients with DILE caused by TNF-α inhibitors.

If DILE and infection are both ruled out, bone marrow aspiration and biopsy to evaluate for the presence of a primary hematologic diagnosis or CT of the chest, abdomen, and pelvis to evaluate for lymphadenopathy suggestive of underlying lymphoma would be indicated.

Testing of rheumatoid factor and anti–cyclic citrullinated peptide (CCP) antibodies is not appropriate, because the patient has had a clear diagnosis of rheumatoid arthritis, and, even if a flare were present, rheumatoid factor and anti-CCP antibodies would not necessarily increase.

KEY POINT

- Drug-induced lupus erythematosus caused by tumor necrosis factor α inhibitors is characterized by fever, rash, arthritis, and hematologic abnormalities in the presence of positive antinuclear antibodies and anti–double-stranded DNA antibodies.

Bibliography

Williams EL, Gadola S, Edwards CJ. Anti-TNF-induced lupus. Rheumatology. 2009;48(7):716-720. [PMID: 19416947]

Item 2   Answer: D

Educational Objective: Manage reactive arthritis with sulfasalazine.

Treatment with sulfasalazine is appropriate for this patient with reactive arthritis. Reactive arthritis is characterized by the presence of inflammatory arthritis that manifests within 2 months of an episode of bacterial gastroenteritis or nongonococcal urethritis or cervicitis in a genetically predisposed patient. Approximately one third of patients manifest the classic triad of arthritis, urethritis, and conjunctivitis. Reactive arthritis is usually self-limited and remits within 6 months without causing erosive damage; approximately 25% of patients develop a chronic persistent arthritis that can be refractory to treatment with NSAIDs. This patient has reactive arthritis related to an episode of gastroenteritis. NSAIDs and corticosteroids have been ineffective in improving her condition. Data on the use of disease-modifying antirheumatic drugs in reactive arthritis are limited; however, sulfasalazine has been shown to have some efficacy in patients with chronic reactive arthritis and may be beneficial for this patient. The benefits of sulfasalazine in peripheral musculoskeletal manifestations of other forms of spondyloarthritis, including psoriatic arthritis, inflammatory bowel disease–associated arthritis, and ankylosing spondylitis, also support the use of sulfasalazine in reactive arthritis.

Colchicine is used to control inflammation in patients with crystal-associated arthritis as well as some autoinflammatory syndromes but is not used for patients with reactive arthritis.

Glucosamine may have a limited role in pain relief in some patients with osteoarthritis but has not been studied or suggested for use in patients with reactive arthritis.

Despite the association between reactive arthritis and bacterial infection, antibiotics are indicated primarily for acute infection and generally are of dubious benefit for reactive joint disease. In some studies, a 3-month trial of minocycline or a similar agent was shown to improve the clinical course of reactive arthritis, particularly when this condition was associated with *Chlamydia trachomatis* infection. There is no role for nitrofurantoin in the treatment of this patient.

KEY POINT

- Treatment with sulfasalazine is appropriate for a patient with chronic reactive arthritis who does not respond to NSAIDs or corticosteroids.

Bibliography

Carter JD, Hudson AP. Reactive arthritis: clinical aspects and medical management. Rheum Dis Clin North Am. 2009;35(1):21-44. [PMID: 19480995]

Item 3   Answer: D

Educational Objective: Manage advanced knee osteoarthritis.

No additional diagnostic testing is indicated for this patient who has osteoarthritis, which is a clinical diagnosis. According to the American College of Rheumatology's clinical criteria, knee osteoarthritis can be diagnosed if knee pain is accompanied by at least three of the following features: age greater than 50 years, stiffness lasting less than 30 minutes, crepitus, bony tenderness, bony enlargement, and no palpable warmth. These criteria are 95% sensitive and 69% specific but have not been validated for clinical practice. Additional diagnostic testing is not appropriate, because it has no impact on the management of advanced disease.

CT of the knee is very sensitive for pathologic findings in bone and can be used to look for evidence of an occult fracture, osteomyelitis, or bone erosions. However, none of these are suspected in this patient.

Small- to moderate-sized effusions can occur in patients with osteoarthritis, and the fluid is typically noninflammatory. Joint aspiration in this patient without evidence of joint inflammation and evident osteoarthritis is not useful diagnostically but is often done in the context of intra-articular corticosteroid injection or viscosupplementation.

MRI is useful to evaluate soft-tissue structures in the knee such as meniscal tears. Patients with meniscal tears may report a clicking or locking of the knee secondary to loose cartilage but often have pain only on walking, particularly going up or down stairs. Patients with degenerative arthritis often have MRI findings that indicate meniscus tears. These tears are part of the degenerative process but do not impact management; arthroscopic knee surgery for patients with osteoarthritis provides no clinical benefit. The one exception may be in patients with meniscal tears that result in a free flap or loose body, producing painful locking of the joint. These symptoms are not present in this patient.

> **KEY POINT**
> - Osteoarthritis is diagnosed clinically and does not require advanced imaging to establish the diagnosis.

Bibliography

Hunter DJ. In the clinic. Osteoarthritis. Ann Intern Med. 2007;147(3):ITC8-1-ITC8-16. [PMID: 17679702]

Item 4   Answer: A

Educational Objective: Diagnose basic calcium phosphate deposition disease.

This patient most likely has basic calcium phosphate (BCP) deposition disease, a crystal disease that should be considered in older persons, especially women, and in the setting of trauma. BCP crystals are most commonly associated with highly destructive inflammatory arthritis such as Milwaukee shoulder, which typically manifests as shoulder pain and a large noninflammatory effusion that may be bloody, often appearing subsequent to trauma. Active motion is markedly limited because of the destruction of articular cartilage and associated tendon structures that develop in this setting, whereas passive motion may be preserved. This patient has an erosive arthritis that developed subacutely subsequent to a trauma; the presence of periarticular diffuse calcification is most consistent with Milwaukee shoulder. Radiographs commonly show both articular and periarticular calcification. BCP crystals cannot be seen under polarized light microscopy but can be visualized as aggregates after alizarin red staining of synovial fluid (although not done routinely), which can confirm the clinical diagnosis.

Calciphylaxis is a condition of soft-tissue calcification that does not typically involve joints and occurs almost exclusively in patients with stage 5 chronic kidney disease.

Calcium pyrophosphate crystals can produce an acute, inflammatory arthritis. In contrast to BCP-induced disease, periarthritis is not a typical feature. Joint fluid examination under polarized light microscopy shows many leukocytes (largely neutrophils) and intra- and extracellular positively birefringent crystals.

Osteoarthritis can affect the shoulder but is typically a chronic rather than acute problem. The joint fluid tends to be noninflammatory, with a leukocyte count of less than 2000/µL (2.0×10^9/L).

> **KEY POINT**
> - Basic calcium phosphate crystals are commonly associated with chronic and highly destructive inflammatory arthritis such as Milwaukee shoulder.

Bibliography

Forster CJ, Oglesby RJ, Szkutnik AJ, Roberts JR. Positive alizarin red clumps in Milwaukee shoulder syndrome. J Rheumatol. 2009;36(12):2853. [PMID: 19966203]

Item 5   Answer: C

Educational Objective: Diagnose early severe atherosclerosis in a patient with systemic lupus erythematosus.

The most appropriate initial diagnostic test is electrocardiography. This patient with long-standing systemic lupus erythematosus (SLE) is at high risk for premature atherosclerosis and myocardial infarction. If her chest and gastrointestinal symptoms reflect an underlying cardiac event, her prognosis depends on rapid diagnosis and treatment.

Mortality in SLE follows a bimodal pattern in which early deaths are most often caused by active disease and infection; however, late deaths (more than 2 years after disease onset) are more often due to cardiovascular disease. Patients with SLE have a greatly increased risk of atherosclerosis and are more likely to develop symptoms at a younger age; women with SLE between the ages of 35 and 44 years are 50 times more likely to develop a cardiovascular event. Risk factors include hypertension, diabetes mellitus, and hypercholesterolemia (all of which may be caused or worsened by chronic corticosteroid therapy) as well as SLE itself. Patients with a longer course and ongoing inflammation are at greatest risk for a cardiovascular event presumably because of inflammation-induced vascular damage. Although symptoms of nausea and vomiting are not typical of acute myocardial infarction, they are not uncommon, especially in women.

CT angiography of the abdomen is appropriate for patients with positive antiphospholipid antibodies and unexplained abdominal symptoms to evaluate for mesenteric thrombosis or ischemia; however, the absence of abdominal tenderness and diarrhea makes this diagnosis less likely.

CT pulmonary angiography would be an important next step if the electrocardiogram were normal in order to rule out pulmonary embolism, which may present with chest pain, fever, tachycardia, and dyspnea. Symptoms of nausea and vomiting would be unusual, however, and pain is usually pleuritic.

This patient may have acute cholecystitis, but this is unlikely in the absence of fever and right upper quadrant tenderness; therefore, a right upper quadrant ultrasonography is not warranted as an initial test.

KEY POINT

- Patients with systemic lupus erythematosus have a greatly increased risk of atherosclerosis and are more likely to develop symptoms at a younger age.

Bibliography
Goldberg RJ, Urowitz MB, Ibanez D, Nikpour M, Gladman D. Risk factors for the development of coronary artery disease in women with systemic lupus erythematosus. J Rheumatol. 2009;36(11):2454-2461. [PMID: 19833754]

 Item 6　　Answer: B
Educational Objective: Diagnose Löfgren syndrome.

Chest radiography is warranted for this patient who has progressive oligoarthritis involving the ankles and right knee. He also has periarthritis (tendon inflammation), erythema nodosum lesions on the shins, anterior uveitis, and fever. The triad of hilar lymphadenopathy, acute oligoarthritis, and erythema nodosum is characteristic of acute sarcoidosis, also known as Löfgren syndrome. The diagnosis can be made without tissue biopsy if symmetric bilateral hilar lymphadenopathy is demonstrated on chest radiograph. Bronchoscopy or mediastinoscopy with lymph node biopsy is indicated to evaluate for lymphoma if hilar or mediastinal lymphadenopathy is asymmetric, because patients with lymphoma can also present with fever and arthritis. Biopsy of erythema nodosum lesions is never

indicated because pathology always reveals a septal panniculitis regardless of etiology. Angiotensin-converting enzyme levels can be elevated in patients with sarcoidosis, but test results are abnormal in only half of patients with the disease, and results are not available immediately.

ANCA-associated vasculitis, particularly granulomatosis with polyangiitis (also known as Wegener granulomatosis) can be associated with arthritis and uveitis, but erythema nodosum is not usually seen in this condition. Patients usually present with upper or lower respiratory tract disease, glomerulonephritis, and/or mononeuritis multiplex, none of which occurs in this patient.

Although inflammatory bowel disease also can present with oligoarthritis, erythema nodosum, and anterior uveitis, this patient has no gastrointestinal symptoms, making this diagnosis less likely. However, if his chest radiograph is normal, a colonoscopy would be indicated.

Disseminated gonorrhea can present with fever and tenosynovitis of the ankles, but it is not generally associated with uveitis. The rash associated with gonorrhea is generally painless and consists of a few scattered vesicular or pustular lesions. Erythema nodosum rarely occurs.

KEY POINT

- In patients with acute lower extremity arthritis and erythema nodosum, Löfgren syndrome can be diagnosed without tissue biopsy if symmetric bilateral hilar lymphadenopathy is demonstrated on chest radiograph.

Bibliography
Iannuzzi MC, Rybicki BA, Teirstein AS. Sarcoidosis. N Engl J Med. 2007;357(21):2153-2165. [PMID: 18032765]

Item 7　　Answer: C
Educational Objective: Manage inflammatory muscle and joint symptoms associated with systemic sclerosis.

Treatment with methotrexate is appropriate for this patient. The presence of symmetric digital swelling in this patient with Raynaud phenomenon, gastroesophageal reflux, and dilated nailfold capillaries is most consistent with systemic sclerosis. This patient's findings include generalized pruritus antedating the onset of skin induration and the presence of anti-topoisomerase I (anti–Scl-70) antibodies, both of which are common characteristics of early diffuse cutaneous systemic sclerosis (dcSSc). Musculoskeletal features of dcSSc may include a symmetric synovitis involving the peripheral joints, tendon sheath inflammation, or (less commonly) a mild inflammatory myopathy; these manifestations often benefit from treatment with weekly methotrexate in doses employed to manage synovitis in patients with rheumatoid arthritis.

Cyclophosphamide is of modest benefit in the treatment of alveolitis in patients with dcSSc and may have some benefit in suppressing other immune-mediated disease manifestations, including joint and muscle inflammation. However, this patient has a normal D$_{LCO}$, making alveolitis an unlikely diagnosis.

Hydroxychloroquine, an agent commonly used to treat systemic lupus erythematosus (SLE), is not indicated; this patient does not have lupus-specific antibodies (anti–double-stranded DNA or anti-Smith antibodies) or clinical features of SLE not otherwise attributable to systemic sclerosis. Furthermore, hydroxychloroquine is not an effective agent to treat myositis.

NSAIDs such as naproxen are not effective in managing acute dermal inflammation or inflammatory myopathy symptoms in patients with systemic sclerosis. This patient is already using ibuprofen, and adding a second NSAID will likely result in increased renal or gastrointestinal toxicity.

> **KEY POINT**
> - Methotrexate can be used to manage musculoskeletal features of diffuse cutaneous systemic sclerosis.

Bibliography
Quillinan NP, Denton CP. Disease-modifying treatment in systemic sclerosis: current status. Curr Opin Rheumatol. 2009;21(6):636-641. [PMID: 19726995]

Item 8   Answer: D
Educational Objective: Manage knee osteoarthritis.

Weight loss and exercise are indicated for this patient with knee osteoarthritis. Her knee pain, which is worse with weight bearing, is suggestive of tibiofemoral knee osteoarthritis, a diagnosis supported by the presence of medial joint line tenderness and radiographic findings of medial tibiofemoral compartment joint-space narrowing. The strongest risk factors for osteoarthritis are advancing age, obesity, female gender, joint injury (caused by occupation, repetitive use, or actual trauma), and genetic factors. Obesity, in particular, is the most important modifiable risk factor for knee osteoarthritis. Several trials have demonstrated that weight loss and/or exercise programs can offer relief of pain and improved function comparable to the benefits of NSAID use. In long-term studies, sustained weight loss of approximately 6.8 kg (15 lb) has resulted in symptomatic relief.

Celecoxib carries an increased myocardial risk and is therefore not appropriate for this patient who has coronary artery disease. Although celecoxib has a lower risk of gastrointestinal ulcers than other NSAIDs, it can still cause dyspepsia, which occurred in this patient after taking naproxen and ibuprofen.

There have been several contradictory studies regarding glucosamine sulfate in the management of osteoarthritis. After several favorable smaller studies, a trial sponsored by the National Institutes of Health showed no effectiveness in reducing pain. A recently conducted meta-analysis also found negative results for the use of glucosamine sulfate.

MRI of the knee would be indicated to evaluate for meniscal or other ligamentous injuries, none of which is suggested by this patient's history (the knee locking or giving way) or examination findings (negative examination for tendinous or ligamentous injury).

> **KEY POINT**
> - Obesity is the most important modifiable risk factor for knee osteoarthritis, and weight loss and exercise are recommended to reduce pain and improve function.

Bibliography
Messier SP. Diet and exercise for obese adults with knee osteoarthritis. Clin Geriatr Med. 2010;26(3):461-477. [PMID: 20699166]

Item 9   Answer: D
Educational Objective: Diagnose rheumatoid arthritis.

Rheumatoid arthritis is the most likely cause of this patient's neuropathy. Rheumatoid arthritis typically involves the wrists and the small joints of the hands and feet in a symmetric pattern, but involvement of the large joints may also occur. Rheumatoid arthritis also is associated with prolonged (>60 minutes) morning stiffness and fatigue. This patient has inflammation of the wrists and small joints of the hands in a symmetric distribution, fatigue, morning stiffness, and synovitis of the wrists and metacarpophalangeal joints, all findings consistent with rheumatoid arthritis. Synovitis of the wrists or subsequent bony changes can compromise the carpal tunnel and cause entrapment of the median nerve. This patient also has bilateral carpal tunnel syndrome, confirmed with electrodiagnostic testing. Carpal tunnel syndrome is the most common neurologic complication of rheumatoid arthritis. Carpal tunnel syndrome is also found more commonly in patients with diabetes mellitus and thyroid disease and in pregnant women relative to the general population.

When osteoarthritis involves the wrists, it may be associated with carpal tunnel syndrome; however, osteoarthritis does not typically involve the metacarpophalangeal joints and is not associated with morning stiffness and fatigue.

Although any wrist flexion may exacerbate symptoms of carpal tunnel syndrome, overuse injury has not been convincingly shown to play a causative role in the pathogenesis of this neuropathy.

Some patients with polymyalgia rheumatica develop a tenosynovitis and synovitis in the hands, wrists, ankles, and tops of feet that may be associated with carpal tunnel syndrome in 10% of patients. Polymyalgia rheumatica occurs in older persons and rarely appears before the age of 50 years.

Bibliography

Muramatsu K, Tanaka H, Taguchi T. Peripheral neuropathies of the forearm and hand in rheumatoid arthritis: diagnosis and options for treatment. Rheumatology Int. 2008;28(10):951-957. [PMID: 18528693]

Item 10   Answer: B

Educational Objective: Manage proliferative lupus nephritis.

A kidney biopsy is indicated to evaluate for proliferative lupus nephritis in this patient who has active systemic lupus erythematosus and abnormal urine findings. Signs of proliferative lupus nephritis on examination may include new-onset hypertension or edema; laboratory studies typically reveal high titers of anti–double-stranded DNA antibodies, hypocomplementemia, proteinuria, hematuria, and erythrocyte and granular casts in the urine. Although this patient's urinalysis findings show proteinuria with only mildly active urine sediment and no erythrocyte casts, kidney biopsy is indicated because of the presence of active clinical disease, positive anti–double-stranded DNA antibodies, and low complements levels. Kidney biopsy will establish the International Society of Nephrology and Renal Pathology Society lupus nephritis class and levels of activity and chronicity, which aid in predicting prognosis. Prompt biopsy followed by aggressive therapy is critical, because the addition of an immunosuppressive agent such as cyclophosphamide or mycophenolate mofetil in conjunction with high-dose corticosteroids is necessary to ensure the best kidney prognosis.

This patient may benefit from intravenous cyclophosphamide after the biopsy-proven diagnosis, which has been the standard of care for diffuse proliferative lupus nephritis; most practitioners currently treat patients with cyclophosphamide for 6 months, followed by azathioprine or mycophenolate mofetil maintenance therapy. Mycophenolate mofetil may be used as an alternative to cyclophosphamide for initial therapy and appears to be as effective in treating lupus nephritis but with less severe toxicity, although long-term data are limited.

MR angiography of the renal arteries is useful to screen for renovascular hypertension and evaluate for renal artery stenosis. Although this patient has hypertension with possible decreased creatinine clearance, the presence of proteinuria and active urine sediment makes renal artery stenosis unlikely, because this does not account for all of his renal findings.

Bibliography

Seshan SV, Jennette JC. Renal disease in systemic lupus erythematosus with emphasis on classification of lupus glomerulonephritis:

advances and implications. Arch Pathol Lab Med. 2009;133(2):233-248. [PMID: 19195967]

Item 11   Answer: C

Educational Objective: Diagnose malignancy in a patient with systemic lupus erythematosus.

A lymph node biopsy is indicated for this patient who has systemic lupus erythematosus (SLE) with two new enlarged supraclavicular lymph nodes. Although patients with SLE often have lymphadenopathy, new large and localized lymph node swelling merits further evaluation. Patients with SLE have a slight increase in cancer risk, especially those treated with long-term immunosuppressive therapy such as cyclophosphamide, azathioprine, or mycophenolate mofetil. Standardized incidence ratio overall for malignancy in patients with SLE is 1.15; increased risk is present for the development of non-Hodgkin and Hodgkin lymphoma, lung cancer, and hepatobiliary cancer. In addition, women with SLE have an 11-fold increased risk of premalignant cervical dysplasia.

An increase in immunosuppressive therapy, including mycophenolate mofetil or prednisone, is not warranted to treat new lymphadenopathy in a patient with SLE. Increased therapy is reserved for worsening clinical symptoms or signs of increased inflammation indicated on laboratory studies, neither of which is noted in this patient.

Tuberculosis may cause lymph node swelling, and this patient is immunocompromised by her SLE therapy, but she has no other findings to suggest tuberculosis such as cough, fever, and weight loss. Her current prednisone therapy will very likely result in a negative tuberculin skin test result regardless of her underlying history of tuberculosis exposure. If tuberculosis is present, staining of the biopsied lymph node tissue for acid-fast bacilli and subsequent culture will reveal the diagnosis. Finally, if the tuberculin skin test results were positive, this would not change the need to evaluate for malignancy in the enlarged lymph nodes.

Bibliography

Bernatsky S, Ramsey Goldman R, Clarke AE. Malignancy in systemic lupus erythematosus: what have we learned? Best Pract Res Clin Rheumatol. 2009;23(4):539-547. [PMID: 19591783]

Item 12   Answer: D

Educational Objective: Diagnose reactive arthritis.

This patient requires urine nucleic acid amplification testing for *Chlamydia trachomatis* and *Neisseria gonorrhoeae*. She has acute arthritis of the right knee, enthesitis of the left ankle, and urethritis, all of which can be seen with disseminated gonorrheal infection; however, in the absence of any recent history of sexual activity, these findings are more suggestive of reactive arthritis as can be seen after *C. trachomatis* infection. Reactive arthritis occurs in both men and women, and enthesitis and oligoarthritis are common. The classic triad of arthritis, urethritis, and conjunctivitis occurs in only one third of patients. Symptoms typically develop 2 to 4 weeks after an infection.

Classic pathogens associated with reactive arthritis include *C. trachomatis* as well as several enteric pathogens. *C. trachomatis* infection may be asymptomatic. Urine sample evaluation with ligase reaction can establish a diagnosis of *C. trachomatis* infection; at that time, antibiotic treatment (azithromycin or levofloxacin) is warranted to prevent potential sequelae of untreated disease. Sexual partners should also be counseled and treated.

Antinuclear antibody testing can be helpful in the diagnosis of systemic lupus erythematosus (SLE). Although arthritis and pyuria can be seen in SLE, the pyuria typically results from glomerulonephritis and is therefore not associated with the lower urinary tract symptoms of frequency and urgency. The patient does not have any other symptoms or signs of SLE.

Rheumatoid factor is present in approximately 70% of patients with rheumatoid arthritis. This disorder typically presents with a symmetric, small joint polyarthritis and does not explain this patient's urinary symptoms and pyuria.

This patient's negative Lyme disease serology results indicate that she does not have Lyme arthritis, and testing the synovial fluid for *Borrelia burgdorferi* infection is not needed. In patients with Lyme arthritis, testing by polymerase chain reaction (PCR) can detect *B. burgdorferi* DNA in synovial fluid. Unlike *B. burgdorferi* serology, synovial fluid PCR testing becomes negative after successful antibiotic treatment. However, synovial fluid PCR testing has not been validated for wide use.

KEY POINT

- Detection of pathogens such as *Chlamydia trachomatis* in patients with arthritis, urethritis, conjunctivitis, and/or enthesitis supports a diagnosis of reactive arthritis.

Bibliography

Hannu T, Inman R, Granfors K, Leirisalo-Repo M. Reactive arthritis or post-infectious arthritis? Best Pract Res Clin Rheumatol. 2006;20(3):419-433. [PMID: 16777574]

Item 13   Answer: D

Educational Objective: Manage knee osteoarthritis with total knee replacement.

This patient has symptoms and radiographic findings consistent with advanced knee osteoarthritis, and total knee replacement surgery is indicated. Patients with knee osteoarthritis who have not responded to conservative therapy and who have functional limitations should be referred to an orthopedic surgeon for consideration of total knee replacement surgery. This is appropriate when no further medical options are available, and the patient and physician together decide that the potential benefits outweigh the risks of this procedure. Patients undergoing joint replacement should be cautioned about the risks of surgery, including general anesthesia (when applicable), deep venous thrombosis/pulmonary embolism, and wound or joint infections. The prosthetic implants may eventually loosen and require surgical replacement, which is a more difficult procedure than original implantation.

A well-conducted randomized trial demonstrated that there is no benefit from knee arthroscopic lavage and/or debridement for patients with advanced knee osteoarthritis. These patients did not have symptoms suggestive of meniscal injury. Unless there are symptoms of meniscal tear (catching or locking), patients with advanced symptoms of knee osteoarthritis are unlikely to benefit from knee arthroscopy.

An osteotomy procedure removes a wedge of bone to realign the axial load on a joint. This procedure has been used in younger patients with knee osteoarthritis with unilateral tibiofemoral arthritis in order to relieve the forces across either the medial or lateral knee compartment. Studies demonstrate improvement in pain, but it is less clear if the improvement exceeds that associated with maximal medical therapy.

Hyaluronate injection is indicated for the management of symptomatic knee osteoarthritis. However, results are best when used for mild to moderate osteoarthritis. The advanced stage of the joint makes it unlikely that this patient would respond to injections.

KEY POINT

- Patients with knee osteoarthritis who have not responded to conservative therapy and who have functional limitations should be referred to an orthopedic surgeon for consideration of total knee arthroplasty.

Bibliography

Hunter DJ. In the clinic. Osteoarthritis. Ann Intern Med. 2007;147(3):ITC8-1-ITC8-16. [PMID: 17679702]

Item 14   Answer: A

Educational Objective: Diagnose chronic calcium pyrophosphate arthropathy.

This patient has chronic calcium pyrophosphate (CPP) arthropathy. CPP arthropathy is a clinical diagnosis made by observing typical osteoarthritis features, along with chondrocalcinosis, in locations atypical for osteoarthritis such as the metacarpophalangeal joints. A chronic inflammatory condition may result, leading to progressive joint destruction. This patient has a polyarthritis with radiologic findings that resemble osteoarthritis (subchondral sclerosis and osteophytes); however, involvement includes the second and third metacarpophalangeal joints, which are not typically involved in osteoarthritis. There also is evidence of calcium deposition in the cartilage of the affected joints and in the wrists. This constellation of findings is pathognomonic for chronic CPP arthropathy.

Hemochromatosis may overlap with CPP arthropathy and can cause osteoarthritis-like arthritis in atypical joints. However, this patient has no evidence of iron overload (normal serum ferritin, iron, total iron-binding capacity, and transferrin saturation) that is characteristic of hemochromatosis.

Although the patient has radiographic findings consistent with osteoarthritis, the involvement of metacarpophalangeal joints and the presence of chondrocalcinosis are not typical for the disorder.

Pseudogout is an acute inflammatory arthritis caused by CPP crystals in the joint. Although this patient has CPP deposition, there is no evidence of a current or prior acute inflammatory arthritis. This patient's 2-year history of joint pain is not consistent with acute pseudogout.

This patient's findings, including involvement of only the second and third metacarpophalangeal joints; limited morning stiffness and soft-tissue swelling; negative rheumatoid factor and anti–cyclic citrullinated peptide antibody results; and no marginal erosions or periarticular osteopenia, do not support a diagnosis of rheumatoid arthritis.

KEY POINT

- Calcium pyrophosphate arthropathy is characterized by osteoarthritis-like arthritis in atypical joints such as the metacarpophalangeal joints along with the presence of chondrocalcinosis.

Bibliography

Schlesinger N, Hassett AL, Neustadter L, Schumacher HR Jr. Does acute synovitis (pseudogout) occur in patients with chronic pyrophosphate arthropathy (pseudo-osteoarthritis)? Clin Exp Rheumatol. 2009;27(6):940-944. [PMID: 20149309]

Item 15   Answer: A

Educational Objective: Manage pregnancy in a patient with rheumatoid arthritis who is taking methotrexate.

Discontinuation of methotrexate 3 months before conception is indicated for this patient with rheumatoid arthritis. Generally, women with rheumatoid arthritis have fertility rates and pregnancy outcomes comparable to those of women without this condition. Preconception counseling is essential for women with active rheumatoid arthritis who are taking disease-modifying antirheumatic drugs (DMARDs), particularly DMARDs that are known to be teratogenic. Methotrexate is highly teratogenic and abortifacient and must be discontinued to avoid fetal toxicity. Methotrexate and leflunomide are considered to be category X drugs (contraindicated in pregnancy) because of the

high risk of fetal harm. Elimination of leflunomide metabolites from the circulation may be accelerated with the use of cholestyramine. Although data are lacking, there also is some concern that male exposure to methotrexate and leflunomide could be associated with reduced fertility and teratogenicity, and discontinuation and elimination of methotrexate and leflunomide prior to conception are advisable for men as well.

Approximately 75% of women with rheumatoid arthritis who become pregnant experience a spontaneous remission of symptoms that usually begins in the second trimester of pregnancy. During pregnancy, most women with rheumatoid arthritis can therefore safely discontinue therapy for this condition. If persistent disease activity occurs during the pregnancy, this patient may benefit from treatment with an alternative agent such as low-dose prednisone, hydroxychloroquine, or sulfasalazine. NSAIDs are often used during the second trimester but should be avoided in the third trimester because of the risk of premature closure of the ductus arteriosus and interference with labor.

Disease activity often flares postpartum. Therapy should then be reinstituted, unless the woman is breast feeding.

KEY POINT

- Women with rheumatoid arthritis who are taking methotrexate must discontinue the medication 3 months before conception.

Bibliography

Neeman N, Aronson MD, Schulze JE, Shmerling RH. Improving pregnancy counseling for women with rheumatoid arthritis taking methotrexate. Am J Med. 2009;122(11):998-1000. [PMID: 19854323]

Item 16   Answer: C

Educational Objective: Diagnose subacute cutaneous lupus erythematosus.

This patient has subacute cutaneous lupus erythematosus (SCLE). The annular form of SCLE is characterized by scaly erythematous circular plaques with central hypopigmentation; the less common papulosquamous variant resembles psoriasis. These rashes most commonly involve the neck, trunk, and extensor surfaces of the arms. They can be chronic and recurrent but do not scar. SCLE may be associated with medications (hydrochlorothiazide, calcium channel blockers, ACE inhibitors, and terbinafine). SCLE occurs in up to 10% of patients with systemic lupus erythematosus (SLE), usually with some of the less serious SLE manifestations (arthritis, serositis), and is associated with anti-Ro/SSA and anti-La/SSB antibodies. This condition also manifests as its own entity; up to 50% of patients with SCLE do not develop systemic manifestations of lupus. This patient's findings of a rash with circular plaques on the chest and arms as well as elevated anti-Ro/SSA antibodies with no evidence of SLE manifestations such as serositis, arthritis, anemia, leukopenia, or kidney involvement are consistent with SCLE. The diagnosis of SCLE is based upon correlating the clinical lesions with the histopathologic findings on skin biopsy.

Livedo reticularis is a lacy, purple, mottling of the skin that frequently occurs in patients with cholesterol emboli syndrome, SLE, Raynaud phenomenon, the antiphospholipid syndrome, and other connective tissue disorders. This condition is caused by poor local cutaneous blood flow (leading to central pallor) with surrounding dilated or congested capillaries. Lesions are exacerbated by the cold or stress but often resolve with warming. Fixed livedo reticularis does not resolve and can be associated with vasculitis.

Erythema migrans, the hallmark manifestation of early Lyme disease, is an oval or circular erythematous rash that often has an inner ring of clearing, giving it the appearance of a "bull's eye." The rash appears within several weeks after exposure and expands slowly over days. Erythema migrans occurs at the site of the tick bite, but patients with disseminated Lyme disease may have multiple lesions caused by hematogenous spread of the bacteria to other skin sites.

Other than SCLE rash, this patient has no other symptoms of SLE and therefore does not fulfill the diagnostic criteria for SLE.

> **KEY POINT**
> - Up to 50% of patients with subacute cutaneous lupus erythematosus do not develop systemic manifestations of lupus.

Bibliography
Walling HW, Sontheimer RD. Cutaneous lupus erythematosus: issues in diagnosis and treatment. Am J Clin Dermatol. 2009;10(6):365-381. [PMID: 19824738]

Item 17   Answer: D
Educational Objective: Manage infectious arthritis in a patient with concurrent gout.

This patient requires empiric therapy with vancomycin plus piperacillin-tazobactam, pending the results of synovial fluid cultures. Based on his history of gout as well as the presence of tophi and intracellular and extracellular negatively birefringent (urate) crystals, the patient is currently having a gout attack. However, an excessively high synovial fluid leukocyte count of the joint (>50,000/µL [50 × 10^9/L]) requires that the acute joint process be presumed infectious until proved otherwise. In this setting, a negative Gram stain is of insufficient sensitivity to rule out infection. Patients with chronic joint damage such as that seen in gout and other arthritides are at greater risk for joint infection. This patient also has diabetes mellitus and is presumed to be immunocompromised and susceptible not only to gram-positive, but also to gram-negative and anaerobic, organisms. Therefore, empiric combination

therapy with vancomycin and piperacillin-tazobactam is an appropriate approach.

Although intra-articular methylprednisolone is an appropriate approach to treat an acute gout attack while minimizing systemic corticosteroid effects, corticosteroids should never be injected into potentially infected joints.

Prednisone is also an effective treatment for acute gout, particularly if polyarticular; however, use in this patient with diabetes and a potential joint infection would not be justifiable unless and until infection were ruled out.

In this patient, infection is empirically assumed but not proved, and the joint has been adequately drained percutaneously for the time being. Surgical debridement and drainage can be considered for a definitively infected joint, particularly if the percutaneous approach is inadequate to fully drain the entire joint, but is premature at this time.

> **KEY POINT**
> - Bacterial infectious arthritis and gout can occur concomitantly in the same joint and should be suspected when there is a very high (>50,000/µL [50 × 10^9/L]) synovial fluid leukocyte count.

Bibliography
Mathews CJ, Weston VC, Jones A, Field M, Coakley G. Bacterial septic arthritis in adults. Lancet. 2010;375(9717):846-855. [PMID: 20206778]

Item 18   Answer: B
Educational Objective: Manage peripheral manifestations of psoriatic arthritis using methotrexate.

Methotrexate is indicated for this patient with peripheral manifestations of psoriatic arthritis. Clinical manifestations of psoriatic arthritis are heterogeneous, and psoriatic arthritis can affect up to 30% of patients with psoriasis, as seen in this patient. Peripheral manifestations of this disorder are notable for a polyarticular pattern, distal interphalangeal joint involvement, nail changes, dactylitis, tenosynovitis, and arthritis mutilans. Because there are various manifestations, choosing a therapeutic regimen must take into account the features of an individual patient's disease, with more severe degrees of inflammation typically requiring more intensive therapy. This patient has psoriatic arthritis with prominent peripheral joint and skin involvement. Methotrexate can be effective in the treatment of both peripheral arthritis and skin manifestations and therefore is warranted for this patient.

NSAIDs such as ibuprofen may be effective for mild peripheral arthritis associated with psoriatic arthritis; however, these agents are generally insufficient in controlling arthritis that is more extensive and limiting, as seen in this patient. Furthermore, NSAIDs are not effective in treating skin manifestations and may worsen the skin manifestations of psoriasis.

Oral corticosteroids such as prednisone typically are avoided in patients with psoriasis and psoriatic arthritis, because they are associated with flares of psoriatic skin disease and may worsen associated comorbidities such as hypertension and dyslipidemia.

Use of rituximab, a chimeric monoclonal antibody that depletes CD20+ B-cell lymphocytes, is limited in the treatment of psoriatic arthritis. There has been a case report of benefit in a patient with psoriatic arthritis treated with rituximab; however, it has also been noted that some patients without psoriasis have developed psoriatic arthritis after rituximab treatment for other conditions. For this patient, treatment with more established therapeutic options is more appropriate.

> **KEY POINT**
>
> - Methotrexate can be effective in the management of both peripheral arthritis and skin manifestations that occur in patients with psoriatic arthritis.

Bibliography

Ritchlin CT, Kavanaugh A, Gladman DD, et al; Group for Research and Assessment of Psoriasis and Psoriatic Arthritis (GRAPPA). Treatment recommendations for psoriatic arthritis. Ann Rheum Dis. 2009;68(9):1387-1394. [PMID: 18952643]

Item 19   Answer: C

Educational Objective: Diagnose secondary osteoarthritis due to hemochromatosis.

Measuring the serum transferrin saturation is indicated for this patient who has signs suggestive of secondary osteoarthritis due to hemochromatosis. Osteoarthritis of the metacarpophalangeal joints in the absence of trauma is unusual and should suggest an investigation for hemochromatosis. Approximately 40% to 60% of patients with hemochromatosis develop arthropathy that is osteoarthritis-like, but characteristically involves the metacarpophalangeal and wrist joints. Hemochromatosis arthropathy also may involve the shoulders, hips, knees, and ankles. Radiographs of the metacarpophalangeal joints may reveal hook-shaped osteophytes that are significantly different from radiographs of patients with primary osteoarthritis. Secondary chondrocalcinosis can also be seen. The initial step in the evaluation of patients in whom hemochromatosis is suspected is measurement of serum transferrin and iron saturation, the most sensitive measure for detecting this disease. Genetic testing for hemochromatosis would also be indicated.

Antinuclear antibody testing for systemic lupus erythematosus (SLE) is not indicated for this patient. SLE can result in inflammatory arthritis in a rheumatoid arthritis–like distribution that is typically nonerosive. However, the patient has no other symptoms of SLE (serositis, rash), and his radiographic changes are not consistent with SLE (presence of osteophytes).

Rheumatoid factor is useful in the diagnosis of rheumatoid arthritis. However, this patient's findings, including asymmetric arthritis and joint-space narrowing with osteophyte formation, are suggestive of osteoarthritis. Testing for rheumatoid factor is therefore not indicated in this patient.

Gouty arthritis of the hands is another form of inflammatory arthritis that can mimic rheumatoid arthritis. However, without cystic changes or tophi, the diagnosis is unlikely, and measurement of serum uric acid levels is not indicated at this time and would not establish the diagnosis of gout.

> **KEY POINT**
>
> - Secondary osteoarthritis typically involves joints not usually affected by primary osteoarthritis, including the metacarpophalangeal joints (which should specifically raise suspicion for hemochromatosis) and the wrists.

Bibliography

Carroll GJ, Breidahl WH, Bulsara MK, Olynyk JK. Hereditary hemochromatosis is characterized by a clinically definable arthropathy that correlates with iron load. Arthritis Rheum. 2011;63(1):286-294. [PMID: 20954257]

Item 20   Answer: A

Educational Objective: Diagnose rheumatoid arthritis.

An anti–cyclic citrullinated peptide (CCP) antibody assay is warranted for this patient in whom rheumatoid arthritis is suspected. Anti-CCP antibodies are present in approximately 40% to 60% of patients with early rheumatoid arthritis, including some patients with a negative rheumatoid factor. These antibodies are 95% specific for rheumatoid arthritis. The presence of higher titers of either rheumatoid factor or anti-CCP antibodies or the presence of both increases the likelihood of disease. Although this patient's rheumatoid factor is negative and his acute phase reactants are normal, rheumatoid arthritis remains a significant concern because he has synovitis of eight small joints and morning stiffness lasting more than 1 hour, common symptoms of rheumatoid arthritis. An anti-CCP antibody assay is therefore appropriate to determine whether this patient's symptoms are caused by rheumatoid arthritis.

Antimitochondrial antibodies are present in patients with autoimmune hepatitis. Patients with this disease can develop arthralgia and arthritis similar to this patient; however, he does not have liver chemistry test abnormalities that are characteristic of autoimmune hepatitis.

Antineutrophil cytoplasmic antibodies are typically associated with vasculitis such as granulomatosis with polyangiitis (also known as Wegener granulomatosis), microscopic polyangiitis, Churg-Strauss syndrome, anti–glomerular basement membrane antibody disease, and drug-induced vasculitis. Arthritis and arthralgia can be associated with these syndromes; however, the presence of these vascular inflammatory disorders would be unusual in the absence of other system involvement.

Antinuclear antibodies (ANA) can be clinically useful when there is clinical suspicion for autoimmune conditions associated with these antibodies such as systemic lupus erythematosus (SLE). SLE may present with arthritis but, in this case, SLE is less likely than rheumatoid arthritis. SLE typically occurs in women of childbearing age, with additional clinical and/or laboratory abnormalities rather than isolated arthritis. ANA are present in some patients with rheumatoid arthritis but are not specific for this disorder.

KEY POINT

- Anti–cyclic citrullinated peptide antibodies are a highly specific marker for rheumatoid arthritis.

Bibliography

Whiting PF, Smidt N, Sterne JA, et al. Systematic review: accuracy of anti-citrullinated peptide antibodies for diagnosing rheumatoid arthritis. Ann Intern Med. 2010;152(7):456-464; W155-166. [PMID: 20368651]

Item 21   Answer: A

Educational Objective: Manage axial spondyloarthritis with NSAIDs.

Treatment with NSAIDs such as diclofenac is appropriate for this patient with axial manifestations of spondyloarthritis. Axial spondyloarthritis is characterized by sacroiliitis revealed on imaging with at least one spondyloarthropathy feature or the presence of HLA-B27 and at least two additional spondyloarthropathy features. Spondyloarthropathy features include inflammatory back pain; arthritis; enthesitis; dactylitis; uveitis; psoriasis; Crohn disease or ulcerative colitis; family history for spondyloarthritis; presence of HLA-B27; elevated C-reactive protein level; and a good response to NSAIDs. This patient has chronic symptoms of inflammatory back pain and radiographic changes of axial spondyloarthritis that occur in ankylosing spondylitis. Axial involvement in ankylosing spondylitis initially involves the sacroiliac joints and lower spine, as seen in this patient. NSAIDs at maximum dosage are recommended as first-line therapy for axial arthritis and are effective in controlling inflammation in this context. Up to 80% of patients respond to anti-inflammatory doses taken on a regular basis. Although existing data suggest that there is little difference in the effectiveness of specific NSAIDs for patients with ankylosing spondylitis, if one NSAID does not provide relief after 2 weeks, another agent may be tried.

Tumor necrosis factor (TNF)-α inhibitors such as etanercept are used to treat both peripheral and axial involvement that occur in spondyloarthritis. However, because of cost and long-term safety concerns, these agents currently are not recommended as first-line therapy. If NSAIDs are insufficient, poorly tolerated, or contraindicated, TNF-α inhibitors are then advised.

Nonbiologic disease-modifying antirheumatic drugs such as methotrexate and sulfasalazine are used to treat peripheral arthritis but are not effective in axial spondyloarthritis.

KEY POINT

- NSAIDs are considered first-line therapy for patients with axial spondyloarthritis.

Bibliography

Song IH, Poddubnyy DA, Rudwaleit M, Sieper J. Benefits and risks of ankylosing spondylitis treatment with nonsteroidal anti-inflammatory drugs. Arthritis Rheum. 2008;58(4):929-938. [PMID: 18383378]

Item 22   Answer: A

Educational Objective: Treat a patient who has polyarteritis nodosa associated with hepatitis B virus infection.

Treatment with entecavir in conjunction with prednisone is indicated for this patient with polyarteritis nodosa who also has hepatitis B virus infection. This patient's constitutional symptoms, abdominal pain, and mesenteric angiogram showing aneurysms of medium caliber and small muscular arteries are consistent with polyarteritis nodosa. Other presenting features include testicular pain, painful cutaneous nodules, skin ulcers, palpable purpura, mononeuropathy, and livedo reticularis. Anemia, leukocytosis, and an elevated erythrocyte sedimentation rate are typical laboratory findings in patients with polyarteritis nodosa. Involvement of the renal arterioles, gastrointestinal tract, and heart may occur. This patient also has hepatitis B virus infection, which is present in up to 50% of patients with polyarteritis nodosa. The initial treatment of patients with polyarteritis nodosa who also have active hepatitis B virus infection is a brief (2-week) course of high-dose corticosteroids in conjunction with antiviral therapy such as entecavir. Using this approach, more than 50% of patients with hepatitis B e antigen–positive polyarteritis nodosa respond with resolution of the arteritis as well as seroconversion to anti–hepatitis B e antibody positivity. High-dose corticosteroids in conjunction with oral cyclophosphamide are standard therapy for patients with refractory disease or severe visceral or neurologic complications and are most commonly reserved for patients who do not have hepatitis B virus infection.

Treatment with rituximab or tumor necrosis factor α inhibitors such as infliximab is relatively contraindicated in this patient because of reported exacerbation of viral replication and hepatitis when administered to patients with active hepatitis B virus infection.

Mycophenolate mofetil can be used as steroid-sparing therapy to prevent relapse in patients with other forms of systemic vasculitis following initial responses to treatment with cyclophosphamide; however, this agent does not have a role in the primary/initial treatment of polyarteritis nodosa.

- Initial treatment of patients with polyarteritis nodosa who also have active hepatitis B virus infection is a limited course of corticosteroids in conjunction with antiviral therapy.

Bibliography

Guillevin L, Mahr A, Callard P, et al; French Vasculitis Study Group. Hepatitis B virus-associated polyarteritis nodosa: clinical characteristics, outcome, and impact of treatment in 115 patients. Medicine (Baltimore). 2005;84(5):313-322. [PMID: 16148731]

Item 23   Answer: E

Educational Objective: Avoid NSAID cardiovascular toxicity in a patient with osteoarthritis.

Treatment with tramadol is indicated for this patient with knee osteoarthritis. Acetaminophen is first-line pharmacologic therapy for osteoarthritis because of its safe profile at approved doses, and it is considered complementary to nonpharmacologic interventions. However, this patient has not responded to acetaminophen in conjunction with physical therapy and topical therapies. Tramadol is a multi-acting agent, and its use in patients with osteoarthritis is well established. This partial opiate agonist also raises serotonin and norepinephrine levels; unlike most opiates, its addictive potential is low, and it does not cause constipation.

Selective cyclooxygenase-2 inhibitors such as celecoxib are useful in the treatment of osteoarthritis but are associated with increased cardiovascular risk in susceptible persons such as this patient who has peripheral vascular disease, hyperlipidemia, and hypertension.

Colchicine has potent anti-inflammatory effects in specific diseases such as gout and familial Mediterranean fever; however, it carries no analgesic potential and is not used to treat osteoarthritis.

Indomethacin is a potent nonselective NSAID with anti-inflammatory effects. Because of its numerous side effects, this agent is not considered first-line therapy in the management of a chronic condition such as osteoarthritis. Its strong association with induction of hypertension and kidney disease makes indomethacin a less desirable agent for this patient. Additionally, indomethacin and most other nonselective NSAIDs are associated with varying degrees of cardiovascular risk and should be employed with caution, especially in high-risk patients. One exception may be naproxen, which in epidemiologic studies has been associated with a lower level of cardiovascular risk and possibly even cardioprotection.

Although corticosteroid injections into the knees may have transient benefit in patients with osteoarthritis, oral prednisone is not standard for osteoarthritis and lacks the analgesic capacity of NSAIDs.

- Selective cyclooxygenase-2 inhibitors are associated with increased cardiovascular risk and should be used cautiously in patients with cardiovascular disease.

Bibliography

Burmester G, Lanas A, Biasucci L, et al. Concise report: the appropriate use of non-steroidal anti-inflammatory drugs in rheumatic disease: opinions of a multidisciplinary European expert panel. Ann Rheum Dis. 2011;70(5):818-822. [PMID: 20833736]

Item 24   Answer: D

Educational Objective: Manage giant cell arteritis.

An ultrasound-guided biopsy of the contralateral temporal artery is indicated for this patient with suspected giant cell arteritis (GCA). Scalp tenderness and headache are common presenting features of GCA with cranial artery involvement. Treatment with corticosteroids is indicated immediately in patients clinically suspected of having GCA to avoid the development of visual loss and should not await temporal artery biopsy results. The initial temporal artery biopsy in this patient with cranial symptoms is negative for findings of GCA; therefore, a biopsy of the contralateral temporal artery is appropriate. Skip lesions are not uncommon in GCA, and ultrasound guidance to identify portions of the artery with transmural thickening and/or halo signal in the vessel has been shown to increase the diagnostic yield in patients with suspected GCA.

CT angiography can be used to identify GCA involvement of large branch vessels of the aorta; however, this test carries the risk of contrast-induced acute kidney injury in this patient with chronic kidney disease.

Until GCA has been thoroughly ruled out in this patient, it is not appropriate to decrease the dose of prednisone and risk visual loss.

MR angiography may be used to diagnose large-vessel vasculitis and can be helpful in cases of a negative temporal artery biopsy. However, patients with an estimated glomerular filtration rate of less than 40 mL/min/1.73 m² are at great risk for developing nephrogenic systemic fibrosis (NSF) after administration of gadolinium, and use of this agent should be avoided in this population group. NSF manifests as a scleroderma-like disease associated with edema, plaque-like rash, and hardening of the skin.

- If temporal artery biopsy results are negative for giant cell arteritis (GCA) in a patient with cranial symptoms, a biopsy of the contralateral temporal artery is then indicated to diagnose GCA.

Bibliography

Arida A, Kyprianou M, Kanakis M, Sfikakis PP. The diagnostic value of ultrasonography-derived edema of the temporal artery wall in giant cell arteritis: a second meta-analysis. BMC Musculoskelet Disord. 2010;11:44. [PMID: 20210989]

Item 25   Answer: A

Educational Objective: Manage methotrexate use and toxicity in rheumatoid arthritis.

This patient has rheumatoid arthritis and must discontinue alcohol consumption before starting therapy with methotrexate. The disease-modifying antirheumatic drug (DMARD) methotrexate is a staple drug for patients with rheumatoid arthritis and other rheumatic conditions and is effective alone or in combination with other agents such as biologics. Although methotrexate is effective and generally well tolerated, this agent has many potential side effects that require management, including methotrexate-induced hepatitis. Patients with preexisting liver disease should rarely, if ever, be treated with methotrexate (and may require regular liver biopsy in that setting to monitor liver function). In addition, the combination of methotrexate and alcohol is a potent one for increasing the risk of methotrexate-induced liver disease. Accordingly, patients taking methotrexate should not drink alcohol regularly, and this patient should be advised to stop drinking alcohol.

Coadministration of folic acid daily reduces the risk of methotrexate-induced side effects, including liver toxicity; its use concurrent with methotrexate is recommended and should not be discontinued in this patient.

Discontinuation of hydroxychloroquine is not necessary, because this agent and methotrexate are frequently coadministered for synergistic effect. Such administration may actually lower the risk for liver abnormalities.

In early rheumatoid arthritis, NSAIDs and systemic low-dose corticosteroids can help control symptoms but do not adequately prevent disease progression. These agents are particularly beneficial early in the disease course until DMARD therapy, which has a slow onset of action, becomes effective. Corticosteroids should be tapered to the lowest effective dose and discontinued when feasible. There is no indication to discontinue prednisone in this patient before starting methotrexate.

Although patients who smoke have an increased risk of rheumatoid arthritis, there is no specific contraindication for smoking among patients with rheumatoid arthritis taking methotrexate. However, it is advised that this patient quit smoking from both a rheumatoid arthritis and an overall health perspective.

KEY POINT

- Discontinuation of alcohol consumption is indicated before initiating therapy with methotrexate.

Bibliography

Thompson AE, Bashook PG. Rheumatologists' recommended patient information when prescribing methotrexate for rheumatoid arthritis. Clin Exp Rheumatol. 2010;28(4):539-545. [PMID: 20663404]

Item 26   Answer: D

Educational Objective: Diagnose pulmonary arterial hypertension in a patient with mixed connective tissue disease.

Right heart catheterization is appropriate for this patient to evaluate for pulmonary arterial hypertension (PAH). She has symptoms and signs suggestive of an underlying diagnosis of mixed connective tissue disease (MCTD), which is characterized by overlapping clinical features of systemic lupus erythematosus, polymyositis, and systemic sclerosis, with high titers of antinuclear and anti-U1-ribonucleoprotein (RNP) antibodies. PAH may also occur, which is the most common disease-related cause of death in patients with MCTD.

This patient has Raynaud phenomenon, hand swelling, joint pain, dysphagia, high-titer speckled antinuclear antibodies, and high-titer RNP antibodies, all of which are typical findings of MCTD. This patient's symptoms of dyspnea on exertion, isolated low D$_{LCO}$, and elevated estimated systolic pulmonary artery pressure on echocardiogram all suggest PAH. Therefore, right heart catheterization is indicated.

Despite the patient's mildly elevated serum creatine kinase level, muscle biopsy is not necessary, because her muscle strength is normal. Patients with MCTD may have subclinical myositis, but respiratory muscle weakness causing dyspnea would be a late finding associated with more profound myositis.

Radionuclide stress test is not indicated for this patient, whose abnormal D$_{LCO}$ and systolic pulmonary artery pressure on echocardiogram are not suggestive of ischemic cardiac disease as the cause for her dyspnea.

In patients with confirmed MCTD without cardiopulmonary symptoms and with normal baseline pulmonary function testing and echocardiogram, yearly repeat tests are appropriate for routine monitoring. It is an inappropriate choice for this symptomatic patient with findings highly suggestive of PAH.

KEY POINT

- Pulmonary arterial hypertension is the most common disease-related cause of death in patients with mixed connective tissue disease.

Bibliography

Jais X, Launay D, Yaici A, et al. Immunosuppressive therapy in lupus- and mixed connective tissue disease-associated pulmonary arterial hypertension: a retrospective analysis of twenty-three cases. Arthritis Rheum. 2008;58(2):521-531. [PMID: 18240255]

Item 27   Answer: D

Educational Objective: Diagnose *Staphylococcus aureus* infection.

This patient has *Staphylococcus aureus* infection. Gram-positive organisms are the most frequent causes of infectious arthritis, with *S. aureus* being the most common. These infections typically are monoarticular, affect the large joints (particularly the knee), and have a rapid onset (hours or 1 to 2 days). This otherwise healthy patient has an acute arthritis following a skin break with cellulitis over the knee, consistent with hematogenous spread of a skin-derived infection. The presence of fever, along with a markedly swollen and inflamed joint, is consistent with *S. aureus* infection.

Acute gouty arthritis typically is monoarticular and frequently involves the knee; however, gout is exceedingly rare in healthy premenopausal women.

Anterior cruciate ligament tear can cause acute swelling, but the joint is usually less inflamed, and this condition is not associated with fever. This patient's knee was not injured after her fall, making an anterior cruciate tear unlikely. In addition, anterior instability ensues (assessed using the anterior drawer and Lachman tests), whereas this patient's knee remained stable.

Although chronic Lyme arthritis can manifest as monoarticular arthritis of the lower extremity, the onset is typically gradual rather than acute, and is not associated with fever.

KEY POINT

- Infectious arthritis caused by gram-positive organisms is typically monoarticular and affects the large joints, particularly the knee, with a rapid onset (hours or 1 to 2 days).

Bibliography

Mathews CJ, Weston VC, Jones A, Field M, Coakley G. Bacterial septic arthritis in adults. Lancet. 2010;375(9717):846-855. [PMID: 20206778]

Item 28   Answer: C

Educational Objective: Manage early rheumatoid arthritis with methotrexate.

Methotrexate is indicated for this patient with early rheumatoid arthritis. Experts recommend that patients begin disease-modifying antirheumatic drug (DMARD) therapy within 3 months of onset. The sooner DMARDs are instituted, the more likely that damage will be limited. Methotrexate is the gold standard DMARD therapy for rheumatoid arthritis and is central to most treatments for the disease. This agent can be effective as initial monotherapy for patients with rheumatoid arthritis of any duration or degree of activity. This patient has synovitis of six metacarpophalangeal joints with a symmetric distribution not involving the distal interphalangeal joints, which is consistent with rheumatoid arthritis. She has swelling, prolonged morning stiffness, an elevated erythrocyte sedimentation rate (ESR), and positive rheumatoid factor, which further support the diagnosis of rheumatoid arthritis, and initial treatment with methotrexate is warranted at this time.

Etanercept is a tumor necrosis factor α inhibitor used for initial therapy in some patients with high disease activity and poor prognostic features. This agent may be necessary for this patient if her disease does not respond to methotrexate.

Hydroxychloroquine as monotherapy may be effective only in mild cases early in the disease course for patients without poor prognostic features. This patient has evidence of moderate disease activity, given the extent of her synovitis and elevated ESR; therefore, hydroxychloroquine as a single agent is unlikely to control this degree of inflammation and is more beneficial as an adjunctive agent.

Reevaluation in 6 weeks is not indicated for this patient whose laboratory studies reveal no evidence of acute parvovirus or hepatitis B infection. Such viral infections can cause an acute polyarthritis syndrome that mimics rheumatoid arthritis. The diagnosis of rheumatoid arthritis previously was predicated on symptoms lasting more than 6 weeks to exclude many self-limiting viral syndromes. However, classification criteria no longer require symptoms to occur for 6 weeks to avoid delays in treatment. The likelihood of rheumatoid arthritis is now calculated on the distribution of joints involved, rheumatoid factor, anti–citrullinated peptide antibodies, acute phase reactants, and duration of symptoms.

KEY POINT

- Methotrexate is the gold standard disease-modifying antirheumatic drug therapy for rheumatoid arthritis and is central to most treatments for the disease.

Bibliography

Saag KG, Teng GG, Patkar NM, et al.; American College of Rheumatology. American College of Rheumatology 2008 recommendations for the use of nonbiologic and biologic disease-modifying antirheumatic drugs in rheumatoid arthritis. Arthritis Rheum. 2008;59(6):762-784. [PMID: 18512708]

Item 29   Answer: A

Educational Objective: Diagnose systemic lupus erythematosus.

An anti–double-stranded DNA antibody assay is the test with the greatest specificity for this patient who has manifestations of systemic lupus erythematosus (SLE). She meets criteria for SLE because of the presence of positive antinuclear antibodies (ANA), along with arthritis, an oral ulcer, and photosensitive rash. The livedo rash may be suggestive of antiphospholipid antibodies. Testing that is indicated in patients with symptoms suggestive of SLE include a complete blood count, erythrocyte sedimentation rate, and urinalysis. Patients with a high pretest probability of SLE and ANA (usually a titer ≥1:160) should undergo confirmatory testing, such as measurement of C3, C4, and CH50 and more specific autoantibody testing. Anti–double-stranded DNA antibodies are present in approximately

50% to 70% of patients with SLE and generally not present in those with other autoimmune diseases. The presence of anti–double-stranded DNA antibodies is correlated with kidney disease in patients with lupus, and rising titers may precede disease flare. Patients with a new diagnosis of SLE should also undergo screening for anticardiolipin antibodies and the lupus anticoagulant.

Anti-Ro/SSA and anti-La/SSB antibodies are present in 10% to 60% of patients with SLE; however, these antibodies are less specific than anti–double-stranded DNA antibodies, because they can also be present in patients with rheumatoid arthritis, systemic sclerosis, and Sjögren syndrome.

Anti-U1-ribonucleoprotein (RNP) antibodies are characteristic of mixed connective tissue disease, which is characterized by features of systemic sclerosis, polymyositis, and SLE. The diagnosis requires the presence of high-titer RNP antibodies, generally in the absence of other autoantibodies. Positive RNP antibodies are also found in 30% to 40% of patients with SLE, but the test is less sensitive and specific than DNA antibodies.

The presence of antiproteinase-3 antibodies (which produces a cANCA pattern on immunofluorescence testing) is suggestive of granulomatosis with polyangiitis (also known as Wegener granulomatosis), a necrotizing vasculitis that typically affects the respiratory tract and the kidneys. This test is not indicated, because this patient does not have findings consistent with the disorder.

KEY POINT
- Anti–double-stranded DNA antibodies are present in approximately 50% to 70% of patients with systemic lupus erythematosus.

Bibliography
D'Cruz DP, Khamashta MA, Hughes GR. Systemic lupus erythematosus. Lancet. 2007;369(9561):587-596. [PMID: 17307106]

Item 30   Answer: D
Educational Objective: Manage peripheral manifestations of inflammatory bowel disease–associated arthritis.

Sulfasalazine is appropriate for long-term treatment of this patient with inflammatory bowel disease (IBD)–associated arthritis, because this drug is effective for both her intestinal and extraintestinal manifestations. Various patterns of arthritis are associated with IBD; this patient has peripheral arthritis, which may be acute and remitting with a pauciarticular distribution commonly involving the knee and usually occurring early in the course of bowel disease. NSAIDs are considered first-line therapy for peripheral arthritis; however, these agents are associated with flares of intestinal inflammation in IBD, as seen in this patient who tried NSAIDs. For patients in whom NSAIDs cannot be used, nonbiologic disease-modifying antirheumatic drugs (DMARDs) can be beneficial in those with moderate or severe peripheral inflammation or mild peripheral inflammation that occurs despite the use of NSAIDs. Peripheral arthritis tends to parallel gastrointestinal inflammation and responds well to the nonbiologic DMARD sulfasalazine. Based on this patient's joint symptoms, bloody diarrhea, and tenesmus, treatment with sulfasalazine is warranted at this time.

Tumor necrosis factor (TNF)-α inhibitors are recommended for patients with ongoing peripheral inflammation, progressive radiographic changes despite nonbiologic DMARD use, or axial inflammation. Although etanercept is effective for peripheral and axial joint inflammation in IBD, it is not effective for intestinal inflammation. Other TNF-α inhibitors, including infliximab, adalimumab, and certolizumab pegol, are effective for both articular and intestinal manifestations.

The nonbiologic DMARD methotrexate is generally used in IBD only after treatment with sulfasalazine has been found to be ineffective. Data on the efficacy of methotrexate in ulcerative colitis are lacking.

Corticosteroids such as prednisone are generally administered as short-term treatment options. The adverse effect profile of corticosteroids limits their use. Corticosteroids are used for long-term treatment only when other medications are contraindicated or have not successfully controlled the patient's symptoms.

KEY POINT
- Treatment with sulfasalazine is indicated in patients with inflammatory bowel disease–associated arthritis.

Bibliography
De Vos M. Joint involvement in inflammatory bowel disease: managing inflammation outside the digestive system. Expert Rev Gastroenterol Hepatol. 2010;4(1):81-89. [PMID: 20136591]

Item 31   Answer: D
Educational Objective: Diagnose morphea.

The most likely diagnosis is morphea. The histology of morphea is similar to that of systemic sclerosis; however, morphea involves only the skin in the absence of other systemic manifestations of systemic sclerosis. Morphea can be further categorized as limited or generalized. Limited morphea consists of one or more discrete plaques of skin involvement, whereas diffuse morphea can diffusely involve the trunk and limbs. In either case, patients do not have the typical extracutaneous manifestations of systemic sclerosis such as gastroesophageal reflux disease, lung disease, bowel dysmotility, or Raynaud phenomenon.

Diffuse cutaneous systemic sclerosis (dcSSc) is characterized by skin thickening that involves areas proximal to the elbows and/or knees.

Limited cutaneous systemic sclerosis (lcSSc) is characterized by skin disease that does not progress proximal to the elbows or knees. A subset of this condition is the

CREST (calcinosis, Raynaud phenomenon, esophageal dysmotility, sclerodactyly, and telangiectasia) syndrome. Both lcSSc and dcSSc can involve the face and neck and both are associated with extracutaneous findings.

Linear scleroderma has an onset typically in childhood and is recognized by skin thickening that follows a dermatomal distribution on one side of the body.

KEY POINT

- Morphea is a category of cutaneous sclerosis that involves only the skin in the absence of other systemic manifestations of systemic sclerosis.

Bibliography

Gabrielli A, Avvedimento EV, Krieg T. Scleroderma. N Engl J Med. 2009;360(19):1989-2003. [PMID: 19420368]

Item 32   Answer: D

Educational Objective: Manage the risk of retinal toxicity in a patient taking hydroxychloroquine.

This patient takes hydroxychloroquine and requires a baseline retinal examination. Hydroxychloroquine is commonly used to treat rheumatoid arthritis and systemic lupus erythematosus. Patients taking hydroxychloroquine are at risk for retinal toxicity by virtue of hydroxychloroquine deposition directly in the retina. Although retinal toxicity is uncommon at currently used doses, the risk of visual problems is best managed by regular retinal examinations by an ophthalmologist, which allows for preclinical detection and drug discontinuation in patients who develop ocular toxicity. The optimal frequency for retinal examination is not well established; prior recommendations for an examination every 6 months may be overly aggressive, with some experts now recommending annual examinations beginning 5 years after initiation. In all patients, if hydroxychloroquine is to be continued, an initial retinal examination either before or shortly after initiation is required to establish a baseline for comparison.

The addition of tumor necrosis factor α inhibitor therapy such as etanercept to a treatment regimen consisting of methotrexate frequently improves rheumatoid arthritis symptoms. However, this patient currently has minimal symptoms, and radiographs show no evidence of progression of joint erosion.

Discontinuation of methotrexate is not indicated. Her symptoms are well controlled on her current regimen, and her liver chemistry tests are within normal limits; she is therefore not experiencing methotrexate toxicity. Because methotrexate controls, but does not remit, rheumatoid arthritis symptoms, discontinuation of the agent may result in recurrence of her symptoms.

Liver biopsy occasionally may be useful in monitoring liver toxicity in patients at high risk for methotrexate-induced toxicity (for example, patients with preexisting liver disease). This patient has no liver disease, and monitoring of liver chemistry tests is considered sufficient to monitor for toxicity.

KEY POINT

- Patients taking hydroxychloroquine are at risk for retinal toxicity and require baseline and follow-up retinal examinations.

Bibliography

Marmor MF, Kellner U, Lai TY, Lyons JS, Mieler WF. Revised recommendations on screening for chloroquine and hydroxychloroquine retinopathy. Ophthalmology. 2011;118(2):415-422. [PMID: 21292109]

Item 33   Answer: A

Educational Objective: Manage rheumatoid arthritis perioperatively.

Cervical spine radiography is the appropriate preoperative diagnostic study for this patient with rheumatoid arthritis who is about to undergo total joint arthroplasty of the left knee. Cervical spine radiography with flexion and extension views is indicated for patients with aggressive or long-standing rheumatoid arthritis to evaluate for atlantoaxial subluxation and dynamic instability. Evaluation for cervical instability is particularly important in the perioperative setting, when extension of the neck for intubation may lead to spinal cord compromise and resultant paraplegia. This patient has evidence of bony changes attributable to erosive arthritis. Similar erosive changes in the cervical spine could increase risk of morbidity, particularly with neck movements that occur during intubation. These radiographic changes may be present in asymptomatic patients. If cervical instability is detected, the surgical team, including the anesthesiologist, must be alerted.

Rheumatoid arthritis is a risk factor for cardiovascular disease; however, this patient's exercise tolerance exceeds four metabolic equivalents. Therefore, exercise cardiac stress testing is not indicated in this context.

Although patients with rheumatoid arthritis can develop interstitial lung disease, preoperative spirometry should not be used routinely for predicting risk for postoperative pulmonary complications. Spirometry does not usually add information beyond what was known or suspected clinically and rarely changes management.

In the absence of a personal or family history of abnormal bleeding, liver disease, significant alcohol use, malabsorption, or anticoagulation therapy, the likelihood of a bleeding disorder is low, and no further preoperative testing is required.

KEY POINT

- Preoperative cervical spine radiography is indicated for all patients with aggressive or long-standing rheumatoid arthritis to evaluate for atlantoaxial subluxation and dynamic instability before intubation.

Bibliography

Grauer JN, Tingstad EM, Rand N, et al. Predictors of paralysis in the rheumatoid cervical spine in patients undergoing total joint arthroplasty. J Bone Joint Surg Am. 2004;86A(7):1420-1424. [PMID: 15252088]

Item 34   Answer: C

Educational Objective: Evaluate potential lipid complications in a patient receiving tocilizumab.

This patient currently receives tocilizumab infusions for rheumatoid arthritis and requires a lipid profile to monitor cholesterol levels. Tocilizumab is FDA approved to treat patients with rheumatoid arthritis who have experienced an inadequate response to tumor necrosis factor α inhibitors. This biologic disease-modifying antirheumatic drug is associated with leukopenia, thrombocytopenia, and elevated serum aminotransferase levels. Tocilizumab also is associated with increases in serum cholesterol levels, a concern given the increased risk for premature cardiovascular disease associated with rheumatoid arthritis. Periodic monitoring for changes in lipid status is therefore indicated for patients receiving tocilizumab, particularly for patients with additional risk factors for coronary artery disease, as noted in this patient who has a family history of the disease.

Tocilizumab is not associated with cardiac toxicities that would require periodic monitoring with echocardiography or electrocardiography.

Given this patient's recent normal liver chemistry test results, further testing is not necessary at this time.

Tocilizumab does not have any significant impact on serum immunoglobulin, and monitoring these levels is not indicated.

KEY POINT

- Periodic monitoring for changes in lipid status is indicated for patients receiving tocilizumab.

Bibliography

Genovese MC, McKay JD, Nasonov EL, et al. Interleukin-6 receptor inhibition with tocilizumab reduces disease activity in rheumatoid arthritis with inadequate response to disease-modifying antirheumatic drugs: the tocilizumab in combination with traditional disease-modifying antirheumatic drug therapy study. Arthritis Rheum. 2008;58(10):2968-2980. [PMID: 18821691]

Item 35   Answer: C

Educational Objective: Manage drug-induced lupus erythematosus.

The most appropriate next step in management is to discontinue infliximab. This patient has drug-induced lupus erythematosus (DILE) caused by the tumor necrosis factor (TNF)-α inhibitor infliximab. Many patients who use TNF-α inhibitors develop autoantibodies, including antinuclear, anti–double-stranded DNA, and anti-Smith antibodies; rarely, these patients develop DILE. Patients with this condition may have typical manifestations of systemic lupus erythematosus but are particularly likely to have cutaneous and pleuropericardial involvement. Kidney and neurologic manifestations are extremely rare.

This patient with previously stable rheumatoid arthritis has increasing joint and constitutional symptoms.

Although arthritis flares and serositis may occur in patients with active rheumatoid arthritis, she also has evidence of a phototoxic skin rash and positive antinuclear antibodies, all of which are features most commonly associated with DILE. Appropriate management of suspected DILE in such patients with rheumatoid arthritis is discontinuation of the offending agent.

Hydroxychloroquine may be used in combination with methotrexate to treat rheumatoid arthritis and is also used to manage non–drug-induced lupus, but the initial appropriate management option in suspected DILE is to discontinue the offending agent.

Combination of biologic agents such as rituximab with TNF-α inhibitors is not recommended in the management of rheumatoid arthritis because of the higher risk of infection complications and marginal additional therapeutic efficacy.

In the absence of DILE manifestations, increasing the dose of methotrexate can be appropriate in a patient on TNF-α inhibitors continuing to have active synovitis; however, the appropriate intervention for this patient is to discontinue the offending agent.

KEY POINT

- Appropriate treatment of patients with drug-induced lupus erythematosus is discontinuation of the offending agent.

Bibliography

Costa MF, Said NR, Zimmermann B. Drug-induced lupus due to anti-tumor necrosis factor alpha agents. Semin Arthritis Rheum. 2008;37(6):381-387. [PMID: 17977585]

Item 36   Answer: D

Educational Objective: Diagnose tuberculous arthritis of the spine.

A vertebral biopsy is appropriate for this patient to evaluate for tuberculous arthritis of the spine. He is immunosuppressed, comes from an area in which tuberculosis is endemic, and has fever, night sweats, and radiographic findings indicating vertebral destruction. In this setting, spinal tuberculosis is the most likely diagnosis; the presence of a normal chest radiograph, as in this case, does not eliminate the possibility of tuberculous skeletal involvement. However, other diagnoses are possible, including other forms of infection, tumors, and occasionally, tophaceous gout. A vertebral biopsy (whether a percutaneous needle biopsy under CT visualization or, in some cases, an open surgical biopsy) can help to establish the diagnosis and eliminate other possibilities to initiate treatment in a timely manner.

CT myelography can further delineate the area of the vertebral damage but would not advance the search for a diagnosis, particularly in the setting of a condition sufficiently advanced to be recognized on plain radiographs, as seen in this case. MRI or CT myelography is

CONT.

valuable in demonstrating compression of the spinal cord and may be considered in the future, particularly if the patient develops neurologic signs, but neither will establish the diagnosis.

Technetium-99m bone scan identifies areas of inflammation but does not provide a microbiologic diagnosis and is less accurate than either CT myelography or MRI in documenting spinal cord compression.

Tuberculin skin testing can be performed as a routine matter, but its interpretation would be difficult in this case—the results may be positive owing to prior exposure rather than active disease; conversely, the patient may be anergic owing to HIV infection.

KEY POINT
- A vertebral biopsy is indicated to diagnose tuberculous spinal osteomyelitis.

Bibliography
Jain AK. Tuberculosis of the spine: a fresh look at an old disease. Bone Joint Surg Br. 2010;92(7):905-913. [PMID: 20595106]

Item 37   Answer: C
Educational Objective: Diagnose knee osteoarthritis.

This patient has advanced knee osteoarthritis. As demonstrated in the radiograph, the medial tibiofemoral compartment is most commonly affected. Symptoms of tibiofemoral disease are exacerbated by weight bearing, whereas patellofemoral osteoarthritis typically causes pain with flexion/extension activities (such as climbing stairs or getting up from a chair). Radiographic findings of osteoarthritis include subchondral sclerosis (bone that appears more dense on radiograph); joint-space narrowing; cystic changes; and the presence of osteophytes, which is the most specific finding associated with osteoarthritis. This patient's radiographic findings include medial compartment joint-space narrowing, sclerosis on both sides of the tibiofemoral joint, small medial osteophytes, and a reactive bone cyst (geode) in the medial tibial plateau.

The hallmark of calcium pyrophosphate (CPP) deposition disease is the presence of chondrocalcinosis. Chondrocalcinosis represents the deposition of CPP crystals in fibrocartilage and articular cartilage. Commonly affected fibrocartilage include the menisci of the knee (usually bilaterally), the symphysis pubis, the triangular disks of the distal radioulnar joint, and the glenoid and acetabular labra. The crystal deposition is recognized as calcific findings in the joint space on radiographs of the knee.

Patients with gout or tophaceous gout may have periarticular masses with internal calcification and adjacent bony erosions with overhanging margins (classic for gouty erosions). Joint-space narrowing is not a primary feature of gouty arthritis; furthermore, the chronic nature of this patient's symptoms without a history of inflammatory attacks makes the diagnosis of gouty arthritis unlikely.

Inflammatory arthritides such as rheumatoid arthritis result in periarticular osteopenia or marginal erosions and generally result in symmetric joint-space narrowing. Soft-tissue swelling and synovial cysts may be detectable. Subchondral sclerosis and osteophytes are typically absent.

KEY POINT
- Radiographic findings of osteoarthritis include subchondral sclerosis, asymmetric joint-space narrowing, and the presence of osteophytes.

Bibliography
Hunter DJ. In the clinic. Osteoarthritis. Ann Intern Med. 2007;147(3):ITC8-1-ITC8-16. [PMID: 17679702]

Item 38   Answer: A
Educational Objective: Diagnose disseminated gonococcal infection.

This patient has disseminated gonococcal infection with associated gonococcal arthritis. This form of infectious arthritis is most commonly found among young, sexually active adults, particularly women. Disseminated gonococcemia is characterized by a prodrome of tenosynovitis, migratory or additive polyarthralgia, and cutaneous lesions that progress from papules or macules to pustules. Fever and rigors are common. As in this patient, subsequent frank arthritis can develop, affecting large and medium-sized joints and accompanied by tendinitis and papulopustular skin lesions. The leukocyte count is typically less than that of other types of bacterial arthritis, and Gram stain and culture results are commonly negative.

Gout also may be highly inflammatory and polyarticular; however, it rarely occurs in premenopausal women, who typically have lower serum urate levels. Furthermore, the first attack of gout is rarely polyarticular, does not typically affect the wrist, usually involves the first metatarsophalangeal joint, and is not associated with papulopustular skin lesions.

Rheumatoid arthritis also is a systemic polyarticular disease. However, onset is typically more gradual; it characteristically involves the proximal small joints of the hands; tendinitis is not present; and papular or pustular skin lesions do not occur. Fever is not a common feature of rheumatoid arthritis.

Staphylococcal arthritis is the most common form of infectious arthritis and can damage joints rapidly. It is more common in children, older patients, and those with previously damaged joints, unlike this 24-year-old patient with no history of, or risk factors for, staphylococcal infection. Staphylococcal arthritis is usually monoarticular, does not produce tenosynovitis, and is not accompanied by systemic skin findings such as the classic papulopustular skin lesions of disseminated gonococcal infection.

KEY POINT

- Gonococcal arthritis presents in the context of a systemic gonococcal infection that typically begins as migratory or polyarticular disease and can affect large and medium-sized joints accompanied by tendinitis and papulopustular skin lesions.

Bibliography

Garcia-De La Torre I, Nava Zavala A. Gonococcal and nongonococcal arthritis. Rheum Dis Clin North Am. 2009;35(1):63-73. [PMID: 19480997]

Item 39   Answer: C

Educational Objective: Evaluate a patient with lung infiltrates due to suspected vasculitis.

This patient has nodular lung infiltrates with hemoptysis, which are highly suggestive of pulmonary vasculitis, and an open lung biopsy, by either minimally invasive video-assisted thoracoscopic surgery or open thoracotomy, is most likely to establish the diagnosis. This patient also has p-ANCA positivity, along with the presence of antimyeloperoxidase (anti-MPO) antibodies, which is suggestive of microscopic polyangiitis. This disorder is characterized by rapidly progressive glomerulonephritis or pulmonary hemorrhage, fever, arthralgia, purpuric skin rash, and mononeuritis multiplex. However, the presence of positive antinuclear antibodies (which, in this patient, may be due to antecedent autoimmune thyroid disease) may result in a false-positive result for ANCA. Furthermore, patients with thyroid disease may also have antithyroperoxidase antibodies that may result in false-positive results for anti-MPO antibodies. The lack of specificity of ANCA testing in these and other circumstances warrants an open lung biopsy in this patient to evaluate for microscopic polyangiitis.

Although demonstration of pauci-immune glomerulonephritis may confirm the presence of ANCA-associated vasculitis, a kidney biopsy is not indicated in the absence of proteinuria or hematuria.

Nasal and sinus mucosa biopsies, although relatively noninvasive, infrequently yield sufficient tissue to evaluate for the presence of ANCA-associated vasculitis.

Because ANCA-associated vasculitis typically involves small arterioles, pulmonary angiography would not provide sufficient diagnostic information.

Transbronchial lung biopsy also typically provides insufficient tissue to establish a diagnosis of pulmonary vasculitis.

KEY POINT

- Histologic confirmation of ANCA-associated vasculitis with open lung biopsy or kidney biopsy is recommended before initiating treatment.

Bibliography

Ramsey J, Amari M, Kantrow SP. Pulmonary vasculitis: clinical presentation, differential diagnosis, and management. Curr Rheumatol Rep. 2010;12(6):420-428. [PMID: 20882372]

Item 40   Answer: B

Educational Objective: Treat a patient with dermatomyositis.

Initial treatment with prednisone is indicated for this patient with dermatomyositis without evidence of severe myositis or extramuscular manifestations. She has Gottron papules, which are pathognomonic for this disorder. This patient also has fatigue, arthralgia, Raynaud phenomenon, nailfold capillary abnormalities with cuticular hypertrophy, proximal muscle weakness, and a photosensitive rash, findings that are consistent with dermatomyositis. She does not have evidence of other extramuscular manifestations such as systemic symptoms of fever and weight loss or pulmonary, cardiac, or gastrointestinal symptoms. High-dose corticosteroids are standard first-line treatment for uncomplicated dermatomyositis and are indicated for this patient. This initial therapy is generally continued for 4 weeks or until serum creatine kinase levels are normalized; treatment is then slowly tapered. For severe cases, intravenous pulse corticosteroids may be administered. Baseline bone mineral density testing is indicated in patients who undergo long-term high-dose corticosteroid therapy. These patients also should begin prophylactic therapy for osteoporosis with calcium and vitamin D supplementation and bisphosphonates. Physical and occupational therapy are crucial adjuncts to pharmacologic therapy in patients with an inflammatory myopathy. Exercise improves aerobic capacity and strength and provides cardiopulmonary benefits. Exercise also is not typically associated with increases in muscle enzyme levels, which are indicative of muscle dysfunction.

Intravenous immune globulin is reserved for patients who require additional therapy in conjunction with corticosteroids or for those who have a contraindication to the use of corticosteroids or other immunosuppressive therapies.

Immunosuppressive therapy such as azathioprine or methotrexate in conjunction with corticosteroids is an important and frequently utilized treatment option for steroid-resistant disease or as steroid-sparing therapy and is often started concurrently with prednisone for severe disease or for those in poor prognosis groups, including patients with extramuscular manifestations of cardiovascular or pulmonary involvement.

KEY POINT

- High-dose corticosteroids are standard first-line treatment for patients with uncomplicated dermatomyositis.

Bibliography

Iorizzo LJ 3rd, Jorizzo JL. The treatment and prognosis of dermatomyositis: an updated review. J Am Acad Dermatol. 2008;59(1):99-112. [PMID: 18423790]

Item 41   Answer: D

Educational Objective: Diagnose ankylosing spondylitis.

This patient most likely has ankylosing spondylitis, and MRI of the sacroiliac joints is most likely to establish a diagnosis. Radiographic evidence of sacroiliitis is required for definitive diagnosis and is the most consistent finding associated with this condition. Onset of ankylosing spondylitis usually occurs in the teenage years or 20s and manifests as persistent pain and morning stiffness involving the low back that is alleviated with activity. This condition also may be associated with tenderness of the pelvis.

Typically, the earliest radiographic changes in affected patients involve the sacroiliac joints, but these changes may not be visible during the first few years from onset; therefore, this patient's normal radiographs of the sacroiliac joints do not exclude sacroiliitis. MRI findings of the sacroiliac joints can include bone marrow edema, synovitis, and erosions. Bone marrow edema is the earliest finding and can precede the development of erosions. MRI, especially with gadolinium enhancement, is considered a sensitive method for detecting early erosive inflammatory changes in the sacroiliac joints and spine and can assess sites of active disease and response to effective therapy.

Bone scan can demonstrate increased uptake of the sacroiliac joints in patients with ankylosing spondylitis but is less sensitive and specific than MRI.

CT is the most sensitive modality available to demonstrate bone changes such as erosions; however, it cannot detect early changes such as bone marrow edema that precede erosive change in patients with ankylosing spondylitis.

In the diagnosis of early ankylosing spondylitis, sacroiliac joint MRI is more sensitive than lumbar spine MRI. Although changes to the lumbar spine can be detected on MRI, they are usually preceded by changes in the sacroiliac joints. Therefore, if imaging of the lumbar spine is negative, subsequent imaging of the sacroiliac joints would still be necessary to exclude ankylosing spondylitis.

KEY POINT

- **MRI is considered the most sensitive method for detecting early erosive inflammatory changes in the sacroiliac joints when radiographs are normal.**

Bibliography

Chary-Valckenaere I, d'Agostino MA, Loeuille D. Role for imaging studies in ankylosing spondylitis. Joint Bone Spine. 2011;78(2):138-143. [PMID: 20851029]

Item 42   Answer: B

Educational Objective: Treat a patient with scleroderma renal crisis.

Treatment with an ACE inhibitor such as lisinopril is indicated for this patient with scleroderma renal crisis (SRC) in the setting of diffuse cutaneous systemic sclerosis (dcSSc). SRC most commonly occurs in patients with dcSSc as a consequence of intimal proliferation and luminal thrombosis in the afferent renal arterioles, resulting in thrombotic microangiopathy with glomerular ischemia and high levels of renin. SRC is characterized by acute onset of hypertension, acute kidney injury, and microangiopathic hemolytic anemia; however, some patients with evolving SRC may be normotensive. Even in patients on dialysis, treatment with an ACE inhibitor is associated with improved outcomes in terms of kidney function and mortality compared with patients not receiving such therapy. For patients with this complication, prompt and aggressive treatment with an ACE inhibitor is essential to restore kidney function and optimally manage hypertension, even for patients who require dialysis and for whom blood pressure has been lowered with other antihypertensive agents.

Bosentan is an endothelin receptor antagonist used to treat pulmonary hypertension or recurring digital ulcers in patients with systemic sclerosis and is not effective therapy for SRC.

Microangiopathic changes with thrombocytopenia can occur in patients with SRC; although plasma exchange has a therapeutic role in other microangiopathies associated with acute kidney injury such as hemolytic uremic syndrome and thrombotic thrombocytopenic purpura, it does not have an established role in the management of SRC.

Sildenafil, a phosphodiesterase inhibitor, is appropriate for patients with pulmonary hypertension or refractory Raynaud phenomenon symptoms but is not effective in the primary management of SRC.

KEY POINT

- **Prompt and aggressive treatment with an ACE inhibitor is essential to restore kidney function and manage hypertension associated with scleroderma renal crisis.**

Bibliography

Denton CP. Renal manifestations of systemic sclerosis—clinical features and outcome assessment. Rheumatology (Oxford). 2008;47(Suppl 5):v54-v56. [PMID: 18784147]

Item 43   Answer: B

Educational Objective: Evaluate rheumatoid arthritis.

Bilateral radiographs of the hands and wrists are indicated for this patient who was diagnosed with rheumatoid arthritis 1 year ago. At that time, radiographs revealed evidence of early erosions of the metacarpophalangeal joints. Control of his disease activity was subsequently achieved, but the erosions may have progressed during the period of ongoing disease activity or even more recently when he has seemed clinically quiescent. Repeat radiographs of the hands and wrists allow for reevaluation of the early erosive changes and establishment of a new baseline. Evidence of progressive erosive changes in the future would suggest the need to change this patient's medical regimen, despite what appears to be clinical control of disease activity otherwise.

The presence of antibodies to anti–cyclic citrullinated peptide (anti-CCP) can be important in the diagnosis and prognosis of rheumatoid arthritis, but CCP titers are not helpful in monitoring disease activity.

There is no recommendation for testing for tuberculosis or hepatitis C virus titers at shorter intervals than 1 year unless there is a particular concern for an exposure or clinical manifestations concerning for an active infection.

The presence of varicella virus antibodies correlates with prior exposure to varicella and protection against varicella infection, although the sensitivity and specificity of available serologic tests is imperfect. Health care workers without serologic evidence of IgG antibodies to varicella virus may benefit from vaccination against varicella, but routine screening for US-born adults is not advised given the high prevalence of seropositivity in this population. The zoster vaccine is indicated for prevention of shingles in many older persons. Varicella vaccine and zoster vaccine are both live, attenuated strains of the varicella-zoster virus. Live vaccines are contraindicated in immunosuppressed patients, including those using tumor necrosis factor α inhibitors, given the risk of disseminated infection due to the vaccine.

> **KEY POINT**
>
> - Repeat radiographs allow for reevaluation of early erosive changes and establishment of a new baseline for patients with rheumatoid arthritis.

Bibliography

Østergaard M, Pedersen SJ, Døhn UM. Imaging in rheumatoid arthritis–status and recent advances for magnetic resonance imaging, ultrasonography, computed tomography and conventional radiography. Best Pract Res Clin Rheumatol. 2008;22(6):1019-1044. [PMID: 19041075]

Item 44   Answer: A

Educational Objective: Diagnose granulomatosis with polyangiitis.

This patient most likely has granulomatosis with polyangiitis (also known as Wegener granulomatosis), a systemic necrotizing vasculitis that predominantly affects the upper and lower respiratory tract and kidneys. More than 70% of patients have upper airway manifestations such as sinusitis; orbital, nasal, inner ear, and laryngotracheal inflammation also can occur. Pulmonary manifestations include cough, hemoptysis, and pleurisy. Characteristic radiographic findings include multifocal infiltrates or nodules, some of which may cavitate. Pauci-immune glomerulonephritis occurs in up to 80% of patients. Although glomerulonephritis may be the presenting manifestation, it is most often preceded by respiratory tract manifestations.

Initial clinical features also may include inflammation of the major salivary glands. When such lesions are present in the setting of lower respiratory tract lesions and kidney abnormalities consistent with glomerulonephritis, as seen in this patient, the most likely diagnosis is granulomatosis with polyangiitis. This disorder is highly destructive if untreated, potentially resulting in cartilage erosion with nasal septal perforation and saddle nose deformity.

Sarcoidosis may cause inflammatory lesions of the orbits and trachea as well as nodular lung infiltrates (necrotizing sarcoid granulomatosis) and an interstitial nephritis but is not associated with significant glomerular disease.

Patients with Sjögren syndrome may have salivary gland enlargement and lung infiltrates; however, significant tracheal inflammation and nodular or cavitary lung lesions are rare. Sjögren syndrome may cause an interstitial nephritis but is not associated with significant glomerular disease.

Tuberculosis may involve the cervical lymph nodes (scrofula), but this rarely occurs in adults. Tuberculosis may also rarely involve submandibular glands or ocular structures but does not account for the glomerulopathy in this patient.

> **KEY POINT**
>
> - Granulomatosis with polyangiitis (also known as Wegener granulomatosis) is a systemic necrotizing vasculitis that predominantly affects the upper and lower respiratory tract and kidneys.

Bibliography

Holle JU, Laudien M, Gross WL. Clinical manifestations and treatment of Wegener's granulomatosis. Rheum Dis Clin North Am. 2010;36(3):507-526. [PMID: 20688247]

Item 45   Answer: B

Educational Objective: Evaluate relapsing polychondritis.

Pulmonary function testing with flow volume loops is indicated for this patient with suspected relapsing polychondritis and pulmonary findings. This autoimmune inflammatory disorder affects the cartilage of the ears and nose, and up to 50% of patients also have a rheumatoid arthritis–like polyarthritis. Relapsing polychondritis also can affect the cartilaginous tracheal rings of the larynx, trachea, and bronchi, which can lead to obstructive findings on flow volume loop diagrams. There are no serologic tests for relapsing polychondritis; diagnosis can be made by biopsy of the affected cartilage but is not necessary if sufficient clinical criteria are present, as seen in this patient with chondritis of the ears and nose, along with a polyarthritis. Because respiratory tract involvement is prevalent, pulmonary function testing with flow volume loops is indicated for patients diagnosed with or suspected of having relapsing polychondritis. This testing can detect the presence of large upper airway involvement, which might require more aggressive treatment.

Saddle nose deformity also can occur in patients with granulomatosis with polyangiitis (also known as Wegener granulomatosis) and is caused by destructive sinusitis with erosion into the cartilage, which can be detected by performing a CT of the sinuses. This patient's previous ear inflammation, negative ANCA, and absence of sinus disease argue against granulomatosis with polyangiitis as the cause of saddle nose deformity, and CT is not warranted.

Rheumatoid factor is present in many patients with rheumatoid arthritis, a disorder that is not associated with destructive facial lesions.

Patients with nasal deformity suspected to be caused by cocaine-induced midline destructive disease or vasculitis would require a urine toxicology screen. These patients often have a positive ("atypical") pANCA due to antibodies to elastase (rather than myeloperoxidase). Based on this patient's findings, including ear damage, arthritis, and negative ANCA, a urine toxicology screen is not warranted.

KEY POINT

- Pulmonary function testing with flow volume loops is indicated for patients diagnosed with or suspected of having relapsing polychondritis to evaluate for large upper airway involvement.

Bibliography

Rafeq S, Trentham D, Ernst A. Pulmonary manifestations of relapsing polychondritis. Clin Chest Med. 2010;31(3):513-518. [PMID: 20692543]

Item 46   Answer: E

Educational Objective: Diagnose early-stage Takayasu arteritis.

This patient has Takayasu arteritis, a disorder that affects the aorta and its major branches as well as the pulmonary arteries and most commonly occurs in young women. The initial inflammatory phase of Takayasu arteritis is characterized by low-grade fever, fatigue, malaise, and weight loss, along with varying degrees of myalgia and arthralgia that may persist for months; laboratory studies typically reveal elevations in erythrocyte sedimentation rate (ESR) and C-reactive protein (CRP) level, along with mild anemia and thrombocytosis. During this phase, imaging of the entire aorta and major branch vessels with MR angiography may detect fusiform narrowing of involved vessels with delayed enhancement in the vessel wall to help establish the diagnosis. As the disease progresses, bruits over affected arteries may become apparent, followed by pulse deficits and manifestations of organ or limb ischemia. A diagnosis of Takayasu arteritis should therefore be considered in the differential diagnosis of this young woman presenting with many of these clinical and laboratory features.

Patients with adult-onset Still disease may have similar laboratory findings; however, this disorder is associated with high spiking fever and additional clinical features, including arthritis, serositis, and skin rash, which are not present in this patient.

Microscopic polyangiitis usually presents with mononeuropathy, signs of glomerulonephritis, and/or pulmonary hemorrhage, and is associated with ANCA having specificity for myeloperoxidase.

Polyarteritis nodosa may present with constitutional symptoms, fever, and myalgia but is usually associated with hypertension, mononeuropathy symptoms, and/or abdominal pain. Further, bruits over large arteries are not a feature of polyarteritis nodosa.

Myalgia and weight loss may be presenting features of polymyositis; however, this diagnosis is unlikely in this patient because of the absence of elevated serum creatine kinase levels and demonstrable weakness.

KEY POINT

- The initial inflammatory phase of Takayasu arteritis is characterized by low-grade fever, fatigue, malaise, myalgia, and weight loss; anemia, thrombocytosis, and elevated erythrocyte sedimentation rate and C-reactive protein level are characteristic laboratory features.

Bibliography

Andrews J, Mason JC. Takayasu's arteritis–recent advances in imaging offer promise. Rheumatology (Oxford). 2007;46(1):6-15. [PMID: 17043053]

Item 47   Answer: A

Educational Objective: Diagnose erosive hand osteoarthritis.

This patient most likely has erosive hand osteoarthritis, which is associated with episodic attacks of inflammatory pain and erosions revealed on radiograph. One or two joints usually are inflamed during an attack, which can help distinguish this condition from the more common polyarticular onset associated with rheumatoid arthritis. Between attacks, the physical examination findings are typical for osteoarthritis, with bony enlargement of the proximal or distal interphalangeal joints (Bouchard or Heberden nodes, respectively). There may be other findings suggestive of hand osteoarthritis such as squaring of the carpometacarpal joint. Radiographs reveal numerous osteophytes in association with more central erosions or cystic changes rather than the marginal erosions of rheumatoid arthritis. Patients with erosive osteoarthritis also may have mildly elevated inflammatory markers, as seen in this case.

Psoriatic arthritis often involves distal interphalangeal joints. The absence of psoriasis rash does not rule out this condition. However, this patient's distribution is suggestive of hand osteoarthritis. Furthermore, the inflammation associated with psoriatic arthritis involves the tenosynovial junction, causing swelling beyond the affected joint (sausage digits). The erosions of psoriatic arthritis can be quite aggressive and show much more destruction than that seen in hand osteoarthritis.

Late-onset rheumatoid arthritis can develop in addition to hand osteoarthritis, making the rheumatoid onset difficult to diagnose. The examiner needs to be vigilant for signs suggestive of rheumatoid arthritis, including a change in the pattern of arthritis with new metatarsophalangeal involvement and morning stiffness.

Tophaceous gout can cause erosive arthritis of the hands; however, this patient does not have tophaceous deposits, which would be seen on physical examination and would appear as a radiographic finding.

KEY POINT
- Erosive hand osteoarthritis is characterized by flares of joint inflammation involving the proximal and distal interphalangeal joints that are associated with erythema, swelling, and severe pain.

Bibliography
Punzi L, Frigato M, Frallonardo P, Ramonda R. Inflammatory osteoarthritis of the hand. Best Pract Res Clin Rheumatol. 2010;24(3):301-312. [PMID: 20534365]

Item 48   Answer: C
Educational Objective: Diagnose type I cryoglobulinemic vasculitis.

This patient most likely has type I cryoglobulinemic vasculitis. Type I cryoglobulins are monoclonal immunoglobulins seen as a complication of monoclonal paraproteins, which are not uncommonly seen in patients with Sjögren syndrome. Cryoglobulinemic vasculitis is characterized by cutaneous palpable purpura, mononeuritis multiplex, and an immune complex glomerulonephritis; serum C3 and C4 levels are usually low.

Microscopic polyangiitis is associated with the presence of p-ANCA. However, the nephritis associated with this disorder is not characterized by significant immune deposits. Moreover, the finding of a positive p-ANCA is not interpretable in the presence of antinuclear antibodies, as the latter may yield positive results in assays for p-ANCA.

An immune complex glomerulonephritis with hypocomplementemia is characteristically seen in patients with lupus-associated glomerulonephritis. The kidney histologic features may be identical to those seen in cryoglobulinemic glomerulonephritis; however, this patient has no other clinical features of systemic lupus erythematosus.

Type II cryoglobulins (mixed/monoclonal) most commonly occur in the context of active infection with hepatitis C virus. This patient has positive hepatitis C virus antibodies but does not have active infection (negative hepatitis C virus RNA).

KEY POINT
- Type I cryoglobulinemic vasculitis may occur as a complication of paraproteins associated with Sjögren syndrome.

Bibliography
Mukhtyar C, Guillevin L, Cid MC, et al.; European Vasculitis Study Group. EULAR recommendations for the management of primary small and medium vessel vasculitis. Ann Rheum Dis. 2009;68(3):310-317. [PMID: 18413444]

Item 49   Answer: B
Educational Objective: Evaluate a patient with interstitial lung disease associated with the inflammatory myopathies.

High-resolution CT of the chest and pulmonary function tests are the appropriate next steps for this patient with polymyositis who is at high risk for interstitial lung disease (ILD). ILD is one of the leading causes of death in patients with polymyositis and dermatomyositis. ILD may be prominent at the onset of myopathy or develop over the course of the disease. This patient's normal chest radiograph does not rule out ILD; 10% of patients with biopsy-proven ILD have normal chest radiographs. This patient has anti–Jo-1 antibody positivity, which is associated with an increased risk for ILD. In patients with pulmonary symptoms or abnormal pulmonary function tests, high-resolution CT (HRCT) of the chest is useful to identify the presence, extent, and severity of disease and may help discriminate between fibrotic disease and active inflammation. Pulmonary function tests typically show a restrictive ventilatory defect with decreased D_{LCO}.

Echocardiography to evaluate for pulmonary arterial hypertension (PAH) is indicated if the HRCT results are negative and pulmonary function test results show an isolated decrease in D_{LCO}, or if results show severe ILD (which may lead to secondary PAH), which is very unlikely in this minimally symptomatic patient with a normal chest radiograph.

Although this patient may ultimately require increased immunosuppressive therapy for ILD, it is appropriate to document the presence and severity of ILD before beginning more aggressive therapy.

Right heart catheterization would be indicated only if there was a high level of suspicion for PAH—for example, if the patient had a negative HRCT scan, isolated decrease in D_{LCO}, and an echocardiogram showing elevated pulmonary artery pressures.

KEY POINT
- Anti–Jo-1 antibodies are highly specific for the inflammatory myopathies and are associated with an increased risk for interstitial lung disease.

Bibliography
Labirua A, Lundberg IE. Interstitial lung disease and idiopathic inflammatory myopathies: progress and pitfalls. Curr Opin Rheumatol. 2010;22(6):633-638. [PMID: 20827201]

Item 50   Answer: A

Educational Objective: Diagnose *Mycobacterium marinum* infection.

This patient has *Mycobacterium marinum* infection. *M. marinum* is a free-living (survives and replicates in the environment without requiring a host) freshwater or saltwater mycobacterial species, and infection is acquired by local inoculation through swimming, handling fish, boating, or other marine activities. The initial manifestation typically is a granulomatous skin lesion; if untreated, the organism can subsequently be transmitted via lymphatics to infect joints locally. *M. marinum* infection is usually localized to the area of the puncture, mainly in the skin, tendons, and adjacent joint (such as in a small joint of the hands). Nodular papules may form and then ulcerate. Diagnosis involves culturing of the joint fluid for mycobacterial infection.

Naegleria fowleri is a free-living freshwater amoeba that typically grows in warm freshwater pools such as lakes or inadequately chlorinated swimming pools and is contracted via nasal exposure, typically during swimming. *N. fowleri* does not cause joint infection, as seen in this patient, but a nearly universally fatal meningoencephalitis.

Neisseria gonorrhoeae is typically transmitted through sexual activity and most commonly occurs in young women; however, the local presentation of this patient's infection after a skin break and marine exposure, the nodular rather than pustular nature of her skin lesion, and local nature of her arthritis (proximal to the skin break and in a small joint) argue against *N. gonorrhoeae* as the likely agent.

Sporothrix schenckii is a soil fungus that can enter the skin through local breaks. Similar to *M. marinum*, it can cause a granulomatous, papular skin infection that may spread lymphatically or hematogenously and occasionally infect a joint. This patient has no specific soil exposure, making such an infection unlikely.

KEY POINT

- *Mycobacterium marinum* infection is acquired by local inoculation through swimming, handling fish, boating, or other marine activities.

Bibliography

Cheung JP, Fung B, Wong SS, Ip WY. Review article: Mycobacterium marinum infection of the hand and wrist. J Orthop Surg (Hong Kong). 2010;18(1):98-103. [PMID: 20427845]

Item 51   Answer: D

Educational Objective: Manage spinal fracture risk in a patient with ankylosing spondylitis.

A repeat radiograph of the spine is indicated for this patient with ankylosing spondylitis. Vertebral fractures often occur in patients who have ankylosing spondylitis with minor or without significant trauma. Ossification of the intervertebral disks, ligaments, and joints of the spine leads to rigidity, which can impair functionality and the ability to dissipate

energy from an applied force. Low bone mineral density is associated with this disorder, although densitometry measurements can be challenging in the setting of the skeletal changes associated with ankylosing spondylitis. Spinal fracture risk appears to be increased beyond peripheral fracture risk, and outcomes from spinal fractures are worse in patients with ankylosing spondylitis than in other populations. This patient has mid back pain. Although the pain may relate to muscular strain due to recent lifting or could be a manifestation of ongoing or recurrent inflammation, this patient must be evaluated for spinal fracture using radiography. Mistakenly attributing back pain to other causes can lead to delays in diagnosis and treatment.

Prednisone is used to treat acute inflammation in rheumatoid arthritis and other conditions but is not typically beneficial in ankylosing spondylitis. Furthermore, corticosteroids can contribute to bone loss and fracture risk.

In patients who have ankylosing spondylitis with persistent or recurrent symptoms related to arthritis, switching from one tumor necrosis factor α inhibitor to another agent in the same class can be appropriate. In this case, however, it is important to evaluate the patient for possible spine fracture before changing immune modulators.

Epidural corticosteroid injections can be helpful in the management of radicular back pain, although the effect may be modest and limited to short-term reduction in pain. These injections have not been found to provide clear benefit in spinal stenosis or nonspecific low back pain.

KEY POINT

- Vertebral fractures often occur in patients who have ankylosing spondylitis with minor or without significant trauma.

Bibliography

Vosse D, Feldkeller E, Erlendsson J, et al. Clinical vertebral fractures in patients with ankylosing spondylitis. J Rheumatol. 2004;31(10):1981-1985. [PMID: 15468363]

Item 52   Answer: E

Educational Objective: Treat a patient with asymptomatic hyperuricemia.

No treatment is required for this patient with asymptomatic hyperuricemia. This condition is characterized by a moderately elevated serum urate level without evidence of gout symptoms. Patients with asymptomatic hyperuricemia have an increased risk for gout over the long term but a low likelihood of a gout attack in the short term; thus, a pharmacologic intervention at this time is not indicated. Although studies suggest that hyperuricemia may contribute to several undesirable comorbidities (hypertension, kidney disease, cardiovascular disease), there is not yet consensus that these risks are sufficient to independently warrant chronic urate-lowering therapy. In patients with asymptomatic hyperuricemia, dietary and lifestyle considerations are always worth reviewing. Decreasing consumption of high-purine

Answers and Critiques

foods (particularly meat and seafood), alcohol, and high-fructose foods may lower serum urate concentrations. An increase in dairy consumption as well as weight loss may also help lower serum urate concentrations. In making recommendations for lifestyle changes, the ability of the patient to comply should always be taken into account.

Allopurinol is an effective urate-lowering agent used to treat symptomatic hyperuricemia. Colchicine is an anti-inflammatory agent that can treat or prevent gout attacks. Probenecid is a uricosuric drug also used to treat symptomatic hyperuricemia. All of these agents may be useful in patients with gout; however, based on this patient's findings, none of these treatment options is warranted at this time.

The diuretic hydrochlorothiazide is used to treat hypertension and promotes increases in serum urate concentration by inhibiting kidney urate excretion; this patient does not have hypertension, and such a strategy would increase the patient's risk of future gout attacks for no specific benefit. In patients who are on thiazide diuretics and require urate lowering, switching to an alternative antihypertensive agent that does not raise serum urate concentration is a reasonable intervention.

> **KEY POINT**
> • Treatment is not indicated for patients with asymptomatic hyperuricemia.

Bibliography

Mandell B. Clinical manifestations of hyperuricemia and gout. Cleve Clin J Med. 2008;75(Supp 5):S5-S8. [PMID: 18822469]

Item 53   Answer: D

Educational Objective: Diagnose polymyositis.

This patient most likely has polymyositis, a disorder characterized by acute or subacute onset of proximal muscle weakness without rash or distal muscle involvement. Electromyography (EMG) cannot reliably distinguish polymyositis from other forms of inflammatory myopathy. Muscle biopsy is the gold standard for diagnosing the idiopathic inflammatory myopathies. On pathologic examination, there is a predominantly lymphocytic muscle infiltration with evidence of necrosis and regeneration. Characterization of the infiltration pattern and cell markers allows for the diagnosis of polymyositis, dermatomyositis, or inclusion body myositis.

Muscle biopsy results from a patient with polymyositis characteristically show CD8-positive T-cell infiltration of the endomysium, often with invasion of intact major histocompatibility complex–I–expressing muscle fibers. Importantly, the muscle biopsy is not performed on the same side as the EMG, because the EMG can disrupt muscle architecture, cause local inflammation, and affect the biopsy results.

Dermatomyositis is characterized by similar myopathic symptoms in the setting of typical rash (heliotrope rash, photosensitive rashes involving the shoulders, neck, and anterior chest) and Gottron papules (hyperkeratotic red papules and plaques over boney prominences); however, biopsy results differ and are notable for CD4-positive T cells in perivascular and perimysial areas.

Hypothyroid-related muscle symptoms are unlikely in this patient with a normal thyroid-stimulating hormone level; in addition, his muscle biopsy results are clearly consistent with an inflammatory process.

Inclusion body myositis usually affects older persons with an insidious course characterized by proximal and distal muscle weakness. Typical biopsy results are similar to that of polymyositis but also include rimmed vacuoles and reddish inclusions; in addition, deposits of amyloid are reported and the degree of inflammation is generally minimal.

> **KEY POINT**
> • Muscle biopsy is the gold standard for diagnosing the idiopathic inflammatory myopathies.

Bibliography

Chahin N, Engel A. Correlation of muscle biopsy, clinical course, and outcome in PM and sporadic IBM. Neurology. 2008;70(6):418-424. [PMID: 17881720]

Item 54   Answer: C

Educational Objective: Treat a patient with parvovirus B19 infection.

This patient has parvovirus B19 infection and requires treatment with ibuprofen. Parvovirus B19 infection is most common in children and manifests as erythema infectiosum, consisting of polyarthralgia, flu-like symptoms, and a characteristic facial rash ("slapped cheek"). Adults usually contract the virus from children. Because the slapped cheek appearance is atypical in adults, the diagnosis should be suspected in the setting of fever and a symmetric polyarthritis, particularly after exposure to a sick child. This patient presents with an acute onset of a polyarticular arthritis accompanied by a morbilliform rash. A positive anti-parvovirus IgM antibody test further supports a diagnosis of parvovirus B19 infection. (Anti-parvovirus IgG antibodies confirm a past infection but are not suitable for diagnosing current parvovirus infection.) Parvovirus B19 infection is usually self-limited and resolves after several weeks; therefore, treatment is directed at control of symptoms, and the use of an NSAID such as ibuprofen is a reasonable strategy to address fever and joint pain.

Azithromycin and penicillin are used to treat bacterial infections, including streptococcal infections that can cause rheumatic fever. Rheumatic fever is usually a disease of childhood but may present in adults as a migratory polyarthritis and fever. The knees, ankles, elbows, and wrists are most commonly affected. Cutaneous findings in patients with rheumatic fever manifest as erythema marginatum, an evanescent, pink macular rash that affects the trunk and sometimes the limbs but not the face. This rash tends to expand centrifugally with clearing in the center.

Rheumatic fever is unlikely in this patient because she did not have a preceding pharyngitis, anti–streptolysin O antibodies are negative, and IgM antibodies against parvovirus B19 are positive.

Hydroxychloroquine is useful in lupus and rheumatoid arthritis. Although this patient's symmetric arthritis and rash could potentially have been due to either of these conditions, the rapid onset of symptoms and the clinical context do not support either of these two diagnoses. Low titers of antinuclear antibodies or rheumatoid factor may also be seen during parvovirus B19 infection; however, when present in this setting, they do not indicate lupus or rheumatoid arthritis.

> **KEY POINT**
> - Parvovirus B19 infection can cause fever and symmetric polyarthritis.

Bibliography

Vassilopoulos D, Calabrese LH. Virally associated arthritis 2008: clinical, epidemiologic, and pathophysiologic considerations. Arthritis Res Ther. 2008;10(5):215-222. [PMID: 18828883]

Item 55   Answer: B
Educational Objective: Diagnose giant cell arteritis.

CT angiography of the neck and chest is indicated for this patient with suspected giant cell arteritis (GCA). Patients with GCA typically have fever and fatigue; therefore, GCA should be considered in the differential diagnosis of fever of unknown origin in patients over the age of 50 years. Polymyalgia rheumatica symptoms such as hip and shoulder girdle stiffness and pain may be the predominant feature. Although many patients with GCA have symptoms referable to the cranial arteries, including temporal or scalp tenderness and jaw claudication, such symptoms may be absent in patients with arteritis confined to the great vessels. Imaging of the great vessels, including the aortic arch, common carotid, innominate, and subclavian arteries, is appropriate for patients with unexplained fever and polymyalgia rheumatica or for patients with suspected GCA whose temporal artery biopsy results are negative. MR angiography is also a suitable diagnostic test.

In the absence of leukopenia or thrombocytopenia and a normal peripheral blood smear, a bone marrow biopsy is not likely to be informative in revealing the cause of fever and joint symptoms in this patient.

Kidney and mesenteric angiography are useful in establishing a diagnosis of polyarteritis nodosa; however, this patient does not have findings associated with this disorder such as hypertension, abdominal pain, kidney dysfunction, or mononeuritis multiplex.

MRI of the shoulder and hip joints is unlikely to yield useful diagnostic information in a patient with limited findings on physical examination.

> **KEY POINT**
> - CT angiography or MR angiography of the neck and chest is appropriate for patients with unexplained fever and polymyalgia rheumatica or for patients with suspected giant cell arteritis whose temporal artery biopsy results are negative.

Bibliography

Marie I, Proux A, Duhaut P, et al. Long-term follow-up of aortic involvement in giant cell arteritis: a series of 48 patients. Medicine (Baltimore). 2009;88(3):182-192. [PMID: 19440121]

Item 56   Answer: A
Educational Objective: Manage the side effects of chronic corticosteroid use.

Alendronate is indicated for this patient with giant cell arteritis (GCA) who is being treated with high-dose prednisone. Corticosteroids enhance bone resorption and decrease bone formation directly through their action on osteoblasts and osteoclasts and indirectly by inhibiting calcium absorption. Although the degree of corticosteroid-induced bone loss is related to the total cumulative dosage, bone loss is highest (up to 30% in some studies) in the initial months of treatment. According to the recommendations of the American College of Rheumatology, prevention of corticosteroid-induced osteoporosis in postmenopausal women ≥50 years of age, who otherwise have low risk for fracture, is warranted and should include the addition of calcium, vitamin D, and a bisphosphonate such as alendronate if corticosteroid treatment is expected to continue for at least 3 months at a dose of ≥7.5 mg/d.

Calcitonin is not a first-line drug for postmenopausal osteoporosis treatment; its fracture efficacy is low, and its effects on bone mineral density are less than those of other agents.

The United States Preventive Services Task Force advises against using estrogen or estrogen plus progestin for the prevention of chronic diseases, including osteoporosis after menopause, because of a trend toward an increased risk of breast cancer, coronary heart disease, stroke, venous thromboembolism, and urinary incontinence.

A thiazide diuretic and sodium restriction effectively decrease calcium loss in the urine, but there are no data regarding bone density or fracture rate for this treatment.

Calcitriol is a more active vitamin D metabolite than vitamin D and is effective in increasing the bone mineral density of the spine, but its effect on fracture rate is unknown. In addition, calcitriol is associated with hypercalcemia and hypercalciuria and is not as effective as a bisphosphonate in preventing corticosteroid-induced fractures. It is not considered a first-line agent for prophylaxis when administering corticosteroids.

KEY POINT

- Prevention of corticosteroid-induced osteoporosis in postmenopausal women requiring long-term corticosteroid use includes the addition of calcium, vitamin D, and a bisphosphonate.

Bibliography

Grossman JM, Gordon R, Raganath VK, et al. American College of Rheumatology 2010 recommendations for the prevention and treatment of glucocorticoid-induced osteoporosis. Arthritis Care Res (Hoboken). 2010;62(11):1515-1526. [PMID: 20662044]

Item 57   Answer: B

Educational Objective: Diagnose diffuse idiopathic skeletal hyperostosis.

This patient most likely has diffuse idiopathic skeletal hyperostosis (DISH). He has neck and low back pain and limited mobility throughout the spine. This patient is male, obese, and has diabetes mellitus, all of which are risk factors for DISH. This disorder is characterized by calcification of the enthesis regions (where the tendons or ligaments insert into bone) and the spinal ligaments. The diagnosis is confirmed on radiograph by the presence of flowing osteophytes along the anterolateral aspect of at least four contiguous vertebral bodies (most easily detected in the thoracic spine), preserved vertebral height, and absent findings typical for ankylosing spondylitis. Although radiographic involvement of the thoracic spine is characteristic of DISH, this area is often asymptomatic.

Although symptoms of ankylosing spondylitis can be similar to that of DISH, patients with ankylosing spondylitis are typically younger. Furthermore, ankylosing spondylitis demonstrates vertical bridging syndesmophytes, whereas DISH demonstrates flowing linear calcification and ossification along the anterolateral aspects of the vertebral bodies that continue across the disk space. Importantly, sacroiliitis, which occurs in ankylosing spondylitis, is absent in DISH.

Lumbar spinal stenosis leads to chronic low back pain and "pseudoclaudication," with pain and radiating symptoms down one or both legs that occur with walking and are relieved by rest. The pain is also characteristically relieved by leaning forward as when climbing stairs, walking uphill, or leaning onto a shopping cart or walker. Spinal stenosis can be demonstrated radiographically by MRI, showing narrowing of the spinal canal by disks and/or osteophytes.

Spondylolisthesis involves the subluxation of one vertebra over another vertebra. The vertebrae should be in linear alignment. Because of lax ligaments (associated with degenerative disk disease) or damaged ligaments, there can be too much anterior–posterior movement between the vertebrae. Spondylolisthesis can result in nerve root impingement with symptoms of sciatica or chronic low back pain. Diagnosis can be made on plain radiographs of the spine. Findings can be more obvious on flexion–extension lateral views of the spine. This patient's radiographs do not reveal spondylolisthesis.

KEY POINT

- Diffuse idiopathic skeletal hyperostosis is confirmed on radiograph by the presence of flowing osteophytes along the anterolateral aspect of at least four contiguous vertebral bodies.

Bibliography

Olivieri I, D'Angelo S, Palazzi C, Padula A, Mader R, Khan MA. Diffuse idiopathic skeletal hyperostosis: differentiation from ankylosing spondylitis. Curr Rheumatol Rep. 2009;11(5):321-328. [PMID: 19772826]

Item 58   Answer: A

Educational Objective: Manage immunizations in a patient receiving biologic therapy.

Administration of intramuscular influenza vaccine before initiation of rituximab is indicated for this patient with rheumatoid arthritis. There are two influenza vaccine types, a trivalent inactivated virus appropriate for all age groups given intramuscularly, and an intranasal live attenuated influenza vaccine appropriate for persons aged 2 to 49 years. The live attenuated vaccine should be avoided in pregnant women as well as patients with chronic metabolic diseases, diabetes mellitus, kidney dysfunction, hemoglobinopathies, immunosuppression, and chronic diseases that can compromise respiratory function or the handling of respiratory secretions. There is no evidence that tumor necrosis factor α inhibitor therapy alters primary immune response to vaccination; however, treatment with rituximab or abatacept may attenuate primary immune responses due to associated blockade of T-cell costimulation by antigen-presenting dendritic cells (abatacept) or B cells (rituximab and abatacept). As such, whenever possible, updating of immunization schedules is best undertaken before initiation of treatment with rituximab or abatacept. Other than previous allergy to eggs or vaccine adjuvants, there is no contraindication to administering killed virus influenza vaccine to patients with rheumatoid arthritis or other autoimmune disorders.

Live attenuated virus vaccines as constituted in intranasal vaccine preparations are contraindicated in patients on immunosuppressive or biologic immunomodulating therapies because of the risk of disseminated viral infection.

Antiviral chemoprophylaxis with agents such as oseltamivir or zanamivir provides immediate protection and may be useful in persons who have not been vaccinated or who are not expected to respond to a vaccine or until vaccine-induced immunity becomes effective; however, antiviral chemoprophylaxis is expensive and can be associated with side effects. Persons who are candidates include residents in an assisted-living facility during an influenza outbreak, those who are at higher risk for influenza-related complications and have had recent household or other close contact with a person with influenza, and health care workers who have had recent close contact with a person with influenza. This patient meets none of these indications for antiviral prophylaxis.

Bibliography

van Assen S, Holvast A, Benne CA, et al. Humoral responses after influenza vaccination are severely reduced in patients with rheumatoid arthritis treated with rituximab. Arthritis Rheum. 2010;62(1):75-81. [PMID: 20039396]

Item 59　　Answer: B

Educational Objective: Diagnose lateral epicondylitis.

This patient most likely has lateral epicondylitis, or tennis elbow, a common cause of lateral elbow pain. Lateral epicondylitis is a periarthritic disorder that affects the soft tissues surrounding, but not involving, the joint. No diagnostic laboratory tests can differentiate periarthritis from arthritis; therefore, the diagnosis is made on the basis of the history and physical examination. Lateral epicondylitis is caused by repetitive movement of the forearm, which can lead to injury and inflammation of the tendon. Patients typically experience pain when carrying, lifting, or gripping objects. This patient has tenderness of the lateral epicondyle and pain on resisted wrist extension and hand gripping, examination findings that are consistent with lateral epicondylitis. Treatment with NSAIDs and physical therapy can relieve symptoms. Use of a counterbrace (a forearm band worn just distal to the elbow) can disperse the forces felt by the tendon and relieve pain.

Cervical radiculopathy can cause pain to radiate into the forearm; however, the pain is usually accompanied by numbness, tingling, or weakness, symptoms that can be reproduced by lateral bending of the neck. Extension of the wrist against resistance does not cause pain, as noted in this patient.

Olecranon bursitis causes pain over the olecranon process at the tip of the elbow and is associated with bursa swelling and, occasionally, erythema. Causes of this condition include traumatic (aseptic) bursitis, gouty bursitis, or septic bursitis (typically *Staphylococcus aureus*). Aspiration of the bursa may be diagnostic and therapeutic if aseptic.

Osteoarthritis of the elbow is rare and generally occurs in a patient with prior trauma to the joint; this disorder causes pain localized to the elbow joint itself and tenderness along the joint line. Unlike this case, physical examination reveals pain on active and passive range of motion, and flexion contracture may occur.

Bibliography

Van Hofwegen C, Baker CL 3rd, Baker CL Jr. Epicondylitis in the athlete's elbow. Clin Sports Med. 2010;29(4):577-597. [PMID: 20883898]

Item 60　　Answer: B

Educational Objective: Diagnose Marfan syndrome.

This patient has Marfan syndrome, one of the most common inherited connective tissue disorders. Diagnosis of Marfan syndrome is dependent upon recognition of its classic signs involving the ophthalmologic, cardiovascular, and musculoskeletal systems. Major diagnostic criteria include four of eight typical skeletal manifestations; ectopia lentis; aortic root dilatation; lumbosacral dural ectasia (diagnosed with imaging); and family history. This patient has evidence of overgrowth of long bones (with an arm span that is greater than his height), arachnodactyly (long digits), and pectus excavatum caused by rib overgrowth. He also has scoliosis, micrognathia, a high arched palate, ligamentous laxity, mitral regurgitation, a dilated aortic root, a history of ectopia lentis (lens dislocation), and a family history of a ruptured aortic aneurysm. These features are consistent with Marfan syndrome.

Patients with classic Ehlers-Danlos syndrome (EDS) have ligamentous laxity that is dramatic rather than mild as well as velvety, hyperextensible skin and atrophic scarring, which are not seen in this patient. Patients with classic EDS do not generally develop arterial aneurysms.

Although patients with osteogenesis imperfecta may have scoliosis, they generally have a history of fracture and are shorter than average height. They also typically have blue sclerae and dentinogenesis imperfecta (poorly developed teeth).

Patients with vascular EDS can have aneurysmal dilatation of many blood vessels as well as ligamentous laxity; however, they do not develop ectopia lentis or have skeletal abnormalities such as a high arched palate or pectus excavatum, and they often have thin, translucent skin.

Bibliography

Judge DP, Dietz HC. Marfan's syndrome. Lancet. 2005;366(9501):1965-1976. [PMID: 16325700]

Item 61 Answer: E

Educational Objective: Manage acute digital ischemia in a patient with systemic sclerosis.

Treatment with intravenous epoprostenol is appropriate for this patient with acute digital ischemia in the setting of limited cutaneous systemic sclerosis (lcSSc). Sequelae of digital ischemia in patients with systemic sclerosis include Raynaud phenomenon, digital pitting, ulceration, and gangrene. The initial management of this patient with an acutely ischemic digit occurring in this setting includes maintaining a warm ambient environment, prompt attention to pain control to decrease sympathetic vasoconstriction, and institution of vasodilating therapy, preferably with a prostacyclin analogue such as epoprostenol.

Bosentan has been shown to be effective in preventing recurrences of digital ulcers in patients with severe Raynaud phenomenon but is not of significant benefit in managing an acutely ischemic digit.

An ACE inhibitor such as enalapril is appropriate treatment for scleroderma renal crisis; however, this patient's elevated blood pressure and the attendant tachycardia are most likely attributable to an increased sympathetic response due to pain, and the normal serum creatinine level, complete blood count, and peripheral blood smear argue against scleroderma renal crisis.

Arteriography of the ipsilateral upper extremity should be considered in patients who have evidence of proximal arterial lesions or who develop digital ischemia in the setting of suspected thromboembolic disease, decreased radial pulse, or otherwise unexplained digital ischemia. Absent such findings on physical examination, arteriography is unlikely to provide additional diagnostic information required for the management of digital ischemia in a patient with established systemic sclerosis.

Digital sympathectomy may be a very useful intervention in patients with severe digital ischemia who do not respond to vasodilating agents but is not indicated in this patient at this time.

KEY POINT

- **Treatment with an intravenous prostacyclin analogue such as epoprostenol is indicated for acute digital ischemia in the setting of limited cutaneous systemic sclerosis.**

Bibliography

Kowal-Bielecka O, Landewé R, Avouac J, et al; EUSTAR Co-Authors. EULAR recommendations for the treatment of systemic sclerosis: a report from the EULAR Scleroderma Trials and Research group (EUSTAR). Ann Rheum Dis. 2009;68(5):620-628. [PMID: 19147617]

Item 62 Answer: C

Educational Objective: Diagnose psoriatic arthritis.

This patient has psoriatic arthritis, a systemic chronic inflammatory arthritis associated with numerous clinical manifestations. Typically, psoriasis predates the arthritis by years, whereas arthritis develops before skin disease in 15% of patients. Although there is a poor correlation between the severity of skin and joint disease, there is a good correlation between the severity of nail disease and the severity of both skin and joint disease. Psoriatic findings may also be limited to nail pitting and onycholysis. There are five patterns of joint involvement in psoriatic arthritis: involvement of the distal interphalangeal joints; asymmetric oligoarthritis; symmetric polyarthritis (similar to that of rheumatoid arthritis); arthritis mutilans (extensive osteolysis of the digits with striking deformity); and spondylitis. Characteristic features of psoriatic arthritis include enthesitis, dactylitis, and tenosynovitis. This patient has findings characteristic of psoriatic arthritis, including inflammation of a distal interphalangeal joint and dactylitis of a toe. He also has nail changes, including pitting and onycholysis.

Lyme arthritis typically involves medium- or large-sized joints rather than distal interphalangeal joints and does not typically cause tenosynovitis. Furthermore, this disorder does not cause nail changes, as seen in this patient.

Osteoarthritis can involve the distal interphalangeal joints but does not cause dactylitis or nail changes.

Rheumatoid arthritis can initially present with an asymmetric pattern, although it classically takes on a symmetric distribution with time. In contrast to this case, rheumatoid arthritis typically spares the distal interphalangeal joints, involving the proximal interphalangeal joints and metacarpophalangeal joints preferentially. Finally, this condition does not cause nail changes.

KEY POINT

- **Psoriatic arthritis is associated with various patterns of joint involvement, most notably distal interphalangeal joint involvement, and is characterized by enthesitis, dactylitis, tenosynovitis, and cutaneous involvement such as nail pitting.**

Bibliography

Taylor W, Gladman D, Helliwell P, Marchesoni A, Mease P, Mielants H; CASPAR Study Group. Classification criteria for psoriatic arthritis: development of new criteria from a large international study. Arthritis Rheum. 2006;54(8):2665-2673. [PMID: 16871531]

Item 63 Answer: C

Educational Objective: Manage gout with urate-lowering agents.

This patient has frequent, symptomatic gout attacks and requires initial treatment with colchicine concurrent with urate-lowering therapy such as allopurinol. Gout manifests as acute, intermittent attacks of severe pain, redness, and swelling of a joint accompanied by intracellular urate crystals seen on polarized light microscopy of the synovial fluid. NSAIDs, corticosteroids, and colchicine are appropriate management strategies for acute gout attacks; choice of treatment is based on relative efficacy and, most importantly, the side-effect profiles of the agents and the risk of toxicity in the individual patient.

Gout is associated with hyperuricemia, and patients with recurrent episodes (≥2 attacks in 1 year) require urate-lowering therapy to prevent both future attacks and occult urate deposition. However, the addition of urate-lowering therapy transiently increases the risk for acute gout attacks for at least 3 to 6 months; accordingly, prophylaxis with an anti-inflammatory agent such as colchicine, at least during that period, is indicated concurrent with urate-lowering therapy.

Along with this treatment regimen, management of risk factors can help to lower serum urate concentrations, including reducing purine and fructose and increasing dairy intake, within the limits of individual tolerance; weight loss; and reducing alcohol consumption. Medications that raise serum uric acid levels, including thiazide diuretics and low-dose salicylates, should be discontinued if alternative therapy is appropriate.

Use of either allopurinol or febuxostat would be appropriate but only in the setting of concurrent prophylaxis. Both febuxostat and allopurinol should be dosed to achieve a serum urate level ≤6.0 mg/dL (0.35 mmol/L), rather than at a fixed dose. The relative effectiveness of these two agents is not well established; febuxostat is more potent on a per-mole basis but is also more expensive than allopurinol.

Treatment with colchicine alone might lower the risk of gout attacks in this patient but would not address the underlying problem of urate deposition, which would likely worsen progressively over time.

KEY POINT

- Colchicine or other anti-inflammatory therapy is indicated concurrent with initiation of urate-lowering agents in patients with frequently recurring gout attacks.

Bibliography
Yang LP. Oral colchicine (Colcrys) in the treatment and prophylaxis of gout. Drugs. 2010;70(12):1603-1613. [PMID: 20687623]

Item 64   Answer: B

Educational Objective: Treat a patient with urticarial vasculitis.

Treatment with hydroxychloroquine is indicated for this patient with urticarial vasculitis, a disorder that lies within the spectrum of small-vessel vasculitis. Urticarial plaques that are fixed in location for more than 24 hours should be biopsied to rule out urticarial vasculitis. If urticarial vasculitis is diagnosed on skin biopsy, the next diagnostic step is measurement of serum complement levels. The presence of hypocomplementemia predicts the presence of systemic vasculitis, most commonly systemic lupus erythematosus (SLE).

Urticarial lesions are the most common manifestations of vasculitis involving the skin in patients with SLE and may be the presenting feature of the disorder. Although most cases of urticarial vasculitis are idiopathic and self-limited, cases associated with underlying systemic vasculitis tend to be chronic or relapsing. Treatment of cutaneous small-vessel vasculitis is best directed toward the underlying cause. For this patient with recurring episodes of urticarial lesions who has a significant titer of antinuclear antibodies, treatment with hydroxychloroquine is appropriate to decrease the frequency and severity of urticarial outbreaks.

Cyclophosphamide is a treatment option for severe, refractory cutaneous vasculitis with skin ulcers or other organ complications that has not responded to treatment with less toxic medications such as hydroxychloroquine or dapsone.

Methotrexate may be of benefit for patients with more severe forms of cutaneous lupus not responding to antimalarial therapy or low-dose corticosteroids but is not presently indicated for this patient unless she does not respond to a trial of antimalarial agents or develops other, more significant manifestations of SLE.

Mycophenolate mofetil can be used as steroid-sparing therapy for patients with steroid-dependent cutaneous lesions not responding to hydroxychloroquine, dapsone, or methotrexate.

KEY POINT

- Hydroxychloroquine is used to treat recurring urticarial lesions associated with cutaneous small-vessel vasculitis or lupus.

Bibliography
Stigall LE, Sigmon JR, Leicht SS. Urticarial vasculitis: a unique presentation. South Med J. 2009;102(5):531-533. [PMID: 19373142]

Item 65   Answer: D

Educational Objective: Distinguish between inflammatory and noninflammatory arthritis.

The presence of symmetric swelling of the proximal interphalangeal joints, elbows, and ankles in this patient is strongly suggestive of an inflammatory arthritis, most likely rheumatoid arthritis. Rheumatoid arthritis can affect most joints; however, the lumbar and thoracic spine as well as the distal interphalangeal joints are spared. Joint involvement is usually symmetric and can involve both large joints and the small joints of the hands and feet. This patient has a history of noninflammatory back pain, which is not typical of rheumatoid arthritis, and is likely an unrelated condition. In contrast, patients with inflammatory back pain and new peripheral inflammatory arthritis should be evaluated for a spondyloarthritis such as psoriatic arthritis.

Although rheumatoid arthritis typically results in prolonged morning stiffness and inflammatory joint fluid, some patients have milder disease. Morning stiffness lasting 15 minutes and a synovial fluid leukocyte count of

$2000/\mu L$ ($2.0 \times 10^9/L$) are on the "borderline" between inflammatory and noninflammatory findings. Morning stiffness lasting more than 1 hour and a synovial fluid leukocyte count greater than $5000/\mu L$ ($5.0 \times 10^9/L$) are more typical of an inflammatory arthritis such as rheumatoid arthritis.

Fibromyalgia is characterized by chronic widespread musculoskeletal pain for at least 3 months. The onset of fibromyalgia in women typically occurs between the ages of 20 and 50 years. The physical examination in patients with fibromyalgia usually is normal except for widespread pain and tenderness. Active synovitis is not consistent with a diagnosis of fibromyalgia.

Osteoarthritis can affect the hips, knees, lumbar and cervical spine, and the proximal and distal interphalangeal joints; however, involvement typically is asymmetric, and the pain does not begin in multiple joints abruptly and simultaneously, as noted in this patient. The elbows and ankles are not commonly affected in patients with osteoarthritis unless these areas have suffered prior trauma.

Polymyalgia rheumatica is characterized by aching in the shoulders, neck, and hip girdle region; fatigue; and malaise that develop over weeks to months. This patient's symptoms and the objective findings of synovitis are not consistent with polymyalgia rheumatica.

KEY POINT

- Morning stiffness lasting more than 1 hour and a synovial fluid leukocyte count greater than $5000/\mu L$ ($5.0 \times 10^9/L$) are associated with inflammatory arthritis.

Bibliography

Huizinga TW, Pincus T. In the clinic. Rheumatoid arthritis. Ann Intern Med. 2010;153(1):ITC1-1-ITC1-15; quiz ITC1-16. [PMID: 20621898]

Item 66   Answer: B

Educational Objective: Manage systemic lupus erythematosus in a patient considering pregnancy.

Treatment with hydroxychloroquine is indicated for this patient with systemic lupus erythematosus (SLE). Although hydroxychloroquine has been used anecdotally for many years in patients with SLE, numerous recent studies document significant benefits of this agent. High levels of evidence show that hydroxychloroquine prevents lupus flares and increases survival in patients with SLE; there also is moderate evidence suggesting protection against irreversible organ damage, thrombosis, and bone mass loss. Hydroxychloroquine should be continued indefinitely to prevent disease reactivation, even if the disease has been quiescent for many years. This patient has mild SLE without evidence of significant internal organ involvement; she is also trying to conceive, which further impacts choice of medication. Although hydroxychloroquine is a pregnancy

category C medication, expert consensus states that this agent is relatively safe in pregnancy, and studies support a reduction in flares without harm to the fetus. Given the demonstrated benefits of hydroxychloroquine in patients with SLE, which are suggested to be time-dependent, it is appropriate to treat this patient at this time, unless the patient refuses or has a contraindication to therapy. Pregnancy outcomes in patients with SLE are better in the absence of active disease, and patients should be counseled to wait to try to conceive until they have had quiescent disease for a minimum of 6 months.

Azathioprine and mycophenolate mofetil have a steroid-sparing effect and have been shown to improve outcomes in patients with severe SLE, particularly those with kidney involvement. Azathioprine, but not mycophenolate mofetil, is generally considered the most acceptable of these agents for use during pregnancy, despite its pregnancy category D rating. This patient does not have severe disease and is not currently taking corticosteroids; therefore, treatment with these medications is not indicated.

This patient is stable with minimal disease activity, both clinically and serologically; therefore, there is no indication for treatment with prednisone unless her symptoms worsen. Prednisone, when necessary, is considered relatively safe for use in pregnancy; about two thirds of the active drug is metabolized by placental enzymes to an inactive form, limiting the amount of fetal exposure.

KEY POINT

- Although hydroxychloroquine is a pregnancy category C medication, this agent is relatively safe in pregnancy and can reduce lupus flares without harm to the fetus.

Bibliography

Ruiz-Irastorza G, Ramos-Casals M, Brito-Zeron P, Khamashta MA. Clinical efficacy and side effects of antimalarials in systemic lupus erythematosus: a systematic review. Ann Rheum Dis. 2010;69(1):20-28. [PMID: 19103632]

Item 67   Answer: B

Educational Objective: Manage early rheumatoid arthritis.

Treatment with methotrexate is indicated for this patient who most likely has rheumatoid arthritis. Once rheumatoid arthritis is suspected, promptly confirming the diagnosis and initiating aggressive therapy are critical. Applying the 2010 American College of Rheumatology Classification Criteria for rheumatoid arthritis, this patient scores 3 points for the distribution of her arthritis (involvement of 4 to 10 small joints), 1 point for the duration of her symptoms (≥6 weeks), 2 points for the presence of an elevated rheumatoid factor at low titer, and 1 point for the presence of an elevated C-reactive protein level, for a total of 7 points. A score of 6 or greater is consistent with a diagnosis of rheumatoid arthritis in patients who have synovitis not otherwise explained by an alternative diagnosis. This patient's lack of radiographic findings does not rule out rheumatoid arthritis, as radiographs may appear normal this early in the disease course.

Early, aggressive disease control is essential with disease-modifying antirheumatic drugs (DMARDs) such as methotrexate to slow the progression of joint damage, to stabilize or prevent functional limitations, and to prevent the complications of long-term uncontrolled inflammation. Damage in rheumatoid arthritis is irreversible once it has occurred, even when aggressive DMARD therapy is used. Evidence shows that rapidly escalating therapy with a multidrug regimen is the most effective means of controlling disease.

Colchicine can reduce inflammation related to crystalline arthropathies and certain autoinflammatory syndromes but is not effective in the treatment of rheumatoid arthritis.

NSAIDs can also be helpful adjunctive agents in the management of pain in patients with rheumatoid arthritis but do not modify disease course.

Shoe inserts can be helpful to reduce mechanical stress but would not address the underlying inflammatory process in this patient.

KEY POINT

- In patients with rheumatoid arthritis, early, aggressive disease control using disease-modifying antirheumatic drugs is essential to slow the progression of joint damage, to stabilize or prevent functional limitations, and to prevent the complications of long-term uncontrolled inflammation.

Bibliography

Aletaha D, Neogi T, Silman AJ, et al. 2010 Rheumatoid arthritis classification criteria: an American College of Rheumatology/European League Against Rheumatism collaborative initiative. Arthritis Rheum. 2010;62(9):2569-2581. [PMID: 20872595]

Item 68   Answer: D

Educational Objective: Manage azathioprine drug-drug interactions.

Treatment with probenecid is indicated for this patient. Probenecid promotes renal urate excretion and is efficacious in patients who underexcrete uric acid (documented by a 24-hour urine collection) in the setting of a normal estimated glomerular filtration rate (GFR). (Its efficacy is limited in patients with significant decreases of estimated GFR.) Probenecid may increase the risk of kidney stones; therefore, patients taking probenecid must hydrate aggressively and may need to alkalinize their urine, and the drug should be used with caution in patients at high risk for stones (for example, a history of stones or tophaceous gout). This patient has frequent gout attacks in the setting of hyperuricemia and requires urate-lowering

therapy. In this setting, probenecid would be both effective and compatible with this patient's azathioprine treatment for granulomatosis with polyangiitis (also known as Wegener granulomatosis).

Allopurinol and febuxostat each lower serum urate by inhibiting xanthine oxidase, an enzyme that converts xanthine to urate. Because azathioprine's active metabolite (6-mercaptopurine) is also metabolized by xanthine oxidase, both allopurinol and febuxostat increase the risk of azathioprine toxicity and are contraindicated in the setting of azathioprine use.

Pegloticase has the capacity to lower serum urate levels through enzymatic digestion of urate; however, it is immunogenic and approved only for treatment-failure gout and is therefore not appropriate for this patient at the present time.

KEY POINT

- Allopurinol and febuxostat are contraindicated in the setting of azathioprine.

Bibliography

Neogi T. Clinical practice. Gout. N Engl J Med. 2011;364(5):443-452. [PMID: 21288096]

Item 69   Answer: A

Educational Objective: Diagnose axial spondyloarthritis using HLA-B27 testing.

HLA-B27 testing is recommended for this patient with suspected axial spondyloarthritis. This condition should be considered in patients with chronic back pain and onset before the age of 45 years. In such patients with evidence of sacroiliitis on radiographs or MRI, the classification criteria for axial spondyloarthritis can be fulfilled if the patient has one or more of the following features: inflammatory back pain; arthritis; enthesitis of the heel; uveitis; dactylitis; psoriasis; Crohn disease or ulcerative colitis; good response to NSAIDs; family history of spondyloarthritis; elevated C-reactive protein (CRP) level; or the presence of HLA-B27. In patients without evidence of radiographic sacroiliitis, the criteria can still be fulfilled if the patient is HLA-B27 positive and has at least two additional spondyloarthritis features.

HLA-B27 is the strongest genetic risk factor for spondyloarthritis; the utility of HLA-B27 testing depends on the setting in which it is evaluated. This patient does not have radiographic evidence of sacroiliitis; however, he has findings compatible with inflammatory back pain; has an elevated CRP level; and has a family history of spondyloarthritis. If this patient is HLA-B27 positive, he would meet the classification criteria. When the presence of HLA-B27 would alter diagnosis and treatment, HLA-B27 testing is recommended.

Human antichimeric antibodies (HACAs) are present in patients treated with proteins that incorporate human and nonhuman elements such as infliximab. Infliximab is used to treat spondyloarthritis, rheumatoid arthritis, and other conditions, and patients treated with this agent often develop HACAs. This patient has not been treated with chimeric molecules and would not be expected to have significant titers of HACAs.

Although the cervical spine can be involved in spondyloarthritis, this patient has low back pain without symptoms or signs of cervical spine involvement; therefore, radiographs of the cervical spine are not warranted.

Rheumatoid factor is present in approximately 80% of patients with rheumatoid arthritis but is uncommon in spondyloarthritis. Furthermore, low back pain is not associated with rheumatoid arthritis.

KEY POINT

- HLA-B27 testing may be useful in patients with inflammatory back pain but no radiologic evidence of sacroiliitis or spondylitis.

Bibliography

Rudwaleit M, van der Heijde D, Landewé R, et al. The development of Assessment of SpondyloArthritis International Society classification criteria for axial spondyloarthritis (part II): validation and final selection. Ann Rheum Dis. 2009;68(6):777-783. [PMID: 19297344]

Item 70   Answer: A

Educational Objective: Diagnose Churg-Strauss syndrome.

This patient most likely has Churg-Strauss syndrome, a form of systemic vasculitis that most often occurs in the setting of antecedent asthma, allergic rhinitis, or sinusitis. Patients typically have eosinophilia, migratory pulmonary infiltrates, purpuric skin rash, and mononeuritis multiplex; fever, arthralgia, and myalgia also are common presenting features. Up to 40% of patients have p-ANCA positivity with specificity for antimyeloperoxidase antibodies. Patients who have positive ANCAs are more likely to have glomerulonephritis, alveolar hemorrhage, mononeuritis multiplex, and purpura.

Granulomatosis with polyangiitis (also known as Wegener granulomatosis) is a necrotizing vasculitis that typically affects the respiratory tract and the kidneys. Radiographs show infiltrates or nodules that are often cavitary, as well as pulmonary hemorrhage. Microscopic polyangiitis is a necrotizing vasculitis that typically involves the kidneys and lungs. Affected patients frequently present with rapidly progressive glomerulonephritis; 50% of patients have pulmonary involvement that usually manifests as pulmonary hemorrhage. Fever, arthralgia, purpura, and mononeuritis multiplex can also occur. Microscopic polyangiitis or granulomatosis with polyangiitis could account for the lung and kidney lesions in this patient; however, his findings of profound eosinophilia and antecedent allergic rhinitis, as well as his history of reactive airways disease, are more suggestive of Churg-Strauss syndrome. Further, granulomatosis with polyangiitis is commonly associated with antiproteinase-3 antibodies.

Patients with polyarteritis nodosa typically present with fever, abdominal pain, arthralgia, and weight loss that develop over days to months. Two thirds of these patients have mononeuritis multiplex, and one third have hypertension, testicular pain, and cutaneous involvement, including nodules, ulcers, purpura, and livedo reticularis. Polyarteritis nodosa may be associated with mild eosinophilia; however, lung involvement is uncommon and ANCA test results typically are negative.

KEY POINT

- Churg-Strauss syndrome is characterized by eosinophilia, migratory pulmonary infiltrates, purpuric skin rash, and mononeuritis multiplex in the setting of antecedent asthma, allergic rhinitis, or sinusitis.

Bibliography

Baldini C, Talarico R, Della Rossa A, Bombardieri S. Clinical manifestations and treatment of Churg-Strauss syndrome. Rheum Dis Clin North Am. 2010;36(3):527-543. [PMID: 20688248]

Item 71   Answer: B

Educational Objective: Diagnose inclusion body myositis.

This patient most likely has inclusion body myositis (IBM), the most common form of myositis in patients older than 60 years, which typically occurs in men. This condition typically manifests as proximal and distal muscle weakness. Although muscle involvement in IBM is typically symmetric, it may be asymmetric in up to 15% of cases. The quadriceps, wrist, and finger flexor muscles are commonly involved. IBM characteristically has an insidious onset and is associated with only moderately elevated serum creatine kinase levels that are typically less than 1000 units/L. This patient's findings of asymmetric quadriceps and wrist muscle weakness, an elevated serum creatine kinase level, absence of autoantibodies, and absence of extramuscular manifestations such as rash, fever, and pulmonary involvement are consistent with this disorder.

Dermatomyositis is characterized by symmetric proximal muscle weakness and positive autoantibodies but includes prominent rash (Gottron papules, heliotrope rash, V sign, or shawl sign).

Polymyositis is more likely to occur in younger patients, is more common in women, and is characterized by symmetric proximal muscle weakness and frequent extramuscular manifestations. Up to 90% of patients have positive autoantibodies, with 80% of patients positive for antinuclear antibodies.

Although statins can cause myalgia, myositis, asymptomatic serum creatine kinase elevation, and even (rarely) rhabdomyolysis, the clinical presentation most commonly is one of muscle pain, tenderness, and cramping. These symptoms usually occur within the first 6 months of therapy and resolve within 2 months of discontinuation of the medication. Statin-induced muscle symptoms are usually dose related, and risk is increased in patients with impaired kidney function. Statin-induced myopathy is unlikely in this patient who had been taking lovastatin for many years.

> **KEY POINT**
> • Although muscle involvement in inclusion body myositis is typically symmetric, it may be asymmetric in up to 15% of cases.

Bibliography
Amato AA, Barohn RJ. Inclusion body myositis: old and new concepts. J Neurol Neurosurg Psychiatry. 2009;80(11):1186-1193. [PMID: 19864656]

Item 72   Answer: C

Educational Objective: Evaluate a patient with limited cutaneous systemic sclerosis.

Pulmonary function testing and echocardiography are indicated for this patient with suspected limited cutaneous systemic sclerosis (lcSSc), which is characterized by skin involvement restricted to the face and extremities distal to the elbow. Diagnosis of systemic sclerosis is based on the presence of tightness, thickening, and swelling/induration of the digits extending proximal to the metacarpophalangeal joints. In the absence of these skin changes, diagnosis also can be established in patients with two of the following: sclerodactyly, terminal digital pitting or ulceration, or basilar interstitial fibrosis on chest radiography. Antinuclear antibodies (ANA) are present in more than 95% of patients with systemic sclerosis. Most patients with lcSSc have an antecedent history of Raynaud phenomenon and are more likely to develop pulmonary arterial hypertension in the absence of other pulmonary manifestations.

This patient has classic manifestations of lcSSc, including Raynaud phenomenon, digital swelling, telangiectasias, and positive ANA in a nucleolar pattern. Periodic assessments with pulmonary function testing and/or echocardiography for early detection of pulmonary arterial hypertension are therefore recommended.

Esophageal dysmotility is common in patients with lcSSc or diffuse cutaneous systemic sclerosis (dcSSc); however, barium esophagography is not indicated unless dysphagia symptoms are present.

High-resolution CT of the chest is recommended to evaluate patients with systemic sclerosis who have dyspnea or otherwise unexplained impairment of oxygen diffusion and a restrictive pattern on pulmonary function testing. High-resolution CT of the chest is not indicated in the absence of pulmonary symptoms or abnormal findings on pulmonary function testing.

A right heart catheterization is indicated in patients with dyspnea or those who have evidence of possible pulmonary arterial hypertension noted on echocardiogram or a low D_{LCO}/FVC ratio.

> **KEY POINT**
> • Most patients with limited cutaneous systemic sclerosis have an antecedent history of Raynaud phenomenon and are more likely to develop pulmonary arterial hypertension in the absence of other pulmonary manifestations.

Bibliography
Hsu VM, Moreyra AE, Wilson AC, et al. Assessment of pulmonary arterial hypertension in patients with systemic sclerosis: comparison of noninvasive tests with results of right-heart catheterization. J Rheumatol. 2008;35(3):458-465. [PMID: 18203320]

Item 73   Answer: A

Educational Objective: Diagnose dermatomyositis.

This patient most likely has dermatomyositis. This inflammatory myopathy is characterized by progressive or intermittent proximal weakness; photosensitive rash such as the shawl sign (involves the posterior neck, upper back, and shoulders) or V sign (involves the anterior neck and chest); heliotrope rash (violaceous discoloration of the eyelids accompanied by periorbital edema); and Gottron papules (violaceous to pink plaques with scaling overlying the extensor surface of the hand joints, knees, and elbows). Other findings include fever, fatigue, Raynaud phenomenon, nailfold capillary abnormalities, including periungual erythema and telangiectasias, as well as cuticle hypertrophy, arthritis, pulmonary manifestations, cardiac involvement, and gastrointestinal symptoms. Up to 80% of patients have positive antinuclear antibodies (ANA). Although this patient's symptoms are consistent with several connective tissue diseases, including systemic lupus erythematosus (SLE), polymyositis, and mixed connective tissue disease (MCTD), the presence of a heliotrope rash and Gottron papules over the elbows, metacarpophalangeal joints, and proximal interphalangeal joints are classically diagnostic for dermatomyositis.

Inclusion body myositis is most common in older men and presents with insidious weakness affecting both proximal and distal muscles; there are no associated rashes or autoantibodies, and extramuscular manifestations are rare.

MCTD is an overlap syndrome of systemic sclerosis, SLE, and myositis; this patient's clinical presentation, including the myositis and positive ANA, is consistent with MCTD with the exception of the dermatomyositis-associated rash.

Manifestations of polymyositis are similar to those of dermatomyositis; however, rash does not occur.

This patient's symptoms, including mild myositis, can be associated with SLE. However, SLE is characterized by malar, subacute cutaneous, or discoid rash, unlike the rashes associated with dermatomyositis.

> **KEY POINT**
> - Gottron papules and heliotrope rash are pathognomonic for dermatomyositis.

Bibliography

Callen J. Cutaneous manifestations of dermatomyositis and their management. Curr Rheumatol Rep. 2010;12(3):192-197. [PMID: 20425525]

Item 74   Answer: E

Educational Objective: Diagnose Sjögren syndrome–associated lymphoma.

Parotid gland biopsy is indicated for this patient who has Sjögren syndrome and progressive parotid swelling suggesting possible non-Hodgkin lymphoma. Patients with Sjögren syndrome have up to a 44-fold increased incidence of lymphoma, which may be confined to glandular tissue. Risk factors for the development of lymphoma include disappearance of rheumatoid factor, the presence of mixed monoclonal cryoglobulinemia, cutaneous vasculitis, and low C4 levels, all of which are seen in this patient. Although benign parotid gland swelling can occur and be unilateral or bilateral in patients with Sjögren syndrome, this patient's high-risk profile and new asymmetric parotid enlargement should prompt a biopsy to evaluate for extranodal lymphoma in the parotid gland. Extranodal marginal zone B-cell lymphomas of the mucosa-associated lymphoid tissue (MALT) are the most common lymphomas in patients with Sjögren syndrome, and salivary glands are the most common location; other extranodal sites include the stomach, nasopharynx, skin, liver, and lungs. The risk of nodal lymphoma is also increased in Sjögren syndrome. Although benign lymphadenopathy is a common disease manifestation, the presence of new or rapidly enlarging lymph nodes may indicate development of nodal lymphoma and should prompt biopsy.

Pilocarpine is effective for reducing dry mouth symptoms but is not used to treat parotid enlargement.

Prednisone is generally used to treat inflammatory symptoms of Sjögren syndrome, including arthritis, vasculitis, and cytopenias, but does not reduce parotid swelling or treat symptoms of keratoconjunctivitis sicca and xerostomia (dry eyes and dry mouth).

Patients with Sjögren syndrome often have elevated immunoglobulin levels with monoclonal gammopathy; stability of this during the patient's disease course, as well as normal hemoglobin, calcium, and alkaline phosphatase levels, suggests that bone marrow biopsy to evaluate for myeloma is not warranted. Extranodal lymphoma in Sjögren syndrome involves the bone marrow in less than 10% of patients.

Hydroxychloroquine is used to treat arthritis associated with Sjögren syndrome; however, it is unclear if this agent has efficacy in reducing sicca symptoms or parotid swelling.

> **KEY POINT**
> - Patients with Sjögren syndrome have up to a 44-fold increased incidence of lymphoma, which may be confined to glandular tissue.

Bibliography

Voulgarelis M, Moutsopoulos HM. Mucosa-associated lymphoid tissue lymphoma in Sjögren's syndrome: risks, management, and prognosis. Rheum Dis Clin N Am. 2008;34(4):921-933. [PMID: 18984412]

Item 75   Answer: A

Educational Objective: Manage rheumatoid arthritis with a tumor necrosis factor α inhibitor.

The addition of adalimumab is appropriate for this patient with rheumatoid arthritis. He has ongoing moderate disease activity, including synovitis and an elevated C-reactive protein level, despite taking methotrexate at a maximum dose for 3 months. Evidence supports aggressive treatment of rheumatoid arthritis to optimize outcomes and minimize sequelae of inflammation. Use of methotrexate in conjunction with a tumor necrosis factor (TNF)-α inhibitor such as adalimumab is associated with further reductions in disease activity and radiographic progression. The currently available agents (etanercept, infliximab, adalimumab, golimumab, and certolizumab pegol) all have similar efficacy. Individual patients may respond better to one of these agents, but no currently available methods predict the likelihood of response to a particular agent. Screening for tuberculosis is indicated before beginning therapy with any biologic agent, and patients who test positive for latent tuberculosis should be treated with isoniazid before beginning biologic therapy.

Folic acid can decrease gastrointestinal and hepatic toxicity of methotrexate. Discontinuation of folic acid does not result in significant improvements in efficacy of methotrexate and would increase the risk of adverse effects.

The combination of methotrexate with a TNF-α inhibitor is associated with greater efficacy than therapy with methotrexate or a TNF-α inhibitor alone. Unless there is a contraindication to methotrexate use, it is used in conjunction with TNF-α inhibitors. Therefore, discontinuation of methotrexate and the use of a TNF-α inhibitor such as infliximab as monotherapy is not appropriate for this patient.

Sulfasalazine as monotherapy is less effective than methotrexate in patients with poor prognostic features and would not improve control of inflammation in this patient.

Methotrexate was appropriate as first-line therapy but is now insufficient; therefore, maintaining this patient's current regimen is not appropriate, because additional treatment is warranted.

KEY POINT

- Use of methotrexate in conjunction with a tumor necrosis factor α inhibitor is associated with further reductions in disease activity and radiographic progression in patients with rheumatoid arthritis.

Bibliography

Visser K, Katchamart W, Loza E, et al. Multinational evidence-based recommendations for the use of methotrexate in rheumatic disorders with a focus on rheumatoid arthritis: integrating systematic literature research and expert opinion of a broad international panel of rheumatologists in the 3E Initiative. Ann Rheum Dis. 2009;68(7):1086-1093. [PMID: 19033291]

Item 76   Answer: D

Educational Objective: Diagnose trochanteric bursitis.

This patient most likely has trochanteric bursitis, a common cause of lateral hip pain. A bursa is a connective tissue sac with a potential space that facilitates smooth movement of one tissue over another. Bursitis results when a bursa becomes inflamed (usually from trauma or an overuse syndrome) or infected. As with other forms of periarthritis, the physical examination distinguishes bursitis from involvement of an adjacent joint. The trochanteric bursa lies directly over the greater trochanter, making it amenable to examination. This condition can be confirmed in patients in whom active hip abduction intensifies the pain or in those in whom the examination reveals pain and tenderness over the bursa, which is located over the lateral projection of the greater trochanter. Passive range of motion does not always elicit pain. Furthermore, patients describe pain when lying on their side or swinging their leg into a car. Relief of pain with lidocaine injection into the bursa can be diagnostic. Treatment includes relative rest, NSAIDs, and topical modalities such as ice or heat. Range-of-motion activities may speed healing. Additional treatment modalities include aspiration of the bursa with or without injection of an anesthetic (lidocaine) and corticosteroid mixture.

Iliotibial band syndrome most commonly occurs in young athletes such as runners or cyclists. This condition also can cause lateral hip pain; however, patients often describe pain that radiates down the outside of the leg. Patients with iliotibial band syndrome exhibit pain to palpation along the band down to the knee. Stretching of the iliotibial band by adducting the knee often reproduces the pain. In contrast, patients with trochanteric bursitis have more localized pain on examination.

Lumbar radiculopathy can cause pain localized to the lateral hip; however, the area is not generally tender, and straight-leg-raising test results are often positive. Lumbar radiculopathy can also result in paresthesia and weakness of the leg. Pain is often felt while sitting but is not generally exacerbated by walking.

Hip joint pathology (osteoarthritis and synovitis) often causes groin or gluteal pain, and passive range of motion elicits pain in these areas. Patients often demonstrate guarding or reduced range of motion.

KEY POINT

- Trochanteric bursitis can be confirmed in patients in whom active hip abduction intensifies the pain or in those in whom the examination reveals pain and tenderness over the bursa.

Bibliography

Strauss EJ, Nho SJ, Kelly BT. Greater trochanteric pain syndrome. Sports Med Arthrosc. 2010;18(2):113-119. [PMID: 20473130]

Item 77   Answer: C

Educational Objective: Diagnose eosinophilic fasciitis.

This patient most likely has eosinophilic fasciitis. This scleroderma spectrum disorder is characterized by woody induration of the extremities sparing the hands and face. The diagnosis is established with a full-thickness skin biopsy extending down to the fascia overlying muscle demonstrating lymphocytes, plasma cells, and eosinophils infiltrating the deep fascia. Although peripheral eosinophilia is often associated with eosinophilic fasciitis, it is not invariably present. This patient has skin induration sparing the digits in the absence of Raynaud phenomenon, which is consistent with eosinophilic fasciitis.

Diabetic scleredema typically involves the skin of the upper torso and shoulder girdle and usually occurs in patients with long-standing insulin-requiring diabetes mellitus.

Diffuse cutaneous systemic sclerosis (dcSSc) is characterized by skin involvement proximal to the distal forearms and knees. Additionally, subcutaneous calcinosis occurs in patients with dcSSc but is a more common finding in patients with limited cutaneous systemic sclerosis. Raynaud phenomenon is the initial clinical manifestation in 70% of patients and eventually occurs in more than 95% of these patients, making dcSSc an unlikely diagnosis for this patient.

Gadolinium contrast administered for MRI studies is an established risk factor for nephrogenic systemic fibrosis (NSF), a condition that can also cause extremity induration that may spare the digits. Patients with an estimated glomerular filtration rate of less than 30 mL/min/1.73 m^2 are believed to be at the greatest risk for developing NSF after administration of gadolinium, and use of this agent should be avoided in this population group. This patient's normal kidney function and absence of gadolinium contrast exposure make NSF an unlikely diagnosis.

KEY POINT

- Eosinophilic fasciitis is characterized by woody induration of the extremities sparing the hands and face in the absence of Raynaud phenomenon.

Bibliography

Boin F, Hummers LK. Scleroderma-like fibrosing disorders. Rheum Dis Clin North Am. 2008;34(1):199-220. [PMID: 18329541]

Item 78   Answer: C

Educational Objective: Diagnose familial Mediterranean fever.

This 16-year-old male adolescent has familial Mediterranean fever (FMF), an autosomal recessive disorder characterized by recurrent 12- to 72-hour episodes of fever with serositis (most commonly abdominal or pleural), synovitis (most often monoarticular and affecting the lower extremities), and erysipeloid rash. Symptoms typically begin in childhood or adolescence; however, 10% of patients experience their first episode in adulthood. FMF is most prevalent in persons of Mediterranean ethnicity but is not restricted to this group. Laboratory studies are consistent with acute inflammation, and serology results for connective tissue and rheumatoid disease are negative. Proteinuria revealed on urinalysis may represent kidney amyloidosis, which can develop in untreated persons. Colchicine is standard therapy and reduces the likelihood of acute attacks and amyloidosis.

Adult-onset Still disease (AOSD) is characterized by fever, rash, and joint pain, and serositis (usually pleuritis or pericarditis) may occur. However, fever associated with AOSD is quotidian, lasts less than 4 hours, and peaks in the early evening; rash is evanescent, salmon-colored, not painful, and appears on the trunk and proximal extremities. Abdominal pain is rare. Finally, a markedly elevated serum ferritin level occurs in most patients with AOSD.

Patients with Crohn disease typically have progressive fatigue, prolonged diarrhea with abdominal pain, weight loss, and fever; extra-abdominal manifestations may include arthritis and skin rash (erythema nodosum or pyoderma gangrenosum). The brief episodic nature of this patient's abdominal and joint symptoms is unusual for Crohn disease, as is the fact that he is completely well between episodes.

Monoarticular arthritis of the lower extremities may occur in patients with reactive arthritis, but fever and abdominal pain are uncommon. Patients with this disorder may have a history of conjunctivitis, oral or genital ulcers, and/or inflammatory back pain. The brief duration of this patient's episodes, with complete resolution between attacks, is not typical of reactive arthritis.

KEY POINT

- **Familial Mediterranean fever is characterized by recurrent 12- to 72-hour episodes of fever with serositis, synovitis, and erysipeloid rash.**

Bibliography

Ben-Chetrit E, Touitou I. Familial Mediterranean fever in the world. Arthritis Rheum. 2009;61(10):1447-1453. [PMID: 19790133]

Item 79   Answer: E

Educational Objective: Manage intercritical gout and hyperuricemia.

Discontinuation of hydrochlorothiazide is indicated for this patient. He has early intercritical gout with hyperuricemia and a family history of gout. However, the limited number and frequency of his attacks (three attacks in 2 years) do not yet meet current guidelines for prophylactic treatment. He has hypertension and takes hydrochlorothiazide, a diuretic that raises serum uric acid levels and increases the risk of gout. Switching to a urate-neutral or urate-lowering antihypertensive agent such as lisinopril is appropriate in this patient.

This patient consumes significant amounts of low-fat dairy products; this type of diet promotes lower uric acid levels and should continue to be encouraged.

Although some leafy green vegetables are high in purines, these vegetables do not appear to raise serum urate levels; therefore, decreased intake of these vegetables is not warranted.

Although consumption of alcoholic beverages can raise serum urate levels, wine appears to be the least, and beer the most, potent alcoholic beverage in this regard. Drinking up to one glass of wine per day is not associated with elevated urate levels.

An increase in fruit intake is not a strategy to prevent gout attacks. Fruits are high in fructose, which is associated with increases in urate levels.

KEY POINT

- **Hydrochlorothiazide raises serum uric acid levels and increases the risk of gout in patients with hyperuricemia.**

Bibliography

Palmer BF, Naderi AS. Metabolic complications associated with use of thiazide diuretics. J Am Soc Hypertens. 2007;1(6):381-392. [PMID: 20409871]

Item 80   Answer: B

Educational Objective: Diagnose Henoch-Schönlein purpura.

This patient has clinical features most consistent with Henoch-Schönlein purpura, a syndrome that most commonly occurs in children but can affect adults with greater severity. Characteristic features are a purpuric rash predominantly affecting the distal lower extremities, arthritis, abdominal pain, and hematuria. Skin biopsy specimens reveal the presence of leukocytoclastic vasculitis with deposits of IgA. Kidney biopsies obtained in patients with persistent hematuria and proteinuria or kidney disease following an attack reveal a glomerulonephritis with IgA deposition consistent with lesions seen in IgA nephropathy. Kidney disease may be aggressive in some patients, with transition to diffuse proliferative glomerulonephritis. In men over the age of 50 years, Henoch-Schönlein purpura has been reported to occur in association with solid tumors or myelodysplastic syndrome. In this 62-year-old man, additional evaluation for underlying malignancy is indicated because of this greater prevalence of cancer, particularly gastrointestinal tumors.

Churg-Strauss syndrome is a vasculitis that typically occurs in the context of a history of asthma; common associated laboratory features include peripheral eosinophilia and the presence of p-ANCA.

Microscopic polyangiitis typically involves small arterioles and may be associated with a glomerulonephritis and purpuric skin lesions; however, immune deposits in the skin are not characteristic of this disorder, and most affected patients have positive ANCA.

Polyarteritis nodosa is a small- to medium-vessel vasculitis that may be associated with renal artery involvement and hypertension; purpura with immune deposits is not a characteristic cutaneous feature.

Subacute cutaneous lupus erythematosus presents as a maculopapular rash, most commonly appearing on the torso and proximal extremities. Antinuclear antibody test results may be negative, but antibodies to Anti-Ro/SSA are frequently present in such patients. Glomerulonephritis is not a complication seen in patients with this disorder.

KEY POINT

- Onset of Henoch-Schönlein purpura may occur in adults and can be associated with solid tumors or myelodysplastic syndrome.

Bibliography

Mitsui H, Shibagaki N, Kawamura T, Matsue H, Shimada S. A clinical study of Henoch-Schönlein Purpura associated with malignancy. J Eur Acad Dermatol Venereol. 2009;23(4):394-401. [PMID: 19207675]

Item 81   Answer: A
Educational Objective: Manage carpal tunnel syndrome.

Electromyography (EMG) and a nerve conduction study are indicated for this patient with probable carpal tunnel syndrome, the most common peripheral neuropathy. Symptoms include aching and paresthesias in the hand and forearm (particularly at night) and weakness of grip strength in advanced cases. On physical examination, there is loss of sensation in the median nerve territory (including the palmar surface of the first three fingers and the radial aspect of the fourth) and thenar atrophy. The Phalen and Tinel signs have limited ability to discriminate carpal tunnel syndrome from other causes of hand dysesthesia. An EMG and a nerve conduction study are useful when the diagnosis is uncertain, when a patient is not responding to therapy, or when surgery is under consideration. In this patient with forearm symptoms, other causes need to be excluded, including a more proximal nerve entrapment or cervical radiculopathy. Therefore, an EMG and nerve conduction study would evaluate the severity of a carpal tunnel diagnosis and exclude other possible diagnoses.

MRI of the wrist has been advocated by some as the imaging study to evaluate for carpal tunnel syndrome.

However, the diagnostic utility of MRI is unclear and is not recommended as a first management step.

Although NSAIDs are recommended and widely used as the initial drug therapy, there is no strong evidence that they are useful.

Carpal tunnel release surgery is indicated for severe carpal tunnel syndrome (by clinical or EMG evidence) but is not indicated in this patient pending confirmation of the diagnosis, categorization of its severity, and possibly pending response to more conservative intervention.

KEY POINT

- In patients with symptoms of suspected entrapment neuropathy, electromyography and a nerve conduction study are useful when the diagnosis is uncertain, when a patient is not responding to therapy, or when surgery is under consideration.

Bibliography

D'Arcy CA, McGee S. The rational clinical examination. Does this patient have carpal tunnel syndrome? [Erratum in: JAMA 2000;284(11):1384.] JAMA. 2000;283(23):3110-3117. [PMID: 1086530]

Item 82   Answer: D
Educational Objective: Manage contraception options for a woman with systemic lupus erythematosus.

The progesterone-containing intrauterine device is the most appropriate contraceptive option for this patient with systemic lupus erythematosus (SLE), the antiphospholipid syndrome, and osteoporosis. She is not a candidate for estrogen-containing hormonal contraceptives of any form, including oral, transdermal, or transvaginal, because of her increased risk of thrombosis associated with high-titer antiphospholipid antibodies. Antiphospholipid antibodies are found in 30% to 40% of patients with SLE and predispose patients to both arterial and venous thromboembolism. These antibodies also are associated with second- and third-trimester pregnancy losses involving multiple mechanisms, including placental thrombosis and placental insufficiency. Progesterone-only forms of hormonal contraception such as the progesterone-containing intrauterine device are appropriate for patients with high-titer antiphospholipid antibodies such as in this case. The progesterone-only pill is another option for this patient, but it is less effective and has a higher rate of side effects, including breakthrough bleeding.

Combination oral contraceptives had been avoided in all women with SLE owing to concern about flare but are now regarded as an effective contraceptive choice for some. The SELENA trial showed no increased risk of flare in stable antiphospholipid antibody–negative patients with SLE taking oral contraceptives. However, patients with SLE who have active disease, moderate- to high-titer antiphospholipid antibodies, history of thrombosis, or other contraindications to estrogen therapy should not receive combination hormonal contraceptive products.

Medroxyprogesterone acetate is given intramuscularly every 3 months; unlike the progesterone-containing intrauterine device and the oral daily progesterone-only pill, it inhibits ovulation and is not recommended for long-term use. Importantly, this agent is associated with a significant risk of osteoporosis and is relatively contraindicated for long-term contraceptive use in this patient who already has osteoporosis.

> **KEY POINT**
>
> - Estrogen-containing hormonal contraceptives are contraindicated in patients with antiphospholipid antibodies.

Bibliography

Culwell KR, Curtis KM, del Carmen Craviato M. Safety of contraceptive method use among women with systemic lupus erythematosus: a systematic review. Obstet Gynecol. 2009;114(2):341-353. [PMID: 19622996]

Item 83   Answer: A
Educational Objective: Diagnose Behçet disease.

This patient most likely has Behçet disease. Behçet disease is a rare systemic disorder characterized by vasculitis and involvement of multiple visceral organs. The most important diagnostic clues are intermittent mucous membrane ulcerations and ocular involvement. Gastrointestinal, pulmonary, musculoskeletal, and neurologic manifestations also may be present. This patient has a 2-year history of recurrent oral ulcerations, erythema nodosum, and arthritis and now presents with panuveitis, retinal vasculitis, and a pulmonary artery aneurysm, manifestations that are strongly suggestive of Behçet disease.

Patients with granulomatosis with polyangiitis (also known as Wegener granulomatosis) can present with uveitis, retinal vasculitis, arthritis, and oral ulcers, as seen in this patient. However, the vasculitis associated with granulomatosis with polyangiitis involves small, rather than large, blood vessels, and aneurysms are not seen. Patients with granulomatosis with polyangiitis often have a history of upper airway disease such as sinusitis or epistaxis and often have glomerulonephritis, none of which is present in this patient.

Although polyarteritis nodosa can result in arterial aneurysms, it typically affects medium-sized mesenteric and renal arteries rather than pulmonary arteries and commonly results in intestinal ischemia and renovascular hypertension. Oral ulcers, uveitis, and erythema nodosum typically do not occur.

Sarcoidosis can manifest as arthritis and uveitis, and rarely can be associated with a large-vessel vasculitis. Pulmonary artery aneurysms are not typical. Chest radiograph usually demonstrates hilar lymphadenopathy with or without parenchymal lung disease.

> **KEY POINT**
>
> - Behçet disease is characterized by oral and genital ulcers, ocular disease, and involvement of the dermatologic, articular, gastrointestinal, and nervous systems.

Bibliography

Calamia KT, Kaklamanis PG. Behçet's disease: recent advances in early diagnosis and effective treatment. Curr Rheumatol Rep. 2008;10(5):349-355. [PMID: 18817637]

Item 84   Answer: D
Educational Objective: Diagnose fungal arthritis.

Synovial biopsy is indicated for this patient with probable fungal arthritis. Fungal arthritis is rare, typically occurs in patients who are immunocompromised, and manifests as subacute monoarthritis. This patient has long-standing, indolent, chronic monoarticular arthritis; a history of diabetes mellitus; and recurrent skin breaks with likely soil exposure. In this setting, infection with a fungus, particularly *Sporothrix schenckii*, is the likely cause. *S. schenckii* is associated with plant litter and other organic materials. *S. schenckii* arthritis usually manifests as progressive joint pain, swelling, and loss of range of motion. The diagnosis of fungal arthritis requires a high degree of suspicion and is most commonly made by synovial biopsy and/or culture of joint fluid. Because joint fluid culture may take weeks, obtaining a synovial biopsy is appropriate at this time.

Alizarin red staining of synovial fluid is not done routinely but is theoretically helpful for identifying basic calcium phosphate (BCP) crystals, which are invisible under polarized light microscopy. However, the chronic nature of the patient's condition, along with his relatively young age and an absence of calcification seen on radiographs, makes a diagnosis of BCP arthritis unlikely.

Obtaining anti–streptolysin O antibody titers aids in the diagnosis of rheumatic fever; however, this patient lacks the systemic signs (such as cardiac and/or neurologic involvement) that warrant consideration of rheumatic fever.

MRI of the knee would help delineate the extent of the joint damage but would not provide insight into the nature of the infectious process.

> **KEY POINT**
>
> - Fungal arthritis is rare, typically occurs in patients who are immunocompromised, and manifests as subacute monoarthritis.

Bibliography

Appenzeller S, Amaral TN, Amstalden EM, et al. Sporothrix schenckii infection presented as monoarthritis: report of two cases and review of the literature. Clin Rheumatol. 2006;25(6):926-928. [PMID: 16333559]

Item 85   Answer: D

Educational Objective: Manage fibromyalgia in a patient without depression.

Treatment with a serotonin and norepinephrine reuptake inhibitor (SNRI) is appropriate for this patient with fibromyalgia. Fibromyalgia is characterized by widespread pain and tenderness of at least 3 months' duration. Other manifestations include fatigue, sleep disturbance, mood disorder, and cognitive dysfunction. Nonpharmacologic therapy is the cornerstone of fibromyalgia treatment and should be initiated in all affected patients. Regular aerobic exercise has been shown to be effective in this setting. High-impact aerobic exercises frequently are poorly tolerated, whereas walking and/or water aerobics are better tolerated. Cognitive behavioral therapy has been shown to be beneficial but is not always covered by insurance plans. This patient has a 1-year history of widespread pain and tenderness along with fatigue and difficulty sleeping, features consistent with fibromyalgia. She tried pregabalin, which was discontinued because of an allergic reaction; therefore, treatment with an SNRI is warranted. Duloxetine and milnacipran are SNRIs approved by the FDA to treat fibromyalgia with or without mood disorder and are similarly as effective as pregabalin.

Fibromyalgia is not an inflammatory condition and does not respond to corticosteroids or NSAIDs. Use of anti-inflammatory medications is not only ineffective, but in the case of corticosteroids, exposes the patient to possible serious side effects. NSAIDs can help control pain caused by conditions such as osteoarthritis but are not effective as monotherapy for fibromyalgia symptoms; however, NSAIDs can be useful when combined with centrally acting drugs such as duloxetine or milnacipran in patients with resistant symptoms. This patient does not have evidence of another source of pain that requires treatment with NSAIDs and has not yet had a trial of a centrally acting medication.

Data on the use of selective serotonin reuptake inhibitors in fibromyalgia are conflicting, and none are currently FDA approved for this condition. Neurotransmitters other than serotonin may be important in fibromyalgia.

KEY POINT

- The serotonin and norepinephrine reuptake inhibitors duloxetine and milnacipran are FDA approved to treat patients who have fibromyalgia with or without depression.

Bibliography

Russell IJ, Mease PJ, Smith TR, et al. Efficacy and safety of duloxetine for treatment of fibromyalgia in patients with or without major depressive disorder: results from a 6-month, randomized,

double-blind, placebo-controlled, fixed-dose trial. Pain. 2008;136(3):432-444. [PMID 18395345]

Item 86   Answer: D

Educational Objective: Treat a patient with prosthetic joint infection.

This patient has a prosthetic knee joint infection caused by methicillin-sensitive *Staphylococcus aureus* and requires surgical removal of the prosthesis. Prosthetic joints may become infected late after implantation (>3 months to years) via hematogenous spread of organisms or a delayed response to low-intensity pathogens. The joint may be swollen and inflamed or only painful. Leukocyte counts may be only modestly elevated; erythrocyte sedimentation rate (ESR) and C-reactive protein (CRP) levels are usually elevated. Radiographs may reveal erosion or loosening around the implantation site. Diagnosis requires synovial fluid aspiration or open debridement, along with Gram stain and cultures. Treatment of prosthetic joint infection typically involves removal of the infected prosthesis.

This patient's findings, including joint pain and elevated leukocyte count, ESR, and CRP level, along with positive synovial fluid cultures, prosthetic loosening, and periprosthetic bone erosion, are consistent with prosthetic joint infection. Antibiotic use may be reasonable (and in infections occurring early after implantation, may be sufficient); however, this patient has already not responded to antibiotic treatment and therefore requires removal of the prosthetic knee joint. After removal, an antibiotic spacer is inserted, and long-term (weeks to months) antibiotic therapy is initiated. Only after complete resolution of the infection can reimplantation be considered.

Diclofenac is a potentially useful therapy for joint pain but does not address the prosthetic joint infection.

Some evidence suggests that rifampin may improve outcomes in patients with methicillin-sensitive *S. aureus* prosthetic joint infection who undergo early extensive surgical debridement; however, this patient did not undergo debridement, and there is no indication for use of rifampin in this patient.

Intravenous vancomycin is useful for infection with methicillin-resistant *S. aureus*; however, this patient's infection should be sensitive to nafcillin or oxacillin along with joint removal, and no additional benefit from vancomycin would be expected.

KEY POINT

- Treatment of delayed-onset prosthetic joint infection typically involves removal of the infected prosthesis.

Bibliography

Del Pozo JL, Patel R. Clinical practice. Infection associated with prosthetic joints. N Engl J Med. 2009;361(8):787-794. [PMID: 19692690]

Item 87   Answer: A

Educational Objective: Diagnose adult-onset Still disease.

This patient most likely has adult-onset Still disease (AOSD), a systemic inflammatory disorder characterized by quotidian fever, evanescent rash, arthritis, and multisystem involvement. Diagnosis is based on typical clinical presentation with exclusion of infection and malignancy, particularly leukemia and lymphoma. Laboratory abnormalities in patients with AOSD include leukocytosis, anemia, thrombocytosis, elevated erythrocyte sedimentation rate, elevated serum ferritin level (≥1000 ng/mL [1000 µg/L]), and abnormal liver chemistry tests; antinuclear antibodies and rheumatoid factor typically are negative. This patient has the typical fever, rash, arthralgia, anemia, leukocytosis, thrombocytosis, and markedly elevated serum ferritin level that are classic for AOSD.

Lymphadenopathy and fever may suggest lymphoma; however, the constellation of other signs and symptoms in this patient, as well as the negative bone marrow biopsy results, suggests AOSD. Further, elevated ferritin levels are not associated with lymphoma or leukemia.

Patients with parvovirus B19 infection have arthritis and rash lasting days to weeks, often after flu-like illness. Spiking fevers, lymphadenopathy, and an elevated leukocyte count and ferritin level are not associated findings.

Fever, arthritis, and lymphadenopathy occur in patients with systemic lupus erythematosus (SLE), but the presence of elevated (rather than decreased) leukocyte and platelet counts and the markedly elevated ferritin level point toward AOSD. An evanescent, salmon-colored rash also is not associated with SLE.

KEY POINT

- Adult-onset Still disease is a systemic inflammatory disorder characterized by quotidian fever, evanescent salmon-colored rash, arthritis, multisystem involvement, and markedly elevated ferritin levels.

Bibliography

Efthimiou P, Paik PK, Bielory L. Diagnosis and management of adult onset Still's disease. Ann Rheum Dis. 2006;65(5):564-572. [PMID: 16219707]

Item 88   Answer: E

Educational Objective: Manage anemia in a patient with systemic sclerosis.

An upper endoscopy is appropriate for this patient with diffuse cutaneous systemic sclerosis (dcSSc). Significant iron deficiency due to gastrointestinal blood loss may develop as a consequence of gastric antral venous ectasia (GAVE) in patients with systemic sclerosis. This possibility should be considered in patients with dcSSc who have increasing fatigue or dyspnea and/or evidence of iron deficiency anemia. Upper endoscopy can be performed to establish the diagnosis of GAVE; the condition can be effectively managed with one or more treatments with laser/photocoagulation.

Erythropoietin may be required to maintain optimal hemoglobin levels in patients with chronic kidney disease. Erythropoietin should not be started until iron status and other causes of anemia have been evaluated and is therefore not indicated in this patient.

Although a bone marrow biopsy can confirm low iron stores, this would add little additional information to the low serum ferritin level and microscopic erythrocyte indices, and is not indicated in the absence of other cytopenias.

Colonoscopy would be an appropriate initial diagnostic test in an older patient at increased risk for colorectal cancer or any patient with altered bowel movements and iron deficiency anemia and may be necessary in this patient if upper endoscopy does not reveal a source of blood loss. However, in this young person with systemic sclerosis, the upper gastrointestinal tract is the most likely source of blood loss and iron deficiency anemia.

A hydrogen breath test is a noninvasive test used to diagnose bacterial overgrowth as a cause of malabsorption. Bacterial overgrowth due to dysfunctional motility may cause chronic diarrhea, alternating diarrhea and constipation, and/or malabsorption. Manifestations of bacterial overgrowth include bloating, abdominal pain, and steatorrhea. This patient has no symptoms to suggest malabsorption, and malabsorption of iron is a relatively uncommon cause of iron deficiency.

KEY POINT

- Iron deficiency due to gastrointestinal blood loss may develop as a consequence of gastric antral venous ectasia in patients with systemic sclerosis.

Bibliography

Ingraham KM, O'Brien MS, Shenin M, Derk CT, Steen VD. Gastric antral vascular ectasia in systemic sclerosis: demographics and disease predictors. J Rheumatol. 2010;37(3):603-607. [PMID: 20080908]

Item 89   Answer: E

Educational Objective: Manage chondrocalcinosis.

No treatment is necessary for this patient with asymptomatic chondrocalcinosis, a manifestation of calcium pyrophosphate (CPP) deposition disease. CPP crystals can deposit directly within cartilage (chondrocalcinosis) or may be released into the joint, stimulating joint space inflammation (acute pseudogout). CPP deposits within the cartilage typically are linear and parallel to the cartilage surface and are commonly located at the cartilaginous structures of the knee and wrist. Hypophosphatasia, hypomagnesemia, hypothyroidism, hemochromatosis, and hyperparathyroidism may be associated with CPP deposition disease;

screening is typically indicated, along with appropriate therapy for any underlying conditions.

Treatment using NSAIDs, corticosteroids, or colchicine is directed toward suppressing inflammation. However, this patient has asymptomatic chondrocalcinosis, which was detected incidentally on radiography; treatment is not warranted because inflammation is not present; possible predisposing causes and associations have been ruled out (hypomagnesemia, hypothyroidism, and hyperparathyroidism); and, at present, there is no way to directly alter the deposition process.

Studies have generally shown that intra-articular hyaluronan injection has comparable efficacy to NSAID therapy in patients with knee osteoarthritis. Hyaluronan levels in the synovial fluid are decreased in patients with osteoarthritis, but the mechanism of action of hyaluronan agents in this setting remains unclear. There is no known benefit in treating patients with asymptomatic CPP deposition disease with hyaluronan injection therapy.

KEY POINT

- Chondrocalcinosis is an asymptomatic condition; in the absence of inflammation or joint destruction, no treatment is necessary.

Bibliography

Rosenthal AK. Update in calcium deposition diseases. Curr Opin Rheumatol. 2007;19(2):158-162. [PMID: 17278931]

Item 90   Answer: A

Educational Objective: Diagnose the antiphospholipid syndrome.

This patient most likely has the antiphospholipid syndrome. Criteria for diagnosis include the presence of a positive lupus anticoagulant, moderate- to high-titer anticardiolipin antibodies, or moderate- to high-titer anti-β2-glycoprotein I antibodies in the setting of arterial thrombosis, vascular thrombosis, pregnancy loss, or specific pregnancy complications. Thrombocytopenia, valvular heart disease, livedo reticularis, and microangiopathic kidney insufficiency frequently are associated, nondiagnostic findings. The antiphospholipid syndrome may be primary or secondary to another connective tissue disease, typically systemic lupus erythematosus.

This patient has symptoms and findings strongly suggestive of the antiphospholipid syndrome, including thrombocytopenia; history of recurrent pregnancy loss; livedo reticularis; a murmur consistent with mitral regurgitation; and elevated serum creatinine level, proteinuria, and noninflammatory urine sediment suggestive of microangiopathic kidney insufficiency. While not conclusive, this patient's elevated activated partial thromboplastin time suggests a possible presence of a lupus anticoagulant (which requires further testing). She has migraines and Raynaud phenomenon, both of which also may be associated with the antiphospholipid syndrome.

Although this patient has thrombocytopenia and easy bruising, immune thrombocytopenic purpura is an unlikely diagnosis, because it does not explain the presence of her other symptoms and findings.

Myelodysplastic syndrome is a possible diagnosis for unexplained cytopenia, although it is more common in older persons and typically involves more than one cell line. If this patient had both negative antiphospholipid antibodies and negative lupus serologies, then hematologic evaluation with bone marrow aspiration and biopsy would be an appropriate next step.

This patient does not have the typical inflammatory symptoms such as rash (malar, discoid, or photosensitive), fever, arthritis, and pleuropericarditis that are associated with systemic lupus erythematosus, making this a less likely diagnosis.

KEY POINT

- Criteria for the diagnosis of the antiphospholipid syndrome include the presence of a positive lupus anticoagulant, moderate- to high-titer anticardiolipin antibodies, or moderate- to high-titer anti-β2-glycoprotein I antibodies in the setting of arterial thrombosis, vascular thrombosis, pregnancy loss, or specific pregnancy complications.

Bibliography

Palomo I, Segovia F, Ortega C, Pierangeli S. Antiphospholipid syndrome: a comprehensive review of a complex and multisystemic disease. Clin Exp Rheumatol. 2009;27(4):668-677. [PMID: 19772805]

Item 91   Answer: C

Educational Objective: Evaluate anterior uveitis.

A chest radiograph is warranted in this patient with anterior uveitis. Patients with anterior uveitis present with the abrupt onset of eye pain and redness. The redness is typically adjacent and circumferential to the iris. Patients may have photophobia, tearing, decreased vision, and headache. As the inflammation involves the iris and ciliary body, patients may have an irregular pupil. Uveitis requires urgent ophthalmologic consultation. Rheumatic diseases associated with uveitis include spondyloarthritis, sarcoidosis, Behçet disease, juvenile inflammatory arthritis, and granulomatosis with polyangiitis (also known as Wegener granulomatosis). In some patients, uveitis is the presenting manifestation of their disease. In patients with isolated anterior uveitis of unknown cause, most experts obtain a chest radiograph as the first diagnostic test to evaluate for the presence of sarcoidosis. In one cohort of more than 1000 patients, eye inflammation was the initial manifestation of sarcoidosis in 21% of patients, and of those, 76% had anterior uveitis. Other diagnostic tests that may be helpful include HLA-B27 (found in patients with spondyloarthritis), ANCA (seen in granulomatosis with polyangiitis and other ANCA-associated vasculitides), and a rapid plasma reagin test (to rule out syphilis). Posterior uveitis involves inflammation of the choroid and/or retina. Differential diagnosis of posterior uveitis includes sarcoidosis, tuberculosis, and histoplasmosis. Syphilis and Lyme disease can also cause posterior uveitis.

Anti–double-stranded DNA antibodies are specific for systemic lupus erythematosus, which can be associated with retinal vasculitis. Anti-Ro/SSA antibodies can be present in patients with Sjögren syndrome, a disorder associated with dry eyes that may lead to corneal ulceration. The presence of rheumatoid factor is associated with rheumatoid arthritis, which can be associated with dry eyes, episcleritis, and scleritis. However, these rheumatic conditions are not associated with uveitis.

KEY POINT

- In patients with isolated anterior uveitis of unknown cause, a chest radiograph is recommended to evaluate for the presence of sarcoidosis.

Bibliography

Heiligenhaus A, Wefelmeyer D, Wefelmeyer E, Rösel M, Schrenk M. The eye as a common site for the early clinical manifestation of sarcoidosis. Ophthalmic Res. 2010;46(1):9-12. [PMID: 21099232]

Item 92   Answer: C

Educational Objective: Treat a patient with acute pseudogout.

Administration of intra-articular triamcinolone is appropriate for this patient. She has intra-articular, intracellular, and extracellular positively birefringent rhomboid-shaped (calcium pyrophosphate) crystals, which are consistent with a diagnosis of acute pseudogout. The presence of linear calcium deposits in the cartilage (chondrocalcinosis), although neither proving nor disproving the current diagnosis, also supports the diagnosis of calcium pyrophosphate deposition disease. Treatment is directed exclusively toward relieving the inflammation and is tailored to the individual patient. This patient's diabetes mellitus, chronic kidney disease, and history of peptic ulcer disease make local therapy with an intra-articular corticosteroid the most desirable option.

Oral allopurinol is a urate-lowering strategy for patients with established gout. Because urate does not play a role in pseudogout, allopurinol is not indicated in the treatment of this patient.

NSAIDs such as ibuprofen can be useful for managing an acute attack of pseudogout; however, this patient has numerous comorbid illnesses, all of which may be exacerbated by NSAIDs.

Intravenous vancomycin is appropriate for patients in whom infection with gram-positive organisms is likely and may be administered empirically pending culture results. This patient's established pseudogout diagnosis, along with

a negative Gram stain and a moderately low (but nonetheless inflammatory) synovial fluid leukocyte count ($<50,000/\mu L$ [$50 \times 10^9/L$]) make an infection unlikely.

Administration of a tapering dose of prednisone could be effective in treating this patient's pseudogout attack but would be undesirable owing to her diabetes.

KEY POINT

- Treatment of a patient with acute pseudogout is directed exclusively toward relieving the inflammation using NSAIDs, intra-articular or systemic corticosteroids, or colchicine.

Bibliography

Announ N, Guerne PA. Treating difficult crystal pyrophosphate dihydrate deposition disease. Curr Rheumatol Rep. 2008;10(3):228-234. [PMID: 18638432]

Item 93   Answer: B

Educational Objective: Diagnose alveolitis in a patient with diffuse cutaneous systemic sclerosis.

A high-resolution CT of the chest is indicated for this patient with diffuse cutaneous systemic sclerosis (dcSSc). Lung involvement due to interstitial lung disease (ILD) or pulmonary arterial hypertension is the primary cause of morbidity and mortality in patients with systemic sclerosis. A low D_{LCO} and a restrictive pattern on pulmonary function testing are highly suggestive of ILD with or without alveolitis. ILD most commonly occurs in patients with dcSSc, and those with positive anti-topoisomerase I (anti-Scl-70) antibodies have the highest risk for developing ILD. Alveolitis may precede ILD; presenting manifestations include dyspnea, nonproductive cough, and exercise intolerance. Therefore, high-resolution CT of the chest is appropriate for this patient to evaluate for alveolitis or early ILD, findings which may not be apparent on chest radiographs.

Pulmonary emboli could account for the attenuation in measured D_{LCO} in this patient. However, he has no risk factors for thrombosis, and his echocardiogram does not suggest the presence of right heart strain; as such, pulmonary emboli cannot explain the restrictive pattern on pulmonary function testing. CT angiography of the chest is therefore not appropriate at this time.

Although patients with long-standing systemic sclerosis are at risk for coronary ischemia due to coronary microangiopathy, a radionuclide exercise stress test is not indicated for this patient who has relatively recent onset of disease and no other coronary risk factors or symptoms of angina.

A right heart catheterization would be indicated if pulmonary function tests were normal and there was evidence of pulmonary hypertension on physical examination (loud pulmonic component of S_2, fixed splitting of the S_2, jugular venous distention) or echocardiogram.

KEY POINT

- Patients with diffuse cutaneous systemic sclerosis and positive anti-topoisomerase I (anti–Scl-70) antibodies have the highest risk for developing interstitial lung disease.

Bibliography

Gabrielli A, Avvedimento EV, Krieg T. Scleroderma. N Engl J Med. 2009;360(19):1989-2003. [PMID: 19420368]

Item 94   Answer: D

Educational Objective: Recognize the risk factors for rheumatoid arthritis.

Smoking is associated with an increased risk of developing rheumatoid arthritis, and cessation is recommended for this and other health reasons. Heritable factors convey susceptibility for developing rheumatoid arthritis. Environmental factors seem to modify this risk. Duration and intensity of smoking correlate with this risk. Users of smokeless tobacco do not have an increased risk of developing rheumatoid arthritis, suggesting it is not simply an effect of nicotine. Smoking cessation is associated with a decline in the risk of developing rheumatoid arthritis, although this benefit is not immediate.

Alcohol use is not associated with an increased risk of rheumatoid arthritis. The patient may be advised to moderate her consumption of alcohol, but it will not alter her risk of developing rheumatoid arthritis.

Hormonal factors may play a role. The risk of developing rheumatoid arthritis is higher in women, but lower in women who have had children. Breastfeeding is associated with a decreased risk of developing rheumatoid arthritis and may account for some or all of the protective effect of parity. The risk of rheumatoid arthritis is inversely associated with duration of lifetime breastfeeding. In one study, use of oral contraceptive pills for 7 or more years was associated with a decreased risk of rheumatoid arthritis. Discontinuing oral contraceptives in this patient may be associated with increased risk or no change in her risk but not a decreased risk.

Obesity and sedentary lifestyle are associated with a number of health risks but have not been clearly linked to the development of rheumatoid arthritis. In patients with rheumatoid arthritis, range of motion exercises help preserve joint motion; in patients with osteoarthritis, aerobic exercise helps maintain muscle strength, joint stability, and physical performance, and weight reduction reduces joint stress on weight-bearing joints.

KEY POINT

- Smoking is associated with an increased risk of developing rheumatoid arthritis, and cessation is recommended for this and other health reasons.

Bibliography

Costenbader KH, Feskanich D, Mandl LA, Karlson EW. Smoking intensity, duration and cessation, and the risk of rheumatoid arthritis in women. Am J Med. 2006;119(6):503.e1-e9. [PMID: 16750964]

Item 95   Answer: C

Educational Objective: Evaluate a patient with a suspected osteoporotic fracture.

CT of the thoracic spine is indicated for this patient. Patients with systemic lupus erythematosus (SLE) are at an increased risk for osteoporosis and related fracture. Osteoporosis occurs in up to 25% of patients with SLE and is related to corticosteroid use, lupus disease activity, decreased physical activity, and avoidance of the sun. Women with SLE report five times as many fractures as age-matched controls, with half occurring before menopause. This patient has acute-onset mid back pain that is central, nonradiating, and constant, and the plain radiograph is negative for fracture. Initial radiographs may not show acute compression fractures; therefore, CT of the thoracic spine is appropriate to identify compression fractures.

Cyclobenzaprine may be useful in treating symptoms of acute mechanical low back pain; however, this agent causes sedation and an increased risk of dependence. Oral analgesic medications such as acetaminophen or NSAIDs are first-line therapy for patients with acute osteoporotic vertebral fracture. There is some evidence that calcitonin may provide more rapid relief of pain from vertebral fractures in patients not responding to simple analgesia.

Patients should be advised to stay active and continue normal activities if possible; enforced bed rest is not an effective treatment plan and may actually lengthen disability.

Physical therapy may be recommended, but at a later point, after both the confirmation of osteoporotic fracture and adequate pain control. Longer-term exercise should be encouraged, as it may have beneficial effects on bone mineral density.

KEY POINT

- CT of the thoracic spine is indicated for patients at increased risk for osteoporotic vertebral fracture who have negative plain radiographs.

Bibliography

Mendoza-Pinto C, Garcia-Carrasco M, Sandoval-Cruz H, et al. Risk factors of vertebral fractures in women with systemic lupus erythematosus. Clin Rheumatol. 2009;28(5):579-585. [PMID: 19224131]

Item 96   Answer: B

Educational Objective: Diagnose Kawasaki disease.

This patient most likely has Kawasaki disease. Although most commonly seen in young children, Kawasaki disease may occur in adults, in particular those with HIV infection such as this patient. His initial findings, including fever with nonexudative conjunctivitis, pleomorphic erythematous rash, and oral mucositis, are consistent with this disorder. Other

CONT.

clinical features include cervical lymphadenopathy and an oligoarticular or polyarticular inflammatory arthritis. Laboratory abnormalities include anemia, leukocytosis, thrombocytosis, and sterile pyuria. As the disease evolves, the rash desquamates, initially in the periungual areas and then proximally over the hands and feet. Recognition of the typical features associated with Kawasaki disease is important to prevent possible coronary artery complications. The preferred initial treatment is administration of intravenous immune globulin, and salicylates are used to manage associated articular symptoms. Moderate doses of corticosteroids can be used for patients with more severe constitutional symptoms who are unresponsive to intravenous immune globulin and salicylates.

Although pyuria and arthralgia can occur with gonococcal infection, the skin lesions associated with disseminated infection are typically papular with central pustules and not a desquamating distal rash as seen in this patient.

Patients with HIV infection may develop severe variants of psoriasis and psoriatic arthritis. However, this patient's skin lesions are not the papular or pustular lesions associated with psoriasis.

Toxic shock syndrome (TSS) is an infrequent, but life-threatening, infection in which bacterial toxins are produced and lead to septic shock. Patients are febrile, hypotensive, have a diffuse malar rash with subsequent desquamation, and have at least three of the following manifestations: nausea, vomiting, or diarrhea; severe myalgia or elevated serum creatine kinase level; hyperemia of the vagina, conjunctiva, or pharynx; acute kidney injury; acute liver injury; thrombocytopenia; or disorientation without focal findings. This patient does not meet the diagnostic criteria for TSS.

KEY POINT

- **Although most commonly seen in young children, Kawasaki disease may occur in adults, in particular in those with HIV infection.**

Bibliography
Sève P, Stankovic K, Smail A, Durand DV, Marchand G, Broussolle C. Adult Kawasaki disease: report of two cases and literature review. Semin Arthritis Rheum. 2005;34:785-792. [PMID: 15942913]

Index

A — NAME AND ADDRESS (Please complete.)

Last Name _____ First Name _____ Middle Initial _____

Address _____

Address cont. _____

City _____ State _____ ZIP Code _____

Country _____

Email address _____

ACP
AMERICAN COLLEGE OF PHYSICIANS
INTERNAL MEDICINE | Doctors for Adults

Medical Knowledge
Self-Assessment
Program® 16

TO EARN *AMA PRA CATEGORY 1 CREDITS™* YOU MUST:

1. Answer all questions.
2. Score a minimum of 50% correct.

==

TO EARN *FREE* SAME-DAY *AMA PRA CATEGORY 1 CREDITS™* ONLINE:

1. Answer all of your questions.
2. Go to **mksap.acponline.org** and access the appropriate answer sheet.
3. Transcribe your answers and submit for CME credits.
4. You can also enter your answers directly at **mksap.acponline.org** without first using this answer sheet.

To Submit Your Answer Sheet by Mail or FAX for a $10 Administrative Fee per Answer Sheet:

1. Answer all of your questions and calculate your score.
2. Complete boxes A–F.
3. Complete payment information.
4. Send the answer sheet and payment information to ACP, using the FAX number/address listed below.

B — Order Number

(Use the Order Number on your MKSAP materials packing slip.)

C — ACP ID Number

(Refer to packing slip in your MKSAP materials for your ACP ID Number.)

COMPLETE FORM BELOW ONLY IF YOU SUBMIT BY MAIL OR FAX

Last Name _____ First Name _____ MI ___

Payment Information. Must remit in US funds, drawn on a US bank.

The processing fee for each paper answer sheet is $10.

☐ Check, made payable to ACP, enclosed

Charge to ☐ **VISA**   ☐ **MasterCard**   ☐ **AMERICAN EXPRESS**   ☐ **DISCOVER**

Card Number _____

Expiration Date _____ / _____   Security code (3 or 4 digit #s) _____
MM   YY

Signature _____

Fax to: 215-351-2799

Questions?
Go to **mskap.acponline.org** or email **custserv@acponline.org**

Mail to:
Member and Customer Service
American College of Physicians
190 N. Independence Mall West
Philadelphia, PA 19106-1572

1 Ⓐ Ⓑ Ⓒ Ⓓ Ⓔ
2 Ⓐ Ⓑ Ⓒ Ⓓ Ⓔ
3 Ⓐ Ⓑ Ⓒ Ⓓ Ⓔ
4 Ⓐ Ⓑ Ⓒ Ⓓ Ⓔ
5 Ⓐ Ⓑ Ⓒ Ⓓ Ⓔ

6 Ⓐ Ⓑ Ⓒ Ⓓ Ⓔ
7 Ⓐ Ⓑ Ⓒ Ⓓ Ⓔ
8 Ⓐ Ⓑ Ⓒ Ⓓ Ⓔ
9 Ⓐ Ⓑ Ⓒ Ⓓ Ⓔ
10 Ⓐ Ⓑ Ⓒ Ⓓ Ⓔ

11 Ⓐ Ⓑ Ⓒ Ⓓ Ⓔ
12 Ⓐ Ⓑ Ⓒ Ⓓ Ⓔ
13 Ⓐ Ⓑ Ⓒ Ⓓ Ⓔ
14 Ⓐ Ⓑ Ⓒ Ⓓ Ⓔ
15 Ⓐ Ⓑ Ⓒ Ⓓ Ⓔ

16 Ⓐ Ⓑ Ⓒ Ⓓ Ⓔ
17 Ⓐ Ⓑ Ⓒ Ⓓ Ⓔ
18 Ⓐ Ⓑ Ⓒ Ⓓ Ⓔ
19 Ⓐ Ⓑ Ⓒ Ⓓ Ⓔ
20 Ⓐ Ⓑ Ⓒ Ⓓ Ⓔ

21 Ⓐ Ⓑ Ⓒ Ⓓ Ⓔ
22 Ⓐ Ⓑ Ⓒ Ⓓ Ⓔ
23 Ⓐ Ⓑ Ⓒ Ⓓ Ⓔ
24 Ⓐ Ⓑ Ⓒ Ⓓ Ⓔ
25 Ⓐ Ⓑ Ⓒ Ⓓ Ⓔ

26 Ⓐ Ⓑ Ⓒ Ⓓ Ⓔ
27 Ⓐ Ⓑ Ⓒ Ⓓ Ⓔ
28 Ⓐ Ⓑ Ⓒ Ⓓ Ⓔ
29 Ⓐ Ⓑ Ⓒ Ⓓ Ⓔ
30 Ⓐ Ⓑ Ⓒ Ⓓ Ⓔ

31 Ⓐ Ⓑ Ⓒ Ⓓ Ⓔ
32 Ⓐ Ⓑ Ⓒ Ⓓ Ⓔ
33 Ⓐ Ⓑ Ⓒ Ⓓ Ⓔ
34 Ⓐ Ⓑ Ⓒ Ⓓ Ⓔ
35 Ⓐ Ⓑ Ⓒ Ⓓ Ⓔ

36 Ⓐ Ⓑ Ⓒ Ⓓ Ⓔ
37 Ⓐ Ⓑ Ⓒ Ⓓ Ⓔ
38 Ⓐ Ⓑ Ⓒ Ⓓ Ⓔ
39 Ⓐ Ⓑ Ⓒ Ⓓ Ⓔ
40 Ⓐ Ⓑ Ⓒ Ⓓ Ⓔ

41 Ⓐ Ⓑ Ⓒ Ⓓ Ⓔ
42 Ⓐ Ⓑ Ⓒ Ⓓ Ⓔ
43 Ⓐ Ⓑ Ⓒ Ⓓ Ⓔ
44 Ⓐ Ⓑ Ⓒ Ⓓ Ⓔ
45 Ⓐ Ⓑ Ⓒ Ⓓ Ⓔ

46 Ⓐ Ⓑ Ⓒ Ⓓ Ⓔ
47 Ⓐ Ⓑ Ⓒ Ⓓ Ⓔ
48 Ⓐ Ⓑ Ⓒ Ⓓ Ⓔ
49 Ⓐ Ⓑ Ⓒ Ⓓ Ⓔ
50 Ⓐ Ⓑ Ⓒ Ⓓ Ⓔ

51 Ⓐ Ⓑ Ⓒ Ⓓ Ⓔ
52 Ⓐ Ⓑ Ⓒ Ⓓ Ⓔ
53 Ⓐ Ⓑ Ⓒ Ⓓ Ⓔ
54 Ⓐ Ⓑ Ⓒ Ⓓ Ⓔ
55 Ⓐ Ⓑ Ⓒ Ⓓ Ⓔ

56 Ⓐ Ⓑ Ⓒ Ⓓ Ⓔ
57 Ⓐ Ⓑ Ⓒ Ⓓ Ⓔ
58 Ⓐ Ⓑ Ⓒ Ⓓ Ⓔ
59 Ⓐ Ⓑ Ⓒ Ⓓ Ⓔ
60 Ⓐ Ⓑ Ⓒ Ⓓ Ⓔ

61 Ⓐ Ⓑ Ⓒ Ⓓ Ⓔ
62 Ⓐ Ⓑ Ⓒ Ⓓ Ⓔ
63 Ⓐ Ⓑ Ⓒ Ⓓ Ⓔ
64 Ⓐ Ⓑ Ⓒ Ⓓ Ⓔ
65 Ⓐ Ⓑ Ⓒ Ⓓ Ⓔ

66 Ⓐ Ⓑ Ⓒ Ⓓ Ⓔ
67 Ⓐ Ⓑ Ⓒ Ⓓ Ⓔ
68 Ⓐ Ⓑ Ⓒ Ⓓ Ⓔ
69 Ⓐ Ⓑ Ⓒ Ⓓ Ⓔ
70 Ⓐ Ⓑ Ⓒ Ⓓ Ⓔ

71 Ⓐ Ⓑ Ⓒ Ⓓ Ⓔ
72 Ⓐ Ⓑ Ⓒ Ⓓ Ⓔ
73 Ⓐ Ⓑ Ⓒ Ⓓ Ⓔ
74 Ⓐ Ⓑ Ⓒ Ⓓ Ⓔ
75 Ⓐ Ⓑ Ⓒ Ⓓ Ⓔ

76 Ⓐ Ⓑ Ⓒ Ⓓ Ⓔ
77 Ⓐ Ⓑ Ⓒ Ⓓ Ⓔ
78 Ⓐ Ⓑ Ⓒ Ⓓ Ⓔ
79 Ⓐ Ⓑ Ⓒ Ⓓ Ⓔ
80 Ⓐ Ⓑ Ⓒ Ⓓ Ⓔ

81 Ⓐ Ⓑ Ⓒ Ⓓ Ⓔ
82 Ⓐ Ⓑ Ⓒ Ⓓ Ⓔ
83 Ⓐ Ⓑ Ⓒ Ⓓ Ⓔ
84 Ⓐ Ⓑ Ⓒ Ⓓ Ⓔ
85 Ⓐ Ⓑ Ⓒ Ⓓ Ⓔ

86 Ⓐ Ⓑ Ⓒ Ⓓ Ⓔ
87 Ⓐ Ⓑ Ⓒ Ⓓ Ⓔ
88 Ⓐ Ⓑ Ⓒ Ⓓ Ⓔ
89 Ⓐ Ⓑ Ⓒ Ⓓ Ⓔ
90 Ⓐ Ⓑ Ⓒ Ⓓ Ⓔ

91 Ⓐ Ⓑ Ⓒ Ⓓ Ⓔ
92 Ⓐ Ⓑ Ⓒ Ⓓ Ⓔ
93 Ⓐ Ⓑ Ⓒ Ⓓ Ⓔ
94 Ⓐ Ⓑ Ⓒ Ⓓ Ⓔ
95 Ⓐ Ⓑ Ⓒ Ⓓ Ⓔ

96 Ⓐ Ⓑ Ⓒ Ⓓ Ⓔ
97 Ⓐ Ⓑ Ⓒ Ⓓ Ⓔ
98 Ⓐ Ⓑ Ⓒ Ⓓ Ⓔ
99 Ⓐ Ⓑ Ⓒ Ⓓ Ⓔ
100 Ⓐ Ⓑ Ⓒ Ⓓ Ⓔ

101 Ⓐ Ⓑ Ⓒ Ⓓ Ⓔ
102 Ⓐ Ⓑ Ⓒ Ⓓ Ⓔ
103 Ⓐ Ⓑ Ⓒ Ⓓ Ⓔ
104 Ⓐ Ⓑ Ⓒ Ⓓ Ⓔ
105 Ⓐ Ⓑ Ⓒ Ⓓ Ⓔ

106 Ⓐ Ⓑ Ⓒ Ⓓ Ⓔ
107 Ⓐ Ⓑ Ⓒ Ⓓ Ⓔ
108 Ⓐ Ⓑ Ⓒ Ⓓ Ⓔ
109 Ⓐ Ⓑ Ⓒ Ⓓ Ⓔ
110 Ⓐ Ⓑ Ⓒ Ⓓ Ⓔ

111 Ⓐ Ⓑ Ⓒ Ⓓ Ⓔ
112 Ⓐ Ⓑ Ⓒ Ⓓ Ⓔ
113 Ⓐ Ⓑ Ⓒ Ⓓ Ⓔ
114 Ⓐ Ⓑ Ⓒ Ⓓ Ⓔ
115 Ⓐ Ⓑ Ⓒ Ⓓ Ⓔ

116 Ⓐ Ⓑ Ⓒ Ⓓ Ⓔ
117 Ⓐ Ⓑ Ⓒ Ⓓ Ⓔ
118 Ⓐ Ⓑ Ⓒ Ⓓ Ⓔ
119 Ⓐ Ⓑ Ⓒ Ⓓ Ⓔ
120 Ⓐ Ⓑ Ⓒ Ⓓ Ⓔ

121 Ⓐ Ⓑ Ⓒ Ⓓ Ⓔ
122 Ⓐ Ⓑ Ⓒ Ⓓ Ⓔ
123 Ⓐ Ⓑ Ⓒ Ⓓ Ⓔ
124 Ⓐ Ⓑ Ⓒ Ⓓ Ⓔ
125 Ⓐ Ⓑ Ⓒ Ⓓ Ⓔ

126 Ⓐ Ⓑ Ⓒ Ⓓ Ⓔ
127 Ⓐ Ⓑ Ⓒ Ⓓ Ⓔ
128 Ⓐ Ⓑ Ⓒ Ⓓ Ⓔ
129 Ⓐ Ⓑ Ⓒ Ⓓ Ⓔ
130 Ⓐ Ⓑ Ⓒ Ⓓ Ⓔ

131 Ⓐ Ⓑ Ⓒ Ⓓ Ⓔ
132 Ⓐ Ⓑ Ⓒ Ⓓ Ⓔ
133 Ⓐ Ⓑ Ⓒ Ⓓ Ⓔ
134 Ⓐ Ⓑ Ⓒ Ⓓ Ⓔ
135 Ⓐ Ⓑ Ⓒ Ⓓ Ⓔ

136 Ⓐ Ⓑ Ⓒ Ⓓ Ⓔ
137 Ⓐ Ⓑ Ⓒ Ⓓ Ⓔ
138 Ⓐ Ⓑ Ⓒ Ⓓ Ⓔ
139 Ⓐ Ⓑ Ⓒ Ⓓ Ⓔ
140 Ⓐ Ⓑ Ⓒ Ⓓ Ⓔ

141 Ⓐ Ⓑ Ⓒ Ⓓ Ⓔ
142 Ⓐ Ⓑ Ⓒ Ⓓ Ⓔ
143 Ⓐ Ⓑ Ⓒ Ⓓ Ⓔ
144 Ⓐ Ⓑ Ⓒ Ⓓ Ⓔ
145 Ⓐ Ⓑ Ⓒ Ⓓ Ⓔ

146 Ⓐ Ⓑ Ⓒ Ⓓ Ⓔ
147 Ⓐ Ⓑ Ⓒ Ⓓ Ⓔ
148 Ⓐ Ⓑ Ⓒ Ⓓ Ⓔ
149 Ⓐ Ⓑ Ⓒ Ⓓ Ⓔ
150 Ⓐ Ⓑ Ⓒ Ⓓ Ⓔ

151 Ⓐ Ⓑ Ⓒ Ⓓ Ⓔ
152 Ⓐ Ⓑ Ⓒ Ⓓ Ⓔ
153 Ⓐ Ⓑ Ⓒ Ⓓ Ⓔ
154 Ⓐ Ⓑ Ⓒ Ⓓ Ⓔ
155 Ⓐ Ⓑ Ⓒ Ⓓ Ⓔ

156 Ⓐ Ⓑ Ⓒ Ⓓ Ⓔ
157 Ⓐ Ⓑ Ⓒ Ⓓ Ⓔ
158 Ⓐ Ⓑ Ⓒ Ⓓ Ⓔ
159 Ⓐ Ⓑ Ⓒ Ⓓ Ⓔ
160 Ⓐ Ⓑ Ⓒ Ⓓ Ⓔ

161 Ⓐ Ⓑ Ⓒ Ⓓ Ⓔ
162 Ⓐ Ⓑ Ⓒ Ⓓ Ⓔ
163 Ⓐ Ⓑ Ⓒ Ⓓ Ⓔ
164 Ⓐ Ⓑ Ⓒ Ⓓ Ⓔ
165 Ⓐ Ⓑ Ⓒ Ⓓ Ⓔ

166 Ⓐ Ⓑ Ⓒ Ⓓ Ⓔ
167 Ⓐ Ⓑ Ⓒ Ⓓ Ⓔ
168 Ⓐ Ⓑ Ⓒ Ⓓ Ⓔ
169 Ⓐ Ⓑ Ⓒ Ⓓ Ⓔ
170 Ⓐ Ⓑ Ⓒ Ⓓ Ⓔ

171 Ⓐ Ⓑ Ⓒ Ⓓ Ⓔ
172 Ⓐ Ⓑ Ⓒ Ⓓ Ⓔ
173 Ⓐ Ⓑ Ⓒ Ⓓ Ⓔ
174 Ⓐ Ⓑ Ⓒ Ⓓ Ⓔ
175 Ⓐ Ⓑ Ⓒ Ⓓ Ⓔ

176 Ⓐ Ⓑ Ⓒ Ⓓ Ⓔ
177 Ⓐ Ⓑ Ⓒ Ⓓ Ⓔ
178 Ⓐ Ⓑ Ⓒ Ⓓ Ⓔ
179 Ⓐ Ⓑ Ⓒ Ⓓ Ⓔ
180 Ⓐ Ⓑ Ⓒ Ⓓ Ⓔ

MK1019